W9-CTW-359

DATE DUE

			PRINTED IN U.S.A.

SOMETHING ABOUT THE AUTHOR

ISSN 0276-816X

SOMETHING ABOUT THE AUTHOR

**Facts and Pictures about Authors
and Illustrators of Books for Young People**

EDITED BY
ANNE COMMIRE

VOLUME 59

 **Gale Research Inc.** • *DETROIT* • *NEW YORK* • *FORT LAUDERDALE* • *LONDON*

Riverside Community College
Library
4800 Magnolia Avenue
Riverside, California 92506

REF
PN
1009
A1C6
V. 59

Managing Editor: Anne Commire

Editors: Agnes Garrett, Helga P. McCue

Associate Editor: Elisa Ann Ferraro

Assistant Editors: Eunice L. Petrini, Linda Shedd

Sketchwriters: Catherine Coray, Cathy Courtney, Marguerite Feitlowitz,
Mimi H. Hutson, Deborah Klezmer, Dieter Miller, Beatrice Smedley

Researcher: Catherine Ruello

Editorial Assistants: Joanne J. Ferraro, Marja T. Hiltunen, June Lee, Susan Pfanner

Production Manager: Mary Beth Trimper

External Production Assistant: Marilyn Jackman

Production Supervisor: Laura Bryant

Internal Production Associate: Louise Gagné

Internal Production Assistant: Sharana Wier

Art Director: Arthur Chartow

Keyliner: C. J. Jonik

Special acknowledgment is due to the members of the *Something about the Author Autobiography Series* staff
who assisted in the preparation of this volume.

While every effort has been made to ensure the reliability of the information presented in this publication, Gale Research Inc. does not guarantee the accuracy of the data contained herein. Gale accepts no payment for listing; and inclusion in the publication of any organization, agency, institution, publication, service, or individual does not imply endorsement of the editors or publisher.

Errors brought to the attention of the publisher and verified to the satisfaction of the publisher will be corrected in future editions.

Copyright © 1990
Gale Research Inc.
835 Penobscot Bldg.
Detroit, MI 48226-4094

Library of Congress Catalog Card Number 72-27107

ISBN 0-8103-2269-2
ISSN 0276-816X

Printed in the United States

Contents

Introduction

As the only annually published ongoing reference series that deals with the lives and works of authors and illustrators of children's books, *Something about the Author (SATA)* is a unique source of information. The *SATA* series includes not only well-known authors and illustrators whose books are most widely read, but also those less prominent people whose works are just coming to be recognized. *SATA* is often the only readily available information source for less well-known writers or artists. You'll find *SATA* informative and entertaining whether you are:

—a student in junior high school (or perhaps one to two grades higher or lower) who needs information for a book report or some other assignment for an English class;

—a children's librarian who is searching for the answer to yet another question from a young reader or collecting background material to use for a story hour;

—an English teacher who is drawing up an assignment for your students or gathering information for a book talk;

—a student in a college of education or library science who is studying children's literature and reference sources in the field;

—a parent who is looking for a new way to interest your child in reading something more than the school curriculum prescribes;

—an adult who enjoys children's literature for its own sake, knowing that a good children's book has no age limits.

Scope

In *SATA* you will find detailed information about authors and illustrators who span the full time range of children's literature, from early figures like John Newbery and L. Frank Baum to contemporary figures like Judy Blume and Richard Peck. Authors in the series represent primarily English-speaking countries, particularly the United States, Canada, and the United Kingdom. Also included, however, are authors from around the world whose works are available in English translation, for example: from France, Jean and Laurent De Brunhoff; from Italy, Emanuele Luzzati; from the Netherlands, Jaap ter Haar; from Germany, James Krüss; from Norway, Babbis Friis-Baastad; from Japan, Toshiko Kanzawa; from the Soviet Union, Kornei Chukovsky; from Switzerland, Alois Carigiet, to name only a few. Also appearing in *SATA* are Newbery medalists from Hendrik Van Loon (1922) to Paul Fleischman (1989). The writings represented in *SATA* include those created intentionally for children and young adults as well as those written for a general audience and known to interest younger readers. These writings cover the spectrum from picture books, humor, folk and fairy tales, animal stories, mystery and adventure, science fiction and fantasy, historical fiction, poetry and nonsense verse, to drama, biography, and nonfiction.

Information Features

In *SATA* you will find full-length entries that are being presented in the series for the first time. This volume, for example, marks the first full-length appearance of Alan Arkin, Art Clokey, Betsy Maestro, Thomas Malory, Herman Melville, and Diane Paterson.

Obituaries have been included in *SATA* since Volume 20. An Obituary is intended not only as a death notice but also as a concise view of a person's life and work. Obituaries may appear for persons who have entries in earlier *SATA* volumes, as well as for people who have not yet appeared in the series. In this volume Obituaries mark the recent deaths of Geoffrey Household, Emily Kimbrough, Kathleen Irene Nixon, and Margot Zemach.

Revised Entries

Since Volume 25, each *SATA* volume also includes newly revised and updated entries for a selection of *SATA* listees (usually four to six) who remain of interest to today's readers and who have been active enough to require extensive revision of their earlier biographies. For example, when Beverly Cleary first appeared in *SATA* Volume 2, she was the author of twenty-one books for children and young adults and the recipient of numerous awards. By the time her updated sketch appeared in Volume 43 (a span of fifteen years), this creator of the indefatigable Ramona Quimby and other memorable characters had produced a dozen new titles and garnered nearly fifty additional awards, including the 1984 Newbery Medal.

The entry for a given biographee may be revised as often as there is substantial new information to provide. In this volume, look for revised entries on Pauline Baynes, John Burningham, Barbara Cooney, Thomas Anthony de Paola, and Sid Fleischman.

Illustrations

While the textual information in *SATA* is its primary reason for existing, photographs and illustrations not only enliven the text but are an integral part of the information that *SATA* provides. Illustrations and text are wedded in such a special way in children's literature that artists and their works naturally occupy a prominent place among *SATA*'s listees. The illustrators that you'll find in the series include such past masters of children's book illustration as Randolph Caldecott, Walter Crane, Arthur Rackham, and Ernest H. Shepard, as well as such noted contemporary artists as Maurice Sendak, Edward Gorey, Tomie de Paola, and Margot Zemach. There are Caldecott medalists from Dorothy Lathrop (the first recipient in 1938) to Stephen Gammell (the latest winner in 1989); cartoonists like Charles Schulz ("Peanuts"), Walt Kelly ("Pogo"), Hank Ketcham ("Dennis the Menace"), and Georges Rémi ("Tintin"); photographers like Jill Krementz, Tana Hoban, Bruce McMillan, and Bruce Curtis; and filmmakers like Walt Disney, Alfred Hitchcock, and Steven Spielberg.

In more than a dozen years of recording the metamorphosis of children's literature from the printed page to other media, *SATA* has become something of a repository of photographs that are unique in themselves and exist nowhere else as a group, particularly many of the classics of motion picture and stage history and photographs that have been specially loaned to us from private collections.

Index Policy

In response to suggestions from librarians, *SATA* indexes no longer appear in each volume but are included in each alternate (odd-numbered) volume of the series, beginning with Volume 58.

SATA continues to include two indexes that cumulate with each alternate volume: the **Illustrations Index,** arranged by the name of the illustrator, gives the number of the volume and page where the illustrator's work appears in the current volume as well as all preceding volumes in the series; the **Author Index** gives the number of the volume in which a person's Biographical Sketch, Brief Entry, or Obituary appears in the current volume as well as all preceding volumes in the series.

These indexes also include references to authors and illustrators who appear in *Yesterday's Authors of Books for Children* (described in detail below). Beginning with Volume 36, the *SATA* Author Index provides cross-references to authors who are included in Gale's *Children's Literature Review.* Starting with Volume 42, you will also find cross-references to authors who are included in the *Something about the Author Autobiography Series* (described in detail below).

What a *SATA* Entry Provides

Whether you're already familiar with the *SATA* series or just getting acquainted, you will want to be aware of the kind of information that an entry provides. In every *SATA* entry the editors attempt to give as complete a picture of the person's life and work as possible. In some cases that full range of information may simply be unavailable, or a biographee may choose not to reveal complete personal details. The information that the editors attempt to provide in every entry is arranged in the following categories:

1. The "head" of the entry gives

    —the most complete form of the name,
    —any part of the name not commonly used, included in parentheses,
    —birth and death dates, if known; a (?) indicates a discrepancy in published sources,
    —pseudonyms or name variants under which the person has had books published or is publicly known, in parentheses in the second line.

2. "Personal" section gives

    —date and place of birth and death,
    —parents' names and occupations,
    —name of spouse, date of marriage, and names of children,
    —educational institutions attended, degrees received, and dates,
    —religious and political affiliations,
    —agent's name and address,
    —home and/or office address.

3. "Career" section gives

    —name of employer, position, and dates for each career post,
    —military service,
    —memberships,
    —awards and honors.

4. "Writings" section gives

    —title, first publisher and date of publication, and illustration information for each book written; revised editions and other significant editions for books with particularly long publishing histories; genre, when known.

5. "Adaptations" section gives

    —title, major performers, producer, and date of all known reworkings of an author's material in another medium, like movies, filmstrips, television, recordings, plays, etc.

6. "Sidelights" section gives

    —commentary on the life or work of the biographee either directly from the person (and often written specifically for the *SATA* entry), or gathered from biographies, diaries, letters, interviews, or other published sources.

7. "For More Information See" section gives

    —books, feature articles, films, plays, and reviews in which the biographee's life or work has been treated.

How a *SATA* Entry Is Compiled

A *SATA* entry progresses through a series of steps. If the biographee is living, the *SATA* editors try to secure information directly from him or her through a questionnaire. From the information that the biographee supplies, the editors prepare an entry, filling in any essential missing details with research. The author or illustrator is then sent a copy of the entry to check for accuracy and completeness.

If the biographee is deceased or cannot be reached by questionnaire, the *SATA* editors examine a wide variety of published sources to gather information for an entry. Biographical sources are searched with the aid of Gale's *Biography and Genealogy Master Index*. Bibliographic sources like the *National Union Catalog*, the *Cumulative Book Index*, *American Book Publishing Record*, and the *British Museum Catalogue* are consulted, as are book reviews, feature articles, published interviews, and material sometimes obtained from the biographee's family, publishers, agent, or other associates.

For each entry presented in *SATA*, the editors also attempt to locate a photograph of the biographee as well as representative illustrations from his or her books. After surveying the available books which the biographee has written and/or illustrated, and then making a selection of appropriate photographs and illustrations, the editors request permission of the current copyright holders to reprint the material. In the case of older books for which the copyright may have passed through several hands, even locating the current copyright holder is often a long and involved process.

We invite you to examine the entire *SATA* series, starting with this volume. Described below are some of the people in Volume 58 that you may find particularly interesting.

Highlights of This Volume

PAULINE BAYNES......"was a thoroughly rebellious five-year-old,... [who] seemed always to be punished for one thing or another." Though her family moved frequently, Baynes and her sister learned to make the most of their temporary quarters. "In those days hotels...were our homes. We would run up and down their enormous corridors and pin our drawings on the walls wherever we were." In school, art became her obsession: "At the beginning of the term we used to bring back holiday art work, and while other pupils might have done one picture, I would bring back as many as forty." She has illustrated over ninety books, including works by C. S. Lewis and J. R. R. Tolkien, and says she has "enjoyed doing different kinds of books....I never think about what children will like, or whether publishers will make money or not; I only try to knit the text and the illustration together." Baynes now lives a quiet life in a remote country cottage in Surrey where "...as soon as breakfast is finished and the dogs walked, I settle down and work through the day. I've had a charmed life, everything has drifted along and I've been very lucky."

JOHN BURNINGHAM......received his early education at the experimental A. S. Neill's Summerhill School, a "school governed by the children," where he did a great deal of drawing and painting. "I was lucky because the art room at Summerhill didn't restrict you to tiny little bits of paper...we used to have great big bits and large brushes, lots of paint." Before attending art school, Burningham became a conscientious objector doing alternative military service rather than joining the National Service. "[I spent] two and a half years working in hospitals, agriculture, forestry, and humanitarian social work. It was much better than going straight to art school; I learned a great deal more." His first children's book, *Borka: The Adventures of a Goose with No Feathers*, won the Kate Greenaway Medal and marked the beginning of his success as a prolific writer and illustrator. "I always describe my way of producing books as being rather like repertory theater. You are 'performing' one book, you're rehearsing the next, and you're learning the part of the one that's to come."

BARBARA COONEY......believes she "was no more talented...than any other child. I started out ruining the wallpaper with crayons...and making eggs with arms and legs. Most children start this way, and most children have the souls of artists.... I became an artist because I had access to materials and pictures, a minimum of instruction, and a stubborn nature." Cooney first earned a Caldecott Medal for her book *Chanticleer and the Fox*, and twenty-one years later she received a second Caldecott for *Ox-Cart Man*. "During those twenty-one years I went on living in the same beautiful, drafty old house. The wind still whistled through the light switches....Under that roof I went on raising my four children and an uncountable number of cats and dogs.... I kept on planting large back-breaking vegetable gardens. I kept on fussing with flowers. Grandchildren began to appear. I kept illustrating." She is adamant when it comes to maintaining high literary standards for children: "I am *not* making picture books for children. I am making them for *people*....'A man's reach should exceed his grasp.' So should a child's."

TOMIE DE PAOLA......made his career choice at the age of seven. "I didn't like [my teacher] because she insisted that I learn arithmetic. I, who could sing any song after hearing it once, memorize any poem, tell the plot of any movie I had seen, could not memorize my tables.... Arithmetic paper was made to draw on. I informed [her] that she didn't seem to understand. I was not going to be an 'arithmetic-er' when I grew up. I was going to be an artist." On the road to fulfilling his childhood dream, de Paola studied art at the Pratt Institute and then spent six months in a Benedictine monastery. "The monastery gave me a way to view life and realize that culture was an important thing.... If you can add to the culture of the race of man, you're doing a really hot number." De Paola has made his contribution through illustration and writing, talents which for him came with a dream, "a dream that I expressed as a child, that when I grew up I would write and draw pictures for books: a dream that people I've never met would get to know me a little better: a dream that the invisible world could be made visible, and even a dream that I could somehow touch others' lives."

HERMAN MELVILLE......embarked upon his first voyage in his early twenties and began a love of the sea that was to inspire him throughout his life: "Give me this glorious ocean life, this salt-sea life, this briny, foamy life when the sea neighs and snorts, and you breathe the very breath that the great whales respire!" Melville published several books, but unable to support his family, he worked nineteen years as inspector of customs at the Port of New York. "Whoever is not in the possession of leisure can hardly be said to possess independence. They talk of the *dignity of work*. Bosh. True work is the *necessity* of poor humanity's earthly condition. The dignity is in leisure. Besides, ninety-nine hundredths of all the *work* done in the world is either foolish and unnecessary, or harmful and wicked." No doubt Melville's despair was increased by his lack of success as an author, as he saw even his now-famous American classic, *Moby Dick,* poorly received by the reviewers. "A book in a man's brain is better off than a book bound in calf—at any rate it is safer." Melville died in almost total obscurity in 1891, later becoming the most renowned and widely-read American author of the nineteenth century.

These are only a few of the authors and illustrators that you'll find in this volume. We hope you find all the entries in *SATA* both interesting and useful.

Yesterday's Authors of Books for Children

In a two-volume companion set to *SATA, Yesterday's Authors of Books for Children (YABC)* focuses on early authors and illustrators, from the beginnings of children's literature through 1960, whose books are still being read by children today. Here you will find "old favorites" like Hans Christian Andersen, J. M. Barrie, Kenneth Grahame, Betty MacDonald, A. A. Milne, Beatrix Potter, Samuel Clemens, Kate Greenaway, Rudyard Kipling, Robert Louis Stevenson, and many more.

Similar in format to *SATA, YABC* features bio-bibliographical entries that are divided into information categories such as Personal, Career, Writings, and Sidelights. The entries are further enhanced by book illustrations, author photos, movie stills, and many rare old photographs.

In Volume 2 you will find cumulative indexes to the authors and to the illustrations that appear in *YABC*. These listings can also be located in the *SATA* cumulative indexes.

By exploring both volumes of *YABC,* you will discover a special group of more than seventy authors and illustrators who represent some of the best in children's literature—individuals whose timeless works continue to delight children and adults of all ages. Other authors and illustrators from early children's literature are listed in *SATA,* starting with Volume 15.

Something about the Author Autobiography Series

You can complement the information in *SATA* with the *Something about the Author Autobiography Series (SAAS),* which provides autobiographical essays written by important current authors and illustrators of books for children and young adults. In every volume of *SAAS* you will find about twenty specially commissioned autobiographies, each accompanied by a selection of personal photographs supplied by the authors. The wide range of contemporary writers and artists who describe their lives and interests in the *Autobiography Series* includes Joan Aiken, Betsy Byars, Leonard Everett Fisher, Milton

Meltzer, Maia Wojciechowska, and Jane Yolen, among others. Though the information presented in the autobiographies is as varied and unique as the authors, you can learn about the people and events that influenced these writers' early lives, how they began their careers, what problems they faced in becoming established in their professions, what prompted them to write or illustrate particular books, what they now find most challenging or rewarding in their lives, and what advice they may have for young people interested in following in their footsteps, among many other subjects.

Autobiographies included in the *SATA Autobiography Series* can be located through both the *SATA* cumulative index and the *SAAS* cumulative index, which lists not only the authors' names but also the subjects mentioned in their essays, such as titles of works and geographical and personal names.

The *SATA Autobiography Series* gives you the opportunity to view "close up" some of the fascinating people who are included in the *SATA* parent series. The combined *SATA* series makes available to you an unequaled range of comprehensive and in-depth information about the authors and illustrators of young people's literature.

Please write and tell us if we can make *SATA* even more helpful to you.

Acknowledgments

Grateful acknowledgment is made to the following publishers, authors, and
artists whose works appear in this volume.

ARION PRESS. Illustration by Barry Moser from *Moby-Dick; or, The Whale* by Herman Melville. Copyright © 1979 by The Arion Press. Reprinted by permission of The Arion Press.

PETER BEDRICK BOOKS. Illustration by Pauline Baynes from *How the Whale Got His Throat* by Rudyard Kipling. Illustrations © 1983 by Macmillan Publishers Ltd. Reprinted by permission of Peter Bedrick Books, an imprint of Macmillan Publishers Ltd.

BELITHA PRESS LTD. Illustration by Leon Baxter from *Animal Hide and Seek* by Mary Hoffman. Illustrations © 1986 by Leon Baxter. Text and art in this format copyright © by Belitha Press Limited. Reprinted by permission of Belitha Press Limited.

BRESLICH & FOSS LTD. Photograph by Rudolf Betz from *Rigoletto: A Guide to the Opera* by Charles Osborne. Copyright © 1979 by Breslich & Foss. Reprinted by permission of Breslich & Foss Ltd.

CASTLEMARSH PUBLICATIONS. Illustrations by Sharon Saseen Dillon from *Where Did My Feather Pillow Come From?* by Audilee Boyd Taylor. Copyright © 1982 by Castlemarsh Publications. Reprinted by permission of Castlemarsh Publications.

CLARION BOOKS. Illustration by Giulio Maestro from *I Think I Thought and Other Tricky Verbs* by Marvin Terban. Text © 1984 by Marvin Terban. Illustrations © 1984 by Giulio Maestro./ Illustration by Giulio Maestro from *Your Foot's on My Feet! And Other Tricky Nouns* by Marvin Terban. Text © 1986 by Marvin Terban. Illustrations © 1986 by Giulio Maestro. Both reprinted by permission of Clarion Books, a division of Houghton Mifflin Company.

WILLIAM COLLINS SONS. Illustration by Pauline Baynes from *Andersen's Fairy Tales* by Hans Christian Andersen./ Illustration by Pauline Baynes from *Prince Caspian: Book 2 in the Chronicles of Narnia* by C.S. Lewis. Copyright 1951 by C.S. Lewis Pty. Ltd./ Illustration by Pauline Baynes from *The Voyage of the "Dawn Treader": Book 3 in the Chronicles of Narnia* by C.S. Lewis. Copyright 1952 by C.S. Lewis Pty. Ltd./ Illustration by Pauline Baynes from *The Silver Chair: Book 4 in the Chronicles of Narnia* by C.S. Lewis. Copyright 1953 by C.S. Lewis Pty. Ltd./ Illustration by Pauline Baynes from *The Magician's Nephew: Book 6 in the Chronicles of Narnia* by C.S. Lewis. Copyright 1955 by C.S. Lewis Pty. Ltd./ Illustration by Mary Shepard from *Mary Poppins* by P.L. Travers. Copyright © revised edition 1982 by P.L. Travers. All reprinted by permission of William Collins Sons & Co. Ltd.

COWARD-McCANN. Illustration by Diane Paterson from *Fiona's Bee* by Beverly Keller. Illustrations © 1975 by Diane Paterson. Reprinted by permission of Coward-McCann.

THOMAS Y. CROWELL. Illustration by Barbara Cooney from *Chanticleer and the Fox*, adapted by Barbara Cooney from the *Canterbury Tales*. Copyright © 1958 by Thomas Y. Crowell Company, Inc./ Illustration by Barbara Cooney from *A White Heron: A Story of Maine* by Sarah Orne Jewett. Copyright © 1963 by Barbara Cooney./ Illustration by John Burningham from *Mr. Grumpy's Motor Car* by John Burningham. Copyright © 1973 by John Burningham./ Illustration by John Burningham from *The Blanket* by John Burningham. Copyright © 1975 by John Burningham./ Illustration by John Burningham from *Come Away from the Water, Shirley* by John Burningham. Copyright © 1977 by John Burningham./ Illustration by Giulio Maestro from *Ferryboat* by Betsy Maestro. Illustrations © 1986 by Giulio Maestro. All reprinted by permission of Thomas Y. Crowell Company, Inc., a subsidiary of Harper & Row, Publishers, Inc.

CROWN PUBLISHERS. Illustration by Giulio Maestro from *Lambs for Dinner* by Betsy Maestro. Text © 1978 by Betsy Maestro. Illustrations © 1978 by Giulio Maestro./ Illustration by Giulio Maestro from *On the Town: A Book of Clothing Words* by Betsy Maestro. Illustrations © 1983 by Giulio Maestro./ Illustration by John Burningham from *Granpa* by John Burningham. Copyright © 1984 by John Burningham./ Illustration by Giulio Maestro from *Through the Year with Harriet* by Betsy Maestro. Text © 1985 by Betsy Maestro. Illustrations © 1985 by Giulio Maestro./ Illustration by John Burningham from *John Burningham's Opposites* by John Burningham. Copyright © 1985 by John Burningham./ Illustration by John Burningham from *Where's Julius?* by John Burningham. Copyright © 1986 by John Burningham. All reprinted by permission of Crown Publishers, a division of Random House, Inc.

DIAL BOOKS FOR YOUNG READERS. Illustration by Diane Paterson from *Monnie Hates Lydia* by Susan Pearson. Illustrations © 1975 by Diane Paterson./ Illustration by Diane Paterson from *Smile for Auntie* by Diane Paterson. Copyright © 1976 by Diane Paterson./ Illustration by Diane Paterson from *The Bravest Babysitter* by Barbara Greenbert. Illustrations © 1977 by Diane Paterson. All reprinted by permission of the publisher, E.P. Dutton, a division of Penguin Books USA Inc.

DOUBLEDAY. Illustrations by Jane Hyman from *The Gumby Book of Colors* by Art Clokey. Copyright © 1986 by Art Clokey. Reprinted by permission of Doubleday, a division of Bantam, Doubleday, Dell Publishing Group, Inc.

FOUR WINDS PRESS. Illustration by DyAnne DiSalvo-Ryan from *The Mommy Exchange* by Amy Hest. Illustrations © 1988 by DyAnne DiSalvo-Ryan. Reprinted by permission of Four Winds Press, an imprint of Macmillan Publishing Company.

GREENWILLOW BOOKS. Illustration by Peter Sis from *The Whipping Boy* by Sid Fleischman. Illustrations © 1986 by Peter Sis./ Illustration by Peter Sis from *The Scarebird* by Sid Fleischman. Text © 1987 by Sid Fleischman, Inc. Illustrations © 1988 by Peter Sis. Both reprinted by permission of Greenwillow Books, a division of William Morrow & Company, Inc.

HARCOURT BRACE JOVANOVICH. Illustration by Mary Shepard from *Mary Poppins Comes Back* by P.L. Travers. Copyright 1935, 1963 by P.L. Travers./ Illustration by Tomie de Paola from *Miracle on 34th Street* by Valentine Davies. Copyright 1947 by Twentieth Century-Fox Film Corporation. Copyright renewed by Elizabeth S. Davies. Illustrations © 1984 by Tomie de Paola./ Sidelight excerpts from *The Melville Log* by Jay Leyda. Copyright 1951 by Harcourt Brace Jovanovich, Inc. Renewed 1979 by Jay Leyda./ Illustration by Tomie de Paola from *Helga's Dowry: A Troll Love Story* by Tomie de Paola. Copyright © 1977 by Tomie de Paola./ Illustration by Tomie de Paola from *Big Anthony and the Magic Ring* by Tomie de Paola. Copyright © 1979 by Tomie de Paola./ Illustration by Tomie de Paola from *The Legend of Old Befana: An Italian Christmas Story*, retold by Tomie de Paola. Copyright © 1980 by Tomie de Paola./ Illustration by Tomie de Paola from *The Comic Adventures of Old Mother Hubbard and Her Dog* by Tomie de Paola. Copyright © 1981 by Tomie de Paola. All reprinted by permission of Harcourt Brace Jovanovich, Inc.

HARMONY BOOKS. Sidelight excerpts by Louis Kaplan and Scott Michaelson and illustrations by Art Clokey from *The Authorized Biography of the World's Favorite Clayboy GUMBY* by Louis Kaplan, Scott Michaelson, and Art Clokey. Copyright © 1986 by Louis Kaplan, Scott Michaelson, and Art Clokey. Reprinted by permission of Harmony Books, a division of Random House, Inc.

HARPER & ROW. Illustration by Joan Sandin from *The Lemming Condition* by Alan Arkin. Illustrations © 1976 by Joan Sandin./ Sidelight excerpt from *Halfway Through the Door: An Actor's Journey Toward the Self* by Alan Arkin. Copyright © 1979 by Alan Arkin./ Illustration by Giulio Maestro from *Comets* by Franklyn M. Branley. Illustrations © 1984 by Giulio Maestro./ Illustration by Giulio Maestro from *Hurricane Watch* by Franklyn M. Branley. Illustrations © 1985 by Giulio Maestro./ Jacket illustration by Griesbach/Martucci from *The Clearing* by Alan Arkin. Copyright © 1986 by Alan Arkin. Jacket design by Anita Soos. All reprinted by permission of Harper & Row, Publishers, Inc.

HARVARD UNIVERSITY PRESS. Sidelight excerpts from *Herman Melville* by Eleanor Melville Metcalf. Copyright 1953 by the President and Fellows of Harvard University. Renewed 1981 by Paul C. Metcalf and David M. Metcalf. Reprinted by permission of Harvard University Press.

COLLINS HARVILL. Illustration by Carolyn Dinan from *The Search After Hapiness* by Charlotte Bronte. Illustrations © 1969 by Harvill Press Ltd. Reprinted by permission of Collins Harvill.

HASTINGS HOUSE. Illustration by Barbara Cooney from *The Little Juggler*, adapted by Barbara Cooney from an Old French Legend. Copyright © 1961, 1982 by Barbara Cooney Porter. Reprinted by permission of Hastings House, Publishers, Inc.

HOLIDAY HOUSE. Illustration by Tomie de Paola from *The Cloud Book* by Tomie de Paola./ Illustration by Tomie de Paola from *Fin M'Coul: The Giant of Knockmany Hill* by Tomie de Paola. Copyright © 1981 by Tomie de Paola./ Illustration by Olivier Dunrea from *Fergus and Bridey* by Olivier Dunrea. Copyright © 1985 by Olivier Dunrea. All reprinted by permission of Holiday House, Inc.

HENRY HOLT & COMPANY. Illustration by Pauline Baynes from *Noah and the Ark*. Text from the Revised Standard Version of the Bible. Illustrations © 1988 by Pauline Baynes. Reprinted by permission of Henry Holt & Company, Inc.

HOUGHTON MIFFLIN. Illustration by Pauline Baynes from *The Adventures of Tom Bombadil* by J.R.R. Tolkien. Copyright © 1962 by George Allen & Unwin Ltd./ Illustration by Pauline Baynes from *Farmer Giles of Ham* by J.R.R. Tolkien. Copyright © 1976 by George Allen & Unwin Ltd. Both reprinted by permission of Houghton Mifflin Company.

ALFRED A. KNOPF. Illustration by Barbara Cooney from *The Peacock Pie* by Walter de la Mare. Copyright © 1961 by Barbara Cooney. Reprinted by permission of Alfred A. Knopf, Inc.

LERNER PUBLICATIONS. Cover illustration from *Yesterday's Trucks* by Patrick C. Dorin. Copyright © 1982 by Lerner Publications Co., 241 First Avenue North, Minneapolis, MN 55401. Reprinted by permission of Lerner Publications Company.

LITTLE, BROWN & COMPANY. Illustration by Barbara Cooney from *The Owl and the Pussy-Cat* by Edward Lear. Illustrations © 1961 by Barbara Cooney. Reprinted by permission of Little, Brown & Company.

LOTHROP, LEE & SHEPARD BOOKS. Illustration by Troy Howell from *The Adventures of Pinocchio: Tale of a Puppet* by C. Collodi. Translated from the Italian by M.L. Rosenthal. Translation © 1983 by M.L. Rosenthal. Illustrations © 1983 by Troy Howell./ Illustration by Steven Kellogg from *How Much Is a Million?* by David M. Schwartz. Text © 1985 by David M. Schwartz. Illustrations © 1985 by Steven Kellogg./ Illustration by Giulio Maestro from *The Story of the Statue of Liberty* by Betsy Maestro. Illustrations © 1986 by Giulio Maestro./ Illustration by Giulio Maestro from *A More Perfect Union: The Story of Our Constitution* by Betsy Maestro. Text © 1987 by Betsy Maestro. Illustrations © 1987 by Giulio Maestro. All reprinted by permission of Lothrop, Lee & Shepard Books, a division of William Morrow & Company, Inc.

MACMILLAN. Illustration by Giulio Maestro from *Big City Port* by Betsy Maestro and Ellen DelVecchio. Illustrations © 1983 by Giulio Maestro. Reprinted by permission of Macmillan Publishing Company.

THE MODERN LIBRARY. Illustration by Rockwell Kent from *Moby Dick; or, The Whale* by Herman Melville. Copyright 1930 by R.R. Donnelley and Sons Company. Renewed 1958 by Rockwell Kent. Reprinted by permission of The Modern Library, a division of Random House, Inc.

NEW AMERICAN LIBRARY. Cover illustration from *Over the Hill at Fourteen* by Jamie Callan. Copyright © 1982 by Jamie Callan./ Cover illustration from *Let the Trumpet Sound: The Life of Martin Luther King, Jr.* by Stephen B. Oates. Both reprinted by permission of New American Library, a division of Penguin Books USA, Inc., New York, NY.

PAGODA BOOKS. Illustration by Michael Cole from *A Christmas Carol* by Charles Dickens. Adaptation and illustrations © 1985 by Michael Cole. Reprinted by permission of Pagoda Books.

PRENTICE-HALL. Illustration by Tomie de Paola from *Charlie Needs a Cloak* by Tomie de Paola. Copyright © 1973 by Tomie de Paola./ Illustration by Tomie de Paola from *Strega Nona: An Old Tale* by Tomie de Paola. Copyright © 1975 by Tomie de Paola. Both reprinted by permission of Prentice-Hall, Inc., Englewood Cliffs, NJ.

G. P. PUTNAM'S SONS. Illustration by Tomie de Paola from *Bill and Pete Go Down the Nile* by Tomie de Paola. Copyright © 1987 by Tomie de Paola. Reprinted by permission of G.P. Putnam's Sons.

RANDOM HOUSE. Illustration by John Burningham from *Chitty-Chitty-Bang-Bang: The Magical Car* by Ian Fleming. Copyright © 1964 by Glidrose Production Ltd. and Jonathan Cape Ltd. Reprinted by permission of Random House, Inc.

CHARLES SCRIBNER'S SONS. Jacket illustration by Ronald Himler from *A Bellsong for Sarah Raines* by Bettie Cannon. Jacket illustration © 1987 by Ronald Himler. Reprinted by permission of Charles Scribner's Sons, an imprint of Macmillan Publishing Company.

VIKING KESTREL. Illustration by Barbara Cooney from *The Story of Holly & Ivy* by Rumer Godden. Copyright © 1985 by Barbara Cooney Porter./ Illustration by Gwenda Turner from *Gwenda Turner's PLAYBOOK* by Gwenda Turner. Copyright © 1985 by Gwenda Turner. Both reprinted by permission of Viking Penguin, a division of Penguin Books USA, Inc.

YALE UNIVERSITY PRESS. Sidelight excerpts from *The Letters of Herman Melville*, edited by Menrell R. Davis and William H. Gilman. Copyright © 1960 by Yale University Press. Renewed 1988 by Margaret R. Gilman. Reprinted by permission of Yale University Press.

Sidelight excerpts by Tomie de Paola from "Involved with Dreams," in *Books for Your Children* , Summer, 1980. Copyright © 1980 by *Books for Your Children*./ Sidelight excerpts from "Autobiography and Friends of Tomie," written for the Tomie de Paola Celebration, September 13-15, 1985, sponsored by the Meriden Public Library, Meriden, CT. Reprinted by permission of Tomie de Paola./ Sidelight excerpts by Michael Frierson from "Gumby: Riding the Clay Rollercoaster with Art Clokey," in *Funnyworld*, Spring, 1988./ Jacket photograph by John Howard Griffin from *Thomas Merton: The Daring Young Man on the Flying Belltower* by Cornelia and Irving Sussman. Jacket photographs © by John Howard Griffin. Reprinted by permission of Elizabeth Griffin-Bonnazzi./ Sidelight excerpts by Barbara Cooney from "Caldecott Award Acceptance," in *The Horn Book Magazine*, August, 1959. Copyright © 1959 by The Horn Book, Inc., 14 Beacon St., Boston, MA 02108. Reprinted by permission of The Horn Book, Inc./ Sidelight excerpts by Anna Newton Porter from "Barbara Cooney," from *The Horn Book Magazine*, August, 1959. Copyright © 1959 by The Horn Book, Inc., 14 Beacon St., Boston, MA 02108. Reprinted by permission of The Horn Book, Inc./ Sidelight excerpts by Barbara Cooney from "Caldecott Medal Acceptance," in *The Horn Book Magazine*, August, 1980. Copyright © 1980 by The Horn Book, Inc., 14 Beacon St., Boston, MA 02108. Reprinted by permission of The Horn Book, Inc./ Sidelight excerpts by Sid Fleischman from "Humbug Mountain," in *The Horn Book Magazine*, February, 1980. Copyright © 1980 by The Horn Book, Inc., 14 Beacon St., Boston, MA 02108. Reprinted by permission of The Horn Book, Inc./ Sidelight excerpts by Sid Fleischman from "Newbery Medal Acceptance," in *The Horn Book Magazine*, July/August, 1987. Copyright © 1987 by The Horn Book, Inc., 14 Beacon St., Boston, MA 02108. Reprinted by permission of The Horn Book, Inc.

Sidelight excerpts from "Me and the Man on the Moon-Eyed Horse," in *Junior Literary Guild*, March, 1977./ Sidelight excerpts by Barry Farrell from "Yossarian in Connecticut," in *Life*, October 2, 1970. Copyright © 1970 by Time Inc. Reprinted by permission of *Life*./ Sidelight excerpts from "Hawthorne and His Mosses," in *Literary World*, August 17-24, 1850./ Cover painting, "Peche du Cachalot," by Ambrose Louis Garneray, from *Moby Dick; or, The White Whale* by Herman Melville. Engraved by Martens and published by Goupil & Vibert, Paris. New American Library./ Cover painting, "The Fort and Ten Pound Island, Gloucester, Mass.," by Fitz Hugh Lave, from *Billy Budd and Other Tales* by Herman Melville. New American Library./ Illustration by Imero Gobbato from *The Boy and the Dolphin* by Abraham Rothberg. Illustrations © 1969 by W.W. Norton Company, Inc./ Sidelight excerpts by Jack Friedman from "Gumby's On a Roll and There's an Art (Clokey) Behind It," in *People Weekly*, February 4, 1985. Copyright © 1985 by Time Inc./ Sidelight excerpts by Sean Elder from "Gumby Transcendent," in *San Francisco Examiner*, July 12, 1987. Reprinted by permission of Sean Elder./ Illustration by Mary Shepard from *Prince Rabbit and The Princess Who Could Not Laugh* by A.A. Milne. Illustrations © 1966 by Edmund Ward (Publishers) Limited. Reprinted by permission of Mary Shepard./ Sidelight excerpts by Ronald Smith from "Vintage KidVid," in *Video*, September, 1984./ Sidelight excerpts by Barry Walters from "Let's Twist Again," in *Village Voice*, March 17, 1987. Copyright © 1987 by The Village Voice, Inc./ Jacket illustration by James Watts from *Brats* by X.J. Kennedy. Copyright © by James Watts. Reprinted by permission of James Watts./ Illustration by Kurt Werth from *McBroom Tells the Truth* by Sid Fleischman. Illustrations © 1986 by Kurt Werth./ Illustration by Nadine Bernard Westcott from *The Hey Hey Man* by Sid Fleischman. Illustrations © 1979 by Nadine Bernard Westcott. Reprinted by permission of Nadine Bernard Westcott./ Cover illustration by Joe Yakovetic from *Betsy and the Boys* by Carolyn Haywood. Copyright 1945 by Harcourt Brace Jovanovich, Inc. Renewed 1973 by Carolyn Haywood. Reprinted by permission of Joe Yakovetic.

PHOTOGRAPH CREDITS

Pauline Baynes: Cathy Courtney; John Burningham: Cathy Courtney; Joan Clark: Kathi Robertson; Barbara Cooney (with grandsons): Phoebe Medina; Thomas Anthony de Paola: Mark Haberman; DyAnne Di Salvo-Ryan: Joseph T. Mueller; Vivian Huff: Maurice Haines; David Klein: Edith Klein; Janet T. Lisle: © by 1987 Lauren Shay; Betsy and Giulio Maestro: John Ligos; Donald M. McFarlan: Granville Fox (London); Roy Paul Nelson: Suzanne Ashley; Stephen B. Oates: Stephen Long, UMass Photo Service; Sharon Saseen: © 1985 by Art Smiley Photography; Irving Sussman: John Howard Griffin; Michael Teitelbaum: Sheleigah Grube; James K. M. Watts: A. S. Koudelka.

Appreciation also to the Performing Arts Research Center of the New York Public Library at Lincoln Center for permission to reprint the program cover of "Moby Dick."

something ABOUT THE AUTHOR

ALDERSON, Sue Ann 1940-

PERSONAL: Born September 11, 1940; daughter of Eugene L. (a psychologist) and Ruthe H. (a psychologist) Hartley; married, 1965; children: Rebecca (adopted), Kai (son). *Education:* Attended Exeter University, 1960; Antioch College, B.A., 1962; Ohio State University, M.A. 1964; doctoral study, Berkeley, 1964-67. *Home:* 2065 Fulton Ave., West Vancouver, British Columbia, Canada V7V 1T3.

CAREER: Has worked as an assistant preschool teacher at the Gesell Institute, New Haven, Conn., as an editorial assistant for *Parents' Magazine,* and as instructor in English at Ohio State University, Berkeley, University of Hawaii, Simon Fraser University, and Capilano College; University of British Columbia, Canada, assistant professor, 1980—; free-lance writer. Teaches creative writing to children, Windsor House School, North Vancouver. *Member:* Writers Union of Canada, Canadian Society of Children's Authors, Illustrators, and Publishers.

WRITINGS:

Bonnie McSmithers You're Driving Me Dithers (illustrated by Fiona Garrick), Tree Frog Press, 1974, revised edition, 1987.
Hurry Up, Bonnie! (illustrated by F. Garrick), Tree Frog Press, 1977.
The Finding Princess (illustrated by Jane Wolsak), Fforbez, 1977.
The Adventures of Prince Paul (illustrated by J. Wolsak), Fforbez, 1977.
Bonnie McSmithers Is at It Again! (illustrated by F. Garrick), Tree Frog Press, 1979.
Comet's Tale (illustrated by Georgia Pow Graham), Tree Frog Press, 1983.

The Not Impossible Summer (illustrated by Christine Rother), Clarke, Irwin, 1983.
Ida and the Wool Smugglers (illustrated by Ann Blades), Douglas & McIntyre, 1987, Macmillan, 1988.

FOR MORE INFORMATION SEE:

Irma McDonough, editor, *Profiles 2,* Canadian Library Association, 1982.

ARKIN, Alan (Wolf) 1934-
(Roger Short)

PERSONAL: Born March 26, 1934, in New York, N.Y.; son of David (an artist and teacher) and Beatrice (a teacher; maiden name, Wortis) Arkin; married second wife, Barbara Dana (an actress and author), June 16, 1964; children: (first marriage) Adam, Matthew, (second marriage) Anthony. *Education:* Attended Los Angeles City College, 1951-52, Los Angeles State College, 1952-53, and Bennington College, 1953-55; studied with Benjamin Zemach, 1952-55. *Residence:* Chappaqua, N.Y. *Address:* c/o Triad, 888 Seventh Ave., New York, N.Y. 10106.

CAREER: Actor, director, composer, and author. Member of "The Tarriers," a folksinging group, 1957-59; actor in improvisational theater with Compass Players, St. Louis, Mo., 1959, and with Second City, Chicago, Ill., 1960. Actor in stage productions, including "Heloise," 1958, "From the Second City," 1961, "Man Out Loud, Girl Quiet," 1962, "Enter Laughing," 1963-64, "A View from under the Bridge," 1964, "Luv," 1964, and "The Opening," 1972. Director of stage productions, including revues during the early 1960s, (under

1

Arkin with wife, Barbara Dana, during the filming of the PBS-TV "Wonderworks" special "Necessary Parties."

the pseudonym Roger Short) "Eh?," 1966, "Hail Scrawdyke!," 1966, "Little Murders," 1969, "The White House Murder Case," 1970, "The Sunshine Boys," 1972, "Molly," 1973, "Joan of Lorraine," 1974, and 1976, "The Soft Touch," 1975, "Rubbers," 1975, and "Yanks 3 Detroit 0 Top of the Seventh," 1975.

Actor in films, including (and producer) "That's Me" (short motion picture), 1962; (and producer) "The Last Mohican" (short motion picture), 1963; "The Russians Are Coming! The Russians Are Coming!," 1966; "Woman Times Seven," 1967; "Wait until Dark," 1967; "The Heart Is a Lonely Hunter," 1968; "Inspector Clousseau," 1968; "The Monitors," 1969; "Popi," 1969; "Catch-22," 1970; "The Last of the Red Hot Lovers," 1972; "Deadhead Miles," 1972; "Freebie and the Bean," 1974; (and director) "Hearts of the West," 1975; "Rafferty and the Gold Dust Twins," 1975; (and director) "The Seven Percent Solution," 1976; "The Magician of Lublin," 1979; (and director and producer) "The In-Laws," 1979; "Simon," 1980; "Chu Chu and the Philly Flash," 1981; "Improper Channels," 1981; (voice) "The Last Unicorn," 1982; "Bad Medicine," 1985; and "Joshua Then and Now," 1985.

Director of films, including "Thank God It's Friday" (short motion picture), 1967; (and producer) "People Soup" (short motion picture), 1969; and "Little Murders," 1971.

Appeared in television programs, including "David Susskind Show," 1962; "The Beatnik and the Politician," 1964; "Les Crane Show," 1964-65; "The Love Song of Barney Kempinski," for "ABC Stage 67," 1966; "Natasha Kovolina Pipishinsky," 1976; "To America," 1976; "The Defection of Simon Kudirka," 1978; "Captain Kangaroo"; "The Fourth Wise Man," 1985; "A Deadly Business," 1986; and "Escape from Sobibor,"

1987. Director of television productions, including "Twigs," 1975, and a number of short films. *Member:* American Federation of Television and Radio Artists; American Federation of Musicians; American Society of Composers, Authors, and Publishers; Actors Equity Association; Screen Actors Guild.

AWARDS, HONORS: Antoinette Perry (Tony) Award from the League of American Theatres and Producers for Best Supporting Actor, *Theatre World* Award, and winner of *Variety*'s New York Drama Critics Poll, all 1963, all for "Enter Laughing"; Golden Globe Award from the Hollywood Foreign Press Association for Best Actor in a Musical or Comedy, and Academy Award nomination for Best Actor from the Academy of Motion Picture Arts and Sciences, both 1967, both for "The Russians Are Coming! The Russians Are Coming!"; Academy Award nomination for Best Actor, and New York Film Critics Award for Best Actor, both 1968, both for "The Heart Is a Lonely Hunter; Obie Award from the *Village Voice* for Distinguished Directing, and Drama Desk Award for Outstanding Director, both 1970, both for "The White House Murder Case"; *Tony's Hard Work Day* was selected one of Child Study Association of America's Children's Books of the Year, 1972, *The Lemming Condition*, 1976; Tony Award nomination for Best Director, 1973, for "The Sunshine Boys"; New York Film Critics Award for Best Supporting Actor, 1975, for "Hearts of the West"; *The Lemming Condition* was selected one of *New York Times* Outstanding Books of the Year, 1976; Genie Award from the Academy of Canadian Cinema and Television for Best Performance by a Actor in a Supporting Role, 1986, for "Joshua Then and Now"; Genie Award for Best Performance by a Foreign Actor from the Academy of Canadian Cinema and Television, 1982, for "Improper Channels."

WRITINGS:

(Contributor of sketches, music, lyrics, and photographic slides) "A View from under the Bridge," first produced in New York City at Square East Theatre, August 5, 1964.
Tony's Hard Work Day (juvenile; illustrated by James Stevenson), Harper, 1972, reissued, 1988.
The Lemming Condition (juvenile; illustrated by Joan Sandin), Harper, 1976.
Halfway through the Door: An Actor's Journey toward the Self (autobiography), Harper, 1979.
The Clearing (young adult), Harper, 1986.

Recordings include "The Banana Boat Song," 1957, "The Babysitters," 1958, "Songs and Fun with the Babysitters," 1960, "The Family Album," 1965, "Luv: A New Comedy," Columbia, 1965, and "The Babysitters Menagerie," 1968.

Composer for "Man Out Loud, Girl Quiet," first produced in New York City at Cricket Theatre, April 3, 1962. Also composer of more than one hundred songs, including "Cuddle Bug," "That's Me," and "Best Time of the Year."

Contributor of science fiction stories to *Galaxy*.

SIDELIGHTS: Born in Brooklyn on **March 26, 1934,** Alan Wolf Arkin was the son of Russian-German Jewish leftist intellectual parents. His father was an artist and teacher, someone with whom Arkin always felt competitive, his mother was a teacher.

"My mother's father was a terrific guy who studied opera singing well into his 80s. He was a jeweler and optometrist in Brooklyn, and in the middle of the afternoon, the busiest time, he'd close up the shop and go in the back and turn off the lights and play his violin. He had a fantastic sense of humor. A few days after he got married, he bought one of those toys—where you hide a dollar inside and you put a piece of paper in one side and the dollar comes out the other. He brought it to my grandmother and said, 'Selena, I have a confession to make. I told you I was a jeweler and optometrist, but this is what I really do for a living.' And then he turned the little crank and the dollar came out and my grandmother burst into tears and ran into her room and wouldn't come out for days.

"My father's father was something else. He used to love to read letters aloud. I remember walking into his bathroom one day and seeing a pair of feet sticking out from under the bathtub. It was the plumber fixing a pipe. And there stood my grandfather, tears streaming down his face, reading a letter from my uncle in North Africa out loud to the plumber."[1]

From his father, Arkin learned deep appreciation for the arts. "The first time I ever got outside my skin was hearing Beethoven's Seventh. My father made me sit down and listen to it, and afterwards he asked me what it was about, and I told him tremendous sorrow. So he said listen again, it's about sorrow that's beyond emotion. It becomes a solid in space. And so I listened and pretended that I was Beethoven composing it, and I got into a state of such transcendant power that it floated me right out of my chair."[1]

At age ten, Arkin began drama lessons in New York, but two years later, at age twelve, he moved with his family to Los Angeles so his father could get a job as a set designer. Unfortunately, his father lost the job because of a Hollywood strike which closed the studios for eight months.

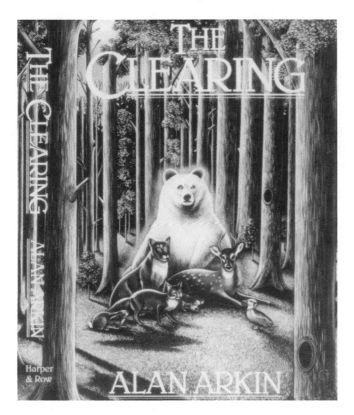

(Jacket illustration by Griesbach/Martucci. Jacket design by Anita Soos from *The Clearing* by Alan Arkin.)

1951. Graduating from Benjamin Franklin High School in Los Angeles, he began studying at Los Angeles City College, then transferred to Los Angeles State College in 1952 and began three years of, at times transcontinental, studies with Benjamin Zemack, a Los Angeles drama teacher.

1953. Arkin went back East and enrolled at Bennington College in Vermont, dropping out in 1956 to join two friends who formed the folksinging group "The Tarriers." He wrote their hit "The Banana Boat Song." Although the group enjoyed success, making several records, playing college campuses and touring the world, Arkin felt uncomfortable in the role. "One day I just looked at myself standing on stage in satin pants with a guitar around my neck and I said, 'What the hell am I?' And the next day I quit."[1]

He had his stage debut with the Compass Players at the Crystal Place in St. Louis in **1959,** then moved on to Chicago to join the Second City troupe, which included Mike Nichols and Elaine May. "I figured that in the Midwest I could have a normal life and a small career as a local actor. . . .At the time that looked about as good as anything I could do."[1]

The troupe was very successful, working almost like a commune. Arkin devoted most of his waking hours to it. They traveled to New York City and became a big hit. "It was fantastic when all these fancy people we'd been cutting up in our routines started showing up in the audience. We were nervous and embarrassed, but then we started hearing how much they loved us, and some of them even came backstage and told us how marvelous we were. The effect of this was to make me doubt the premise of our work. . .I thought there had to be something wrong with either the potency or the aim when the people we thought we were destroying all loved us so much."[1]

1964. Arkin became depressed and moody, questioning the nature of his successes. "I'd been telling myself for years that everything would take care of itself as soon as I became a successful actor. And then I became a good working actor, working six days a week and that was great except that I had absolutely no life at all outside of that. I felt like I was being swept along in some current. I didn't feel that I had any control over my destiny. And then three people in one week told me I ought to see a psychiatrist and that started me fantasizing about going and then I'd be sitting there telling this neutral person all these horrible things about myself."[1] He entered analysis, which he continued for six years. On June 16, he wed Barbara Dana, an actress.

In his Broadway debut, "Enter Laughing," he portrayed a nervous student with no talent. The performance won Arkin a Tony Award. "It was the second year of my analysis, and I had been making quiet, unassuming advances. I was learning to trust my doctor and getting some basic techniques in self-examination, but nothing terribly important had surfaced. At the same time, without my being aware of it, a lot of deeply suppressed material was starting to push at me.

"I was starring very successfully in a play called 'Enter Laughing,' and in the middle of the long run I came down with a case of laryngitis. By this time I was sophisticated enough about myself to suspect that the sickness was attributable to the surfacing of some material in my analysis that I did not want to talk about. Nevertheless, in order to keep the play going, something had to be done to restore my voice. A doctor was recommended, a 'miracle doctor' who was known for his immediate cures of laryngitis among singers and actors. I went to him. It was about noon on a Saturday, just before the matinee, and I was ushered right in. The doctor gave me a

(From the movie "The Russians Are Coming! The Russians Are Coming!," Arkin's feature-film debut. Released by United Artists, 1966.)

cursory examination, followed by an injection that I can still feel. I do not know what it contained—I suspect it was some sort of amphetamine—but it was as if molten lava had been poured into my veins. I do not recall the next few hours very clearly, but I know I felt like a rabid dog.

"I got through the play somehow, but I raged, I fumed, and I wanted to tear the theater apart. I remember cursing a great deal, spewing out all sorts of venom related to my fellow actors, the audience and the management. I imagined I could literally climb the walls, and I am not sure that I did not attempt it. After the show I went back to my dressing room, feeling as if I had burned out years of repressed rage and violence. In this weakened condition, the walls of my subconscious came down and an enormous amount of analytic material started pouring out of my mind. I grabbed a pencil and paper and wrote steadily from four o'clock until curtain time that evening. Revelation upon revelation came to me about my early childhood, and by the time I finished I felt purged, spent and cleaner than I had ever felt in my life. The next day, Sunday, I dragged my good doctor away from his family to read for him what I had put down, and afterward, in a Freudian slip of his own, he referred to me as Doctor Arkin. He quickly corrected himself, but I took it as a great compliment, and a sign that I had done some significant digging. For a week I felt clean and whole and pure.

"The following Saturday I got to the theater a half hour before the show, took a few minutes to shake off the outside world and locate my character, and then got ready to shave. Now, at this theater, as in many theaters, there is a backstage sound system that allows the actors in their dressing rooms to hear the audience and the action on stage, and also to get time checks from the stage manager. It allows the actors to stay in their dressing rooms rather than wait in the wings. I picked up my razor, held it against my face, and at that precise moment the sound system was turned on. What I heard was the roar of the matinee audience scrambling for seats, but the juxtaposition of the two things—the razor against my face and the noise of the crowd—caused my hands and then my feet to go absolutely dead. I did not know what was wrong with me. I shook myself several times to get the circulation going, but it did not help. I felt as if I was in terrible jeopardy, and I could not bring myself either to shave or to go on stage."[2]

Arkin was able to go on stage, but he cites this experience in his memoir, *Halfway through the Door,* as proof that he has lived other lives. It stands out as one of several such experiences which his yoga teacher later revealed to him as residual memories from other lives. Apparently he had once been beheaded by a mob in the French Revolution, and that explains his continuing fear of razors. In this case, the sound of the audience reminded him of the roaring blood lust of the mob.

1966. Arkin made his film debut in "The Russians Are Coming! The Russians Are Coming!" for which he won an Oscar nomination. After playing the role of a lovable Soviet leader, he observed that "everyone thinks I'm a sweet Russian now. Nobody really recognizes me. Of course I don't recognize them either.

"Before a film or play I find myself walking like the character I'm going to be. I find myself looking at clothes that the character would wear and not me. I can't take my mind off the character. I read the script many times and find myself falling into a thought pattern not my own, a speech pattern not my own."[3]

"I prepare for a role in a strange way. I don't read the script very many times. I don't consciously think of it. I just find that it

stays on my mind all the time until I get locked onto an image of the person I'm supposed to be. If that doesn't happen, I consider myself in deep trouble, but usually it means that the character doesn't know who he is. Like when I was doing 'The Russians Are Coming!' I felt terribly strange and awkward and I thought it was because this was my first movie and a lot was riding on it. But then I caught myself and said, wait a minute! this is exactly what Rozanov feels! The strangeness and the sense of not knowing the language were his feelings, not mine. I was giving myself the right signals, but in my insecurity I misinterpreted him. Ah, God, it's very convoluted. What I'm trying to say is that you have to read the signals that come out of the subconscious and find out what they're trying to tell you. If you really listen to yourself, you can trust your instincts to practically never mislead you."[1]

Later, he wrote of this transitional time when he was moving from theater to films: "The theater became my addiction, my obsession, my god. What I did not realize—and this is crucial—is that there is no power whatsoever in the craft of acting itself. Acting is nothing more than a concept. The power I experienced on stage was in me. I invested my performances with that power. Had I been courageous enough to accept the idea that the power was mine to invest anywhere I chose, in whatever craft, sport, profession, social activity, I would have been a much happier person much sooner. But I kept this knowledge from myself. And the reason I did so was because power is dangerous, and I did not trust myself to use it well. Therefore the stage, where all manner of hateful or beautiful things can take place and no one gets hurt.

"Interestingly, I began to lose that power when my name was placed over the title of a play. When I became a star, all of a sudden I could no longer lose myself in a character. I could no longer hide, because people were coming to the theater to see *me*. I was forced to accept the fact that I was not really the character I was portraying, that I was actually on stage, and that the feelings I displayed were really variations of my own emotions. This stifled me to the point that it became uncomfortable to be in front of an audience. I began holding myself carefully in check. I became afraid of taking chances, of having the audience dislike me. And as a result, my flights of liberation now came only with sex, alcohol or marijuana. Fortunately, I was able to work in film, which is more intimate, and although there is never enough time from shot to shot to have an extended feeling of flight, there is still a wonderful fantasy life built around the idea of being a successful actor. Most of these fantasies involved the anticipation of more money, more attention, more ability to control associates scripts; and for a while all this sustained me. I was not happy, mind you, but I was terribly busy."[2]

1967. Arkin played three roles in "Wait until Dark," the parts of father, son, and psychopathic killer.

1968. He received another Academy Award nomination for the role of deaf-mute John Singer in "The Heart Is a Lonely Hunter," and won the New York Film Critics Best Actor Award.

He met his guru, John, a teacher of Agni yoga, a yoga of meditation without exercise. "I was playing the title role in a film called 'Popi.' It was a film I cared about deeply. I felt I was doing good work, I was making a great deal of money, and I was in a period of my career when I was popular and in demand. My marriage was thriving. I had, in fact, achieved everything I had ever set out to do. Through my own efforts and with the help of analysis, I had realized a life that would have been the envy of most of the world. The one problem I could not work

"West!" said Uncle Claude. (From *The Lemming Condition* by Alan Arkin. Illustrated by Joan Sandin.)

around was that I was angry and unhappy most of the time. I was all right as long as I was acting, making love, eating and buying some piece of musical or photographic equipment, but the rest of the time I was actively confused and empty.

"Had I been able to busy myself twenty-four hours a day with creative projects, lovemaking and eating, I probably could have avoided yoga. But sooner or later in the day there was that moment when I was alone or exhausted, and then the endless nightmare of 'Who am I?' would present itself. I knew people who seemed to be able to avoid this nightmare, people who had decided on their limits, the areas in which they were comfortable and those in which they were not. People who simply refused to allow their minds any excursions into unknown territory. I had friends who maintained that they had a clear idea of who they were in the universe, and seemed to be able to live reasonably well in and around their beliefs.

"I found myself envying these people with fixed goals, fixed identities. I would have traded places with any number of them, but I could not. They had an ability that I did not possess. A moment alone, a bad review, a play closing—any one of a hundred things could send me into oblivion. And yet somewhere, even in my darkest moments, I suspected that I knew something they did not know, that lurking in my despair and questioning was more truth than in their rigid certainties."[2]

1969. Arkin produced his third short film, called "People Soup," in which both Matthew and Adam, his older sons, played parts. Earlier films of his were "The Last Mohican" and "That's Me." "'People Soup' is a more positive statement than the other two. What it's really about is the magic of childhood, which is something I believe in. I think it's the best of the three. What bothers me now about the other two is not that they're invalid or untrue or imperceptive but that they represent points of view I no longer feel. They're both caring films, but they're placid. They're not on the side of the possibility for betterment."[1]

1970. "Shortly after 'Popi,' I left for Mexico to play Yossarian in 'Catch-22.' It was another role I cared very much about, from a book I loved, but the film took a direction I could not understand, and this became a source of great pain for me. We were in Mexico for four months, and we of the cast were left to our own resources for long periods of time, waiting for elaborate camera setups that literally took days to organize. Months went by with little or no contact with the outside world, and my lack of personal resources plus feeling at odds with the project in which I was engaged kept me isolated and on edge, so that I remained in an emotional limbo for most of the eight months it took to shoot the film. Although I suspect that a lot of things were beginning to formulate subconsciously, I don't recall spending one moment thinking about either yoga or John for an entire year."[2]

But soon after his return to New York, he became a formal student of John and of yoga.

During the same year, Arkin and his wife bought a summer home in Connecticut. With typical angst, he needed to justify his comfortable existence. "It's like I say to myself in this day and age, what right have I got to peace and happiness and clean air? But then I say, well, because most people can't have it so good, does that mean I should deprive myself? Who would it help?"[1]

1971 While directing his first play, "Little Murders," he decided to end his six-year relationship with his doctor. "I decided to leave analysis, partly because I sensed that I was getting into places my doctor did not know about, care about or feel were part of the analytic process—one or another or all of these reasons. In addition, I felt I was outsmarting myself in several areas. I worked my way around my anger continuously, never got at its roots and was feeling more and more that I never would within the analytic process.

"Also, I discovered that the best I could come up with philosophically was an uneasy existentialism. I found myself trying to say that life is devoid of meaning, that it is all a random joke, that we must laugh at the whole universe and once we have done so, go about our business and behave as if there was meaning. This was the culmination of twentieth-century philosophy. I wanted to fall in step with it, but I could get no sense out of it. It made me miserable. What I was approaching gingerly

Arkin starred in the 1985 Canadian film "Joshua Then and Now."

with Guru seemed, on the other hand, to be totally irrational, but it was beginning to make me happy, or at least peaceful for the first time in my life. I decided to opt for irrational joy rather than rational misery. My doctor and I parted warmly and amicably, and I thank him still for the work that we accomplished—the beginning tools for self-examination and an enjoyment of the process of change.

"I continued to see John. Perhaps once a week I would travel up to Mount Vernon, where he lived in what he called his ashram, or spiritual school, with his lovely, unbelievable warm and happy wife, his mother and one disciple. I was for the most part uncomfortable in this environment. It was just too peaceful. Feeling capable of explosions that would be damaging to this place, I disliked it and was unhappy with myself. For there was no tension here that I could relate to; nothing askew, nothing hidden. In other words, I saw nothing of myself in this environment, and I kept looking for familiar things in the people and the place, but without much success. I came there because the tension I constantly felt was impossible to live with, but when I placed myself in an environment where it was missing, I was mistrustful and uncomfortable."[2]

1972. Arkin starred in two films: "Last of the Red Hot Lovers" and "Deadhead Miles." He also published his first children's book, *Tony's Hard Work Day,* about a little boy whose family was fixing up a summer house. When they rebuffed him in his offers to help, he went off and built his own imaginary house, and the family was so impressed they moved in there instead.

No doubt the idea came from his son Tony, who was four at the time.

1976. He published *The Lemming Condition* for older readers. The story tells about a young lemming named Bubba who questions the age-old tradition among lemmings of throwing themselves into the sea.

Constantly working on films, television movies and despite his variety of accomplishments as singer, song-writer, actor, director and writer, Arkin remains ambiguous about success: "Success is doing what you've set out to do, so it can be a million different things and you yourself are the only one who can know it when it comes."[1]

He says that a "capsule philosophy" card he once saw in a New York City bus sums up his idea of important activity: "I thought it would be Demosthenes or Socrates or someone, but who was it? Benny Goodman. It was Benny Goodman's capsule philosophy. So I chuckled to myself and then I read it, and what he was saying was that he'd spent years trying to find the right wood for reeds. And he said, 'A lot of people think this is a shameless waste of time but it is terribly important to me, because I have found that the one thing a man must have is an activity that destroys time's terrible rush.' *Time's terrible rush* that said the whole thing to me."[1]

Of all his important activities, he seems to find directing most satisfying: "When I'm really working well as a director, it's as

(From the short motion picture "People Soup." Written and directed by Arkin, starring his sons Adam and Matthew.)

if the script is somewhere back of my head, and the actors are out in front and I'm suspended on a beam of light in between. It's the greatest feeling you can possibly have. I think directing is a more mature activity than acting. When you're acting, you're re-creating someone else's vision of the world. When you're directing, you're interpreting someone else's vision and incorporating your own into it. But in acting I have such a feeling of confidence that I can't just leave it behind. It's the only thing that gives me that good feeling of potency, where you trust yourself. It's too much of a feeling to learn to live without. Acting in a movie is going to be like a vacation now. I suppose it's the German tradition or the Jewish or whatever that tells you that everything has to have a reason for being, that it's not enough to just have a good time. But I think I've come about as far as I can with the idea of working out of discipline and dedication. From now on I'm going to try to work out of *joy*. I guess, I'm going to learn to trust myself to the extent where I feel that whatever I'm in contact with is going to be worth something.

"I used to be panicky. There used to be a time when I thought that if I couldn't act I was going to have to jump out a window. But I don't feel that anymore. Now I have a life of my own. I can get through a day very, very well involving myself in a thousand things that have nothing to do with acting. I can spend time with my wife. I can devote good constructive time to my children, I can play tennis. I can garden. I used to just question my existence all the time. I guess a lot of people do—it's the 20th Century disease, you know, *whom am I?* Well, I don't ask

anymore. I don't wake up in the morning and say, *who am I? What do I have to do to feel like I'm alive? I already know I'm alive, and since I already know, I don't have to ask.*"[1]

FOOTNOTE SOURCES

[1] Barry Farrell, "Yossarian in Connecticut," *Life,* October 2, 1970. Amended by Alan Arkin.
[2] A. Arkin, *Halfway through the Door: An Actor's Journey toward the Self,* Harper, 1979.
[3] *Contemporary Authors,* Volume 112, Gale, 1985.

AUSTIN, Oliver L(uther), Jr. 1903- 1988

OBITUARY NOTICE:—See sketch in *SATA* Volume 7: Born May 24, 1903, in Tuckahoe, N.Y.; died December 31, 1988, in Gainesville, Fla. Biologist, administrator, editor, and author. Austin was a specialist in ornithology and his 1961 book, *Birds of the World: A Survey of the 27 Orders and 155 Families*, was considered definitive in the field.

Working as a biologist with the U.S. Department of Agriculture early in his career, he helped his father establish the Austin Ornithological Research Station in Wellfleet, Massachusetts, in 1929. The younger Austin directed the station from 1932 until 1957, when he became ornithological curator of the Florida State Museum. In 1931, at the age of twenty-eight, he was elected to membership in the American Ornithological Union. He was also a member of the Explorer's Club.

During the 1940s and 1950s he worked for the U.S. armed forces, first as a commander in the Naval Reserve, then as a technical specialist in Tokyo, Japan, and at Maxwell Air Force Base, Alabama. Austin's books include *The Birds of Japan*, written with Nagahisa Kuroda, and *The Random House Book of Birds*, a children's book written with his wife, Elizabeth. For the "Golden Field Guide" series, published by Golden Press, he wrote *Families of Birds*. Beginning in 1968 he also edited the quarterly journal *Auk*.

FOR MORE INFORMATION SEE:

Martha E. Ward and Dorothy A. Marquardt, *Authors of Books for Young People*, supplement to the 2nd edition, Scarecrow, 1979.
American Men and Women of Science: The Physical and Biological Sciences, 16th edition, Bowker, 1986.

OBITUARIES

New York Times, January 4, 1989.
Chicago Tribune, January 6, 1989.

BARTON, Pat 1928-
(Pat Arrowsmith)

PERSONAL: Born August 20, 1928, in London, England; daughter of Harry (an insurance director) and Olive (a civil servant; maiden name, Flude) Arrowsmith; married John Barton (a writer and bookseller), March 22, 1962; children: Anne-Louise, Jeremy. *Education:* Attended Pitman's College, 1946-47. *Religion:* Anglican. *Home:* 84 Old Kennels Lane, Olivers Battery, Winchester, Hants SO22 4JT, England.

CAREER: Writer, 1947—; Royal London Insurance Company, London, England, 1947; United Society for the Propagation of the Gospel, Westminster, England, beginning 1953, childrens' magazine editor, 1955-62. *Member:* Ephemera Society.

WRITINGS:

"Fleming—Don't Go!" Archibald Lang Fleming, First Bishop of the Arctic, Edinburgh House, 1962.
Glorious Explosion: Stories of North India and Pakistan, Edinburgh House, 1965.
Fighter for the Right: The Story of Trevor Huddleston, Lutterworth, 1967.
Narrow Boat Summer, Blackie, 1974.
Waiting for the Jubilee, Blackie, 1976.
A Week Is a Long Time (illustrated by Jutta Ash), Abelard, 1977.
The Devil's Garden (illustrated by Ken Stott), Abelard, 1978, Scholastic, 1979.
The Last Run, Blackie, 1980.

UNDER NAME PAT ARROWSMITH

Camp Christopher, Blackie, 1948.
Goodbye, Uncle Simon, Blackie, 1950.
Honeycomb Valley, Blackie, 1951.

Contributor of short stories and lesson material for the United Society for the Propaganda of the Gospel and Edinburgh House Press.

WORK IN PROGRESS: Children's books: *The Day the Fog Came Down, Just as Far as Baxton*, and *Christy Is Missing*, a children's mystery.

SIDELIGHTS: "I remember quite clearly the day I decided that I wanted to be a writer. It was during the last war and I had been evacuated to the country with my sister and mother. I was reading a book by Hugh Walpole called *Jeremy* which my father had given me for my birthday, and the characters seemed so real that I felt I could almost touch them. 'I want to write like that,' I told myself. The nearest I got at the time was to win a story competition in the 'Mickey Mouse Comic!' I also started a club with some of the local children and a magazine to go with it. I think the magazine was mainly for my own benefit because I think I wrote most of the items.

"Also, during this time in the country, we lived next door to the writer Graham Seton. He impressed me quite a bit, especially when he used to shout at us, 'How do you expect me to write with all that noise going on?' Years later, when I had children of my own, I was able to appreciate how he felt.

"Back in London after the war, my mother and father, probably not quite knowing what to do with me, sent me to Pitman's College to learn 'secretarial skills.' After all, I wasn't qualified for much else. And at least I was able to advance from typing with two fingers to touch typing. I also advanced from scribbling short stories in exercise books to a full-length book for children. I sent it to Blackie who said that their list was full, but if my manuscript wasn't accepted anywhere else within eighteen months perhaps I would let them see it again? So I sat on the manuscript for eighteen months because I had already started work on a second book. When I eventually sent the first manuscript back to Blackie I was nineteen and had started to work for an insurance company in London. My mother telephoned me at work to say that a letter had arrived from the publisher and should she open it? The relief and joy when she at last said: 'It's all right. They're going to publish it,' was amazing. I don't think there are many moments as great as the acceptance of one's first book.

"*Camp Christopher* was soon followed by *Goodbye, Uncle Simon* and *Honeycomb Valley*. They were all published under my maiden name of Pat Arrowsmith. Later this name was to cause some confusion when Pat Arrowsmith of Campaign for Nuclear Disarmament fame came upon the scene.

"But not everything in the garden was rosy from then on. My fourth book was rejected. This came as quite a shock but, on reflection, perhaps it was for the best. It made me realise that not everything I wrote would automatically be published.

"Eventually I changed my job and went to work for an Anglican missionary society (I had recently joined the Anglican church) in Westminster. It turned out to be one of the liveliest places I have ever worked—and I have worked in quite a few. When the editor of the childrens' magazine left, they asked me if I would take over her job. I did, after some persuasion. I was also helping write childrens' lesson material and because of all this had little time or inclination to go home and write fiction. I stayed on as editor until the time I left to have my first baby. Probably the most important thing I learned as an editor was how to be economical with words.

"I married John Barton in 1962. He worked as a surveyor then with the Ordnance Survey and was sometimes away for weeks at a time. Whilst awaiting the birth of my second baby I was asked by the Lutterworth Press if I would consider writing the

PAT BARTON

story of Bishop Trevor Huddleston for their 'Faith and Fame' series. This was something of a challenge so I agreed. But I found this factual writing far more difficult than fiction. Dialogue could not just be invented; it had at least to be based on the truth. But the book did get written and was published as *Fighter for the Right*.

"We moved to Hampshire in 1968, and because of the children and their friends, the guinea-pigs, the ducks, gerbils, cat, the very large garden, etc., etc., I wrote nothing until my son Jeremy was old enough to go to school with his sister Anne-Louise. 'Now there is absolutely no excuse,' I told myself firmly.

"For some time I had thought about writing a book with a canal background and this was to be the setting of *Narrow Boat Summer*. One of the children had already given me the title of another story 'A Week Is a Long Time!' This was my first attempt at the text for a picture story later to be published by Abelard-Schuman with delightful illustrations by Jutta Ash.

"Creating atmosphere and character I find one of the most fascinating and rewarding parts of writing; working out an interesting and original plot the most difficult. Each book is revised at least three times. Wherever possible I do like to try to bring some history into a book in an unobtrusive sort of way, for example, the canals, the last war, the 1950s, so that readers are not only entertained (I hope) but also learn something new."

BAYNES, Pauline (Diana) 1922-

PERSONAL: Born September 9, 1922, in Brighton, England; daughter of Frederick William Wilberforce (a Commissioner in the Indian Civil Service) and Jessie Harriet Maude (Cunningham) Baynes; married Fritz Otto Gasch (a garden contractor), March 25, 1961 (deceased). *Education:* Attended Farnham School of Art, 1937, and Slade School of Art, 1939-40. *Home and office:* Rock Barn Cottage, Dockenfield, Farnham, Surrey GU10 4HH, England.

CAREER: Illustrator, 1941—; art teacher at School in Camberley, England, 1946-47. Work exhibited at the Royal Academy, and in London and surrounding areas. Worker for British Army's Camouflage Development and Training Centre, 1940-42, and Hydrographic Department of British Admiralty, 1942-45. *Member:* Women's International Art Club. *Awards, honors:* Lewis Carroll Shelf Award, 1962, for *The Lion, the Witch, and the Wardrobe;* Carole Prize, 1964, for *The Puffin Book of Nursery Rhymes;* Kate Greenaway Medal from the British Library Association, and *Book World*'s Spring Book Festival Award, both 1968, both for *A Dictionary of Chivalry; The Joy of the Court* was selected one of Child Study Association of America's Children's Books of the Year, 1971; Kate Greenaway Medal Commendation, 1972, for *Snail and Caterpillar; The Iron Lion* was selected one of *New York Times* Notable Books, 1984.

PAULINE BAYNES

WRITINGS:

ALL SELF-ILLUSTRATED

Victoria and the Golden Bird, Blackie & Sons, 1947.
How Dog Began, Methuen, 1986, Holt, 1987.
Good King Wenceslas, Lutterworth Press, 1987.

ILLUSTRATOR

Victoria Stevenson, *Clover Magic,* Country Life, 1944.
V. Stevenson, *The Magic Footstool,* Country Life, 1946.
J. R. R. Tolkien, *Farmer Giles of Ham,* Allen & Unwin, 1949, Houghton, 1950.
V. Stevenson, *The Magic Broom,* Country Life, 1950.
W. T. Bebbington, *And It Came to Pass,* Allen & Unwin, 1951.
C. S. Lewis, *The Lion, the Witch, and the Wardrobe,* Bles, 1950, (ALA Notable Book), Macmillan, 1951, new edition, 1988.
Henri Pourrat, *A Treasury of French Tales,* Allen & Unwin, 1951, Houghton, 1954.
C. S. Lewis, *Prince Caspian,* Macmillan, 1951, new edition, 1988.
E. J. S. Lay, *Men and Manners,* Macmillan, 1952.
C. S. Lewis, *The Voyage of the "Dawn Treader,"* Macmillan, 1952, new edition, 1988.
Marjorie Phillips, *Annabel and Bryony,* Oxford University Press, 1953.
C. S. Lewis, *The Silver Chair,* Macmillan, 1953, new edition, 1988.
C. S. Lewis, *The Horse and His Boy,* Macmillan, 1954, new edition, 1988.

A. Hitchcock and L. J. Hitchcock, *Great People Thru' the Ages,* Blackie & Sons, 1954.
A. Hitchock and L. J. Hitchcock, *The British People,* Blackie & Sons, 1955.
C. S. Lewis, *The Magician's Nephew* (ALA Notable Book), Macmillan, 1955, new edition, 1988.
Llewellyn, *China's Court and Concubines,* Allen & Unwin, 1956.
C. S. Lewis, *The Last Battle: A Story for Children,* Macmillan, 1956, new edition, 1988.
Emmeline Garnett, *The Tudors,* Blackie & Sons, 1956.
E. Garnett, *Queen Anne,* Blackie & Sons, 1956.
E. Garnett, *Civil War,* Blackie & Sons, 1956.
Amabel Williams-Ellis, *The Arabian Nights,* S. G. Phillips, 1957.
Rhoda Power, *From the Fury Northmen,* Riverside Press, 1957.
Denton, *Stars and Candles,* Benn, 1958.
Monica Backway, *Hasan of Basorah,* Blackie & Sons, 1958.
Joan Mary Bete, *The Curious Tale of Cloud City,* Blackie & Sons, 1958.
Anne Malcolmson, *Miracle Plays,* Houghton, 1959.
A. Williams-Ellis, *Fairy Tales from the British Isles,* Blackie, 1960, F. Warne, 1964.
Loretta Burrough, *Sister Clare,* Houghton, 1960.
Dorothy Ensor, *The Adventures of Hakim Tai,* Harrap, 1960, Walck, 1962.
Mary C. Borer, *Don Quixote,* Longmans, Green, 1960.
Edmund Spenser, *Saint George and the Dragon,* Methuen, 1961, Houghton, 1963.

"Why do you think that, Daughter of Eve?" asked the Lion. (From *The Magician's Nephew: Book 6 in the Chronicles of Narnia* by C. S. Lewis. Illustrated by Pauline Baynes.)

Gladys Hickman and E. G. Hume, *Pilgrim Way Geographies,* Volumes I, II, III, and IV, Blackie & Sons, 1961.

Lynette Muir, *The Unicorn Window,* Abelard, 1961.

James Morris, *The Upstairs Donkey and Other Stolen Stories,* Pantheon, 1961.

Alison Uttley, *The Little Knife That Did All the Work,* Faber, 1962.

J. R. R. Tolkien, *The Adventures of Tom Bombadil,* Allen & Unwin, 1962, Houghton, 1963.

Hans Christian Andersen, *Andersen's Fairy Tales,* Collins, 1963.

Iona Opie and Peter Opie, editors, *The Puffin Book of Nursery Rhymes,* Puffin, 1964.

Allan, *Come into My Castle,* Macmillan, 1964.

K. G. Lethbridge, *The Rout of the Ollafubs,* Faber, 1964.

M. Gail, *Avignon in Flower,* Houghton, 1965.

M. C. Borer, "Famous Lives" (series), Longman, 1965.

A. Uttley, *Recipes from an Old Farmhouse,* Faber, 1966.

Radost Pridham, *A Gift from the Heart: Folk Tales from Bulgaria,* Methuen, 1966, World, 1967.

Abigail Homes, *Education by Uncles,* Houghton, 1966.

J. R. R. Tolkien, *Smith of Wootton Major,* Allen & Unwin, 1967.

Jennifer Westwood, *Medieval Tales,* Hart-Davis, 1967, Coward, 1968.

Grant Uden, *A Dictionary of Chivalry,* Longman Young, 1968, Crowell, 1969.

Joseph W. Krutch, *The Most Wonderful Animals That Never Were,* Houghton, 1968.

Lady Jekyll, *Kitchen Essays,* Collins, 1970.

Richard D. Blackmore, *Lorna Doone,* Collins, 1970.

Constance Hieatt, *The Joy of the Court,* Crowell, 1970.

Naomi Mitchison, *Graeme and the Dragon,* Cambridge University Press, 1970.

J. Westwood, *Isle of Gramarye: An Anthology of the Poetry of Magic,* Hart-Davis, 1970.

Leonard Clark, *All Along Down Along,* Longman, 1971.

J. Westwood, *Tales and Legends,* Coward, 1971.

Philippa Pearce, *Stories from Hans Andersen,* Collins, 1972.

Helen Piers, *Snail and Caterpillar,* American Heritage, 1972.

Katie Stewart, *The Times Cookery Book,* Collins, 1972.

Enid Blyton, *Land of Far Beyond,* Methuen, 1973 (Baynes was not associated with the earlier edition).

John Symonds, *Harold,* Dent, 1973.

H. Piers, *Grasshopper and Butterfly,* McGraw, 1975.

Geoffrey Squire, *The Observer's Book of European Costume,* F. Warne, 1975.

G. Markham, *The Compleat Horseman,* Houghton, 1976.

Eileen Hunter, *Tales from Way Beyond,* Deutsch, 1979.

Richard Barber, *A Companion to World Mythology,* Kestrel, 1979.

Christopher Towers, *Oultre Jourdain,* Weidenfeld & Nicolson, 1980.

Rosemary Harris, *The Enchanted Horse,* Kestrel, 1981.

H. Piers, *Frog and Shrew,* Kestrel, 1981.

Overhead was the great patch of lurid light on the roof of the Underworld. (From *The Silver Chair: Book 4 in the Chronicles of Narnia* by C. S. Lewis. Illustrated by Pauline Baynes.)

Eustace. . .found himself standing on the frame; in front of him was not glass but real sea. (From *The Voyage of the "Dawn Trader": Book 3 in the Chronicles of Narnia* by C. S. Lewis. Illustrated by Pauline Baynes.)

Rumer Godden, *The Dragon of Oq*, Macmillan, 1981.

Mary Norton, *The Borrowers Avenged*, Kestrel, 1982.

R. Godden, *Four Dolls*, Greenwillow, 1983.

Peter Dickinson, *The Iron Lion*, Blackie & Sons, 1983, Peter Bedrick Books, 1984.

Rudyard Kipling, *How the Whale Got His Throat*, Macmillan, 1983.

Althea Peppin, *National Gallery Children's Book*, National Gallery, 1983.

David Harvey, *Dragon Smoke and Magic Song*, Allen & Unwin (Australia), 1984.

Anna Sewell, *Black Beauty*, Puffin, 1984.

Ursula Moray Williams, *The Further Adventures of Gobbolino and the Little Wooden Horse*, Penguin, 1984.

The Song of the Three Holy Children, Holt, 1986.

Mrs. Alexander, *All Things Bright and Beautiful*, Lutterworth Press, 1986.

George Macbeth, *Daniel*, Lutterworth Press, 1986.

Beatrix Potter, *Country Tales*, Warne, 1987.

B. Potter, *Wag-by-Wall*, Warne, 1987.

Noah and the Ark, Holt, 1988.

Rosemary Harris, compiler, *Love and the Merry-Go-Round*, Hamish Hamilton, 1988.

R. Harris, *Colm of the Islands*, Walker, 1989.

Jenny Koralek, *The Cobweb Curtain*, Holt, 1989.

ALL BY CLAUDE NICOLAS; ALL ORIGINALLY PUBLISHED IN FRANCE BY L'ECOLE DES LOISIRS

The Roe Deer, Chambers, 1974.

The Frog, Chambers, 1974.

The Butterfly, Chambers, 1974.

The Duck, Chambers, 1974.

The Bee and the Cherry Tree, Chambers, 1976.

The Salmon, Chambers, 1976.

The Dolphin, Chambers, 1977.

WORK IN PROGRESS: Illustrations for J. R. R. Tolkien's *Bilbo's Last Song,* for Houghton; *Praise Be to God,* collected prayers, for Lutterworth Press; illustrations for *The Land of Narnia* by Brian Sibley, for Collins.

SIDELIGHTS: **September 9, 1922.** "Shortly after I was born in Brighton, my parents returned to India where my father was posted as deputy commissioner in the Indian civil service. My mother was a very beautiful woman with an outgoing manner, an ability to tell a good story, and had been trained as a pianist.

(From *The Adventures of Tom Bombadil* by J. R. R. Tolkien. Illustrated by Pauline Baynes.)

(Frontispiece from *Farmer Giles of Ham* by J. R. R. Tolkien. Illustrated by Pauline Baynes.)

Baynes with husband, Fritz, in front of their cottage, 1988. (Photograph by Cathy Courtney.)

"My older sister, Angela, was the beacon of my life and had a great influence on me. She was a spendid artist and I copied everything she did. We had the same upbringing that many other children in India had, with an Indian ayah [nurse] to look after us. My mother was with us all the time, of course, and had a difficult life looking after two young children in remote jungle stations.

"My mother was not well in India, and she, my sister and I returned to England. My first recollection is of parting with my ayah at the Gare de Lyon in Paris where she left us to go back to India with another family. Watching my ayah disappear forever was the first dreadful thing that happened to me, and I still remember screaming at the parting.

"When my mother went to a nursing home for treatment, Angela and I were placed in my mother's old school, Farnborough Convent, which was close by. It had once been the home of the Empress Eugenie and was a very religious establishment—we came home at holiday time with corns on our knees. I can remember the strange, rather nice, smell of my missal, but it was in Latin, and, of course, I didn't understand a word of it. It was a horrific change after being spoilt by my mother and ayah to suddenly be in this enormous convent with five hundred other girls. I hardly had any contact with my sister, as I was in kindergarten, and she in the middle school, and the nuns were very strict.

"I was a thoroughly rebellious five-year-old, unaccustomed to discipline and seemed always to be punished for one thing or another. I remember being made to kneel down in the long gallery in disgrace, and the whole school filed past. I can't imagine what a five-year-old child could have done to merit that sort of punishment, but you don't query things as a child, and it may have been a first lesson in independence! About this time I distinctly remember being very crafty when I wanted to get my way. In order to make myself cry, for instance, I went into the lavatory, imagined my mother in a snow storm, and emerged weeping and seeking sympathy. Children can be very devious: they do those things automatically, without reasoning. But I believe that early convent experience had a lot to do with an eventual suspicious and belligerent character.

"I learned to read when I was five. I remember the *Nowadays and the Everyday Fairy Book* very vividly by Anna Alice Chapin, illustrated by Jessie Willcox Smith. It was my first book, and I have it by my bed to this day. I read anything and everything: school stories, the classics, and particularly books that were well illustrated like those by Rackham and Dulac.

"After about two years at Farnborough Convent, I returned to live with my mother in hotels and guest houses going daily to school. It was not until I went to my final boarding school that I realized that I was the only person with fifteen addresses in everybody's address book!

"It wasn't easy to keep pets in a guest house, but I was always interested in animals and had a large collection of stuffed wooden and china animals with whom I played. I disliked dolls, but still have my sixty-five-year-old teddy bear. I was

They noticed a delicious smell. (From *Prince Caspian: Book 2 in the Chronicles of Narnia* by C. S. Lewis. Illustrated by Pauline Baynes.)

passionately fond of dogs, but had to wait to have my first dog, Darcy, a bull terrier, until we eventually had a family house when my father retired and returned to England. Dogs have played a major part in my life ever since. At one time I had four, but now only two.

"My mother was an inveterate film-goer and we saw all the early films with her. She also gave us a musical education, and we were taught to play the piano. My sister was an excellent pianist but I stopped my lessons at the convent because the nuns used to hit my knuckles if I didn't get it right. I took up playing again when I was older, but was very lazy with practicing and stopped when I left school.

"When I was nine I went to a very proper and rather Victorian boarding school with forty-four pupils, in Camberley, Surrey, where I stayed until I was fifteen. We were taught elegant manners and stood up every time someone entered a room. The school was divided into five patrols, rather like a Girl Guide system, each with its own song composed and written by former pupils. We sang them on Saturday evenings, and it was all taken very seriously. There were many rules with the most extraordinary system of conduct, order, punctuality, neatness, and rudeness marks, and if you swore you were supposed to take an order mark for yourself. I went through the whole gamut of punishments, and even once began a school term 'in silence' until the following holidays. I was asked to leave twice for being thoroughly impertinent and out of hand. I was always rebelling against any sort of authority and particularly resented older girls telling me what to do. I must have been very tiresome, difficult, and nonconformist. All in all, however, I

was happy there and was asked to come back to teach the art class although I had no qualifications, so the headmistress must have seen some good in me."

During her school days Baynes' father came back and forth to England on leave from the Indian civil service. "I just took it for granted and accepted that it was his job to be away. My mother wrote him regularly, and he sent us hundreds of photographs, so we kept well in touch.

"When my father returned home he was taxed if he remained in England for more than six months, so we usually spent part of his leave in Switzerland. In those days hotels were very cheap and, as far as we were concerned, they were homes. We would run up and down their enormous corridors and pin our drawings on the walls wherever we were. They were magic times; I loved Switzerland."

Influenced by her sister, Baynes began to draw at an early age. "Angela left school when she was fifteen and went to Farnham Art School. There were always paints and other art materials around. She was patient and encouraging and would help me do the things she was learning. Mostly I drew theatre design and costumes. Angela loved the theatre and ballet and I was always included in visits with her and her friends. We saw a great many Shakespearean productions and, at the other end of the scale, went with my mother to see what she enjoyed—variety shows (vaudeville, that is).

"At school there was a policy to keep one from becoming big headed. I was brought up to keep very quiet and wait for somebody else to applaud if I had done something worthwhile, so my drawing did not get much encouragement. Whereas today you have to sell yourself and get some publicity. However, 'art' was my obsession at school and the only thing I was good at. At the beginning of the term we used to bring back holiday art work, and while other pupils might have done one picture, I would bring back as many as forty. We did have one or two devastating girls who came back with pictures of birds they'd copied from books with every feather perfect, and they would be the ones who would be applauded! It was quite fashionable in those days to read us a poem and ask us to do a border around it. We also did a lot of plant drawing and still life. The four best pictures were selected and put up on the wall, and I would be very upset if one of mine was not among them."

1937. Entered Farnham Art School. "I knew only too well that I would not pass my school certificate examinations like the rest of my class, and that I didn't want to be the only one that failed. The only thing I had been good at was English. I won a couple of prizes for writing, but my arithmetic was abysmal. I'm one of those lazy characters where a curtain comes down if I'm not interested in a subject and I can't get any further. My sister hadn't taken her school certificate either, so I persuaded my mother to let me leave school and go straight to art school when I was fifteen, as my sister had done.

"Art school was not quite as easy as I had imagined it would be, but I took it seriously and went every day. I didn't enjoy the discipline of drawing perspective, or drawing from the antique (Greek and Roman), or even life drawing. I found those things terribly difficult and, in consequence, have never been able to understand perspective. Luckily, the design school teacher, Ann Heywood, was an enchanting person who inspired everyone and left us free to do our own thing. She taught me painting on silk, lacquer painting, and tempera painting which I enjoyed, and encouraged my leaning towards design and all things decorative. Eventually, I went to work in the design school with Ann Heywood full time. I was elected to the

(From "Thumbelina" in *Andersen's Fairy Tales* by Hans Christian Andersen. Illustrated by Pauline Baynes.)

Women's International Art Club when I was sixteen, mainly because Ann Heywood knew the right sort of work to send to their exhibition.

"The bedrooms at the school were named after different English painters: Watts, Millais, Rommey, and so on. In time I slept in most of the rooms and got to know the pictures, which were mostly reproduced in brown and white. It was a good method of learning about paintings. One of my favorite has always been Millais' 'Ophelia.' I loved it then, and still do.

"After a few very happy terms at the Farnham School of Art, life changed completely with the outbreak of World War II. My sister was at the Slade School, which had been evacuated to Oxford, and was finishing her diploma course. I was allowed to work alongside her, without taking the usual preliminary exams as a special concession. I worked in the new Bodleian building, which was then still being built, doing tempera painting on my own, until my sister had completed her course.

"Wartime Oxford was an exciting place to be, and it was a happy time for me. I made a lot of friends, went to theatres, parties, and dances. My sister married a fellow Slade student who then went off to the war. It was a time when J. R. R. Tolkien and C. S. Lewis were Dons at Oxford and writing their first books, some of which I was later to illustrate. The atmosphere was inspiring. However, my sister finshed her course and the family returned to Farnham."

During the early '**40s,** Baynes and her sister found voluntary war work. "We did curious jobs like looking after evacuee babies at the house J. M. Barrie lived in when he was writing *Peter Pan.* It had a special atmosphere, and so everything had been built very small, and you had to bend your head to get into

the room. There were about forty babies to be looked after by a nursing staff of three.

"I was also a volunteer at an army canteen a couple of nights a week. By this time I was engaged to a lieutenant whom I had met while he was still at school. We had a long engagement of seven years, as he was overseas most of the time. When he returned at the end of the war, we realized that we had both changed and the engagement was broken off.

"Eventually my sister and I went to work full time making demonstration models for instruction courses at the Camouflage Development and Training Centre, an army establishment at Farnham Castle. This was the beginning of another totally different life for me. Everybody I met was involved in some way with an artistic career. There were art masters, men who worked with stained glass, illustrators, gallery owners, and painters. James Gardener, who went on to design the Festival of Britain, was there as was theatre designer Oliver Messel and painter Julian Trevelyan. I made a lasting friendship with Berkley Sutcliffe who was designing for the theatre in London at that time. It was exciting working with all these established artists whose careers had been momentarily stopped by the war.

"Perry Powell, a telephonist at Farnham Castle, was a marvelously eccentric printer whose mother owned a small publishing business producing government brochures among other things. He had time on his hands in the army, and decided to publish children's books in paperback, based on the popular Puffin collection. He got us all involved illustrating the books. My first was *Question Mark*, about a little boy, Mark, who asked questions. There were restrictions on printing during the war and it was done in an economical way with black, red, and green ink. It was lovely to have a book in 'print.' I did a book

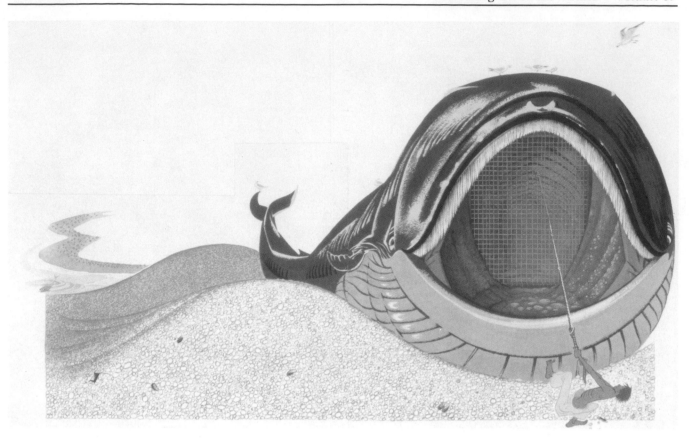

**"By means of a grating
I have stopped your ating."**
(From *How the Whale Got His Throat* by Rudyard Kipling. Illustrated by Pauline Baynes.)

about the names of flowers, one on mythical monsters, and quite a few others.

"I had a great passion for reading anything about ghosts and used to frighten myself to death. I started a correspondence with Harry Price, author of *The Most Haunted House in Britain,* who was interested in various psychic phenomena. I decorated one of my letters to him with a ghost hanging on a nail and he showed the letter to Frank Whittaker, the editor of *Country Life.*" In consequence Baynes' career as illustrator took off and she was commissioned to illustrate Victoria Stevenson's *Clover Magic* as well as two others by her. "These were 'proper' books, in hardback."

Baynes moved to Bath in **1942** to take a position drawing maps and charts for the Hydrographic Department of the Admiralty, but continued with her illustration in the evenings and on weekends. At the end of the war, in 1945, she moved back to Farnham to be with her mother. "A few years later, my father retired from the Indian civil service and we finally acquired a house where we could all live together as a family, with my sister and her family nearby. Eventually I found a cottage close by where I could live independently and yet be close to my mother and father, and where I have lived for more than thirty years.

"I had by this time—for the only time in my life—got an agent. She found me jobs designing everything from cigarette packets, scent bottles, and magazine illustration to tea towels and Christmas wrapping paper and cards. I prefer designing to illustrating on the whole, so this was great fun, and something I found quite easy.

"I was also sending my folio of drawings to different firms, looking for illustration work on my own. J. R. R. Tolkien had turned down an illustrator for *Farmer Giles of Ham,* and the art editor of one firm showed him my drawings. A pseudo Anglo-Saxon drawing caught his eye, and he liked the style, feeling it would be right for his book.

"As far as I can remember Tolkien didn't send me any instructions. I was given the brief on how many half-pages and full-pages were needed, and it was common sense to scatter them throughout the book. When the book was finished Tolkien wrote to me, and he and his wife became friends. I still have a letter from him saying, 'I hope we can get together on a book I'm writing at the moment. I envisage having borders on each page.' That book was *The Lord of the Rings* and, of course, the publishers didn't envisage anything of the kind (there were eventually 1069 pages!), so I just did the cover."

1951. *The Lion, the Witch, and the Wardrobe* which Baynes illustrated was published. "My reputation seemed to rest on the Lewis books, but they were done during a short period right at the beginning of my career. I only met C. S. Lewis twice. My diary entry for our meeting in London reads, 'Had lunch with C. S. Lewis. Came home. Made rock cakes,' and my chief memory is that he looked at his watch all the time. Another time I joined a lunch party he gave at Magdalen College and I was rather nervous—going on to meet Tolkien the same day for the first time. Lewis was very well known because of his broadcast talks to the troops during the war, and he had already established a reputation with his theological books and as a lecturer. Even my father, coming back from India, had some of his books and was terribly impressed when I said I'd been offered a book to illustrate by Lewis.

"*The Lion, the Witch, and the Wardrobe* was very moving and I actually shed a few tears at the sad bits. The story required naturalistic drawings that were not too decorative. At this point I hadn't had that much experience with books, or had proper art training in anatomy, so my legs and arms tended to come out of the wrong part of the body and the figures were rather stiff. I can always *see* far better than I can *draw* and have never been able to translate on paper what I see in my head. You've got to be honest with the text and pick up things that really matter. Of course one researches details like the lamppost and Mrs. Beaver's sewing machine (you can't keep all that in your head). Near Farnham we have woods like those in Narnia where you almost double up under the the larch trees."

In the beginning of Baynes' career, she was advised by the editor of *Country Life* that an artist could get by with not-so-good drawings if he had a reputation for accuracy. Through the succession of books which followed, many of them school books, Baynes has always tried to remember this. From her historical books over the years she has managed to acquire considerable knowledge of period costumes.

"I hope my work improved all the way through the 'Narnia' books, and that the last volume is better than the first. At first I drew too lightly and was asked to make the drawings a bit stronger. There were only two things Lewis ever criticized: I drew someone rowing the wrong way and he very gently asked if I could possibly turn him around; his other request was that I pretty the children up a little. One thing my sister had learned from art school was not to make things too 'chocolate boxy' and perhaps subconsciously I veered away from making the children too attractive.

"Things were changing in England—designing was being done by advertising agents, consortiums and studios, so I had to rely on books exclusively. I remember asking Ernest Shepard, who became a good friend, if he thought I'd have enough work as a free-lance book illustrator, and he answered, 'You'll have to live off the smell of an oily rag, but I'm sure you'll be alright.' I worked terribly hard doing nearly everything that was offered: cookery books, geography books, and a whole series of history books. I learned all the time from them and after I'd done a whole range of 'period work,' I could look at other people's drawings and see if they had the wrong shoe for that time period or recognize what they'd lifted out of other pictures. Nevertheless, I spent one day a week teaching foreign sailors in a TB sanatorium and one day teaching mentally subnormal girls to supplement my income, and because I enjoyed it."

1961. Married Fritz Gasch. "Before I met my husband, Fritz, I was quite happy living by myself. Then I discovered companionship and love I had never known. He came to England as a German prisoner of war and stayed on the advice of his parents who were in East Germany, the Russian zone. He first worked as a nurseryman then as a driver for a big concern in Ascot, followed by garden contracting with his own business. We only knew each other a few months before we decided to get married. Meeting Fritz was the best thing that ever happened to me; he was a splendid man and a wonderful husband who was completely tolerant of his wife's obsession to draw!

"I have enjoyed doing different kinds of books. Alison Uttley's *Recipes from an Old Farmhouse* ranks among my favorites because it was such awkward material to work with, lots of torn-up paper on which she'd written her recipes and notes. The text was mainly about what happened to her as a small girl, and

the publisher asked me to somehow shape the whole thing into a book. I did an introductory picture for each category of recipes with a chapter head for her reminiscences. It came out well: my eyes were still good and I was able to do some detailed drawings, which I'm still quite pleased with!

"The oddest book I've done was Christopher Towers' *Oultre Jourdain*. There were 327 pages of blank verse to do with Christianity and Mohammedism, and there can't be too many people who have read it from beginning to end. It was left to me to decide how to illustrate it. I put black and white wherever I could and a few full pages in color to break it up. Another unusual book, one I was flattered to be asked to do, was the *National Gallery's Children's Book*. One of the illustrations had to be Michelangelo painting the ceiling of the Sistine Chapel. I can't imagine anything more tricky, but nothing daunted me, I found a diagram of a movable crane which I could use and got on and did it, and, hopefully, it wasn't too bad.

"I'm afraid I never think about what children will like, or whether publishers will make money or not; I only try to knit the text and illustrations together. It is the text that is important and that's why it's useful to be able to change one's style slightly to suit a particular book. When I did the *The Arabian Nights* I did them in a totally Persian style whereas *Noah* needed a Byzantine, ecclesiastical type of treatment. With *How Dog Began* I wanted to do pictures like prehistoric cave painting, but I hope my own style came through as well.

"Very often you don't get feedback on your work. I can count on one hand the number of criticisms I've had. I rarely had to do anything twice, and when I look at my drawings, some should have been redone, but publishers don't seem to query what you send them. I would have appreciated it if someone had said at the time 'that arm's awfully long isn't it?' or something like that. When you draw for months on end, it's nice to get a reaction, but, hopefully, *before* it is printed!"

Baynes' most unusual work was her design for the world's largest crewel embroidery for Plymouth Congregational Church in Minneapolis. "I got a letter from the church in Minneapolis saying they had a huge blank wall in their Guild Hall and would I do a design for them? They liked my Tolkien drawings and thought a semi-medieval style would be good for an embroidery. I didn't really believe in the project until a lady minister from the church arrived in England and told me they were really serious about it. They sent me some literature about the church, the general background and the first meeting with the Indians. I did a design in a month which took them three years to stitch! My only brief was to keep it simple; they decided on the best stitches to use. During all that time they kept in touch and sent me photographs. The 'needlers,' as they called themselves, were marvellous people and have become great friends. My design was absolutely nothing compared with the time, trouble, and exquisite work of the Plymouth Church ladies who stitched it. The finished embroidery is brilliant and fantastic.

"I went to the unveiling which was an amazing experience. It was so beautiful and so vast that I was dumbfounded at what they had made of my little design. The material did a lot for the design, and they had stitched it in little squares which were so carefully put together that none of the joins showed at all. People come from all over America to see it."

1989. Baynes lives a very quiet life in a remote country cottage near Farnham in Surrey. "If I'm working on a book, I generally don't go out or bother with the house. I have two dogs, Bertha and Mighty. Mighty sits behind me on my chair while I work, and Bertha is never very far away from my side. As soon as

Then he sent forth a dove from him, to see if the waters had subsided. (From *Noah and the Ark*. Text from the revised standard version of *The Bible*. Illustrated by Pauline Baynes.)

breakfast is finished and the dogs walked, I settle down and work through the day. I've had a charmed life, everything has drifted along and I've been very lucky.

"My sister was indeed a beacon that I could follow, and my husband the light of my life; they are both dead, alas, but the slow-burning candle that is my obsession with illustrating still glows hopefully on!"[1]

FOOTNOTE SOURCES

[1]Based on an interview by Cathy Courtney for *Something about the Author*.

BLUMBERG, Leda 1956-

PERSONAL: Born July 19, 1956, in Mount Kisco, N.Y.; daughter of Gerald (a lawyer) and Rhoda (an author; maiden name, Shapiro) Blumberg; married Thomas Volk (a cabinet-maker), September 4, 1983; children: Dana, Eliza. *Education:* Attended Franconia College, 1974-76. *Home and office:* 378 Baptist Church Rd., Yorktown Heights, N.Y. 10598.

CAREER: Teatown Lake Nature Reservation, Ossining, N.Y., teacher and creator of nature exhibits, 1974; horseback riding instructor and horse trainer, 1974—; veterinarian's assistant,

LEDA BLUMBERG

Bedford, N.Y., 1980; author of children's books, free-lance writer and photographer, 1980—. Leader, 4-H Club, 1980-83. *Member:* Authors Guild, Society of Children's Book Writers, United States Dressage Association, American Horse Shows Association.

WRITINGS:

Pets, F. Watts, 1983.
(With Rhoda Blumberg) *The Simon and Schuster Book of Facts and Fallacies* (illustrated by Paul Frame), Simon & Schuster, 1983 (published in England as *Hamlyn Book of Facts and Fallacies,* Hamlyn, 1985).
The Horselover's Handbook: An Introduction to Owning, Caring for, and Riding Horses (illustrated with photographs by Murray Tinkelman), Avon, 1984.
(With R. Blumberg) *Lovebirds, Lizards, and Llamas: Strange and Exotic Pets* (self-illustrated with photographs), Messner, 1986.
Breezy (illustrated by June V. Evers), Avon, 1988.

Contributor of articles and photographs to periodicals including *Chronicle of the Horse, Cobblestone, Horse and Rider, Suburban Horseman, Pet Lovers' Gazette,* and *Junior Riders.* Manuscript editor for *Junior Riders,* 1985.

WORK IN PROGRESS: A young adult novel.

SIDELIGHTS: "I feel fortunate to have combined my love of animals with the ability to write. I grew up on a farm and learned to love nature at an early age. Caring for our menagerie of animals and horseback riding took up most of my spare time, but I always loved to write.

"After college, I apprenticed with an Olympic-level horse trainer and thought that training horses and teaching riding would be my sole career. When the opportunity to work on a children's encyclopedia arose, I was hesitant. Fortunately I decided to give it a try and discovered that I love writing for children.

"*Pets,* my first book, was fun to research and write because while growing up I'd had a wide variety of pets—everything from turtles and hamsters to a goat that slept on the porch. Several years later I had the opportunity not only to write about pets again, but to photograph them in *Lovebirds, Lizards, and Llamas,* a book I co-authored with my mother, Rhoda Blumberg. Since the book was about unusual pets, I had a wonderful time finding and photographing odd creatures like hermit crabs, tarantulas, boa constrictors, and llamas. We had already collaborated on *The Simon and Schuster Book of Facts and Fallacies* and knew that we worked well together.

"Every morning I wrote and photographed. The afternoons were devoted to horses. From my typing desk, I looked out over pastures filled with horses—a real inspiration for my writing.

"I was thrilled to see my first horse book, *The Horselover's Handbook: An Introduction to Owning, Caring for, and Riding Horses,* which quickly became a popular book in the United States and Canada.

"My latest book, *Breezy,* a story about a girl and her adopted mustang, is my first piece of fiction. The freedom of fiction writing enticed me and I plan to write many more young adult novels.

"I live on a farm forty miles north of New York City with my husband, Tom, and our two young daughters, Dana and Eliza. Raising children has temporarily slowed down my writing, but I keep notebooks filled with ideas for future books. Writing has become a fulfilling way for me to communicate my thoughts, feelings, and knowledge about topics I love."

BOISSARD, Janine 1932-

PERSONAL: Born December 18, 1932, in Paris, France; daughter of Adeodat (a banker) and Renaudin (a housewife) Boissard; married Michel Oriano (a teacher), 1954; children: Francois, Ivan, Marianne, Fanny. *Religion:* Catholic. *Home:* 9 rue de Villersexel, 75007 Paris, France. *Agent:* Max Becker, 115 East 82nd St., New York, N.Y. 10028.

CAREER: Free-lance writer, 1954—. *Awards, honors: A Matter of Feeling* was selected one of New York Public Library's Books for the Teen Age, 1981, 1982; Palmes Academiques, for her young adult books.

WRITINGS:

IN ENGLISH TRANSLATION

Claire et le bonheur, Fayard, 1979, translated by Mary Feeney, published in United States as *Christmas Lessons,* Little, Brown, 1984, published under title *A Question of Happiness,* Ballantine, 1985.
A Matter of Feeling, translated by Elizabeth Walter, Little, Brown, 1980.
Moi, Pauline!, Fayard, n.d., translated by M. Feeney, published in United States as *A Time to Choose,* Little, Brown, 1985.

A New Woman, Little, Brown, 1982.
Cecile: A Novel (originally published in France under the titles, *Cecile, la poison* and *Cecile et son amour*), translated by M. Feeney, Little, Brown, 1988.
A Different Woman, Little, Brown, 1988.

OTHER

"L'esprit de famille" (television series; title means "Family Spirit"), Fayard (Paris), 1977.
L'Avenir de Bernadette (title means "Bernadette's Future"), Fayard, 1978.
Rendez-vous avec mon fils (title means "A Date with My Son"), Fayard, 1981.
Les miroirs de L'ombre (title means "The Looking- Glass of Shadows"), Fayard, 1982.
Cecile et son amour (title means "Cecile and Her Love"), Fayard, 1984.
Cecile, la poison (title means "Cecile, the Poison"), Fayard, 1984.
Une femme reconciliee (title means "A Woman at Peace"), Fayard, 1986.
Vous verrez—, vous m'aimerez (title means "You'll See, You'll Love Me"), Plon (Paris), 1987.

WORK IN PROGRESS: Three Women and One Emperor tells about the three women in Napoleon I's life.

SIDELIGHTS: "I grew up in a very happy family, where I was regarded as the 'different' (though much loved) child. Unhappy at boarding school, I had decided by the time I was twelve that I would become famous so that other people would know what I was really like, and love me. Why not become a writer? I took up my pen and have not let go of it since. My first novel was published by a large French publishing house when I was twenty, and apart from the novels which have appeared in America, I have also written detective stories and television scripts. My novels about the Boissard family were the basis for an extremely successful and long-running series in France.

"Writing is as necessary to me as breathing."

BRADFORD, Richard (Roark) 1932-

PERSONAL: Born May 1, 1932, in Chicago, Ill.; son of Roark (a writer) and Mary Rose (a literary agent; maiden name, Sciarra) Bradford; married Julie Dollard, September 15, 1956 (divorced, May 18, 1972); married Lee Head (a writer), June 25, 1977 (deceased); children: (first marriage) Thomas Conway. *Education:* Tulane University, B.A., 1952. *Politics:* Democrat. *Religion:* None. *Home and office address:* P.O. Box 1395, Santa Fe, N.M. 87504. *Agent:* McIntosh & Otis, 475 Fifth Ave., New York, N.Y. 10017.

CAREER: Novelist. New Mexico State Tourist Bureau, Santa Fe, staff writer, 1956-59; New Orleans Chamber of Commerce, New Orleans, La., editor, 1959-61; Zia Co., Los Alamos, N.M., editor, 1962-64; New Mexico Department of Development, Santa Fe, research analyst, 1967-68; Universal Pictures, Universal City, Calif., screenwriter, 1968-70. *Military service:* U.S. Marine Corps, 1953-56; became sergeant. *Member:* Writers Guild of America, Authors Guild, Authors League of America, Edouard Manet Society, Sigma Chi, Quien Sabe Club. *Awards, honors:* Litt.D., New Mexico State University, 1979.

WRITINGS:

Red Sky at Morning (novel), Lippincott, 1968.
So Far from Heaven, Lippincott, 1973.

ADAPTATIONS:

"Red Sky at Morning" (motion picture), starring Richard Thomas, Desi Arnaz, Jr., Claire Bloom, and Catherine Burns, Universal, 1971.

RECORDINGS

"Red Sky at Morning" (cassette), Books on Tape, 1976, Recorded Books, 1987.
"So Far from Heaven" (cassette), Books on Tape, 1977.

WORK IN PROGRESS: A novel.

SIDELIGHTS: Bradford's first novel, *Red Sky at Morning*, has been a tremendous success, going through multiple printings and spawning a popular Universal film of the same title. Many reviewers compared the book favorably with *Catcher in the Rye*.

The book tells the story of Josh Arnold, a seventeen-year-old Alabaman who moves to New Mexico with his mother when his father joins the Navy to serve in World War II. The action centers on Josh, who surprisingly experiences little difficulty in adapting to life in rural New Mexico after growing up in big-city Mobile, on his friends, and, to a lesser extent on his mother, who finds it impossible to get used to the racially-mixed area that is so different from the race-conscious, class-conscious Alabama of the early forties.

JANINE BOISSARD

BRANDIS, Marianne 1938-

PERSONAL: Born October 5, 1938, in Amersfoort, The Netherlands. *Education:* Attended University of British Columbia, 1956-58, and St. Francis Xavier University, 1958-59; McMaster University, B.A., 1960, M.A., 1964. *Home:* 105 Isabella St., Apt. 505, Toronto, Ontario, Canada M4Y 1N9.

CAREER: Canadian Broadcasting Corp., writer of promotional material, 1964-66; Ryerson Polytechnic, Toronto, Ontario, Canada, instructor in English, 1967-89; writer. *Member:* Writers Union of Canada. *Awards, honors:* Imperial Order of the Daughters of the Empire Award (Canada), and Young Adult Canadian Book Award from the Saskatchewan Library Association, both 1986, both for *The Quarter-Pie Window; The Tinderbox* was named an *Our Choice/Your Choice* Book by the Canadian Children's Book Centre, 1982-85, and *The Quarter-Pie Window*, 1986-89.

WRITINGS:

This Spring's Sowing (novel), McClelland & Stewart, 1970.
A Sense of Dust (short story; illustrated by Gerard Brender a Brandis), Brandstead, 1972.
The Tinderbox (novel; illustrated by G. Bender a Brandis), Porcupine's Quill, 1982.
The Quarter-Pie Window (novel; illustrated by G. Brender a Brandis), Porcupine's Quill, 1985.
Elizabeth, Duchess of Somerset (adult biographical novel), Porcupine's Quill, 1989.

WORK IN PROGRESS: A sequel to *The Quarter-Pie Window;* a short novel.

SIDELIGHTS: "Because I was born in The Netherlands, English is my second (though now most comfortable) language. We came to Canada just before my ninth birthday, and as part of the process of learning English I read a great deal. Knowing more than one language meant that I was aware of the various ways in which different languages work; therefore I was constantly exploring alternative ways of saying things. That, I have found, is a very useful habit for a writer to have.

"I began writing because I wanted to do what my favourite writers did—create imaginary worlds and explore the real one. I took one course in creative writing; the most important thing it taught me was how to read other people's books so as to learn from them. For the rest, I have learned by trial and error, and by means of useful criticism from my friends and readers.

"I do not see myself as specifically a children's writer. I write for adults as well and find that there is a great deal of common ground.

"My hobbies and other activities are mostly connected with writing. I read a great deal, and most of what I read is relevant to the subjects or style of my own work. I am very interested in history; when I travel I make a point of visiting museums and historical places. For me it is impossible to distinguish 'hobby' from 'research.' My novels are concerned with the way people actually lived in the past, or with the more private side of the lives of prominent people. Wherever I go, and in whatever I read, I look for facts and insights which illuminate this."

BRANDT, Sue R(eading) 1916-

PERSONAL: Born June 16, 1916, in Curryville, Mo.; daughter of William Francis (a farmer) and Virginia Lee (a homemaker; maiden name Ball) Reading; married Charles J. Brandt (a public relations man), June 14, 1957. *Education:* University of Chicago, A.B., 1942. *Home:* 417 East Kiowa, Apt. 706, Colorado Springs, Colo. 80903.

CAREER: Former teacher in public and private schools; Scott, Foresman & Co., Chicago, Ill., editor, 1950-56; Charles Scribner's Sons, New York City, editor, 1956-62; Grolier, Inc., New York City, and Danbury, Conn., member of editorial staff of *New Book of Knowledge*, 1962-66, 1977-84, and *Encyclopedia Americana*, 1966-77.

WRITINGS:

How to Write a Report (juvenile; illustrated by Anne Canevari), F. Watts, 1968, revised edition, 1986.
Facts about the Fifty States (juvenile), F. Watts, 1969, revised edition, 1988.

BRIERLEY, (Louise) 1958-

PERSONAL: Born February 15, 1958, in Glossop, England, daughter of Kenneth and Kathleen Brierley. *Education:* Manchester Polytechnic, England, B.A. (first class honors), 1980; Royal College of Art, England, M.A., 1983. *Home:* 65 Highbury, New Park, London NS2 ET, England. *Office:* 45 Charlotte Rd., London EC2, England.

CAREER: Illustrator. *Awards, honors:* Merit Certificate from the Deloitte Haskins and Sells Book Cover Competition, and Prize for Best Illustrated Book, both 1987, for *The Twelve Days of Christmas*.

WRITINGS:

King Lion and His Cooks (self-illustrated), Anderson, 1981, Holt, 1982.

ILLUSTRATOR

Rudyard Kipling, *The Elephant's Child*, Macmillan (London), 1984, Bedrick Books, 1985.
The Twelve Days of Christmas, Holt, 1986.
Selina Hastings, reteller, *The Singing Ringing Tree*, Holt, 1988.
Walter de la Mare, *Peacock Pie*, Holt, 1989.

WORK IN PROGRESS: Fisher-Woman, a self-illustrated story.

SIDELIGHTS: "Books are a means of expressing dream-like images with weird and wonderful themes. They allow me to invent a whole personal world and present it within a package that anyone may own. I like to use images that work with the text—as a key for the audience to use its own imagination within this fictitious world. I don't like to give too much away.

"I should like to develop these ideas for adult books; images are as important to adults as well as children, enhancing the text, but never replacing one's imagination."

BROOK, Judith (Penelope) 1926-
(Judy Brook)

PERSONAL: Born December 22, 1926, in Weymouth, England; daughter of Charles Geoffrey (in Royal Navy) and Evelyn (an artist; maiden name, Moore) Brook. *Education:* Chelsea School of Art, National Diploma in Design, 1949. *Politics:* Labour ("but I am not a member of the party"). *Home:* 27 Short Rd., Chiswick, London W4 2QU, England.

CAREER: Artist and illustrator; has worked for Hans Schleger & Associates. *Member:* Friends of the Earth, Campaign for Nuclear Disarmament, London Wildlife Group, Friends of Chiswick House. *Awards, honors:* Carnegie Medal Commendation from the British Library Association, 1960, for *The Rescuers; Tim Mouse and the Major* was selected one of Child Study Association of America's Children's Books of the Year, 1967, *Tim Mouse Visits the Farm,* 1969, and *Darwin and the Voyage of the Beagle,* 1985; *Hector and Harriet* and *Darwin and the Voyage of the Beagle* were both exhibited at the Bologna International Children's Book Fair, 1985.

WRITINGS:

JUVENILE; SELF ILLUSTRATED; UNDER NAME JUDY BROOK

Tim Mouse, World's Work, 1966, Platt & Munk, 1968.
Tim Mouse and the Major, World's Work, 1967, Lothrop, 1975.
Tim Mouse Visits the Farm, World's Work, 1968, Platt & Munk, 1969.
Tim Mouse Goes Down the Stream, World's Work, 1970, Lothrop, 1975.
Tim and Helen Mouse, World's Work, 1970.
Tim Mouse and Father Christmas, World's Work, 1971.
Noah's Ark, World's Work, 1972, F. Watts, 1979.
This Little Pig, World's Work, 1973.
Alfred the Helpful Donkey, World's Work, 1974.
The Friendly Letter Box, World's Work, 1975.
Belinda, World's Work, 1976.
Mrs. Noah and the Animals, World's Work, 1977.
Belinda and Father Christmas, World's Work, 1978.
Mrs. Noah's ABC 123, World's Work, 1979.
Around the Clock, World's Work, 1980.
Dicky and Geoff, the Jaunting Gerbils, Deutsch, 1984.
Hector and Harriet, the Night Hamsters: Two Adventures, Deutsch, 1984, Dutton, 1985.
(With Pam Royde) *The Wind in the Willows Activity Book,* Deutsch, 1984.
Charlie Clown at the Seaside, Kingfisher Books, 1986.
Charlie Clown at the Circus, Kingfisher Books, 1986.

ILLUSTRATOR

Amabel Williams-Ellis, *Princesses and Trolls: Twelve Traditional Stories,* J. Barrie, 1950.
Ursula Hourihane, *Little Pig Barnaby and Other Stories,* Oxford University Press, 1952.
Alison Uttley, *Magic in My Pocket,* Puffin, 1957.
Margery Sharp, *The Rescuers,* Collins, 1959.
(With Pat Schleger) S. E. Bell, *Old Dog Tom Work Book,* Ginn, 1963.
(With P. Schleger) S. E. Bell, *Little Chick Chick,* Ginn, 1963.
Felicia Law, *Darwin and the Voyage of the Beagle,* Dutton, 1985.

Also illustrator of Janet Nichols' *Brock and Bruin,* for Heinemann, "Brock and Bruin" comic strip in *TV Land,* and for BBC *Radio Times* and educational publications.

SIDELIGHTS: "I was educated at various schools, including Dunhurst, Brickwall girls' school, Beacon Hill, and finally (most important) Beltane, where I was from 1939 until the end of the war. Arthur Wragg taught us art, and he has been the main influence in my life. I never took any exams at school, being interested only in painting, history, and English.

"After the war I attended Chelsea School of Art, where my main teacher was Brian Robb. I won two scholarships there and obtained my National Diploma in Design. Before I left I painted a large mural for a Hertfordshire school, and I illustrated a small book of folk tales by Amabel Williams-Ellis.

"I then worked for ten years or more, part time, at the studio of Hans Schleger & Associates, while also illustrating a number of small books. In the 1960s, after illustrating *Brock and Bruin* by Janet Nichols, I drew the same characters for an ITV comic. This enabled me to save enough money to concentrate on my own books. As a result, over the last several years I have produced the six 'Tim Mouse' books and quite a few others. Some of these are still available, and a number of them have been translated.

"I was politically active with Campaign for Nuclear Disarmament (CND) during the sixties and still attend large gatherings. I was also very active over the problem of the military dictatorship in Greece until democracy was established in that country. My other interests are ecology, history, and the preservation of old buildings and the English countryside. I have recently joined Friends of the Earth. I am also a member of the London Wildlife Group, and we have saved five-and-one-half acres of woodland in Chiswick from development. In addition, I belong to Friends of Chiswick House and have a nice little cottage and garden next to the grounds."

HOBBIES AND OTHER INTERESTS: Gardening, walking, collecting children's books.

BROOKS, Bill 1939-

PERSONAL: Born September 27, 1939, in Toronto, Canada; son of Arthur John (a stockbroker) and Edith (a homemaker; maiden name, Forbes) Brooks; married Betty Okura (vice-president of Bill Brooks Photography Ltd.), February 8, 1969. *Education:* University of Toronto, B.A., 1962. *Agent and office:* Masterfile Stock Photo Agency, 415 Yonge St., Suite 200, Toronto, Ontario, Canada M5B 2E7.

CAREER: McGraw Hill Co. of Canada, Toronto, advertising assistant, 1962-63; Ashley & Crippen (photo studio), Toronto, studio manager, 1963-65; Polaroid Corporation of Canada, Toronto, technical representative, 1966-67; McClelland & Stewart Publishers, Toronto, photo editor, 1967-72; free-lance stock photographer, 1972—; owner of Bill Brooks Photography Ltd., Toronto, 1967—. Member of advisory board of photo program, Humber College, Toronto, 1975—; evaluator of photo collections, Royal Ontario Museum, Toronto, 1985—.

WRITINGS:

SELF-ILLUSTRATED WITH PHOTOGRAPHS

Wildlife of Canada, Hounslow, 1976.
The Colour of Ontario, Hounslow, 1977.
The Colour of Alberta, Hounslow, 1978.
The Colour of British Columbia, Hounslow, 1980.

BILL BROOKS

ILLUSTRATOR; ALL WITH PHOTOGRAPHS

(With Chic Harris and Tom Hall) Val Clery, *Canada in Colour,* Hounslow, 1972.

Sheila Bennet, *Ottawa,* Hounslow, 1973.

Janice Tyrwhitt, *The Mill* (illustrated by Helen Fox), McClelland & Stewart, 1976.

V. Clery, *Seasons of Canada,* Hounslow, 1978.

Stuart Trueman, *The Colour of New Brunswick,* Hounslow, 1981.

Raymond Souster, *Queen City,* Oberon, 1984.

SIDELIGHTS: "I am a professional stock photographer with book publishing experience who used the contents of his stock photo files to produce illustrated books. I did one book a year for ten years to finance the creation of a stock photo file. I'm not doing books at present, but my stock photos are leased to book publishers the world over.

"I travel the world constantly as a photographer and speak broken French as a second language. I photograph a wide range of subject matter, but I am most concerned about the world's ecology. I, therefore, do my best work in the wilderness areas of the world.

"In the early 1980s with the instant remainder, the sixth month shelf life, the book business changed and I switched my photographic business toward stock advertising photography. I still maintain my publishing contacts and would still be interested in the right project."

BROOKS-HILL, Helen (Mason) 1908-

PERSONAL: Born December 16, 1908, in Toronto, Ontario, Canada; daughter of James Cooper (a banker) and Florence (a homemaker; maiden name, MacArthur) Mason; married Frederick Brooks-Hill (a retired financial analyst), September 9, 1939; children: Heather (Mrs. James Kranias), Frederick, Robin, Gillian (Mrs. Gerald Lee). *Education:* Havergal College, Toronto, matriculation degree, 1926. *Religion:* Roman Catholic. *Home:* 41 Second St., Oakville, Ontario, Canada L6J 3T1.

CAREER: Royal Bank of Canada, Toronto, Ontario, Canada, ledger keeper and secretary, 1925-29; Manufacturers Life Insurance Co., Toronto, medical underwriter, 1929-39. Red Cross driver in Newfoundland during World War II.

WRITINGS:

The Special Little Donkey (illustrated by June Bramall), privately printed, 1969.

Castor Chats with Young Canadians, privately printed, 1974, reissued, 1985.

On the Way to Visit Elizabeth (illustrated by granddaughters, Kathy Kranias and Gillian Kranias), privately printed, 1975.

Alison's Dream, Mosaic Press, 1981, reissued, 1989.

SIDELIGHTS: "I originally wrote these children's stories for my grandchildren. On request I had them printed—and donated the sales of two of them to 'Canadian Save the Children' Fund. They are all sold out except for a few copies I have kept."

HELEN BROOKS-HILL

BROWN, Joseph E(dward) 1929-

PERSONAL: Born December 14, 1929, in San Francisco, Calif.; son of LeRoy D. (a technical writer) and Ora E. (Ackley) Brown, married Anne Ensign (a writer), 1976. *Education:* Attended University of Wisconsin, 1952, and University of Hawaii, 1953. *Residence:* Coronado, Calif.

CAREER: San Diego Union, San Diego, Calif., reporter and foreign correspondent, 1959-69; *Oceans,* San Diego, editor, 1969-71; free-lance writer, 1971-82, 1984—; *Sea & Pacific Skipper,* Newport Beach, Calif., 1982-84. *Military service:* U.S. Navy, 1948-52. *Member:* Authors Guild. *Awards, honors:* Outstanding Science Trade Book for Children from the National Science Teachers Association and the Childrens Book Council, 1974, for *Wonders of a Kelp Forest; The Sea's Harvest* was selected one of Child Study Association of America's Children's Books of the Year, 1975, and *Wonders of Seals and Sea Lions,* 1976; Louisiana Library Association and Louisiana State University Press Special Award, 1983, for *Return of the Brown Pelican.*

WRITINGS:

JUVENILE NONFICTION

Wonders of a Kelp Forest, Dodd, 1974.
The Sea's Harvest: The Story of Aquaculture (illustrated by wife, Anne Ensign Brown), Dodd, 1975.
Wonders of Seals and Sea Lions, Dodd, 1976.
(With A. E. Brown) *Harness the Wind: The Story of Windmills,* Dodd, 1976.
Oil Spills: Danger in the Sea, Dodd, 1978.
Rescue from Extinction, Dodd, 1981.

ADULT NONFICTION

The Golden Sea, Playboy Press, 1974.
The Mormon Trek West, Doubleday, 1980.
Yesterday's Wings, Doubleday, 1982.
Return of the Brown Pelican, Louisiana State University Press, 1983.
Off-Season: A Guide to Visiting the Western National Parks without the Crowds, Harcourt, 1988.

Contributor of nonfiction articles to more than eighty-five publications, including *Reader's Digest, Smithsonian, Science Digest, Discover, Islands, Arizona Highways, National Wildlife, Sierra Club Bulletin,* and *Nautical Quarterly.*

WORK IN PROGRESS: Collaborating with wife, Anne Ensign Brown on a children's book about historic military forts of the Old West, and a guidebook to Padre Island National Seashore, Texas, both to be published by the Southwest Parks and Monuments Association.

SIDELIGHTS: "Born in San Francisco and living most of my life near saltwater instilled in me a deep respect early on, and this fascination for the sea is reflected in many of my writings of the past forty years or so. Marine science, oceanography, ships and sailing, marine birds and mammals, navigation—these are topics to which I am drawn time and again by a burning personal interest although I do not consider myself a 'sea writer' but rather a 'generalist.'

"I am interested in many things and, by virtue of experience and curiosity, I think I have been able to translate many subjects into meaningful and understandable form for other people.

"Almost anything fascinates me: how life comes to a new island, how one large corporation has successfully turned garbage into useful oil, the decline and comeback of that most marvelous of all seabirds, the pelican; volcanos, earthquakes, and other natural phenomena; the careers of such colorful people as attorney Melvin Belli, psychic Peter Hurkos, Nobel Laureate Linus Pauling. A forty-year history of smoking which led to coronary bypass surgery became a personal account published in *Reader's Digest.* These and dozens of other subjects have turned from curiosity to printed word, either as magazine articles or as books.

"Writing juvenile books has been a special source of pride and satisfaction for me. Greater than any monetary reward are the occasional letters I receive from school children who have used my books as reference for school projects, and who have taken the time to write and tell me so.

"Oddly, perhaps, I became a writer almost by accident. As a junior high school student in Burbank, California, I played trumpet in the school band. I played it so poorly, in fact, that my teacher suggested I drop music (which I happen to love) and select an alternate course. My grandfather, a San Francisco area newspaperman for more than fifty years, was visiting at the time. I explained my dilemma. 'Why not change to journalism?' he offered.

"I did, and I haven't left the writing field in the forty or more years since. And I've never regretted my ineptitude for playing the trumpet."

BURNINGHAM, John (Mackintosh) 1936-

PERSONAL: Born April 27, 1936, in Farnham, Surrey, England; son of Charles and Jessie (Mackintosh) Burningham; married Helen Gillian Oxenbury (a designer, author and illustrator of children's books), August 15, 1964; children: Lucy, William Benedict, Emily. *Education:* Central School of Art, London, national diploma in design, 1959. *Home:* 5 East Heath Rd., London NW3 1BN, England. *Address:* c/o Jonathan Cape Ltd., 30 Bedford Sq., London WC1B 3EL, England.

CAREER: Author, illustrator and free-lance designer. Worked at farming, slum-clearance, forestry, in the Friend's Ambulance Unit and school building as an alternative to military service, 1953-55; free-lance illustrator traveling through Italy, Yugoslavia, and Israel, 1953-55; worked for a year on set designs, models, and puppets for an animated puppet film in the Middle East, 1959-60; designed posters for London Transport and the British Transport Commission, early 1960s; author and illustrator of children's books 1963—; free-lance designer of murals, exhibitions, three-dimensional models, magazine illustrations and advertisements.

AWARDS, HONORS: Kate Greenaway Medal from the British Library Association for Illustration, 1963, for *Borka; The Extraordinary Tug-of-War* was selected one of the American Institute of Graphic Arts Books, 1967-68; Kate Greenaway Medal, Honorary Award from the Biennale of Illustrations Bratislava, one of *New York Times* Best Illustrated Children's Books of the Year, one of *New York Times* Outstanding Books, and one of *School Library Journal*'s Best Books, all 1971, *Boston Globe-Horn Book* Award for Illustration, and a Children's Book Showcase selection, both 1972, all for *Mr. Gumpy's Outing; Seasons* and *Mr. Gumpy's Outing* were each selected one of Child Study Association of America's Chil-

JOHN BURNINGHAM

dren's Books of the Year, 1971, and *Mr. Gumpy's Motor Car*, 1976.

Mr. Gumpy's Motor Car was included in the Children's Book Showcase of the Children's Book Council, 1977; *Come Away from the Water, Shirley* was selected one of *New York Times* Best Illustrated Children's Books of the Year, 1977, and *Granpa*, 1985; Deutscher Jugendliteraturpreis (German Youth Literature Prize) from the Federal Ministery of the Interior, 1980, for *Would You Rather. . .;* Kurt Maschler/Emil Award runner-up from the National Book League (Great Britain), 1983, for *The Wind in the Willows*, and 1986, for *Where's Julius?;* Kurt Maschler/Emil Award, 1985, for *Granpa.*

WRITINGS:

SELF-ILLUSTRATED

Borka: The Adventures of a Goose with No Feathers, Random House, 1963.
John Burningham's ABC, J. Cape, 1964, Bobbs-Merrill, 1967, new edition, Crown, 1985.
Trubloff: The Mouse Who Wanted to Play the Balalaika, J. Cape, 1964, Random House, 1965.
Humbert, Mister Firkin, and the Lord Mayor of London, J. Cape, 1965, Bobbs-Merrill, 1967.
Cannonball Simp: The Story of a Dog Who Joins a Circus, J. Cape, 1966, Bobbs-Merrill, 1967.
Harquin: The Fox Who Went Down to the Valley, J. Cape, 1967, Bobbs-Merrill, 1968.
Seasons, J. Cape, 1969, Bobbs-Merrill, 1971.

Mr. Gumpy's Outing (ALA Notable Book; Junior Literary Guild selection), Holt, 1970.
(Adapter) *Around the World in Eighty Days*, J. Cape, 1972.
Mr. Gumpy's Motor Car, J. Cape, 1973, Macmillan, 1975.
Come Away from the Water, Shirley (*Horn Book* honor list), Crowell, 1977.
Time to Get Out of the Bath, Shirley (*Horn Book* honor list), Crowell, 1978.
Would You Rather. . ., Crowell, 1978.
The Shopping Basket, Crowell, 1980.
Avocado Baby, Crowell, 1982.
John Burningham's Colors, Crown, 1985.
John Burningham's 123, Crown, 1985.
John Burningham's Opposites, Crown, 1985.
Where's Julius?, Crown, 1986.
John Patrick Norman McHennessey: The Boy Who Was Always Late (*Horn Book* honor list), Crown, 1988.

"LITTLE BOOK" SERIES

The Rabbit, J. Cape, 1974, Crowell, 1975.
The School, J. Cape, 1974, Crowell, 1975.
The Snow, J. Cape, 1974, Crowell, 1975.
The Baby, J. Cape, 1974, Crowell, 1975.
The Blanket, J. Cape, 1975, Crowell, 1976.
The Cupboard, J. Cape, 1975, Crowell, 1976.
The Dog, J. Cape, 1975, Crowell, 1976.
The Friend, J. Cape, 1975, Crowell, 1976.
Granpa, J. Cape, 1984, Crown, 1985.

"NUMBER PLAY" SERIES

Count Up: Learning Sets, Viking, 1983.

(From *Chitty-Chitty-Bang-Bang: The Magical Car* by Ian Fleming. Illustrated by John Burningham.)

Five Down: Numbers as Signs, Viking, 1983.
Just Cats: Learning Groups, Viking, 1983.
Pigs Plus: Learning Addition, Viking, 1983.
Read One: Numbers as Words, Viking, 1983.
Ride Off: Learning Subtraction Viking, 1983.

"FIRST WORDS" SERIES (ENGLAND); "NOISY WORDS" SERIES (UNITED STATES)

Sniff Shout, Viking, 1984.
Skip Trip, Viking, 1984.
Wobble Pop, Viking, 1984.
Slam Bang!, Viking, 1985.
Cluck Baa, Viking, 1985.
Jangle Twang, Viking, 1985.

ILLUSTRATOR

Ian Fleming, *Chitty-Chitty-Bang-Bang: The Magical Car,* Random House, 1964.
Letta Schatz, editor, *The Extraordinary Tug-of-War,* Follett, 1968.
Kenneth Grahame, *The Wind in the Willows,* Viking, 1983.

WALL FRIEZES

Birdland, Braziller, 1966.
Lionland, J Cape, 1966, Braziller, 1967.
Storyland, J. Cape, 1966, Braziller, 1967.
Jungleland, J. Cape, 1968.
Wonderland, J. Cape, 1968.
Around the World, J. Cape, 1972.

ADAPTATIONS:

FILMSTRIPS

"Mr. Gumpy's Outing," Weston Woods.
"Come Away from the Water, Shirley," Weston Woods.
"Mr. Gumpy's Motor Car" (filmstrip with cassette), Weston Woods, 1982.
"Cannonball," Finehouse/Evergreen.

Burningham's books have been published in Afrikaans, Danish, Dutch, Finnish, French, German, Japanese, Norwegian, Swedish, Spanish, and Zulu.

WORK IN PROGRESS: Get Off My Train, a book for children; a film of *Grandpa;* a book about England for adults.

SIDELIGHTS: John Burningham was born on **April 27, 1936,** in Farnham, Surrey. "I grew up in England the youngest of three. My sisters were very kind to me, but were often at different schools, and as my father was away a lot, we weren't a particularly close family. My father was a salesman who worked all over the country and my parents were always buying and selling houses—the combination of the two meant we moved about. As a consequence, I went to ten different schools, missing quite often. I didn't like being dumped at boarding school, there is nothing pleasant about the first day. I often went

(From *The Blanket* by John Burningham. Illustrated by the author.)

(From *Come Away from the Water, Shirley* by John Burningham. Illustrated by the author)

to stay with my grandparents. I was quite fond of my grandfather; he was good at making up stories and could have been a writer if he had put his mind to it.

"I was read to as a child by my mother and grandmother. Later I read to myself, but was not a great reader. I loved reading *Rupert* (I still think Bestall's drawings are very good), although I don't think I went through all the classics. I have a queue of books which I want to read, and the pile grows more enormous every year. I've got to go through Dickens for a start."[1]

At twelve, Burningham went to A. S. Neill's famous Summerhill School, an experiment in liberal teaching methods. "It was a school governed by the children; we made the rules. These were not practical rules about outside safety—those had been thought out—but the pupils generally discussed the best way to organise the day. Lessons were not compulsory, you didn't have to go, but most people felt bored and left out if they stayed away. We had a meeting every week, and we used to fine or punish people who broke the rules. We were about forty or fifty pupils; it was a very happy school.

"I did a lot of drawing and painting as a child. Most of what I was doing was representative. My pictures were large and free; mostly in boats or conveyances. I was lucky because the art room at Summerhill didn't restrict you to tiny little bits of paper—so many kids get a hard, greasy crayon and a small bit of sugar paper to draw on—we used to have great big bits and large

brushes, lots of paint. I get hundreds of letters from kids sending drawings as a teachers' project. You can tell the kind of facilities they're given—minute, restrictive. Art is just not rated in our schools. If you don't rate something then you don't produce. But artists seem to battle through in spite of it.

"I had a pretty easy adolescence. I suppose there's always the next generation saying, 'You've had your fun, but what are you going to do next?' It's awful when people ask you at the age of eighteen. You've had this great time as a student, but at the end of it you've got to move on. I hadn't a clue what to do when I left school. I came out with one 'O' level in English, and I had failed art. I couldn't see the point of exams. They were always given on lovely days when it was wonderful outside."[1]

1953-1955. As an alternative to National Service, Burningham joined The Friends' Ambulance Unit. "In my day there was still conscription and so I became a Conscientious Objector. It was nothing to do with religion. I'm not a pacifist in the sense that I believe there are no circumstances under which I would kill someone, because I think there are, but I certainly am a pacifist in terms of believing we should not fill the world with weapons. I wouldn't go in the army, but I was prepared to do alternative military service: two and a half years working in hospitals, agriculture, forestry and humanitarian social work. It was much better than going straight to art school; I learned a great deal more. I also traveled. I worked in Israel doing demolition, in Calabria [Southern Italy] building a school, in Goven [Scotland] rehabilitating slum areas. I worked in the National

push

(From *John Burningham's Opposites* by John Burningham. Illustrated by the author.)

Hospital for Nervous Diseases as a porter, and I chopped down trees for nine months."[1]

1956-1959. Student at the Central School of Art and Craft in London. "I met a friend who'd been at Summerhill with me who was doing graphics and illustration at the Central School and I thought, 'Well, that sounds interesting.' I had been drawing in my free time—something I never do now—so I applied and got in.

"I was quite sociable and worked reasonably hard. I hadn't lived in London before and that was tricky since I didn't know the city well. I'm still not particularly rooted in London. I live in Hampstead which is a compromise; it's as near to the country as you can get.

"I wasn't a hippy. I don't think any hippies came out of Summerhill. A hippy is usually someone who is reacting to an uptight upbringing. If you suddenly don't have to wear school uniforms, you perhaps go completely mad and dye your hair orange. Summerhill people were fairly conformist because they could do everything they wanted at school.

"I met Helen [Oxenbury] at Central. I think I was in my last year and she was in her second. The first time we met was in the canteen, and we had a very boring conversation about cigarettes. It wasn't love at first sight; we didn't get married for years. I'd had some serious relationships before, but not one I'd thought about finalising."[1]

1960. "After I left Central I worked for a few months in a graphics design studio. Then I came across a man who asked me if I'd like to work on an animated film about the biblical Joseph and his brothers. I went to Israel with him and stayed for about a year. Eventually Helen came out to join me and began to work with the National Theatre. She stayed while I came back to look for a job in London.

"I thought one had to look smart to get a job. I never wore suits, but I had one terrible, heavy, hairy suit—God knows where it came from. I put on a tie, which nearly killed me, and I staggered into the art department of the *Observer* with this portfolio full of the most ridiculous things—life drawings, all sorts of oddments. I went into this very hot office feeling absurd, and the man I was seeing was sitting there across the

Mr. Gumpy was going for a ride in his car. (From *Mr. Gumpy's Motor Car* by John Burningham. Illustrated by the author.)

desk in just his undershirt. After that, I went round and round endlessly looking for work.

"Finally I got lucky. I was staying as a lodger in the house of Harold Hutchinson, then art director for London Transport. He gave me a commission to do posters; I was most grateful. It paid one-hundred pounds and was the first big full-color print job I had. When the first poster came out, it was everywhere, outside the station, at the bus stands. I expected to see groups of people discussing it—I was so naive—instead, they'd be standing up against it completely oblivious.

"Nowadays London Transport posters are really appalling. The art of the poster has diminished in this country since the thirties."[1]

Despite the London Transport commission, Burningham found it no easier to find work as an illustrator. "When you're starting, publishers and agencies are all terrified to give you the first commission. They'd say, 'Ah, but you do posters don't you? If you do illustration or somebody else come back to us afterwards.' They'd write my name down on a piece of paper and then chuck it in the basket before I was out of the room. I

wanted to do illustration work, but I failed to get any in eighteen months. I'd always been confident that in the end it would be alright, but you do get depressed.

"Then I went to New York and made rounds. I got an agent who found me various bits and pieces which paid very well compared to what was going on at home. I started off with one or two contacts and then went on from there. When I came back to London, I was still able to do educational work for America, and I got a job in an art school teaching two days a week. Nowadays, unfortunately, they're cutting back on part-time teaching, which is diabolical. Art schools need part-time teachers, they have more to inject because they're working themselves, rather than just teaching. It kept me going a bit."[1]

1963. "In the meantime I'd written a rough of my first book, *Borka: The Adventures of a Goose with No Feathers*, and somebody suggested I try Jonathan Cape. I liked children's books because of all the drawing. Tom Maschler had just joined Jonathan Cape and said, 'If you develop it, we'll publish it.' It's wonderful the first time you see a book of yours in print and you know there are thousands of copies.

Julius was throwing snowballs at the wolves. (From *Where's Julius?* by John Burningham. Illustrated by the author.)

"*Borka* won the Kate Greenaway Medal, and I've gone on from there. I often wonder if life had taken another course whether I would actually have done something quite different. Supposing I'd put up a watercolor for the Summer Exhibition? Maybe now I'd be doing watercolors."[1]

In **1964**, Burningham married Helen Oxenbury. Their first child, Lucy, was born in 1967, their son, Bill, in 1968, and Emily in 1980. "I never thought about fatherhood. I never thought, 'Gosh, I'd like to have children.' It's something you tackle. Babies are quite alarming, because for the first couple of weeks they're so fragile. I have a close relationship with my children, and they've had a much more settled childhood than I did. I was around, working at home. When they were little they crawled around my workroom. Children can give you wonderful jolts, they'll suddenly walk past and say, 'That crow isn't touching the telephone wires,' and they'll be right. But I've never believed in testing books on my children. I think that shows you don't know what you're doing. Besides a lot of my later books are not specifically for children."[1]

Homebound while the children were small, Oxenbury too began to illustrate children's books. "Helen starting to do books wasn't at all threatening. When she was stuck at home with the kids it just came about. Our work is very different, but we've always given each other criticism. We do it at a stage when we're strong enough to take it. When somebody's just scratching around, it's not the right moment to say, 'This doesn't work.' There's a point at which you *can* say that."[1]

1970. Commissioned by Jonathan Cape to illustrate Jules Verne's *Around the World in Eighty Days* for its centenary, Burningham undertook to make the journey described in the book. "I did this ludicrous trip round the world in eighty days. It was timed so that I left the Reform Club [London] at eight o'clock in the morning, as Verne did in the story, and I got back to the Cafe Royal [London] at whatever time he did. Jules Verne never made that trip, nobody ever did, the whole thing was purely fictitious. S. J. Perelman tried it once, got fed up, and packed it in.

"The problem was that the itinerary was very carefully worked out by Thomas Cook Tours. In order to take in the different places, a very intricate program had to be set up. Although, you can go round the world in five hours—or whatever it is—in a fighter plane, it was a question of how to make it all work with train, boat, and plane connections in eighty days. There were fantastic things I saw and did, but by and large it was about checking in for my next flight, terrified of losing my cases and tickets. When you put your cases in the luggage office in Istanbul, you don't expect to see them again.

"There were continents I'd never been to before. First, I got the boat across to Calais, from there I got the Orient Express to Istanbul. No one told me they take the restaurant car off in Italy. I traveled through Yugoslavia, Bulgaria and Rumania on an empty stomach. Next I went to Cyprus, on to Egypt from there to Ethiopia. Then to Kenya, India, Nepal, Hong Kong, Bangkok, Japan, Australia, New Zealand, Fiji, Tonga, Mexico, across the United States, up to Canada, across Canada and back to London. When I got back to Heathrow I got down and kissed the tarmac and said, 'I'm never going to travel again.' People say how lucky I must have been to see all those places, and of course I was, but it is terrible to do that amount of traveling.

"Usually I was in the wrong place. I would be stuck in Northern Australia for five days with nothing to do, then have two days somewhere with plenty to explore. I was in Mexico City for twenty-four hours, in some places half a day. I went round Kenya National Parks with the Kenyan Tourist Board in a Land Rover; I saw the animals and stayed in all the marvelous lodges. The India Tourist Board took me round India, but at the end of ten days I was almost saying, 'Don't show me another temple, please. They're wonderful, but just don't show me anything more.'

"It would have been much more fun if I hadn't had to do a book at the end of it. You tend to panic if you're in Tonga in the Pacific and think 'My God, I've got to draw this when I get back.' What the hell makes Tonga different from Fiji? It's all palm trees. So I photographed things like pillar boxes, license plates, little details that I thought I might want to use.

"I had the impression that I was keeping a diary, but in fact I had very little to show. I'd kept curious things: dead butterflies, labels, and bits of napkin. I used them all on the end-papers of the book. But I did almost no drawing at all, and I'd had the idea that I was going to have done all these drawings by the time I reached England.

"I don't like to draw when I'm traveling; I can't bear sitting around with everybody looking over my shoulder. It's too much like work. In fact, when people get out their box of paints I just think, 'Can't you think of something else to do; it's so nice out here?'"[1]

1978. Burningham worked on films for the BBC, all made on the kitchen table. "I put masses and masses of work and detail into them, but when they came out—they were little five-minute films for children. The camera picked out so few details; it had been a complete waste of time. I have had films made of my work, and that's fine if somebody does it sympathetically, but I'm not really interested in it. The Americans made a very good film of *Cannonball Simp*—with live actors rather than animation.

"Film and television aren't an influence on my work. Television is very soporific. None of my family will watch it if they have an alternative. I don't go out to the cinema often, but I'm a great admirer of Jacques Tati. He's totally underrated. His observation of humanity and his introduction of new film techniques have never been given the credit they deserve."[1]

1983. "When asked to illustrate *The Wind in the Willows,* I only agreed because I hadn't read it. I said, 'Send me a copy, but will you please paste over the pictures?' There are several versions: Arthur Rackham's, E. H. Shepard's, and various other decorative ones. I wouldn't have done *Rupert* if I'd been asked, or *Winnie the Pooh*. It would have been impossible because I knew those were classic Shepard drawings that couldn't be re-done and bettered; they're brilliant.

"I'm a great fan of Shepard, but I don't think his drawings for *The Wind in the Willows* are very good. The character of Toad, Mole and Badger don't actually come across. They are very difficult characters. I had to battle with how to do them, which generally happens, but they are particularly difficult. When you dress Toad you have the problem of what to do with webbed feet in shoes. The Water Rat is probably the most problematic because a water rat is extremely hairy—like one of those eye-hidden dogs covered in fur. If you're trying to change the expression on that animal, you can't have all that hair. Therefore, I made him more of a rat-type water rat.

"In the case of Badger, you have a definite character, a sort of plodding figure. I based him on a retired school master living on his own. Animals are often trouble, their markings come in the

(From *Granpa* by John Burningham. Illustrated by the author.)

wrong place. A zebra's stripes will come cross the eyes. When you try and give them some sort of expression you can't because there's a bit of camouflage there. I messed around with the Badger's camouflage in order to get his expressions right. We used to live in a cottage in Dorset where the badgers shuffled about at night. You very rarely saw them but you got an idea of the way they operate.

"I think it's essential to get the characteristic of the animal as it is in nature. It mustn't be sentimental; I can't bear that. It's difficult to define 'getting it right' because it can be slightly out of proportion, if you've got the essence of the character. Facsimile models of animals or dolls are actually rather boring; they don't really work when somebody models them. Equally, drawings are slightly dead if someone makes them near to nature. You have to get the essence."[1]

Despite his success and the number of books published, Burningham still finds the work process difficult. "Nobody kicks me down to my work room, I have to kick myself down there. It's a curious dilemma: there is nothing more satisfying, reassuring, and pleasing than to have done some good work, but I tend to escape given any opportunity. I'll play passionately bad tennis, or go to a sale of antiques. I can go down the road to post a letter and find myself on the other side of London, not be quite sure why, except that I've avoided what I should be doing. A deadline is quite a good thing because working in a vacuum is difficult. It's much better when someone says 'If this book is coming out next spring, we've got to have proofs to take to Frankfurt or Bologna and you've got to get a move on,' otherwise there are so many things that are more important to do than work.

"And there is this awful business of never believing that I'll be able to do another piece of work. I sometimes feel I have absolutely no ability. When I go to my room, where I've got all the equipment and paper and cardboard, chances are that I'll produce a deadly drawing with awful colors. If I were a bricklayer, once I'd learn to lay bricks, I could always lay bricks; they might be a bit rough one day and not as well laid, but nevertheless I could lay bricks.

"When I get to the point where I have produced enough drawings to believe in the project, it starts to get slightly less awful and I can listen to the radio and work away. For *John Patrick Norman McHennessey*, I probably did hundreds of sketches of the authoritarian character before I could draw him quickly. I'm sure actors go through the same thing to *be* that person while they are acting.

"I rarely work with other people's texts, apart from *Around the World in Eighty Days, The Wind in the Willows*, and Ian Fleming's *Chitty-Chitty-Bang-Bang*. If somebody's written the story, it's a *fait accompli*. It's actually easier to illustrate. When I do the text as well, I walk around for months, even years, turning over images and sections, thinking how to put things together. The images and the text have got to come together because the balance is important between the two. I bring them to the boil at the same time. I make sketches endlessly, get exasperated, go to post a letter. Usually, the problem with a story is how you're going to end it. Then finite tuning— spending hours over the actual use of a few words, the structuring. When it is over you look back and think, 'What on earth was the problem?'"[1]

Burningham finds that some adults have more difficulty understanding his work than children. *Grandpa* and *Come*

Away from the Water, Shirley are two examples: "In *Grandpa* the grandfather dies, there is an empty chair—and as far as children are concerned, it's a matter of fact. It is only adults who write to me to ask, 'Is he dead. . .?'

"Two things are happening in *Come Away from the Water, Shirley*. The little girl's fantasy adventure on one side; the parents on the other side saying, 'Don't touch that dog, don't do this, watch out about that.' A lot of adults have said to me, 'Oh those awful parents!' and I have said, 'No, they're not awful parents—it's just that they have to get back on the bus, and if she does get her feet wet it's a damn nuisance.' The noise one makes as a parent is just like music—in one ear and out the other. So, yes, there's a lesson in the story, but it is not a moral lesson."[2]

"Choosing books for children is quite a problem. There's so much *manufacturing* of children's books, it's become an industry and that's a pity. Although production standards have gone up in some ways, it's really the publishers kidding the parents who then kid the children that they're getting what they want—but they're not. Usually it's an outdated vision of childhood from the nineteenth century, which no longer means anything. Children want a good story, whether it's pictorial or verbal.

"I think critics for children's books are better in America than they are in Britain. There are very few people who actually pull books apart here. There are reviewers for some of the major papers in the States who do it very well."[1]

Over the past few years Burningham has been working on a book about England—a picture book for adults. "I have planned to do this book for years, trying to define England and the English. England is changing, but only superficially; actually it remains very much as it was. It is not a beautiful Thomas-Hardy-cottage-country type of book. It's a mixture. The text is mostly selected quotations, I'm not writing it.

"The traveling for *Around the World in Eighty Days* was good practice, except that you always think you know how to do a book until you do. I had a miserable year driving round England, seeing lovely things and awful things, and worrying that they just didn't do anything for me. I was looking too hard. Now that I'm getting much further into it, I know what the missing pieces actually are. I've learned to recognize them.

"I hope I'm a ruthless editor of my own work. There are some things I don't mind, for instance a finger print on some part of the drawing. Drawing is a bit like music in that 'Tea for Two' is a very good tune. Whether you play it on a harmonica or with a symphony orchestra doesn't really matter, the tune is good and will stand any amount of different treatment. By the time your work has been printed, the essence of what you wanted is more important than perfection. Perfection in printing can be deadly.

"I always describe my way of producing books as being rather like repertory theater. You are 'performing' one book, you're rehearsing the next, and you're learning the part for the one that's to come. I've always got ideas fermenting. I've never had a sabbatical, although I'd quite like one."[1]

Burningham has other interests which take him away from his drawings. "I like the world of building. We have a wooden boat house right on the water on the east coast of England where Helen was brought up. We also have had a house in southwest France for years. It must have been the cheapest house ever— we bought it for eighty pounds; it didn't have any floors or windows or a roof. It was just stone walls; we put in the rest.

I'm an impatient person, but I like doing up buildings and collecting materials from all over.

"I go to art galleries sometimes, but it has to be on my terms. I like looking at pictures, but not with lots of other people. I've been in a museum in Vienna where they've got an amazing room with four Rembrandt portraits and no half-asleep guide tottering on a stool guarding them. It's quite remarkable because you're in there with nobody else. I've gone to Chartres at four o'clock in the morning before the buses got there."[1]

Burningham is positive about the future. "I don't let myself worry for my children. What chance have you got if you do that? You think, 'There'll be another Chernobyl, there must be, if some fundamentalist Christian or Moslem doesn't let off a bloody great rocket first.' We've used up the ozone layer, we've got the greenhouse effect in the southern hemisphere, the North Sea is rising, the ice flows are melting. If you want to look at it that way, there is no hope. Every civilization has done itself in one way or another, and we're due for it mighty soon because we have no respect for nature or resources. But then you can say, 'Well, we're quite clever, maybe we can think of some ozone substitute to pump into the atmosphere.' I'm an optimist."[1]

FOOTNOTE SOURCES

[1]Based on an interview by Cathy Courtney for *Something about the Author*.

[2]Michele Field, "PW Interviews: John Burningham and Helen Oxenbury," *Publishers Weekly*, July 24, 1987.

CALLAN, Jamie 1954-

PERSONAL: Born January 26, 1954, in Long Island, N.Y.; daughter of John (a personnel administrator) and June (a secretary; maiden name, Dingwall) Callan; married Eugene Silver (an actor), June 20, 1981; children: Callan Vallancourt. *Education:* Norwalk Community College, A.A., 1973; Bard College, B.A., 1975; Goddard College, M.A., 1980; currently working on M.F.A. at University of California at Los Angeles, 1987—. *Religion:* Unitarian. *Residence:* North Hollywood, Calif. *Address:* c/o New American Library, 1633 Broadway, New York, N.Y. 10019. *Agent:* Kay Kidde, Kidde, Hoyt & Picard, 335 East 51st St., New York, N.Y. 10022.

CAREER: Western Union International, New York City, editor of *TelexTalk,* 1976-78; Mid-Orange Correctional Facility, Warwick, N.Y., teacher, 1980; Fiction Project, New York City, teacher of creative writing at New York Hospital/Cornell Medical Center's Psychiatric Unit, 1982-86. Sales promotion coordinator for Estee Lauder, 1981-86. *Member:* Society of Children's Book Writers, Authors Guild, PEN American Center, West. *Awards, honors:* New York State Creative Artists Public Service Grant, 1980, for unpublished novel "Andrea Darcy"; Fellow at Millay Colony for the Arts, summer, 1981; Doubleday/Columbia University Fellowship, 1982; Fellow at Virginia Center for the Arts, winter, 1983, and fall, 1985; PEN Syndicated Fiction Award, 1985, for short story "The Naked Man"; Bread Loaf Writers Conference Fellowship, 1986; University of California at Los Angeles Fellowship in screenwriting, 1987.

WRITINGS:

YOUNG ADULT NOVELS

Over the Hill at Fourteen (Scholastic Book Club selection), New American Library, 1982.
The Young and the Soapy, New American Library, 1984.
Just Too Cool, New American Library, 1987.

Contributor of articles, stories, and poems to magazines, including *Greenfield Review, Back Bay View, Wellspring, Washington Square Writes,* and *Buckle.*

WORK IN PROGRESS: "Thrill Rides," "Big Babies," and "In the Heat of the Kitchen," screenplays; *Mixed Messages,* a short story collection.

SIDELIGHTS: "My career as an author of novels for young adults started by accident. My very first novel, 'Andrea Darcy,' won an award in 1980, and because of this, several publishers, including New American Library, contacted me. While New American Library could not publish 'Andrea Darcy,' they

asked me if I would be interested in writing a book on assignment about a teenage fashion model. I did a great deal of soul-searching before I accepted, then decided that it is better to write, even if it's not on a truly heartfelt subject, than not to write at all.

"To my surprise, I began to enjoy writing *Over the Hill at Fourteen,* and when it was complete I was thrilled by the response. Scholastic Book Club bought it, and it was favorably reviewed in several publications. The most exciting result was getting fan mail. Teenagers from all over the country wrote to me, and my book seemed important and meaningful to them.

"With my move to California, I've expanded my horizons, and am now getting involved in screenwriting. This seems to be a great way to reach a large audience. UCLA is a wonderful school and I've found it creatively stimulating. This will be my second master's degree, but I seem to be addicted to education! I need to feel as if I'm constantly learning something new. It feeds me creatively."

CANNON, Bettie (Waddell) 1922-

PERSONAL: Born November 13, 1922, in Detroit, Mich.; daughter of William Ross (a businessman) and Willie Ruth (a homemaker; maiden name, Whitehead) Waddell; married Charles Joseph Cannon (a hydraulic engineer and business owner), July 22, 1944; children: Charles Joseph III, Sallie Jane Cannon Clover, Kathleen Laura Cannon Rafferty, Suzannah Whitehead Cannon Milling. *Education:* Attended Michigan State University, 1940-42, and Oakland University, 1972-74.

CAREER: Cannon Engineering and Equipment Co., Troy, Mich., vice-president 1963—; writer, 1968—. Conference coordinator at Oakland University, 1970-74; member of board of directors of Readings for the Blind, Southfield, Mich. *Member:* Authors Guild, Society of Children's Book Writers, Detroit Women Writers (president, 1975-77), Greater West Bloomfield Historical Society (member of board of directors). *Awards, honors:* Award of Merit from the Historical Society of Michigan, 1980, for *All about Franklin.*

WRITINGS:

All about Franklin: From Pioneer to Preservation, Four Corners Press, 1980.
A Bellsong for Sarah Raines (young adult novel), Scribner, 1987.

Contributor of stories and articles to local newspapers, including *Passages North.*

WORK IN PROGRESS: A young adult novel entitled *Begin the World Again,* about "a teenager who has lived in communes all her life. She has grown up as part of the 'alternative culture' with her hippie parents and their friends. The story is about her quest for her own place in the world which takes her to her grandmother's home in the suburbs and back to her Kentucky farm"; research on "the life of a young girl captured by Indians in the 1850s and how she tries to return to her former life"; a short story, "The Piano Player."

I am a model. I am a sex goddess. And yes, I'm also a spoiled brat. (Cover illustration from *Over the Hill at Fourteen* by Jamie Callan.)

SIDELIGHTS: "'Inspire' means to breathe in/animate/enliven/motivate. Seeing these meanings again in my *Webster's Second* helps me now to understand my everlasting reluctance to talk

BETTIE CANNON

about inspiration. It seems too lofty for me. Besides, my father used to say, 'Production is ninety-nine percent perspiration and one percent inspiration.' I guess this is why writing does not arrive for me in a sudden clap of thunder from On High, but rather comes naturally as breathing out and breathing in. Things happen in life and I write to understand what I feel or think. The motivating event for *A Bellsong for Sarah Raines* was the alcoholism and the eventual suicide of my father. Although I wrote long before his death, I think our intertwined stories circled, paced my brain, and maybe 'inspired' me to write my first novel. I wish I could say I set out to write a young adult novel. But it would be a lie. I just wrote the book and my voice emerged as that of a young girl. And if the voice of a young girl is what comes to the page and young readers like it, I am pleased.

"Two data points in my memory bank seem to describe my journey toward becoming a writer. First, is a photograph of myself at ten or eleven. I wear a pilot's leather helmet and a bomber jacket handed down to me by my rich cousin Tommy. I gaze at the camera through horn-rimmed, thick glasses and hold my beloved copy of *Little Women* at camera-eye level. I point at the author's name. The old photo is the symbol of my dramatic 'I'm-going-to-be-a-writer-like-Louisa- May-Alcott' period. In addition to Louisa May Alcott, there were two uncles, Kyle and Don Whitehead, who were newspapermen in Harlan, Kentucky. Watching them work when I visited Harlan every summer, I understood that I could be a writer. My idea of heaven was going to the *Daily Enterprise* where my uncles fitted me with a printers devil's hat fashioned from a sheet of newsprint and let me work the linotype machine. (Kyle was a columnist for the *Harlan Daily Enterprise*, its editor, and teacher of journalism at Murray State in Kentucky. Don became an AP war correspondent, book author, and two-time Pulitzer Prize winner.) And, during one school year back in Detroit's Tappan Intermediate, I wrote two Civil War novels a la *Gone with the Wind;* worked on the gossip-cum-scandal sheet

'Homeroom Hotstuff"; and wrote long impassioned letters to both my grandmothers.

"My second data point is letters *from* my two grandmothers. I'm in MacKenzie High School now. My grandmother from Kentucky writes that she is pleased I want to be a writer, and 'I know you will, if you try.' My Ohio grandmother says, 'Last letter you said you want to be an actress and singer now. Well, make up your mind.' I think these two different grandmothers tell me more than anything can about the two parts of myself. As if to show my Ohio grandmother I could make up my mind, I moved into my 'I'm-going-to-be-a-singer-actress-like-my-Aunt-Esther' period. Aunt Esther was a coloratura soprano known as the 'Florida Nightingale.' Oh, I still worked on the school newspaper but all I did was keep the real writers from their deadlines. When I won the lead in the school play 'Come Out of the Kitchen' (which seems not to be a prophetic title), applause at the end of Act III turned me away from my writing. I majored in drama at Michigan State, fell in love, married, and immediately produced four children. I became Donna Reed and Harriet Nelson but in my heart I was still Louisa May Alcott and Aunt Esther.

"My singing was confined to church choirs and P.T.A. Mother Singers; my acting to the Children's Community Theatre of Kansas City. I portrayed complex characters like green-bearded gnomes and bellicose zoo-keepers and wrote nothing but Christmas cards and laundry lists for years. One day after a performance in Shawnee Mission, Kansas, as I tried to peel off enough of my false beard to get home with dignity, I thought, 'I

(Jacket illustration by Ronald Himler from *A Bellsong for Sarah Raines* by Bettie Cannon.)

can write a play as good as this one.' I did and the play, while it never saw the light of day, did win a local prize. From that day to this, I never looked back.

"In a kind of informal apprenticeship, I was a 'stringer' for a local paper, wrote feature articles for the *Detroit News Sunday Magazine,* wrote the beginnings of several short stories and novels, took writing courses, sold poetry, humor pieces, did two corporate histories, and wrote *All about Franklin: From Pioneer to Preservation* which won the Michigan Historical Society's Award of Merit that year. This was all in preparation for writing my novel *A Bellsong for Sarah Raines.*

"I am grateful for the help I've had along the way— first, by my maternal grandmother and those two uncles, then by writing teachers from Kansas to Iowa to North Carolina, and by the members of Detroit Women Writers in whose workshops and conferences I began to see myself as a real writer. (I'm a past-president of Detroit Women Writers, and I speak to writers at the annual two-day conference held at Oakland University.)

"Writers who have influenced me are Eudora Welty, Mary Lee Settle, Christina Stead, and Peter Taylor; and the Russian writers who first taught me that characters could be good and evil at the same time, the way we are."

HOBBIES AND OTHER INTERESTS: Needlework, gardening, history, reading, antiques, talking to my eight grandchildren.

CHESLER, Bernice 1932-

PERSONAL: Born October 3, 1932, in New Bedford, Mass.; daughter of Myer Aaron and Ethel (Margolis) Goldberg; married David Alan Chesler (a research engineer), November 4, 1956; children: Mark, Lisa and Stanford (twins). *Education:* Attended Syracuse University, 1950-53; Northeastern University, B.A., 1955. *Home:* 40 Columbus St., Newton Highlands, Mass. 02161.

CAREER: Lowell Institute Cooperative Broadcasting Corp., Cambridge, Mass., member of public relations department staff, WGBH-TV and WGBH-FM, 1955-57; former resource chairman of Creative Arts Council of Newton Schools and representative of Metropolitan Council for Educational Opportunities; research and publications coordinator for national children's television program "Zoom," 1972-75; currently free-lance writer.

WRITINGS:

In and out of Boston with Children, Barre, 1966, 3rd edition published as *In and out of Boston with (or without) Children* (illustrated by Joan Drescher), 1975, 4th edition, Globe Pequot, 1982.
(Editor) *Do a Zoom Do,* Little, Brown, 1975.
(With Evelyn Kaye) *The Family Guide to Cape Cod: What to Do When You Don't Want to Do What Everyone Else Is Doing* (illustrated by J. Drescher), Barre, 1976.
Bed and Breakfast in the Northeast, Globe Pequot, 1983.
Bed and Breakfast Coast to Coast, Stephen Green, 1986.
Bed and Breakfast in New England, Globe Pequot, 1987, 2nd edition, 1989.
Bed and Breakfast in the Mid-Atlantic States, Globe Pequot, 1987, 2nd edition, 1989.

Editor of "People You'd Like to Know" series of ten booklets on awareness of the handicapped, Enyclopaedia Britannica

Educational Corp., 1979. Publications coordinator for *The Zoom Catalog,* Random House, 1972.

CLARK, Joan 1934-

PERSONAL: Born October 12, 1934, in Liverpool, Nova Scotia, Canada; daughter of W. I. and Sally (Dodge) MacDonald; married Jack Clark (a geotechnical engineer), 1958; children: two sons, one daughter. *Education:* Acadia University, B.A., 1957; attended University of Alberta, 1960. *Home:* 6 Dover Place, St. John's, Newfoundland, Canada A1B 2P5. *Address:* c/o Writers' Union of Canada, 24 Ryerson Ave., Toronto, Canada M5T 2P3.

CAREER: Teacher in Sussex, New Brunswick, 1957-58, Edmonton, Alberta, 1960-61, Calgary, Alberta, 1962-63, and Dartmouth, Nova Scotia, 1969-70; co-founder and co-editor of *Dandelion* (magazine), 1974-81; free-lance writer. *Member:* Writers' Union of Canada, PEN International, Writers' Guild of Alberta, Writers' Alliance of Newfoundland and Labrador. *Awards, honors: Wild Man of the Woods* was exhibited at the Bologna International Children's Book Fair, 1985, and runner-up, Canadian Library Association Book of the Year for Children Award, 1986; shortlisted for Governor Generals Award, 1989; Canadian Authors Association Award for *The Victory of Geraldine Gull,* 1989.

WRITINGS:

JUVENILE

Girl of the Rockies, Ryerson, 1968.
Thomasina and the Trout Tree (illustrated by Ingeborg Hiscox), Tundra Books, 1971.
The Hand of Robin Squires (illustrated by William Taylor and Mary Cserepy), Clarke, Irwin, 1977.
The Leopard and the Lily (fable; illustrated by Velma Foster), Oolichan Books, 1984.
Wild Man of the Woods, Penguin Books Canada, 1985, Viking Kestrel, 1986.
The Moons of Madeleine, Viking Kestrel, 1986.

ADULT

From a High Thin Wire (short stories), NeWest, 1982.
The Victory of Geraldine Gull (novel), Macmillan of Canada, 1988.
Swimming toward the Light (short stories), Macmillan of Canada, 1990.

Contributor of short stories to magazines, including *Canadian Fiction, Waves, Dalhousie Review, Saturday Night, Journal of Canadian Fiction,* and *Wascana Review.*

WORK IN PROGRESS: Two novels, one for adults and one for children.

SIDELIGHTS: "I have read extensively to children in libraries and schools across Canada. This is one of the delights of writing children's stories. I want children to connect the work with the person, to understand how literature grows out of a particular time and place. This is something I did not understand until I was in my late twenties and began to write. For a long time I was intimidated by the fact that I hadn't recognized the writer in myself at an earlier age. That, too, changed when I realized the book I will write at fifty-four is not the book I would have

JOAN CLARK

written at twenty-four. By being a late starter, I feel I have gained more than I have lost."

CLOKEY, Art 1921-

PERSONAL: Born in 1921, in Detroit, Mich.; adopted son of Joseph Clokey (a composer); divorced; married second wife Gloria Stamm; children: (first marriage) Ann (deceased), Joe. *Education:* Pomona College, liberal arts degree, 1948; attended University of Southern California, 1950. *Home:* Sausalito, Calif.

CAREER: Motion picture producer. Creator of characters Gumby, 1956, and Davy and Goliath. *Military service:* U.S. Armed Forces, during World War II.

WRITINGS:

TELEVISION; ALSO DIRECTOR AND PRODUCER

"Gumby" (130 six-minute episodes), syndicated 1956, new syndicated TV series (99 seven-minute episodes), Lorimar-Telepictures, 1988.
"Davy and Goliath," syndicated, 1961.

Also produced the film, "Mandala" in 1975 which examines time and mind expanding experience and the evolution of consciousness.

ADAPTATIONS:

VIDEO

"Gumby's Incredible Journey," Family Home Entertainment, 1956.
"Gumby Adventures," Family Home Entertainment, 1956.
"Gumby and the Moon Boggles," Family Home Entertainment, 1956.
"Gumby's Supporting Cast," Family Home Entertainment, 1986.

SIDELIGHTS: Born in Detroit, Michigan, in 1921. When he was ten years old his parents separated; his mother remarried, and Clokey went to live with his father. "I remember when I was six or seven, I would draw in school. I was watching Saturday matinees of 'Hell's Angels,' and I'd draw these dog fights in the air."[1]

A year later, his father died in a car accident, and Clokey relocated to Southern California with his mother, and adoptive father composer Joseph Clokey. "My whole life opened up."[2] My foster father played the organ and was a musician."[3] "I absorbed a lot of the creative impulse from him."[1]

Attended Pomona College in Claremont, California, leaving to serve in the U.S. Armed Forces in World War II and returning to earn a degree in liberal arts in 1948. Clokey briefly studied for the ministry at an Episcopal seminary in Connecticut, and in 1950, enrolled in the University of Southern California film department. There he studied with his first important teacher, Slavko Vorkapich, who taught him ". . .the kinesthetic principles of organized movement.

"I call them kinesthetic film forces, because we stimulate the eye cells when we see all that light and shadow moving on the screen. It induces a sense of motion in your nervous system. If you can organize [these patterns] properly, you can make your film—any film—have much more vitality. An extreme example is in Cinerama, when you're going down a roller coaster and you can feel those forces dragging at you."[1]

"It's similar to music. You build to a climax through use of timing and intensity of the stimuli—the duration, syncopation, and so on. All deal with the same thing . . . . Vorkapich . . .taught that it's more like poetry and music. He would refer to the shots and the definite cuts as notes. Visual notes to combine and use in various ways, to get across your feelings. To delight and create new ideas and things—a new slant on life. You can do amazing things to the autonomic nervous system if you know how to organize these forces. It's the balancing of repetition, variety, tempo. And just a split second of rest. It's all a mysterious combination."[3]

"Vorkapich got down to basics. His theory was that motion pictures dealt only with motion and the illusion of three dimensionality. They're nothing more than the illusion of three dimensional objects created by the director's use of shapes, shadows, colors and motion. He said if you understood how to organize those things through camera angle, camera movement, pace, and so forth, you could make any film more interesting."[4]

Clokey began working in television after making an industrial film for a local soup company, using animation to illustrate the "pea soup making process." "I got my first job doing commercials because people were fascinated how I could make the screen come alive in ways that other people couldn't."[4]

ART CLOKEY

His commercials included Coca-Cola, Budweiser and Sanka. "But I didn't like the deadlines and the competition. It was very stressful. I was happy to get into doing something like Gumby."[1]

"Gumby was a by-product of an art film I made in 1953, called 'Gumbasia.' In 'Gumbasia,' I filmed geometric and amorphous shapes made from modeling clay of many colors. These shapes moved and transformed to the background rhythm of jazz.

"I wanted to avoid as much as possible the distraction of any recognizable forms in 'Gumbasia.' It was an experiment in pure movement, where the whole plane moved out in different shapes this way and that. 'Gumbasia' was filled with movements that, when put together, created a feeling. For instance, there was a shot showing a ball rolling through clay arches and the next shot showed the ball going over a little hill. You begin to *feel* the movement. In the early 1970s, *Playboy* used that scene in a feature called 'Sex in Cinema.' (I could never understand why.)

"Sam Engel, a major movie producer, had asked to see my film. I had met Sam because, at that time, I was tutoring his son in English and Latin at Harvard Military Academy (now Harvard School) in Los Angeles. 'This is the most exciting film I have ever seen in my life!' Sam said. When Sam comments that a film is exciting, God listens; otherwise He might miss out on something big!

"We immediately formed a partnership. Sam had just finished a film starring Burt Lancaster and Sophia Loren, and my

repressed libido was turning out fantasies of helping to direct Sam's next picture, with Sophia, Marilyn Monroe, or Jayne Mansfield. I soon learned, however, that I would turn in my libido for a box of clay. Since Sam had another son who was about three years old, he was interested in the quality of children's fare on television. He could see that my trimensional animation process would be perfect for children's films. Imagine my disappointment at his suggestion that I work on a clay figure instead of Sophia's!

"I trudged home to do my asexual assignment, never having dreamed that I would be involved in making movies for children—prepubescent children at that! For weeks I played around with clay—molding many shapes and colors, looking for the right figure. Although it could never compare with the 'casting couch' routine, tabletop modeling became a fascinating challenge to my imagination.

"Clay is the basic medium for creative conception of new forms. It's malleable and it changes every time you touch it. You push and mash it, and a lump turns into something, just like magic.

"Clay. . .is very basic in the psyche as a substance. Scientists say that we evolved from clay. It's been in our civilization for years as a medium for expression and a very practical medium—making pots for carrying water, storing grain, and used as writing tablets for many thousands of years. What else? Birds use clay to build their nests. Oh, little images and gods, of course. And Jesus used clay to heal.

(Illustration from *The Gumby Book of Colors* by Jane Hyman.)

"I set out to create a shape and size that were functionally practical from the film animating standpoint. Animating clay for hours under hot lights created a problem: I found it necessary to have a shape and size that were easily reproduced, so that a fresh figure could be substituted as the old one became dirty and completely misshapen through excessive manipulation.

"Part of the idea behind 'Gumbasia' was that everything in life is based on geometric forms. Gumby and Pokey are close to that. They are simple forms and combinations of those forms. If you roll some white clay into a ball, slit it in half, and place each on a side of Pokey's head, you have his eyes. And when Pokey's eyes bug out, they come out as rods.

"Gumby's shape is simple. . . . We put a little bump on his head to give him the bump of wisdom that the Buddhists have. The only difference is that they have it in the center and Gumby's is over to the side. Actually, the real inspiration for this bump came from my early childhood. In the living room of my grandfather's farmhouse in Michigan hung a framed photo enlargement of my father, taken when he was eighteen. It showed a cowlick on one side of his head that looked like a large bump. I was so amazed by it. If you superimpose an outline of that portrait over Gumby, you will see that the heads coincide perfectly.

"As for size, I finally settled on a seven-inch Gumby, as this turned out to be the easiest to work with. Rolling out a large slab

of half-inch-thick clay, I was able to create a number of Gumby bodies in a few minutes with a homemade 'cookie cutter.' The arms were rolled separately and cut from lengths of long snakelike pieces of clay. Soft wire was inserted into both the arms and the body to give needed rigidity. The eyes were little disks of white clay, cut and bent for various expression changes, and the pupils were tiny balls of red clay that stuck to the white disks. These balls were easily rolled about to create a variety of expressions. The eyebrows, mouth, and nose were made of yellow stringlike pieces that stuck to the green body.

"Green with a hint of blue was what I chose for Gumby's color. Imagine a luxuriant field on a bright day when the green grass picks up just a pinch of blue sky. Gumby looks like a fat blade of glass. I am sure Walt Whitman would have been pleased. Pokey, on the other hand, is all earth—orange and black. Pokey is skeptical and down to earth, as opposed to Gumby, who has both feet on the ground but his head in the clouds.

"As for Gumby's name, I had learned the term 'gumbo' as a child in Michigan. During the rainy season, before they had pavement through the farm country, the roads got very slippery and mucky. My father would come home and tell us that he had 'gotten stuck in the gumbo' on the farm. From my years of studying Latin, I knew that the diminutive of 'gumbo' is a 'Gumbino' or 'Gumby,' and the mother was 'Gumba,' which is the female declension in Latin. 'Gumbo' is the masculine. Seven years of the language and that's the only way I ever used it.

(Illustration from *The Gumby Book of Colors* by Jane Hyman.)

"I took the Gumby pilot to Tom Sarnoff at NBC, who was immediately charmed by the character and by the style of clay animation. He signed me to produce a series of 'The Adventures of Gumby.' Roger Muir, the producer of 'Howdy Doody,' agreed after seeing the film that it would be a winner, and decided to introduce Gumby on his show. Gumby then graduated to his own show, 'The Gumby Show,' with Pinky Lee as the emcee. Pinky Lee may have chafed under that title; I think he resented playing second fiddle to a piece of clay.

"NBC gave me complete artistic freedom, which is something almost unheard of now at a network. I would just fantasize and daydream.

"Sometimes I would tell my children bedtime stories and turn them into Gumbys. I developed no formulas. Each episode was a separate creation. I never knew what the next episode was going to be about. The love I had for my children rubbed off on those stories. I was. . .enjoying creating."[3]

"I was. . .operating as most artists do, on a subconscious level. There's deep meanings in everything we create. Where does the inspiration come from? Where do dreams come from?"[5]

After a year with NBC, Clokey decided to produce "Gumby" independently, and set about selling the show to stations all over the country. "In a few stations the station managers had a rapport with children and some too had the too dynamic on kids. But most of them were just like sheep. They were just

administering and making sure they made money. There was no ratings they could look at, so I couldn't sell it to them."[1]

A colleague convinced Clokey that "Gumby" could become more popular through the marketing of a toy model of the character; thus the Gumby Toy Co. was created in 1964. "For seven years I resisted commercializing, making Gumby toys. I was afraid, being very idealistic, that the parents and the kids would feel we were exploiting them. We wanted to give them something through the films, not take from them. But I had to make dolls, otherwise I couldn't get the films syndicated."[1]

During the sixties, Clokey and his first wife separated, after attempting to reconcile with the help of counselors. "She would walk out in the middle of sessions, and I walked out on a psychiatrist she chose.

"I had an unfortunate divorce. . . .Oh, it was frightening. [My wife and her lawyer] were threatening to take away things I'd created. I finally got back control, after patience and finding the right lawyers."[1]

The pain of divorce and the general atmosphere of the sixties started Clokey on a spiritual journey that led to the study of various philosophies. "I took a sabbatical to learn how to be happy."[6] "I explored ways to become a better director by getting into all kinds of self-awareness. Encounter groups, psychotherapy. . . .you name it, I tried it."[4] "It was kind of like a quest for my true self, why I wasn't happy, why I got into this mess. So I went and spent maybe $40,000 on all kinds of therapy—group therapies. Gestalt, you name it. It was a fascinating experience and I was able to strenghen myself a great deal."[1]

In Japan, he studied Zen Buddhism with guru, Alan Watts. "One day he said rather humorously that there are two kinds of people in the world, the prickly and the gooey. The prickly are the rigid and uptight, and the gooey are the easygoing and flowing. I then decided to make two characers who symblized these two types. One was a spiked dinosaur, called Prickle, and the other was a little blue mermaid named Goo. The female is more gooey and the male is prickly."[3]

Clokey's continued interest in Eastern thought manifested itself in his 1975 film "Mandala." "I attempted in 'Mandala' to suggest a time and mind expanding experience, the evolution of consciousness, by orchestrating deep cultural symbols from the collective unconscious."[4]

Like many artists of that time, he experimented with hallucinogens. "People often ask me if I did drugs while making Gumby. I never took psychedelics until after I left the show, as a way of exploring my self-awareness. I wanted to improve my skills as a director."[6]

Though he was happily remarried during the 70s to Gloria Stamm, who became his partner in work and in spiritual pursuits, Clokey experienced more tragedy. In 1974, his nineteen-year-old daughter died in a car crash. "I just cried for six months."[2]

He also experienced considerable failure in business, due, he believed, to his failure to make shrewd, tough business deals. "I had a weakness from childhood of wanting to please, a doormat complex."[2]

In 1979, Clokey saw a documentary about spiritual leader, Sathya Sai Baba. "It was mind-blowing. He was the ultimate expression of what I was trying to do with Gumby—and that's to remind us that nothing is impossible.

"He apparently is the fullest manifestion in human form of the infinite creative force of the universe. In other words, he's like Jesus Christ, only more so. He's it. He's like Krishna."[1]

"[A] resurgence in Gumby's popularity started when my wife, Gloria, and I went to India to see avatar Sathya Sai Baba. Sai Baba can materialize objects out of thin air; you can't believe it unless you see it. Strings of beads and gold rings just come out of his hand. I stood there with Gumby and he did this circular motion with his arms. I could see the sacred ash coming out of his hand. He plopped it right on Gumby, and when we came home things started to happen."[3]

At the Art Center in Pasadena, Clokey gave a lecture on animation and discovered how much the young adults in the audience still appreciated Gumby. "The episodes started appearing on TV again, sales of the Gumby toys began to pick up, and then Eddie Murphy did his Gumby skit on 'Saturday Night Live.' My son Joe came to me and asked why I let Eddie Murphy do that to Gumby. I told him that you have to understand humor. Gumby has to laugh at himself too. Gumby is a symbol of the spark of divinity in each of us, the basis of the ultimate value of each person. Eddie Murphy instinctively picked up on this when he asserted, 'I'm Gumby, dammit!' When people watch 'The Adventures of Gumby' today, they get a blissful feeling. After years of being grown up and crushed by life's downers, we yearn again for that Gumby high.

"Gumby reminds the child of who he is and where he came from. Like *Alice in Wonderland* or the land of the fairy tales, where anything can happen. And he reminds them that that's really the way life is. . .but we can't see it. Our eyes are clouded with what is called *maya* in India; what we call lack of awareness. So the kid is reminded that he can do anything."[3]

"[Gumby is] an honest, sincere noncynical expression of love. . . .Strangely, part of the appeal is the clay, the subconscious primordial symbol of the human condition. Children pick up on this right away. The clay is like them. It's always changing."[2]

"And how does Gumby feel about his renewed popularity? Well, he really doesn't have a reaction; he accepts it. He says that everybody is unusual and exciting and interesting, and everybody is like him. There's no situation Gumby can't handle. He might get smashed, but he always comes back."[3]

Lorimar-Telepictures produced an all-new Gumby syndicated TV series, aired in 1988, viewed in eighty-four percent of the domestic market and overseas from Central America to Italy. Clokey and company were engaged in creating ninety-nine seven- minute episodes. "With one camera and one animator and two or three artists, we can shoot possibly twenty seconds a day. Here we'll have at least ten or eleven animators, ten to twelve cameras. I've never heard of a project on this scale before."[1]

With a budget of $7.5 million from Lorimar Telepictures, a lot more time and money has gone into producing each show with better sets, larger crowd scenes, finely crafted soundtracks,

Pokey and Gumby. (From *The Authorized Biography of the World's Favorite Clayboy GUMBY* by Louis Kaplan and Scott Michaelsen in harmony with Art Clokey.)

complex computer-controlled camera movements and other features not available during the original series of over two decades ago.

Art Clokey wrote ninety-five of the ninety-nine episodes. Gumby can go anywhere in time and space for his adventures simply by walking through a wall or into a book. Almost all of the animation is done by hand with a variety of tools and materials. Gumby is held in place with T-shaped pins, or thin wires if he is called upon to fly. Petroleum jelly is used to hold the irises in place to affect instant eye movements. Paper mouths create 60 to 70 different mouth positions.

"Plans have been made for a 'Gumby' feature film. He will still be true-blue-green. . .he'll be more sophisticated. He'll deal with computers and do a dance that will make Michael Jackson envious.

"It's amazing, at sixty-three, I'm starting a new career."[2]

"Life is a game: play it. That's what Sai Baba keeps telling people. But the cloaking, the surprise factor, is interesting. I remember my own children. The first thing they really loved was surprise. Peek-a-boo, hide and seek, stuff like that. That's suspense: is it going to turn out this way or that way? How is it going to happen? What's going to happen next? That's the surprise. In the simplest of clowning actions, when Gumby falls into a toaster, when you hear it go click, click, click. . .you don't know what he's going to look like when he pops out.

"The key to life and joy is surprise. The game is to keep a certain part of your life a secret."[3]

FOOTNOTE SOURCES

[1]Sean Elder, "Gumby Transcendent," *San Francisco Examiner,* July 12, 1987.
[2]Jack Friedman, "Gumby's On a Roll and There's an Art (Clokey) behind It," *People Weekly,* February 4, 1985.
[3]Louis Kaplan and Scott Michaelson with Art Clokey, *Gumby: The Authorized Biography of the World's Favorite Clayboy,* Harmony Books, 1986.
[4]Michael Frierson, "Gumby: Riding the Clay Rollercoaster with Art Clokey," *Funnyworld,* spring, 1983.
[5]Ronald Smith, "Vintage KidVid," *Video,* September, 1984.
[6]Barry Walters, "Let's Twist Again: Gumby Bounces Back," *Village Voice,* March 17, 1987.

FOR MORE INFORMATION SEE:

Carlyle Wood, *TV Personalities Biographical Sketch Book,* TV Personalities, 1957.
Les Brown, *Les Brown's Encyclopedia of Television,* New York Zoetrope, 1982.
Stuart Fisher, *Kids TV: The First Twenty-Five Years,* Facts on File, 1983.
Us, June 27, 1988.

COLE, Michael 1947-

PERSONAL: Born June 14, 1947, in Reading, England; son of Percy (a shop manager) and Alice (a homemaker; maiden name, Benham) Cole; married Susan Larner (a sculptor), March 1, 1972; children: Selby Larner (daughter), Rowen Larner (son). *Education:* Attended Berkshire College of Art, 1963-66. *Politics:* Socialist/Democrat. *Religion:* Atheist. *Home and office:* Summerdale, 8 Greenway Lane, Bath BA2 4LJ, England. *Agent:* Mic Cheetham, c/o Anthony Sheil, 43 Doughty St., London WC1N 2LF, England.

MICHAEL COLE

CAREER: Illustrator. *Member:* Society of Industrial Artists and Designers. *Awards, honors:* Two illustrations from *A Christmas Carol* received Best of British Illustration '86 by Association of Illustrators, London Book Exhibition, 1986.

ILLUSTRATOR

Phyllis Arkle, *Magic in the Air,* Viking Penguin, 1980.
Ray Hammond, *The Bytes,* Century Hutchinson, 1983.
Charles Dickens, *A Christmas Carol,* Barron, 1985.

WORK IN PROGRESS: Advertising projects.

SIDELIGHTS: "I cannot remember a time when I did not want or need to draw, and there was no doubt my early childhood fantasies and imaginings were stimulated by comic picture books. Those picture stories would take me off on great adventures in the American West, the England of Robin Hood, the emperors of Ancient Rome or Greece, but most important—into the past! I grew up also in the heyday of film and television, John Ford's westerns, the Hollywood epic, the fantastic animation of Walt Disney and especially two wonderful films by David Lean—Dicken's 'Oliver Twist' and 'Great Expectations.' At this time a superlative comic magazine for children was introduced in England—the *Eagle.* Founded on a very high quality of stories and artwork which avoided cartooning, the *Eagle* proved that illustration could tell stories in a 'strip' format without being vulgar. It went on to be a showcase for some of Britain's and the world's finest 'strip' art by artists such as Frank Hampson, Frank Bellamy, Ron Embleton and many others.

(Detail of the first of three spirits from *A Christmas Carol* by Charles Dickens. Illustrated by Michael Cole.)

"I drew my own wild west stories, Arthurian Legends etc., all through my school and college years only to stop when I became a full-time illustrator in advertising. But the ideas have always continued to germinate, culminating (logically enough with hindsight) in the works of Charles Dickens.

"I read *A Christmas Carol* at school and I've read it dozens of times since and it remains as vivid now as it did then, that first time. Dickens had good relationships with all of his illustrators and there is no doubt that his writing suits illustration and film. Maybe because he was a journalist first and foremost, but I certainly found it possible to illustrate almost every word whilst remaining loyal to his text, and with the use of modern colour printing give a new look to a book that is now over 140 years old. Although not intended as a children's book any more than Dickens himself intended it to be, the visual qualities have attracted younger people to it and perhaps to his other great works. I hope so."

HOBBIES AND OTHER INTERESTS: Acting, wine, cookery.

COLLINGTON, Peter 1948-

PERSONAL: Born April 2, 1948, in Northcotes, England; son of Nick Edward (a draftsman) and Barbara (a homemaker;

maiden name, Pope) Collington; married Bonnie Winfield, February 17, 1979; children: Sasha. *Education:* Attended Bournemouth College of Art, 1964- 67. *Politics:* "Middle of the cul-de-sac." *Religion:* "Born again agnostic." *Agent:* Gina Pollinger, 4 Garrick St., London WC2E 9BH, England.

CAREER: Writer and illustrator, 1984—. Worked as an elevator operator, child minder, and cleaner while writing and drawing, 1967-84. *Awards, honors:* Mother Goose Award runner-up from the British Book Club Books for Children, 1987, for *Little Pickle;* Smarties Prize, 1988, for *The Angel and the Soldier Boy.*

WRITINGS:

SELF-ILLUSTRATED JUNVENILES

Little Pickle, Dutton, 1986.
The Angel and the Soldier Boy, Knopf, 1987.
My Darling Kitten, Knopf, 1988.

WORK IN PROGRESS: On Christmas Eve.

SIDELIGHTS: "When my daughter was born in 1981, I spent a lot of time taking care of her. I would draw little pictures for her of mum and dad, granny and grandpa, and anyone else she was interested in. When Sasha was nearly two she loved to push about her own stroller. One day I did a drawing of a little girl pushing along her sleeping mummy. My daughter was delighted. This was how I got the idea for *Little Pickle*. It took me about nine months to do the illustrations. Every day I would bring to Sasha the latest installment of the book and hold her up to view it. She would have a look and then we would have to act it out. She would be Little Pickle (not too far from the truth), and I would be the sea captain and rescue her from a makeshift boat of cardboard.

"The idea of the rescue at sea has parallels within my own family. My grandfather was a sea captain who took part in the evacuation of Russian refuges from Odessa in 1919. My grandmother was a passenger aboard my grandfather's ship. She had been a private secretary to the commander of the navy base in Odessa and was escaping the Bolsheviks. They met, fell in love, and married. I feel that my grandmother was rescued from impending disaster in the same way as Little Pickle is in my book."

FOR MORE INFORMATION SEE:

New York Times, December 3, 1987.
New York Times Book Review, May 17, 1987.

COONEY, Barbara 1917-

PERSONAL: Born August 6, 1917, in Brooklyn, N.Y.; daughter of Russell Schenck (a stockbroker) and Mae Evelyn (an artist; maiden name, Bossert) Cooney; married Guy Murchie (a war correspondent and author), December, 1944 (divorced, March, 1947); married Charles Talbot Porter (a physician), July 16, 1949; children: (first marriage) Gretel Goldsmith, Barnaby; (second marriage) Charles Talbot, Jr., Phoebe. *Education:* Smith College, B.A., 1938; also attended Art Students League, 1940. *Politics:* Independent. *Home and office:* Pepperell, Mass. 01463.

BARBARA COONEY

CAREER: Free-lance author and illustrator, 1938—. *Military service:* Women's Army Corps, World War II, 1942-43; became second lieutenant.

AWARDS, HONORS: New York Herald Tribune's Children's Spring Book Festival Honor Book, 1943, for *Green Wagons,* and 1952, for *Too Many Pets;* Caldecott Medal from the American Library Association, 1959, for *Chanticleer and the Fox,* and 1980, for *Ox-Cart Man;* Chandler Book Talk Reward of Merit, 1964; *Christmas Folk,* and *The Owl and the Pussy-Cat* were both selected one of Child Study Association of America's Children's Books of the Year, 1969, *Hermes, Lord of Robbers* and *Book of Princesses,* both 1971, *Down to the Beach,* 1973, *Squawk to the Moon, Little Goose,* 1974, *Lexington and Concord, 1775,* 1975, and *The Story of Holly and Ivy, The Little Fir Tree, Christmas in the Barn,* and *Emma,* all 1986.

Squawk to the Moon, Little Goose was included on *School Library Journal*'s Book List, 1974; *Squawk to the Moon, Little Goose* was selected one of *New York Times* Outstanding Books of the Year, 1974, *When the Sky Is Like Lace,* 1975, and *Ox-Cart Man,* 1979; Silver Medallion from the University of Southern Mississippi, 1975, for Outstanding Contributions in the Field of Children's Books; Medal from Smith College, 1976, for body of work; *Ox-Cart Man* was selected one of *New York Times* Best Illustrated Books of the Year, 1979; *Tortillitas para Mama and Other Nursery Rhymes* was selected a Notable Children's Trade Book in the Field of Social Studies by the National Council for Social Studies and the Children's Book Council, 1982, and *The Story of Holly and Ivy,* 1986; American Book Award for Hardcover Picture Book from the Association of American Publishers, 1983, for *Miss Rumphius; Spirit Child* was chosen as a Notable Children's Book by the Association for Library Service to Children of the American Library Association, 1984; Keene State College Children's Literature Festival Award, 1989.

WRITINGS:

SELF-ILLUSTRATED

The King of Wreck Island, Farrar & Rinehart, 1941.
The Kellyhorns, Farrar & Rinehart, 1942.
Captain Pottle's House, Farrar, 1943.
(Adapter) Geoffrey Chaucer, *Chanticleer and the Fox* (ALA Notable Book), Crowell, 1958.
The Little Juggler: Adapted from an Old French Legend (*Horn Book* honor list; Junior Literary Guild selection), Hastings House, 1961, new edition, 1982.
Twenty-Five Years A-Graying: The Portrait of a College Graduate, a Pictorial Study of the Class of 1938 at Smith College, Northampton, Massachusetts, Based on Statistics Gathered in 1963 for the Occasion of Its 25th Reunion, Little, Brown, 1963.
(Adapter) *The Courtship, Merry Marriage, and Feast of Cock Robin and Jenny Wren: To Which Is Added the Doleful Death of Cock Robin* (*Horn Book* honor list), Scribner, 1965.
(Adapter) Jacob Grimm and Wilhelm Grimm, *Snow White and Rose Red,* Delacorte, 1966.
Christmas, Crowell, 1967.
(Editor) *A Little Prayer,* Hastings House, 1967.
A Garland of Games and Other Diversions: An Alphabet Book, Holt, 1969.
Miss Rumphius, Viking, 1982.
(Reteller) J. Grimm, *Little Brother and Little Sister,* Doubleday, 1982.
Island Boy (*Horn Book* honor list), Viking, 1988.

ILLUSTRATOR

Carl Malmberg, *Ake and His World,* Farrar & Rinehart, 1940.
Frances M. Frost, *Uncle Snowball,* Farrar & Rinehart, 1940.
Oskar Seidlin and Senta Rypins, *Green Wagons,* Houghton, 1943.
Anne Molloy, *Shooting Star Farm,* Houghton, 1946.
Phyllis Crawford, *The Blot: Little City Cat,* Holt, 1946.
Nancy Hartwell, *Shoestring Theater,* Holt, 1947.
L. L. Bein, *Just Plain Maggie,* Harcourt, 1948.
Lee Kingman, *The Rocky Summer,* Houghton, 1948.
Ruth C. Seeger, *American Folk Songs for Children in Home, School and Nursery School: A Book for Children, Parents and Teachers* (ALA Notable Book), Doubleday, 1948.
Child Study Association of America, *Read Me Another Story,* Crowell, 1949.
Rutherford Montgomery, *Kildee House,* Doubleday, 1949.
L. Kingman, *The Best Christmas,* Doubleday, 1949, reissued, Peter Smith, 1985.
Phyllis Krasilovsky, *The Man Who Didn't Wash His Dishes,* Doubleday, 1950.
R. C. Seeger, *Animal Folk Songs for Children: Traditional American Songs,* Doubleday, 1950.
Nellie M. Leonard, *Graymouse Family,* Crowell, 1950.
Child Study Association of America, *Read Me More Stories,* Crowell, 1951.
R. Montgomery, *Hill Ranch,* Doubleday, 1951.
Elisabeth C. Lansing, *The Pony That Ran Away,* Crowell, 1951.
L. Kingman, *Quarry Adventure,* Doubleday, 1951 (published in England as *Lauri's Surprising Summer,* Constable, 1957.
E. C. Lansing, *The Pony That Kept a Secret,* Crowell, 1952.
Mary M. Aldrich, *Too Many Pets,* Macmillan, 1952.
M. W. Brown, *Where Have You Been?,* Crowell, 1952, reissued, Scholastic Book Services, 1966.
Barbara Reynolds, *Pepper,* Scribner, 1952.
Miriam E. Mason, *Yours with Love, Kate,* Houghton, 1952. li
Margaret W. Brown, *Christmas in the Barn,* Crowell, 1952.

At once the fox jumped up, grabbed Chanticleer by the throat. . . . (From *Chanticleer and the Fox*, adapted from the *Canterbury Tales*. Illustrated by Barbara Cooney.)

(From *Peacock Pie* by Walter de la Mare. Illustrated by Barbara Cooney.)

Catherine Marshall, *Let's Keep Christmas*, Whittlesey House, 1953.

R. C. Seeger, *American Folk Songs for Christmas*, Doubleday, 1953.

N. M. Leonard, *Grandfather Whiskers, M. D.: A Graymouse Story*, Crowell, 1953.

L. Kingman, *Peter's Long Walk*, Doubleday, 1953.

E. C. Lansing, *A Pony Worth His Salt*, Crowell, 1953.

Jane Quigg, *Fun for Freddie*, Oxford University Press, 1953.

Margaret Sidney, *The Five Little Peppers*, Doubleday, 1954.

M. W. Brown, *The Little Fir Tree*, Crowell, 1954, reissued, 1985.

Margaret G. Otto, *Pumpkin, Ginger, and Spice*, Holt, 1954.

Helen Kay (pseudonym of Helen C. Goldfrank), *Snow Birthday*, Farrar, Straus, 1955.

Louisa May Alcott, *Little Women; or, Meg, Jo, Beth, and Amy*, Crowell, 1955.

Louise A. Kent, *The Brookline Trunk*, Houghton, 1955.

Catherine S. McEwen, *Away We Go! One-Hundred Poems for the Very Young*, Crowell, 1956.

Catherine Marshall, *Friends with God: Stories and Prayers of the Marshall Family*, Whittlesey House, 1956.

H. Kay, *City Springtime*, Hastings House, 1957.

Neil Anderson (pseudonym of Jerrold Beim), *Freckle Face*, Crowell, 1957.

Henrietta Buckmaster, *Lucy and Loki*, Scribner, 1958.

Harry Behn, *Timmy's Search*, Seabury, 1958.

M. G. Otto, *Little Brown Horse*, Knopf, 1959.

Elizabeth G. Speare, *Seasonal Verses Gathered by Elizabeth George Speare from the Connecticut Almanack for the Year of the Christian Era 1773*, American Library Association, 1959.

Le Hibou et la Poussiquette (French adaptation of *The Owl and the Pussycat* by Edward Lear; *Horn Book* honor list), translated by Francis Steegmuller, Little, Brown, 1961.

Walter de la Mare, *Peacock Pie: A Book of Rhymes*, Knopf, 1961.

Noah Webster, *The American Speller: An Adaptation of Noah Webster's Blue-Backed Speller*, Crowell, 1961.

M. G. Otto, *Three Little Dachshunds*, Holt, 1963.

Sarah O. Jewett, *A White Heron: A Story of Maine*, Crowell, 1963.

Virginia Haviland, *Favorite Fairy Tales Told in Spain*, Little, Brown, 1963.

Papillot, Clignot, et Dodo (French adaptation of *Wynken, Blynken, and Nod* by Eugene Field), translated by F. Steegmuller and Norbert Guterman, Farrar, Straus, 1964.

Hugh Latham, translator, *Mother Goose in French*, Crowell, 1964.

A. Molloy, *Shaun and the Boat: An Irish Story* (Junior Literary Guild selection), Hastings House, 1965.

Jane Goodsell, *Katie's Magic Glasses*, Houghton, 1965.

Samuel Morse, *All in a Suitcase*, Little, Brown, 1966.

Aldous Huxley, *Crowns of Pearblossom*, Random House, 1967.

Alastair Reid and Anthony Kerrigan, *Mother Goose in Spanish*, Crowell, 1968.

Edward Lear, *The Owl and the Pussy-Cat*, Little, Brown, 1969.

Natalia M. Belting, *Christmas Folk*, Holt, 1969.

E. Field, *Wynken, Blynken and Nod*, Hastings House, 1970.

William Wise, *The Lazy Young Duke of Dundee*, Rand McNally, 1970.

Homer, *Dionysus and the Pirates: Homeric Hymn Number 7* (*Horn Book* honor list), translated and adapted by Penelope Proddow, Doubleday, 1970.

Felix Salten (pseudonym of Siegmund Salzman), *Bambi: A Life in the Woods*, Simon & Schuster, 1970.

Book of Princesses, Scholastic Book Services, 1971.

Homer, *Hermes, Lord of Robbers: Homeric Hymn Number Four*, translated and adapted by P. Proddow, Doubleday, 1971.

Homer, *Demeter and Persephone: Homeric Hymn Number Two*, translated and adapted by P. Proddow, Doubleday, 1972.

John Becker, *Seven Little Rabbits*, Walker, 1972.

May Garelick, *Down to the Beach*, Four Winds, 1973.

Robyn Supraner, *Would You Rather Be a Tiger?*, Houghton, 1973.

Dorothy Joan Harris, *The House Mouse*, Warne, 1973.

Edna Mitchell Preston, *Squawk to the Moon, Little Goose* (ALA Notable Book), Viking, 1974.

Zora L. Olsen, *Herman the Great*, Scholastic Book Services, 1974.

E. L. Horwitz, *When the Sky Is Like Lace*, Lippincott, 1975.

Jean P. Colby, *Lexington and Concord, 1775: What Really Happened*, Hastings House, 1975.

E. M. Preston, *The Sad Story of the Little Bluebird and the Hungry Cat*, Four Winds, 1975.

Marjorie W. Sharmat, *Burton and Dudley* (Junior Literary Guild selection), Holiday House, 1975.

M. J. Craig, *The Donkey Prince*, Doubleday, 1977.

Aileen Fisher, *Plant Magic*, Bowmar, 1977.

Ellin Greene, compiler, *Midsummer Magic: A Garland of Stories, Charms, and Recipes*, Lothrop, 1977.

Donald Hall, *Ox-Cart Man* (*Horn Book* honor list; Junior Literary Guild selection), Viking, 1979.

Delmore Schwartz, *I Am Cherry Alive, the Little Girl Sang*, Harper, 1979.

Norma Farber, *How the Hibernators Came to Bethlehem*, Walker, 1980.

Wendy Kesselman, *Emma*, Doubleday, 1980.

Margot C. Griego and others, selectors and translators, *Tortillitas para Mama and Other Nursery Rhymes: Spanish and English*, Holt, 1982.

John Bierhorst, translator, *Spirit Child: A Story of the Nativity*, Morrow, 1984.

Rumer Godden, *The Story of Holly and Ivy*, Viking, 1985.

Toni de Gerez, reteller, *Louhi, Witch of North Farm*, Viking, 1986.

Sergei Prokofiev, *Peter and the Wolf*, Viking, 1986.

Elinor L. Horwitz, *When the Sky Is Like Lace*, Lippincott, 1987.

Gloria M. Houston, *The Year of the Perfect Christmas Tree: An Appalachian Tale*, Dial, 1988.

Contributor of illustrations to periodicals.

ADAPTATIONS:

"Chanticleer and the Fox" (sound filmstrip), Weston Woods, 1959.

"Wynken, Blynken and Nod" (sound filmstrip), Weston Woods, 1967.

"Owl and the Pussycat" (sound filmstrip), 1967.

"The Man Who Didn't Wash His Dishes" (sound filmstrip), Weston Woods, 1973.

"Squawk to the Moon" (sound filmstrip), Viking, 1975.

"Miss Rumphius" (filmstrip with cassette), Live Oak Media, 1984.

"Ox-Cart Man" (filmstrip with cassette), Random House.

"How the Hibernators Came to Bethlehem" (filmstrip with cassette; ALA Notable Recording), Random House.

"American Folksongs for Children" (cassette).

WORK IN PROGRESS: Hattie and the Wild Waves, pictures and text; illustrations for *Roxaboxen* by Alice McLerran, for

The young man was delighted to find so clean and comfortable a little dwelling in this New England wilderness. He listened eagerly to the old woman's quaint talk, watched Sylvia's pale face and shining gray eyes with ever growing enthusiasm, and insisted that this was the best supper he had eaten for a month. Afterward the new-made friends sat down in the doorway together watching the moon come up.

(From *A White Heron: A Story of Maine* by Sarah Orne Jewett. Illustrated by Barbara Cooney.)

Lothrop, and *Letting Swift River Go* by Jane Yolen, for Little, Brown.

SIDELIGHTS: "I've been drawing pictures for as long as I can remember. It's in the blood. My great- grandfather carved and painted cigar store Indians. He also did oil paintings on canvas. Well done, but not wonderful, in all honesty. He was a commercial artist, painted all sorts of things, from landscapes to Cleopatra's barge. My mother was an amateur painter, but she really knew how to lay on the paint. Basically she was an impressionist. She gave me all the materials I could wish for and then left me alone, didn't smother me with instruction. Not that I ever took instruction very easily. My favorite days were when I had a cold and could stay home from school and draw all day long."[1]

". . .I was no more talented, however, than any other child. I started out ruining the wallpaper with crayons, like everybody else, and making eggs with arms and legs. Most children start this way, and most children have the souls of artists. Some of those children stubbornly keep on being children even when thay have grown up. Some of these stubborn children get to be

artists. . . .I became an artist because I had access to materials and pictures, a minimum of instruction, and a stubborn nature."[2]

Although Cooney was born in Brooklyn, N.Y., her grandmothers were both from Brooklyn and Maine, and she has spent virtually every summer of her life in Maine, mostly in Waldboro, where her grandmother had a home. "My father was a stockbroker and we lived for the most part in suburbia, which I didn't like as much as Maine. I attended boarding school, and although I was always considered the 'class artist,' I was truly terrible. We had very little in the way of art education. Perhaps because I wasn't exposed to good formal training, I think I didn't have proper respect for what that could be. I never seriously considered going to art school, for example. Now I wish I had gone. I wanted nothing but a liberal arts education, and so went to Smith College. That is a decision I have since regretted. I wish I had gone to the Rhode Island School of Design, which at the time was the best school of its kind. I have felt way behind technically, and what I've learned I have had to teach myself. To this day, I don't consider myself a very skillful artist.

"At Smith, I took mostly art history courses. In those days, the studio art department was not big, but it was adequate. I took what courses were offered, but there wasn't a lot to choose from. As graduation neared, I realized I had to decide what to do with myself in the 'real world.' Book illustration, I thought, might be a way to use what little talent I judged I had. I went to the Art Students League in Manhattan to study etching and lithography, not so much because I wanted to work in those mediums, but because I thought they would help my black-and-white drawing skills. After not too long I put together a portfolio, trudged it around to art directors and landed some work.

"I had the opportunity to do some traveling in Europe before World War II broke out and was very struck, particularly by what I saw going on in Germany. Already you saw swastikas in the streets, people giving the Nazi salute and shouting 'Heil Hitler!' and signs saying, 'Jews Forbidden.' It was horrifying, and hard to make sense of it all. Of course then we had no knowledge of Nazi atrocities. When the war broke out, I felt I wanted to do something to contribute, and so joined the Women's Army Corps [WACS]. I had wanted to join the Navy and actually spoke with a high-ranking officer who said, 'This will never be a women's Navy.' So it was the WACS or nothing. It was not a 'women's army,' either, to be sure. The rationale for bringing women in was to liberate men from desk jobs so that they could be sent into action. I was in Officer's Candidate School, went through basic training and to this day make my bed the way I was taught to in the army. There were some strange rules. For example, when reporting to your Captain, you had to wear a girdle. My military career didn't last long. I married, became pregnant and had to leave."[1]

Cooney has juggled the responsibilities as wife of a country doctor, mother of four children, ambitious gardener, gourmet cook and dedicated artist her entire career. To date, she has illustrated over one hundred books. Her mother-in-law, Anne Newton Porter, on the occasion of Cooney's winning the Caldecott Medal for *Chanticleer and the Fox* said, "[She lives with her family] in a large, rambling, early nineteenth-century

Barnaby looked at the ground. . .saying nothing for fear that words would bring his tears. (From *The Little Juggler,* adapted from an Old French legend. Illustrated by Barbara Cooney.)

house. . , .One could lose oneself in it. . . .But does it have a studio to which she may retire? No indeed. She works in the room where the family most loves to gather, except perhaps for the big brown kitchen. Her long work-table faces the fireplace. Her drawing boards and brushes and half-finished sketches are always about, and seem, miraculously, to be left undisturbed. There is no separation of her creative life from her everyday domestic activity. That is perhaps because she lives as creatively as she works. The children who run and dance across her pages run and dance across her life.

"Barbara is very serious about her work. A 'deadline' is a sacred thing, even if she has to wait until everyone has gone to bed to get on with her pictures. If she likes a book, she lives in it while she is illustrating it. When she did *Little Women* she even wore a bun. Though none of her family felt it was really her style, it may have helped her to understand Miss Alcott's immortal sisters. She went to Concord and sketched the houses where the Marches and 'Aunt March' and Laurie may have lived. She drew the kind of furniture they must have used and walked on the streets where Jo may have strolled with Laurie.

(From *The Owl and the Pussy-Cat* by Edward Lear. Illustrated by Barbara Cooney.)

The snowflakes began to cover the key as Peter ran off. (From *The Story of Holly and Ivy* by Rumer Godden. Illustrated by Barbara Cooney.)

"When she did *Grandfather Whiskers, M.D.*, a cage of mice sat near her work-table to the delight of her children. *Chanticleer* meant a pen of chickens loaned by a neighbor. But more than that, it meant the Middle Ages and with scrupulous and loving care she studied the period of Chaucer until it came alive for her. Indeed, I think there is something a bit medieval in much of her work, a perception of the beauty of humble flowers....Durer expressed the same feeling in the delicate foregrounds of many of his etchings and in his water colors of common weeds and grasses. I have noticed that when Barbara takes a walk in the woods she seldom returns without great armfuls of ferns or branches. She will show you, perhaps, some strange mosses or gray-green lichens or the pale untimely bloom of witch hazel."[3]

In her 1959 Caldecott Award Acceptance, Cooney said, "The question most generally asked me...was how did I happen to do [*Chanticleer and the Fox*], what inspired me. That question is a little embarrassing because the answer is so simple. I just happened to want to draw chickens.

"To answer more exactly....For years I have admired the work of Chinese and Japanese artists, in particular, their landscapes and their birds. But I think that the actual day that *Chanticleer* was conceived was...one autumn day. I had been out in the woods picking witch hazel and was on my way to cook supper. As I came out of the woods I passed a little barn that I had often passed before. But never at that time of day nor when the barn door was wide open. At that hour the sun was getting low and it shone right into the doorway. The inside of the barn was like a golden stage set. At that time of year the loft was full of hay, gold hay. And pecking around the floor of the barn was a most gorgeous and impractical flock of fancy chickens—gold chickens, rust-colored chickens, black ones, white ones, speckled ones and laced ones, some with crests on their heads, some with feathered legs, others with iridescent tails, and all with vermilion-colored wattles and combs.

"I believe that children in this country need a more robust literary diet than they are getting....'a man's reach should exceed his grasp.' So should a child's. For myself, I will never talk down in—or write down to children. Much of what I put into my pictures will not be understood. How many children will know that the magpie sitting in my pollarded window in *Chanticleer and the Fox* is an evil omen? How many children will realize that every flower and grass in the book grew in Chaucer's time in England? How many children will know or care? Maybe not a single one. Still I keep piling it on. Detail after detail. Whom am I pleasing—besides myself? I don't know. Yet if I put enough in my pictures, there will be something for everyone. Not all will be understood, but some will be understood now and maybe more later. That is good enough for me."[4]

Modest as Cooney often is about her skills, she, nonetheless, is known for the technical acumen evident in her drawings and paintings. When in the early 1960s, the *Horn Book* did a series called "The Artist at Work," Cooney was invited to contribute an article on scratchboard illustration, a most painstaking technique and one she has used extensively.

"I have done many, many books in black and white, it is true; but my heart and soul are in color. You just can't beat color for emotional power, range, and subtlety. I've been working a lot with acrylics—I love their warmth and the ease with which they can be used. I'm also trying to incorporate colored pencils, so that I can do color line work. And lately, I've been experimenting with pastel, which is the purest color in the world. Pastels are pure, unadulterated pigment. Nothing refracts light more finely than pastel. The difficulty is that it is very delicate and tends not to reproduce well. But its effects are irresistible, so I must keep experimenting until I have a solution!"[1]

Cooney travels extensively when doing research for her work. "I've made several trips to Mexico, a country I find particularly fascinating. For *Spirit Child*, which deals with the introduction of Bible stories to the Aztecs, I wanted to learn all that I could about sixteenth- and seventeenth-century Mexico. To help me find the right 'tone' and palette for the illustrations, I studied paintings in the art and anthropological museums of Mexico City. I also went to visit Indian villages. For *Tortillitas para Mama*, I knocked around a great deal of Mexico in a little yellow rented Volkswagen. On that trip, I was especially interested in studying the land and light. The colors in Mexico are astonishingly, deliciously brilliant.

"The paintings for *Tortillitas para Mama* are acrylic on fabric (linen and cotton weave) over masonite. This book is a bit smaller format than I usually do. It seemed right, because the text is comprised of rather short poems. I didn't want to overwhelm the words with pictures. And because most of the poems are of equal (or nearly equal) length, I thought it best to do a regular-shaped, nearly square book.

"Usually I ask my editors for as big a format as they can give me. I like to spread out. Books about the sea, or travel, are generally better suited to a horizontal shape. Christmas books (of which I've done many) tend to be more attractive in a vertical shape. Christmas trees are vertical, for example, with lots of interest near the top. Too, Christmas books often feature hovering angels so you want the eye to be able to roam upwards."[1]

She has illustrated a number of folk tales and nursery rhymes from around the world, including editions of *Mother Goose* in French and Spanish. "These materials are extraordinarily rich for an illustrator, allowing him or her the opportunity to work with period detail, and to find new ways to render familiar images, both great challenges.

"A marvellous consequence of my work with folk tales was an invitation to go to Finland. Helsinki has the largest folklore collection in the world. In the several weeks that I spent there, I was able to meet many Finnish artists, writers, folklorists, scholars and librarians. I was so very impressed with Finland. It is very rich culturally and the people are so hospitable."[1]

"I often go to great lengths to get authentic backgrounds for my illustrations. I climbed Mount Olympus to see how things up there looked to Zeus. I went down into the cave where Hermes was born. I slept in Sleeping Beauty's castle. But to illustrate *Ox-Cart Man,* all I had to do was step outside my back door. (It was a lot cheaper, too.)

"*Ox-Cart Man* is the story of a New Hampshire farmer who lived in the last century. The story begins in October, when Ox-Cart Man hitches up his ox, loads up his cart with all the things he and his family have been making and growing all year long, and makes the long trip from the inland hills to Portsmouth Market on the coast. There he sells everything, including the ox, buys a few things, and starts the long trek home. Then the cycle of working and growing begins again.

"Even though the story took place, as I said, just outside my back door, I still had to do some preliminary research. First of all, I had to establish *exactly* when the story could have happened. 'When' is very important to an illustrator because the sets (the landscape and architecture) must be accurate; so must the costumes, the props, the hairdos, everything.

"To begin, I tackled the road that the Ox-Cart Man would have followed. This, I found out, would have been one of the early New Hampshire turnpikes, one which opened to traffic in 1803. This was a toll road. The Ox-Cart Man would have paid one and a half cents a mile for his two-wheeled cart. He paid by the axle, as we still do on the New Hampshire turnpikes. Going to the big markets along the seaboard were great events for New England farmers. Along the road were plenty of wayside inns where they could get hay for their horses and oxen and food for themselves. There were toddy irons in the fire and toddies in the tummy and a good night's sleep for everyone at the end of the day. Every year thousands of carts and wagons passed this way until the railroads arrived in 1847 and commerce took to the rails.

"Next, I investigated Portsmouth and Portsmouth Market to ascertain what buildings would have been there between 1803 and 1847. The main difficulty here was that Portsmouth buildings, including the Market, had a bad habit of periodically burning down. It was a puzzle trying to figure out what was where and when.

"What finally determined the date was the Ox-Cart Man's beard. I wanted him to have a lovely red beard like Leon's. The story, therefore, had to happen between 1803 and 1847, when the turnpikes were busy, at a time when the brick market building in Portsmouth was standing, and when beards were in fashion. Thus, the date of 1832 was settled upon. After that it was downhill sledding all the way.

"Even though we have hard-topped roads and telephone poles and the trappings of the twentieth century, when you get into country up our way, it still looks pretty much like the New England that the Ox-Cart Man knew. In October the leaves are still the colors of fire, and there is a smoky-blue haze over the hills and mountains. After the leaves have fallen, November comes, all tan and gray. The land and the sea lie still, a little sad, waiting for winter. People bank their houses with fir boughs and brace themselves for the cold that is coming. The snow falls. December and January pass, and February. In

March the sap begins to run again. People tap their maple trees and put out buckets to catch the sap. Then comes April. Spring arrives slowly in our part of the country. It is a thin spring. The grass takes its time greening up, but the bluets come up in the fields and pastures. The brooks are overflowing from the melted snow and are full of little trout. On a lucky morning people have trout for breakfast along with their coffee and toast. At last comes the lovely month of May. The orchards are in bloom. Every seed you plant, you think, has a good chance of coming up. And, as all of you know, May is much the best month for being in love.

"Although *Ox-Cart Man* ends with the beautiful month of May, the month of hope, it starts with October, another beautiful month, the month of fulfillment."[2]

Twenty-one years after her first Caldecott, Cooney was awarded her second Medal for *Ox-Cart Man*. "A generation has passed since I stood up to accept my first Caldecott Medal. During those twenty-one years I went on living in the same beautiful, drafty old house. The wind still whistled through the light switches. Occasionally, the roof still leaked. Under that roof I went on raising my four children and an uncountable number of cats and dogs. A golden palomino horse was living in the barn, and a Connemara pony. I kept on planting large back-breaking vegetable gardens. I kept on fussing with flowers. Grandchildren began to appear. I kept on illustrating. And my husband kept on coming home for lunch.

"Luckily for me, during this time there has been an energetic little Frenchwoman, named Solange, to help me take care of my circus. When Solange came in the morning after I had heard the news about this year's Caldecott Award, I said, 'Solange! Guess what! I have won the Caldecott Medal again!'

"'Oh, madame,' she said, 'your cup runneth over!' And, indeed, it does.

"One more biblical quotation, please, 'In the beginning was the Word. . . .' Don't let any illustrator forget that! The other time I was given this lovely medal, the author, Geoffrey Chaucer, was unable to be there. . . .I would like to thank the poet who made the golden chain upon which I strung my beads, the author of *Ox-Cart Man*, Donald Hall."[2]

Cooney has said that she wishes now to do no more than one or two books a year. "While my children were growing up and needing things like college educations, of course I wanted to produce a lot, so as to earn well. Now I want to work more slowly, with time to experiment on new techniques.

"As I look back on the decades I've been making books for children, I feel extremely grateful. I've been able to do the books I wanted in the way I wanted. And I have enjoyed some of the 'trappings' that accompany what we tend to think of as 'success.' But the trappings are of relatively minor importance. What counts is the mark on the page."[1]

When asked why she is an illustrator, Cooney replied: "The answer is that I love stories. Lots of artists have loved stories. The sculptors and vase-painters of ancient Greece were forever illustrating Homer. The Byzantine and Romanesque and Gothic artists spent their lives illustrating the Bible. Stories from the Ramayana were the basis for much of the great art in the Orient. Like all these artists, I love illustrating a good story.

"In the world of illustration, the picture-book field is far and away the most exciting. And I am not making picture books for children. I am making them for *people*."[2]

FOOTNOTE SOURCES

[1]Based on an interview by Marguerite Feitlowitz for *Something about the Author*.
[2]Barbara Cooney, "Caldecott Medal Acceptance," *Horn Book*, August, 1980.
[3]Anna Newton Porter, "Barbara Cooney," *Horn Book*, August, 1959.
[4]B. Cooney, "Caldecott Award Acceptance," *Horn Book*, August, 1959.

FOR MORE INFORMATION SEE:

Bertha E. Mahony and others, compilers, *Illustrators of Children's Books: 1744-1945*, Horn Book, 1947.
B. M. Miller and others, compilers, *Illustrators of Children's Books: 1946-1956*, Horn Book, 1958.
Publishers Weekly, March 23, 1959.
American Library Association Bulletin, April, 1959.
Library Journal, April, 1959.
Horn Book, February, 1961, October, 1969, August, 1980.
Muriel Fuller, editor, *More Junior Authors*, H. W. Wilson, 1963.
Lee Kingman, editor, *Newbery and Caldecott Medal Books: 1956-1965*, Horn Book, 1965.
Diana Klemin, *The Art of Art for Children's Books*, C. N. Potter, 1966.
Jean Poindexter Colby, *Writing, Illustrating and Editing Children's Books*, Hastings House, 1967.
L. Kingman and others, compilers, *Illustrators of Children's Books 1957-1966*, Horn Book, 1968.
Elinor W. Field, *Horn Book Reflections*, Horn Book, 1969.
Bettina Hurlimann, *Picture-Book World*, World Publishing, 1969.
Lee Bennett Hopkins, *Books Are by People*, Citation Press, 1969.
Constantine Georgiou, *Children and Their Literature*, Prentice-Hall, 1969.
Martha E. Ward and Dorothy A. Marquardt, *Authors of Books for Young People*, 2nd edition, Scarecrow, 1971.
Donnarae MacCann and Olga Richard, *The Child's First Books*, H. W. Wilson, 1973.
Contemporary American Illustrators of Children's Books, Rutgers University Art Gallery, 1974.
M. E. Ward and D. A. Marquardt, *Illustrators of Books for Young People*, Scarecrow, 1975.
L. Kingman, editor, *The Illustrator's Notebook*, Horn Book, 1978.
L. Kingman and others, compilers, *Illustrators of Children's Books: 1967-1976*, Horn Book, 1978.
Jim Roginski, compiler, *Newbery and Caldecott Medalists and Honor Book Winners*, Libraries Unlimited, 1982.
L. Kingman, editor, *Newbery and Caldecott Medal Books: 1976-1985*, Horn Book, 1986.
Jeanette K. Cakouros, "Children's Author Talks about 'New Baby,'" *Maine Sunday Telegram*, November 27, 1988 (p. 26A).

COLLECTIONS

Kerlan Collection at the University of Minnesota.
De Grummond Collection at the University of Southern Mississippi. Boston Public Library, Mass.
Free Library of Philadelphia, Penn.
Gary Public Library, Ind.
Milwaukee Public Library, Wis.

JUDY CUTCHINS

CUTCHINS, Judy 1947-

PERSONAL: Born December 6, 1947, in New Orleans, La.; daughter of Amos Price (an engineer) and Mary (Young) Cutchins; married Lamar Furr (a government administrative director), November 27, 1985. *Education:* Georgia State University, B.A., 1969, M.Ed., 1973; Emory University, specialist in elementary education, 1978. *Home:* Decatur, Ga. *Office:* c/o Morrow Junior Books, 105 Madison Ave., New York, N.Y. 10016.

CAREER: De Kalb County School System, De Kalb County, Ga., elementary school teacher, 1970-74; Fernbank Science Center, Atlanta, Ga., life sciences instructor, 1975—. Georgia Conservancy, founder of environmental day camp, 1974-75, member of Board of Trustees, 1978-80, chairperson of Membership Education Committee, 1981-82; Atlanta Environmental Coalition to create the Atlanta Outdoor Activities Center, advisory board member, 1977; Partners of the Americas, Recife, Brazil, guest science instructor, 1979; Earthwatch Program, researcher and photographer, 1981; presents public programs on natural science topics; environmental consultant to Heery & Heery Architects. *Member:* Society of Children's Book Writers, Council of Authors and Journalists in Georgia, Dixie Council of the Arts.

AWARDS, HONORS: Outstanding Science Trade Book Award for Children from the National Science Teachers Association, 1984, for *Are Those Animals Real?,* 1985, for *Andy Bear,* and 1986, for *The Crocodile and the Crane; Andy Bear* was chosen one of Child Study Association of America's Children's Books of the Year, 1986, and *The Crocodile and the Crane,* 1987; Reading Magic Award, and one of *Parenting Magazine*'s Best Books, both 1989, both for *Scaly Babies;* Reader's Choice Award from Silver Burdett and Ginn, and one of *Booklist*'s Children's Editors' Choices, both 1989, both for *Andy Bear.*

WRITINGS:

ALL WITH GINNY JOHNSTON; ALL NONFICTION FOR CHILDREN

Are Those Animals Real? How Museums Prepare Wildlife Exhibits, Morrow, 1984.
Andy Bear: A Polar Bear Grows Up at the Zoo (illustrated with photographs by Constance Noble), Morrow, 1985.
The Crocodile and the Crane: Surviving in a Crowded World, Morrow, 1986.
Scaly Babies: Reptiles Growing Up, Morrow, 1988.
Scoots, the Bog Turtle (illustrated by Frances Smith), Atheneum, 1989.
Windows on Wildlife: Realistic Zoo and Aquarium Exhibits, Morrow, 1990.

Author of bi-monthly environmental newsletter for young readers, for Georgia Conservancy, 1970-78; author of natural science newsletter for elementary schools.

SIDELIGHTS: "Fernbank Science Center's exhibit hall, where my co-author Ginny Johnston and I work as elementary biology instructors, is filled with dioramas featuring very realistic taxidermy. When we teach in the museum's classrooms we often use such visual aids as mounted specimens and lifelike models. We quickly learned that although children love studying about animals and their habitats, they are equally intrigued by the specimens and models. In 1981 we began using vacation time and evenings to compile a simplified explanation, with photos, of ways museums around the country create their wildlife exhibits. Our work resulted in our first children's book, *Are Those Animals Real?* We were pleased with its success in museum book stores and libraries around the United States, and particularly pleased that it was selected by the National Science Teachers Association (NSTA) as an Outstanding Science Book for Children in 1984.

"That got us started. Since that time our research has led us in the direction of zoo and wildlife conservation work. We had the opportunity to work with Constance Nobel, a zookeeper at Zoo Atlanta who almost single-handedly raised a baby polar bear. Her photographs were unprecedented and the story was beautiful. That became our second book; it too was chosen by the NSTA as an Outstanding Children's Science Book in its first year of publication. The story is filled with warmth and information about polar bears. In the kind of writing we do, we believe strongly that nonfiction does not have to be encyclopedic and dull. It can have the entertainment and imagination-stirring value of fiction with the added bonus of education.

"We will probably always be educators first and writers second. We do not just look for subjects for the sake of writing another book. We want to share with young readers some of the fascinating things we discover in the worlds of wildlife, museums, and zoos. We work hard to present current and new information that children will not find in other books. For example, our book *Scaly Babies,* is the only book we know of that details in words and photographs the lives of hatchling and newborn reptiles. It is filled with reptile facts, and we believe it is very accurate, thanks to the expertise of the herpetology staff at Zoo Atlanta and others. Accuracy is perhaps our primary objective, and we have a number of expert readers in all that we do.

"Our first color-illustrated book (all the others are photographed) is called *Scoots, the Bog Turtle;* its pictures were done by Frances Smith in Atlanta. It is a nonfiction book about life in a North Carolina bog. The reader follows a tiny turtle through a bog summer. We worked very closely with Frances to ensure accuracy in both the text and the illustrations. The subject of *Windows on Wildlife* is new natural habitat exhibits in zoos and aquariums across the country. We selected six outstanding examples of exhibits that represent the exciting new trend in zoos toward caring for captive wildlife in zoo habitats that duplicate the wild as closely as possible. The gorilla exhibit at Zoo Atlanta is included.

"Researching a book is always a learning process for us. We read books, articles, everything we can get our hands on. We meet interesting and dedicated people who work with wildlife and other areas of natural science. We write draft after draft trying to reach the most enjoyable and informative product for the eight- to twelve-year-old reader. We edit each other's work, bounce ideas back and forth, and as a team we are very complementary. We have the same goals for our books, similar approaches to teaching, and the same hard work ethic."

DAY, A(rthur) Grove 1904-

PERSONAL: Born April 29, 1904, in Philadelphia, Pa.; son of Arthur Sinclair (a salesman) and Clara Tomlinson (a housewife; maiden name, Hogeland) Day; married Virginia T. Molina (a college instructor), July 2, 1928. *Education:* Stanford University, A.B., 1926, M.A., 1942. Ph.D., 1944. *Religion:* Protestant. *Home:* 1434 Punahou St., Apt. 1223, Honolulu, Hawaii 96822. *Agent:* John Hawkins and Associates, 71 West 23rd St., New York, N.Y. 10010. *Office:* c/o University of Hawaii Press, 2840 Kolowalu St., Honolulu, Hawaii 96822.

CAREER: Columbia University, New York, N.Y., research assistant, Institute of Educational Research, 1926-27; free-lance writer, 1927-30; Stanford University, Stanford, Calif., research assistant, 1932-36, assistant director of engineering, science, and management war training, 1943-44; University of Hawaii, Honolulu, assistant professor, 1944-46, associate professor, 1946-50, chairman of department, 1948-53, professor, 1950-61, senior professor of English, 1961-69, professor emeritus, 1969——. Fulbright senior research fellow in Australia, 1955; Smith-Mundt Visiting Professor of American Studies, University of Barcelona, 1957-58; Fulbright visiting professor of American studies, University of Madrid, 1961-62. *Member:* Authors Guild, Modern Language Association of America, Phi Beta Kappa, Phi Kappa Phi, Adventurer's Club of Honolulu. *Awards, honors:* Hawaii State Award for Literature, 1979.

WRITINGS:

Tommy Dane of Sonora, Century, 1927.
(With Fred J. Buenzle) *Bluejacket,* Norton, 1939, new edition, 1986.
Coronado's Quest: The Discovery of the Southwestern States, University of California Press, 1940, new edition, 1964.
(With Ralph S. Kuykendall) *Hawaii: A History,* Prentice-Hall, 1948, revised edition, 1961.
The Sky Clears: Poetry of the American Indians, Macmillan, 1951, new edition, 1964.
Hawaii and Its People, Duell, Sloan & Pearce, 1955, third edition, 1968.
(With James A. Michener) *Rascals in Paradise,* Random House, 1957.
Hawaii, Fiftieth Star, Duell, Sloan & Pearce, 1960, 2nd edition, Meredith, 1969.
The Story of Australia, Random House, 1960.
James A. Michener, Twayne, 1964, new edition, 1977.
They Peopled the Pacific, Duell, Sloan & Pearce, 1964.

Louis Becke, Twayne, 1966.
Explorers of the Pacific, Duell, Sloan & Pearce, 1966.
Coronado and the Discovery of the Southwest, Meredith, 1967.
Pirates of the Pacific, Meredith, 1968.
Adventurers of the Pacific, foreword by James A. Michener, Meredith, 1969.
Jack London in the South Seas, Four Winds Press, 1971.
Pacific Islands Literature: One Hundred Basic Books, University Press of Hawaii, 1971.
(With Edgar C. Knowlton, Jr.) *V. Blasco Ibanez,* Twayne, 1972.
What Did I Do Right? (auto-bibliography), privately printed, 1974.
Robert D. Fitzgerald, Twayne, 1974.
Kamehameha, First King of Hawaii, Hogarth Press, 1974.
Captain Cook and Hawaii, Hogarth Press, 1975.
Eleanor Dark, Twayne, 1976.
Mad about Islands: Novelists of a Vanished Pacific, Mutual, 1987.

EDITOR

(In Spanish) *Fernando Cortes: Despatches from Mexico,* American Book Co., 1935.
(With Carl Stroven) *The Spell of the Pacific: An Anthology of Its Literature,* Macmillan, 1949.
(With William F. Bauer) *The Greatest American Short Stories,* McGraw, 1953, published as *The Greatest American Short Stories: Twenty Classics of Our Heritage,* 1970.
(With C. Stroven) *A Hawaiian Reader,* introduction by James A. Michener, Appleton, 1959.
(With C. Stroven) *Best South Sea Stories,* Appleton, 1964.
Jack London, *Stories of Hawaii,* Appleton, 1965.
Mark Twain's Letters from Hawaii, Appleton, 1966.
(With C. Stroven) *True Tales of the South Seas,* Appleton, 1966.
Louis Becke, *South Sea Supercargo,* University Press of Hawaii, 1967.
(With C. Stroven) *The Spell of Hawaii,* Meredith, 1968.
(And author of introduction) *Melville's South Seas: An Anthology,* Hawthorn, 1970.
The Art of Narration: The Novella, McGraw, 1971.
(And author of introduction) Robert L. Stevenson, *Travels in Hawaii,* University Press of Hawaii, 1973.
(With Amos P. Leib) *Hawaiian Legends in English: An Annotated Bibliography,* University Press of Hawaii, 1979.
Modern Australian Prose, 1901-1975, Gale, 1980.
History Makers of Hawaii: A Biographical Dictionary, Mutual, 1984.
(With Bacil F. Kirtley) *Horror in Paradise,* Mutual, 1986.
The Lure of Tahiti, Mutual, 1986.

Contributor to *Encyclopedia of Poetry and Poetics,* 1965, and *Encyclopaedia Britannica,* 1968; also contributor of short stories and articles to national magazines. Editor-in-chief, *Pacific Science,* 1947-49.

SIDELIGHTS: "I can't remember a time when I didn't know I was going to become a writer of books; but early on I became aware of the magic of those funny letters on a page. When I was in the first grade, during recess I swapped my treasured pocketknife for a paperback by Horatio Alger (as I remember, it was *Strive and Succeed*). Next day the friend's mother made us exchange back, but by then I had read the whole book. I recall proudly getting a user card from the Philadelphia Public Library when I was six years old. The first book I took out was a children's edition of *Gulliver's Travels*. During most of my life since then, I have read an average of three or four books a week.

A. GROVE DAY

Over almost eighty years, that is a lot of books. By exploring every sort of writing, I gradually learned to find the kinds of authors really worthwhile.

"I wrote a play in the eighth grade, and when I got to high school I spent four years contributing to the semi-weekly paper. At age seventeen, I sent a sixteen-line poem to a national humorous magazine. I was paid a dollar a line, my first money from writing. 'Gee!' I thought; 'what an easy way to make a living!' But ten years were to pass before I next earned a check from my pen or typewriter.

"When I was ten years old, in 1914, my family decided to move to southern Sonora, below the Mexican border, where my uncle worked as an American doctor. My younger brother and I ran barefoot through the sandy, cactus-littered streets of a small mining village, free of school but reading everything that friends would lend us. In the early spring of 1915, we were warned that the notorious bandit and revolutionary, Pancho Villa, and his small army would be attacking the town. On a narrow-gage train to the main line north, we managed to escape only one day ahead of the capture of our homeplace by a wild band of armed fighters. Back in the United States, we went to school in the fifth grade at El Paso, Texas. But my first experience in a foreign country gave me plenty of good background material for my first book.

"As an undergraduate at Stanford University, California, I wrote for all the campus publications. One night I had a vivid dream. I was hunting deer out in the mountains of Sonora, armed with my trusty carbine. From the forest beyond, I heard what I thought was an approaching animal. As I leveled my weapon, in the sights appeared not a deer but a frightened man, a fugitive from some nameless horror.

"Pondering how such an event could happen and what would occur afterwards, I wrote a short story that was helpfully read by my writing professor. The following year I was back in New York at Columbia University. Remembering the pleasure I had found in reading back issues of *St. Nicholas,* a favorite magazine for young people founded in 1873, I dusted off the manuscript and sent it to the current editor. He accepted this yarn about an American boy's adventures in northern Mexico, paid me $50, and kindly asked for more. The upshot was that my Tommy Dane stories appeared in no fewer than twenty-one issues of *St. Nicholas* before its demise in 1935 during the Great Depression. My first book, *Tommy Dane of Sonora,* was a collection of the early magazine tales.

"Trying to please young readers, I learned a great deal that would help me when I began turning out books for adults. In error, I thought it would be easy to break into print by writing for teenagers. The knowledge of adolescents is not wide, but it is deep, and such readers cannot be fooled by technical mistakes. My audience, I knew, would complain to the editor if they sensed something haywire in a printed piece. In one story I had Tommy Dane learn to fly a Curtiss Jenny plane, and never have I had to be so certain that all the details of the fiction were in their exact places!

"About one-fifth of my fifty books were written for teen readers. Friendly editors in New York publishing houses encouraged me to deliver such volumes as *Hawaii, Fiftieth Star, The Story of Australia, They Peopled the Pacific, Explorers of the Pacific, Pirates of the Pacific: Coronado and the Discovery of the Southwest,* and *Jack London in the South Seas.* Many adults have enjoyed these books without knowing that their main audience was the teenage group.

"As a college teacher of literature and writing for most of my life, as well as a free-lance author of books and magazine articles, I have never forgotten that the first duty of a writer is to satisfy the reading needs of his chosen audiences. And it is still harder for me to write a rousing story for young people than it is to compose a learned discourse for a convention of fellow professors."

FOR MORE INFORMATION SEE:

New Statesman, June 23, 1967.
Literary Arts Hawaii, spring/summer, 1988 (p. 22ff).

de PAOLA, Thomas Anthony 1934-
(Tomie de Paola)

PERSONAL: Name pronounced Tommy de-*pow*-la; born September 15, 1934, in Meriden, Conn.; son of Joseph N. (a union official) and Florence (Downey) de Paola. *Education:* Pratt Institute, B.F.A., 1956; California College of Arts and Crafts, M.F.A., 1969; Lone Mountain College, doctoral equivalency, 1970. *Address:* c/o The Putnam & Grosset Group, 200 Madison Ave., New York, N.Y. 10016.

CAREER: Professional artist and designer, and teacher of art, 1956—; Newton College of the Sacred Heart, Newton, Mass., instructor in art, 1962-63, assistant professor of art, 1963-66; writer and illustrator of juvenile books, 1965—; San Francisco College for Women (now Lone Mountain College), San Francisco, Calif., assistant professor of art, 1967-70; Chamberlayne Junior College, Boston, Mass., instructor in art, 1972-73; Colby-Sawyer College, New London, N.H., associate professor, designer, technical director in speech and theater, 1973-76; New England College, Henniker, N.H., associate professor of art, 1976-78, artist-in-residence, 1978-79; Whitebird Books, New York, N.Y. creative director, 1987—.

Painter and muralist, with many of his works done for Catholic churches and monasteries in New England; designer of greeting cards, posters, magazine and catalog covers, record album covers, and theater sets; writer and set and costume designer for Children's Theatre Project at Colby-Sawyer College, 1973-76; member of the advisory board of the Children's Radio Theatre, Washington, D.C., until 1986; member of the National Advisory Council of the Children's Theatre Company of Minneapolis, Minn.; member of board of directors, Ballet of the Dolls Dance Company, Minneapolis, Minn.

EXHIBITIONS:—One-man: Botolph Group, Inc., Boston, Mass., 1961, 1964, 1967; Putnam Art Center, Newton College of the Sacred Heart, Newton, Mass., 1968, 1972; Botolph in Cambridge, Mass., 1971-72, 1975, 1978; Alliance Corporation, Boston, Mass., 1972; Library Arts Center, Newport, N.H., 1975, 1982, 1984; Rizzoli Gallery, New York, N.Y., 1977; Clark County Library, Las Vegas, Nev., 1979; Englewood Library, Englewood, N.J., 1980; Louisiana Arts and

Science Center, Baton Rouge, La., 1981; University of Minnesota, Minneapolis, 1981; Children's Theatre, Minneapolis, 1981; Yuma City-County Library, Yuma City, Ariz., 1981; Charles Fenton Gallery, Woodstock, Vt., 1984; Arts and Science Center, Nashua, N.H., 1985; "Tomie De Paola: A Retrospective," Arts and Science Center, Nashua, 1986; Bush Galleries, Norwich, Vt., 1987; Women's Club, Minneapolis, 1988; Dayton's-Bachman's Annual Flower Show, Minneapolis, 1989.

Group shows: South Vermont Art Center, Manchester, 1958; Grail Festival of the Arts, Brooklyn, N.Y., 1959; Botolph Group, Boston, Ma., 1962, 1964, 1969; San Francisco College for Women, Calif., 1969; Immaculate Heart College, Los Angeles, Calif., 1969; Botolph in Cambridge, Mass., 1971-74; Library Arts Center, Newport, N.H., 1975; "Children's Book Illustrators," Everson Museum, Syracuse, N.Y., 1977; "Twelfth Exhibition of Original Pictures of International Children's Picture Books, sponsored by Maruzen Ltd., and Shiko-Sha Ltd., Japan, 1977; Twelfth Illustrators' Exhibition," Children's Book Fair, Bologna, Italy, 1978; "Art and the Alphabet," Museum of Fine Arts, Houston, Tex., 1978; "Book Forms," Dayton Art Institute, Dayton, Ohio, 1978; "Fourteenth Exhibition of Original Pictures of International Children's Picture Books," sponsored by Maruzen Ltd., and Shiko-Sha Ltd., Japan, 1979.

"Children's Book Illustrators '80," Brattleboro Museum and Art Center, Brattleboro, Vt., 1980; "This Pure Creature: The Unicorn in Art," Wilson Arts Center, Harley School, Rochester, N.Y., 1980; "The Original Art," Master Eagle Gallery, New York, N.Y., 1980-1988; "December Art Exhibit," Port

THOMAS ANTHONY DE PAOLA

Washington Public Library, Port Washington, N.Y., 1981; "Sixteenth Exhibition of Original Pictures of International Children's Picture Books," sponsored by Maruzen Ltd. and Shiko-Sha Ltd., Japan, 1981; "A Decade of the Original Art of the Best Illustrated Children's Books, 1970-1980," University of Connecticut Library, Storrs, Conn., 1982; "Twenty-fourth Annual Exhibition," Society of Illustrators, New York, N.Y., 1982; "Illustrators Exhibition," Metropolitan Museum of Art, New York, N.Y., 1982; "Illustrators Exhibition," New York Public Library, New York, N.Y., 1982, 1983; "A Peaceable Kingdom: Animals in Art," Museum of Fine Art, Houston, Tex., 1982.

"Twenty-fifth Annual Exhibition," Society of Illustrators, 1983; "D Is for Dog," Dog Museum of America, New York, N.Y., 1983; "Once Upon a Time," Boulder (Colo.) Center for Visual Arts, 1983; "Illustrious: Contemporary New Hampshire Illustrators," University Art Galleries, University of New Hampshire, Durham, 1983; "Twenty-sixth Annual Exhibition," Society of Illustrators, 1984; "And Peace Attend Thee," Trustman Art Gallery, Simmons College, Boston, Mass., 1984, Bush Galleries, Norwich, Vt., Congress Square Gallery, Portland, Me., and Richmond Public Library, Richmond, Va, all 1985, and Denver Public Library, Colo., and Colorado Academy, Denver, both 1986; "Daffodil Arts Show," New London Historical Society, New London, N.H., 1985, 1986, 1988; "Twenty-seventh Annual Exhibition," Society of Illustrators, 1985; Aetna Institute Gallery, Hartford, Conn., 1986; "Once Upon a Picture," Miami Youth Museum, Fla., 1986; "New Hampshire Illustrators Exhibit," New Hampshire Historical Society, Concord, N.H., 1988. Works are included in many private collections. *Member:* Society of Children's Book Writers (member of board of directors), Authors Guild.

AWARDS, HONORS: Boston Art Directors' Club Awards for Typography and Illustration, 1968; *Poetry for Chuckles and Grins* was selected one of Child Study Association of America's Children's Books of the Year, 1968, *John Fisher's Magic Book,* 1971, *David's Window* and *Charlie Needs a Cloak,* 1974, *Strega Nona* and *Good Morning to You, Valentine,* 1975, *Strega Nona's Magic Lessons, Tattie's River Journey, Tomie DePaola's Mother Goose,* and *The Quilt Story,* all 1986, and *Teeny Tiny,* and *Tomie de Paola's Favorite Nursery Tales,* 1987; Franklin Typographers (New York) Silver Award, 1969, for poster design.

The Journey of the Kiss was included in the American Institute of Graphic Arts exhibit of Outstanding Children's Books, 1970, *Who Needs Holes?,* 1973, and *Helga's Dowry,* 1979; *Andy, That's My Name* was included on *School Library Journal's* list of Best Picture Books, 1973, and *Charlie Needs a Cloak,* 1974; Friends of American Writers Award for Children's Book Illustration, 1973, for *Authorized Autumn Charts of the Upper Red Canoe River Country; Authorized Autumn Charts of the Upper Red Canoe River Country* was included in the Children's Book Showcase of the Children's Book Council, 1973, and *Charlie Needs a Cloak,* 1975.

Brooklyn Art Books for Children Award from the Brooklyn Museum and Brooklyn Public Library, 1975, for *Charlie Needs a Cloak,* 1977, 1978, and 1979, for *Strega Nona,* and 1978, for *Simple Pictures Are Best;* Caldecott Honor Book from the American Library Association, 1976, and Nakamore Prize (Japan), 1978, both for *Strega Nona; Strega Nona* was included in the Bologna International Children's Book Fair, Bologna, Italy, 1977, and *The Quilt Story,* 1985; books included in international illustrators exhibitions in Japan, 1977, 1978, and 1979; *Helga's Dowry* was included in the American Institute of

Graphic Arts Book Show, 1977, *The Triumphs of Fuzzy Fogtop,* 1980, and *Miracle on 34th Street,* 1984; *The Quicksand Book* and *Simple Pictures Are Best* were both chosen one of *School Library Journal's* Best Books for Spring, 1977; Chicago Book Clinic Award, 1979, for *The Christmas Pageant; Helga's Dowry* was chosen a Children's Choice by the International Reading Association and the Children's Book Council, 1978, *The Popcorn Book, Pancakes for Breakfast, The Clown of God, Four Scary Stories, Jamie's Tiger,* and *Bill and Pete,* 1979, *Big Anthony and the Magic Ring* and *Oliver Button Is a Sissy,* both 1980, *The Comic Adventures of Old Mother Hubbard and Her Dog,* 1982, *Strega Nona's Magic Lessons,* 1983, *The Carsick Zebra and Other Animal Riddles,* 1984, and *The Mysterious Giant of Barletta,* 1985.

Garden State Children's Book Award for Younger Nonfiction from the New Jersey Library Association, 1980, for *The Quicksand Book;* Kerlan Award from the University of Minnesota, 1981, for "singular attainment in children's literature"; Golden Kite Award for Illustration from the Society of Children's Book Writers, 1982, for *Giorgio's Village,* and 1983, for *Marianna May and Nursey; Boston Globe-Horn Book* Award Honor Book for Illustration, 1982, and Critici in Erba commendation from the Bologna Biennale, 1983, both for *The Friendly Beasts;* Regina Medal from the Catholic Library Association, 1983, for "continued distinguished contribution to children's literature"; *Sing, Pierrot, Sing* was chosen one of *School Library Journal's* Best Books, 1983; *Mary Had a Little Lamb* was chosen as a Notable Book by the Association of Library Service to Children (American Library Association), 1984; "Clown of God" was selected a Notable Children's Film, 1984; *Sing, Pierrot, Sing* was selected a Notable Children's Trade Book in the Field of Social Studies by the National Council of Social Studies and the Children's Book Council, 1984, and *The Mysterious Giant of Barletta,* 1985; Award from the Bookbuilders West Book Show, 1985, for *Miracle on 34th Street.*

Tattie's River Journey was exhibited at the Biennale of Illustration, Bratislava, 1985; *Redbook* Children's Picturebook Award Honorable Mention, 1986, for *Tomie de Paola's Favorite Nursery Tales;* Golden Kite Honor Book for Illustration, 1987, for *What the Mailman Brought.*

WRITINGS:

ALL UNDER NAME TOMIE DE PAOLA; ALL SELF-ILLUSTRATED

The Wonderful Dragon of Timlin, Bobbs-Merrill, 1966.
Fight the Night, Lippincott, 1968.
Joe and the Snow, Hawthorn, 1968.
Parker Pig, Esquire, Hawthorn, 1969.
The Journey of the Kiss, Hawthorn, 1970.
The Monsters' Ball, Hawthorn, 1970.
(Reteller) *The Wind and the Sun,* Ginn, 1972.
Nana Upstairs and Nana Downstairs, Putnam, 1973.
Andy, That's My Name, Prentice-Hall, 1973.
Charlie Needs a Cloak (ALA Notable Book; Junior Literary Guild selection), Prentice-Hall, 1973.
The Unicorn and the Moon, Ginn, 1973.
Watch Out for the Chicken Feet in Your Soup (Junior Literary Guild selection), Prentice-Hall, 1974.
The Cloud Book: Word and Pictures ("Reading Rainbow" selection), Holiday House, 1975.
Michael Bird-Boy, Prentice-Hall, 1975.
(Reteller) *Strega Nona: An Old Tale* (ALA Notable Book; *Horn Book* honor list), Prentice-Hall, 1975, published as *The Magic Pasta Pot,* Hutchinson, 1979.
Things to Make and Do for Valentine's Day, F. Watts, 1976.

She lived all alone, and she wasn't very friendly. (From *The Legend of Old Befana: An Italian Christmas Story*, retold by Tomie de Paola. Illustrated by Tomie de Paola.)

When Everyone Was Fast Asleep, Holiday House, 1976.

Four Stories for Four Seasons, Prentice-Hall, 1977.

Helga's Dowry: A Troll Love Story (ALA Notable Book), Harcourt, 1977.

The Quicksand Book (ALA Notable Book), Holiday House, 1977.

Bill and Pete (Junior Literary Guild selection), Putnam, 1978.

(Adapter) *The Clown of God: An Old Story* (ALA Notable Book; *Horn Book* honor list), Harcourt, 1978.

The Christmas Pageant, Winston, 1978, published as *The Christmas Pageant Cutout Book*, 1980.

Pancakes for Breakfast, Harcourt, 1978.

The Popcorn Book (Junior Literary Guild selection), Holiday House, 1978.

(With others) *Criss-Cross, Applesauce*, Addison House, 1979.

Big Anthony and the Magic Ring (ALA Notable Book), Harcourt, 1979.

Flicks (Junior Literary Guild selection), Harcourt, 1979.

Oliver Button Is a Sissy, Harcourt, 1979.

The Kids' Cat Book, Holiday House, 1979.

Songs of the Fog Maiden, Holiday House, 1979.

The Family Christmas Tree Book, Holiday House, 1980.

The Knight and the Dragon (Junior Literary Guild selection), Putnam, 1980.

The Lady of Guadalupe, Holiday House, 1980.

(Reteller) *The Prince of the Dolomites: An Old Italian Tale*, Harcourt, 1980.

The Legend of Old Befana: An Italian Christmas Story, Harcourt, 1980.

The Comic Adventures of Old Mother Hubbard and Her Dog (Junior Literary Guild selection), Harcourt, 1981.

The Friendly Beasts: An Old English Christmas Carol (ALA Notable Book), Putnam, 1981.

(Reteller) *Fin M'Coul: The Giant of Knockmany Hill* (ALA Notable Book), Holiday House, 1981.

Now One Foot, Now the Other, Putnam, 1981.

The Hunter and the Animals: A Wordless Picture Book, Holiday House, 1981.

Strega Nona's Magic Lessons, Harcourt, 1982.

Giorgio's Village (ALA Notable Book), Putnam, 1982.

Francis, the Poor Man of Assisi (ALA Notable Book), Holiday House, 1982.

Noah and the Ark, Winston, 1983.

Sing, Pierrot, Sing: A Picture Book in Mime, Harcourt, 1983.

(Adapter) *The Story of the Three Wise Kings*, Putnam, 1983.

(Adapter) *The Legend of the Bluebonnet: An Old Tale of Texas*, Putnam, 1983.

Marianna May and Nursey, Holiday House, 1983.

(Adapter) *The Mysterious Giant of Barletta: An Italian Folktale*, Harcourt, 1984.

The First Christmas, Putnam, 1984.

Country Farm, Putnam, 1984.

(Adapter) *David and Goliath*, Winston, 1984.

(Adapter) *Queen Esther*, Winston, 1984, revised edition, Harper, 1987.

Esther Saves Her People, Winston, 1984.

Tomie de Paola's Mother Goose Story Streamers, Putnam, 1984.

Tomie de Paola's Mother Goose (*Horn Book* honor list), Putnam, 1985.

Tomie de Paola's Favorite Nursery Tales, Putnam, 1986.

Merry Christmas, Strega Nona, Harcourt, 1986.

Bill and Pete and the Class Trip, Putnam, 1987.

Bill and Pete Go Down the Nile ("Reading Rainbow" selection), Putnam, 1987

The Miracles of Jesus Holiday House, 1987.

But the pasta raised the cover, and Big Anthony as well. (From *Strega Nona: An Old Tale*, retold by Tomie de Paola. Illustrated by Tomie de Paola.)

Tomie de Paola's Book of Christmas Carols, Putnam, 1987.
An Early American Christmas, Holiday House, 1987.
The Parables of Jesus, Holiday House, 1987.
(Editor) *The Legend of the Indian Paintbrush*, Putnam, 1987.
Baby's First Christmas, Putnam, 1988.
Tomie de Paola's Book of Poems, Putnam, 1988.
(Reteller) *Hey Diddle Diddle: And Other Mother Goose Rhymes*, Putnam, 1988.
The Art Lesson, Putnam, 1989.
Too Many Hopkins, Putnam, 1989.
Haircuts for the Woolseys, Putnam, 1989.
Tony's Bread, Whitebird Books, 1989.

ILLUSTRATOR; UNDER NAME TOMIE DE PAOLA

Lisa Miller (pseudonym of Bernice Kohn Hunt), *Sound*, Coward, 1965.
Pura Belpre, *The Tiger and the Rabbit and Other Tales*, Lippincott, 1965.
L. Miller, *Wheels*, Coward, 1965.
Joan M. Lexau, *Finders Keepers, Losers Weepers*, Lippincott, 1967.
Jeanne B. Hardendorff, editor, *Trickey Peik and Other Picture Tales*, Lippincott, 1967.
Melvin L. Alexenberg, *Sound Science*, Prentice-Hall, 1968.
James A. Eichner, *The Cabinet of the President of the United States*, F. Watts, 1968.
Leland Blair Jacobs, compiler, *Poetry for Chuckles and Grins*, Garrard, 1968.
M. L. Alexenberg, *Light and Sight*, Prentice-Hall, 1969.
Samuel Epstein and Beryl Epstein, *Take This Hammer*, Hawthorn, 1969.
Mary C. Jane, *The Rocking-Chair Ghost*, Lippincott, 1969.
Robert Bly, *Morning Glory*, Kayak, 1969.
Nina Schneider, *Hercules, the Gentle Giant*, Hawthorn, 1969.
Duncan Emrich, editor, *The Folklore of Love and Courtship*, American Heritage Press, 1970.
D. Emrich, editor, *The Folklore of Wedding and Marriage*, American Heritage Press, 1970.
Eleanor Boylan, *How to Be a Puppeteer*, McCall, 1970.
S. Epstein and B. Epstein, *Who Needs Holes?*, Hawthorn, 1970.

Barbara Rinkoff, *Rutherford T. Finds 21B*, Putnam, 1970.
Philip Balestrino, *Hot as an Ice Cube*, Crowell, 1971.
S. Epstein and B. Epstein, *Pick It Up*, Holiday House, 1971.
John Fisher, *John Fisher's Magic Book*, Prentice-Hall, 1971.
William Wise, *Monsters of the Middle Ages*, Putnam, 1971.
Peter Zachary Cohen, *Authorized Autumn Charts of the Upper Red Canoe River Country*, Atheneum, 1972.
Jean Rosenbaum and Lutie McAuliffe, *What Is Fear?*, Prentice-Hall, 1972.
Sibyl Hancock, *Mario's Mystery Machine*, Putnam, 1972.
Rubie Saunders, *The Franklin Watts Concise Guide to Babysitting*, F. Watts, 1972, published as *Baby-Sitting: For Fun and Profit*, Archway, 1979.
S. Epstein and B. Epstein, *Hold Everything*, Holiday House, 1973.
Kathryn F. Ernst, *Danny and His Thumb*, Prentice-Hall, 1973.
Valerie Pitt, *Let's Find Out about Communications*, F. Watts, 1973.
S. Epstein and B. Epstein, *Look in the Mirror*, Holiday House, 1973.
Alice Low, *David's Windows*, Putnam, 1974.
Charles Keller and Richard Baker, editors, *The Star-Spangled Banana and Other Revolutionary Riddles*, Prentice-Hall, 1974.
Martha Shapp and Charles Shapp, *Let's Find Out about Houses*, F. Watts, 1975.
Lee B. Hopkins, editor, *Good Morning to You, Valentine*, Harcourt, 1975.
Mary Calhoun, *Old Man Whickutt's Donkey*, Parents Magzine Press, 1975.
Norma Farber, *This Is the Ambulance Leaving the Zoo* (Junior Literary Guild selection), Dutton, 1975.
Barbara Williams, *If He's My Brother*, Harvey House, 1976.
John Graham, *I Love You, Mouse*, Harcourt, 1976.
M. Shapp and C. Shapp, *Let's Find Out about Summer*, F. Watts, 1976.
Eleanor Coerr, *The Mixed-Up Mystery Smell*, Putnam, 1976.
Steven Kroll, *The Tyrannosaurus Game*, Holiday House, 1976.
Bernice K. Hunt, *The Whatchamacallit Book*, Putnam, 1976.
L. B. Hopkins, editor, *Beat the Drum: Independence Day Has Come*, Harcourt, 1977.

"Now isn't that a shame.
   Fin was off workin' on the causeway
   when some important family affair called him away.
   But he'll be home by tea time,
   so why don't you just come right in and sit down."

Poor Fin trembled in the cradle.

(From *Fin M' Coul: The Giant of Knockmany Hill*, retold by Tomie de Paola. Illustrated by Tomie de Paola.)

But when she came back
The poor dog was dead.

(From *The Comic Adventures of Old Mother Hubbard and Her Dog*. Illustrated by Tomie de Paola.)

(From *Charlie Needs a Cloak* by Tomie de Paola. Illustrated by the author.)

Daniel O'Connor, *Images of Jesus,* Winston, 1977.

Belong, Winston, 1977.

Journey, Winston, 1977.

Jean Fritz, *Can't You Make Them Behave, King George?,* Coward, 1977.

Jane Yolen, *The Giants' Farm,* Seabury, 1977.

Stephen Mooser, *The Ghost with the Halloween Hiccups,* F. Watts, 1977.

Tony Johnston, *Odd Jobs,* Putnam, 1977, published as *The Dog Wash,* Scholastic, 1977.

Patricia L. Gauch, *Once upon a Dinkelsbuhl,* Putnam, 1977.

S. Kroll, *Santa's Crash-Bang Christmas,* Holiday House, 1977.

Nancy Willard, *Simple Pictures Are Best* (Junior Literary Guild selection), Harcourt, 1977.

(With others) N. Farber, *Six Impossible Things before Breakfast,* Addison-Wesley, 1977.

Malcolm Weiss, *Solomon Grundy Born on Oneday: A Finite Arithmetic Puzzle,* Crowell, 1977.

Annabelle Prager, *The Surprise Party,* Pantheon, 1977.

L. B. Hopkins, editor, *Easter Buds Are Springing: Poems for Easter,* Harcourt, 1978.

S. Kroll, *Fat Magic,* Holiday House, 1978.

T. Johnston, *Four Scary Stories,* Putnam, 1978.

Jan Wahl, *Jamie's Tiger,* Harcourt, 1978.

Sue Alexander, *Marc, the Magnificent,* Pantheon, 1978.

Naomi Salus, *My Daddy's Moustache,* Doubleday, 1978.

William Cole, editor, *Oh, Such Foolishness!,* Lippincott, 1978.

George Webbe Dasent, translator, *The Cat on the Dovrefell: A Christmas Tale,* Putnam, 1979.

Daisy Wallace, editor, *Ghost Poems,* Holiday House, 1979.

J. Yolen, *The Giants Go Camping* (Junior Literary Guild selection), Seabury, 1979.

Anne Rose, *The Triumphs of Fuzzy Fogtop,* Dial, 1979.

Pauline Watson, *The Walking Coat,* Walker, 1980.

Daniel M. Pinkwater, *The Wuggie Norple Story,* Four Winds, 1980.

P. L. Gauch, *The Little Friar Who Flew,* Putnam, 1980.

Clement C. Moore, *The Night before Christmas,* Holiday House, 1980.

Patricia MacLachlan, *Moon, Stars, Frogs and Friends,* Pantheon, 1980.

A. Prager, *The Spooky Halloween Party,* Pantheon, 1981.

S. Mooser, *Funnyman's First Case,* F. Watts, 1981.

Malcolm Hall, *Edward, Benjamin and Butter,* Coward, 1981.

Michael Jennings, *Robin Goodfellow and the Giant Dwarf,* McGraw, 1981.

J. Fritz, adapter, *The Good Giants and the Bad Pukwudgies* (ALA Notable Book), Putnam, 1982.

Ann McGovern, *Nicholas Bentley Stoningpot III,* Holiday House, 1982.

T. Johnston, *Odd Jobs and Friends,* Putnam, 1982.

Shirley R. Murphy, *Tattie's River Journey,* Dial, 1983.

David A. Adler, *The Carsick Zebra and Other Animal Riddles,* Holiday House, 1983.

S. Mooser, *Funnyman and the Penny Dodo,* F. Watts, 1984.

Valentine Davies, *Miracle on 34th Street,* Harcourt, 1984.

Sara Josepha Hale, *Mary Had a Little Lamb* (ALA Notable Book), Holiday House, 1984.

T. Johnston, *The Vanishing Pumpkin,* Putnam, 1984.

T. Johnston, *The Quilt Story,* Putnam, 1985.

Jill Bennett, reteller, *Teeny Tiny,* Putnam, 1986.

Thomas Yeomans, *For Every Child a Star: A Christmas Story,* Holiday House, 1986.

Katie and Kit and the Sleepover, Simon & Schuster, 1987.

Katie and Kit at the Beach, Simon & Schuster, 1987.

Katie, Kit and Cousin Tom, Simon & Schuster, 1987.

Katie's Good Idea, Simon & Schuster, 1987.

Carolyn Craven, *What the Mailman Brought* (Junior Literary Guild selection), Putnam, 1987.

Elizabeth Winthrop, *Maggie and the Monster,* Holiday House, 1987.

J. Fritz, *Shh! We're Writing the Constitution,* Putnam, 1987.

Sanna A. Baker, *Who's a Friend of the Water-Spurting Whale?,* Cook, 1987.

Nancy Willard, *The Mountains of Quilt,* Harcourt, 1987.

Cindy Ward, *Cookie's Week,* Putnam, 1988.

T. Johnston, *Pages of Music,* Putnam, 1988.

Caryll Houselander, *Petook: An Easter Story,* Holiday House, 1988.

Conceived, designed, and directed puppet ballet, "A Rainbow Christmas," at Botolph in Cambridge, Mass., 1971; de Paola's books have been published in many countries, including

Steady rain or snow falls from nimbostratus clouds. (From *The Cloud Book* by Tomie de Paola. Illustrated by the author.)

Denmark, Germany, Netherlands, Sweden, Norway, Japan, Italy, France and South Africa. Contributor to *Once Upon a Time: Celebrating the Magic of Children's Books in Honor of the Twentieth Anniversary of Reading Is Fundamental*, Putnam, 1986.

ADAPTATIONS:

"Wind and the Sun" (sound filmstrip), Xerox Films/Lumin Films, 1973.

"Andy" (sound filmstrip), Random House, 1977.

"Charlie Needs a Cloak" (filmstrip with cassette), Weston Woods, 1977.

"Strega Nona" (filmstrip with cassette), Weston Woods, 1978, (musical, adapted by Dennis Rosa, based on *Strega Nona, Big Anthony and the Magic Ring,* and *Strega Nona's Magic Lessons*), first produced in Minneapolis, Minn. by the Children's Theatre Company, 1987, (videocassette), CC Studios, 1985.

"Let's Find Out about Houses" (sound filmstrip), Doubleday Multimedia.

"Let's Find Out about Summer" (sound filmstrip), Westport Communications.

"The Surprise Party" (filmstrip with cassette), Random House.

"Pancakes for Breakfast" (filmstrip), Weston Woods.

"Clown of God" (play; adapted by Thomas Olson), first produced in Minneapolis by the Children's Theatre Company, 1981, (16mm film; videocassette), Weston Woods, 1984.

"Strega Nona's Magic Lessons and Other Stories" (record or cassette; includes *Strega Nona's Magic Lessons, Strega Nona, Big Anthony and the Magic Ring, Helga's Dowry; Oliver Button Is a Sissy, Now One Foot, Now the Other, Nana Upstairs and Nana Downstairs*), read by Tammy Grimes, Caedmon, 1984.

"Big Anthony and Helga's Dowry," Children's Radio Theatre, 1984.

"The Night before Christmas" (cassette), Live Oak Media, 1984.

"The Vanishing Pumpkin" (filmstrip with cassette), Random House.

"Sing, Pierrot, Sing," (filmstrip), Random House.

"Why don't you go to the village dance tonight? It would perk you up." (From *Big Anthony and the Magic Ring* by Tomie de Paola. Illustrated by the author.)

"The Legend of the Bluebonnet: An Old Tale of Texas" (filmstrip with cassette; ALA Notable filmstrip), Random House, 1985.

"The Mysterious Giant of Barletta" (cassette), Random House, 1985.

"Mary Had a Little Lamb" (filmstrip with cassette), Weston Woods, 1985.

"Tattie's River Journey" (filmstrip with cassette), Listening Library.

"The Legend of the Indian Paintbrush" (filmstrip with cassette), Listening Library, 1988.

"Tomie De Paola's Christmas Carols" (cassette), Listening Library, 1988.

"Merry Christmas, Strega Nona" (cassette), Listening Library, (play; adapted by T. Olson) first produced in Minneapolis by the Children's Theatre Company, 1988.

"Tomie De Paola's Mother Goose" (play; adapted by Constance Congdon), first produced in Minneapolis by the Children's Theatre Company, January, 1990.

Charlie Needs a Cloak has been adapted into Braille and *Strega Nona* has been produced as a talking book.

WORK IN PROGRESS: Illustrating Tony Johnston's *The Badger and the Magic Fan*, for Putnam; *Tomie de Paola's Bible Stories, The Bacons Go on a Diet, The Webers Go Fishing,* and *The Adventures of Uncle Mr. Satie,* all for Putnam; *Little Grunt and the Big Egg,* for Holiday House.

SIDELIGHTS: "I never had much trouble remembering. Whether it comes from a good memory, old home movies or the fact that I come from a family that loves telling old stories on each other or just because I have always had a very active imagination, I can't really say. I do know, that all the remembering has helped me in my work of writing and illustrating books for children. That memory is my 'thermometer' so to speak. I use it to say 'would I have liked that as a child—if not why?' It keeps me honest."[1]

De Paola was born **September 15, 1934** in Meriden, Connecticut "towards the end of the Depression, just before Roosevelt's first election. My father was lucky, he was a barber in one of the best barbershops in town. So he actually worked throughout the Depression. It's very interesting; people have an image of

He and Pete went inside to find a rest room to brush Bill's teeth. (From *Bill and Pete Go Down the Nile* by Tomie de Paola. Illustrated by the author.)

Italians being robust and loud. My father was just the opposite. He was a quiet and thoughtful man who was loads of fun and loved to cook. I grew up not knowing that men didn't cook.

"My mother and father were very social—the house was always filled with people. At the drop of a hat, there would be a party. I love to give and go to parties now, so I think it rubbed off on me. The big moment of the year was Christmas. We would decorate the house, and then on Christmas Eve, we would have an open house for all the neighbors.

"The other holiday that got the neighborhood together was the Fourth of July. This was after the Second World War, of course. There would be a huge neighborhood picnic with anywhere from one hundred to two hundred people. My father had connections for professional fireworks, so we had fireworks that rivaled those of the city.

"Maybe it was the size of the town—or maybe it was the fact that my tap dancing lessons were reported in the newspaper—but I remember loving that town because everybody knew me. I was the best artist from about fourth grade on, and the yearbook said so. I had made the decision to be an artist and author of books when I was four."[2]

His mother read aloud to the family every night, which "I'm sure had a lot to do with my decision to become an artist. She would read the old fairy tales and legends, especially during the war, when my father was working the graveyard shift at a war plant job. I would come down, not able to sleep, and see my mother curled up in a chair with graham crackers and peanut butter, reading."[2]

School either excited or bored him to tears. "I went to afternoon kindergarten [at King Street School properly called Samuel Huntington] and my teacher was Miss Immick. Nothing really dramatic happened, except that I was furious that we were not going to learn to read until the following year. I wanted to just wait but [my mother] intervened, convincing me that I couldn't get into first grade without kindergarten. That year Jeannie Houdlette who was my neighbor, best friend, and whose mother made wonderful doughnuts got to play the mouse with peas in her mouth in our class production of Peter Rabbit. Johnny Gregory got to play Peter. I was one of the three others—I think Cottontail. I remember that it was not 'Oscar' or 'Tony' material.

"In **March of 1940,** my mother went off to Meriden Hospital to have a baby. I insisted on a baby sister with a red ribbon in her hair. My sister Maureen was born and as far as I was concerned, she was mine. There are so many events surrounding her birth, some of which involved my Italian grandmother, that I could fill a book with them. Suffice it to say, I was suddenly an older brother.

"That year was also the year I started tap dancing lessons at Miss Leah Grossman's Dancing School. I loved them. . . .Not only was I to do the military tap routine with the class but I had been singled out by Miss Leah (whom I adored with all my heart and soul) to do a specialty with Joan Ciotti to 'The Farmer and the Dell.'. . .I would continue to take tap from Miss Leah and others until I went to Art School—years later.

"First grade was great except for 'Dick and Jane.' I hated them, but I loved learning to read and I got a library card. Mildred Kiniry was my teacher. I adored her. (I thought her name was

Title page from the 1977 ALA Notable Book. (From *Helga's Dowry: A Troll Love Story* by Tomie de Paola. Illustrated by the author.)

CANARY.) She let me draw and read and tell her things. I told her I was going to be an artist when I grew up—and sing and dance on stage. She suggested I might consider being a lawyer. I guess my arguing every point with her was quite impressive!

"That year in the dance recital I was a pirate and sang a wonderful song, 'I ain't afraid of the policeman.' I even wore a patch over one eye.

"**September, 1941** I was seven and I was in second grade. Miss Esther Gardner was my teacher. I didn't like her because she insisted that I learn arithmetic. I, who could sing *any* song after hearing it once, memorize *any* poem, tell the plot of *any* movie I had seen, could not memorize my tables! And besides that, arithmetic paper was made to draw on. I informed Miss Gardner that she didn't seem to understand. I was not going to be an 'arithmetic-er' when I grew up. I was going to be an artist.

"Beulah Bowers came to the rescue. Mrs. Bowers was the art teacher who traveled to all the schools. First grade did not 'get her.' She was due to come to King Street School before Thanksgiving and I was sure she'd plead my case. She'd tell Miss Gardner to give me more than one piece of paper that we had to be 'careful of.' She'd let me use my very own Crayola crayons (64 colors including FLESH) instead of the awful school crayons. She'd save me from arithmetic. Well—almost. Actually when Mrs. Bowers arrived in the classroom, it was almost a complete disaster!

"Two boys from an upper grade carried in a large piece of paper torn from the big roll at the end of the hall. They were followed by Mrs. Bowers who was wearing a flowered smock over her dress. She carried a large box of colored chalks.

"The paper monitor. . .handed out the *ONE* piece of paper, the crayon monitor handed out the school crayons that no matter how hard you rubbed no color ever appeared on the paper. I had my own Crayolas waiting inside my desk and I was all set to appeal to Mrs. Bowers to help me escape Miss Gardner and the second grade.

"Mrs. Bowers proceeded to draw a turkey, a pilgrim lady and a pilgrim man on the paper which had been thumbtacked to the board in the front of the classroom. I was disappointed. They weren't very good. 'Now,' she said, 'boys and girls, take your crayons and copy these drawings.' That did it! Everyone knew that *real* artists don't copy! I folded my arms and sat there. Miss Gardner came down the aisle to my desk. Mrs. Bowers was with her. 'What's the matter *NOW?*' she said. I ignored Miss Gardner and pulling my crayons out of my desk, I explained to Mrs. Bowers the great injustice that had been done. I told her about the paper, the crayons, the arithmetic. Then I added, 'I'm going to be an artist when I grow up.' I pointed at the board.

"Instead of strangling me, Mrs. Bowers did a wonderful thing. She made a deal with me. If I copied the turkey and pilgrims like the rest of the class and if there was time, she'd make sure I'd get another piece of paper and I could draw anything I'd like with my *OWN* crayons. That sounded fine to me and from that day on Beulah Bowers and I were friends. She didn't get me out of arithmetic though.

"That year was to bring big changes, not only in Meriden and my life but in the world too. It was a Sunday in December and we were listening to Uncle Tom read the 'funnies.' Suddenly, everything changed. Pearl Harbor entered our vocabularies. Instead of our usual Sunday with my Irish grandfather and grandmother in Wallingford, the grown-ups talked in hushed voices. One thing was clear. My mom's brother, our Uncle Charles who was so much fun and made us laugh was going away to become a soldier.

"All of a sudden, it became the 'War Years.' There were ration books, gas stamps, war stamps to buy in school, black-out curtains, air raids, scrap drives, paper drives and war bond rallies. There was also Rita Hayworth, Fred Astaire, Carmen Miranda, the Jitterbug, the Rhumba and Swing.

"Scheduled to make my First Communion in June, I had to go to Sunday School [at St. Joseph's]. As part of the First Communion deal, I got a little 'set' which was a leatherette case containing a prayer book with an embossed cover, rosary beads and a scapular. (I've always loved sets of things, even to this day—sets of pens, brushes, crayons.)

"Those were also the years that my tap dancing really took off. Instead of being in a 'class,' there were only four of us who were at the same 'level' of instruction. In the recital of 1942, there was a specialty in the first act where Bill Burke and I, in plaid shirts, recited a patriotic poem-song called 'Uncle Sam gets around, but he just don't drift. . . .' Miss Leah had geniune theatre in her blood. But that was also the recital that paired me up with Carol Morrissey. Our number in the recital was titled 'A Couple of Couples.' For the life of me I can't remember who the other girl was. . . .I can remember everything else, our costumes, the music (it was 'Just a Couple in a Castle' from the animated movie 'Mr. Bug Goes to Town. . .').

"From that year on Carol and I were a team, dancing our way through every benefit, minstrel show, Lion's Club meeting, Moose meeting in town. And, we were pretty good, too. We stayed together until 1952 when I went off to art school. I think my favorite title for a routine was 'Senor and Senorita Swing.'

"Third grade was a bit disruptive. Miss Bailey was my teacher. I was crazy about her, but she left mid-year to get married. I wasn't too pleased with that, because Miss Bailey seemed to *really* appreciate talent. . . .I don't remember too much more."[1]

"The years get all mixed up during those 'War Years,' but there are some events that really stick out."[1] "There were many air raids. When you're that age, you don't realize the catastrophic consequences that could exist from a bomb falling on you. Of course, we weren't bombed. So how does one know? It was kind of exciting to go down into the air raid shelter or the basement of the school and sit there huddled around the radio. The air raid warden would knock on the door and say, 'There is a light showing.'

"I was terribly patriotic. We all were. I would go out on paper and scrap metal drives and, because of my tap dancing, was in several bond rally shows. Carol and I entertained for organizations to raise money for the war effort."[2]

"**Christmas of 1943,** when I was nine, was wonderful! All my presents were art supplies: paints, brushes, colored pencils, all sorts of instruction books, watercolors and even an easel. I remember that my father tried his hand with my watercolors to copy a picture from a magazine—sort of 'playing with the electric train' syndrome.

"**Christmas of 1944** was the Christmas that I found *all* the hidden Christmas presents, so it was rotten. I've never snooped for a present, Christmas or birthday since!

"So many memories of the 'War Years' come racing back that they get all jumbled up. One memory though that stands out is mixing the color into the margarine. No matter how yellow the margarine became it still tasted like Crisco.

"Fourth grade was a drag—one of the worst years. Miss Early did not like me drawing all the time, so I was constantly in trouble. But it was during the fourth grade, that I sent a drawing to Walt Disney and received a letter back from a secretary saying how pleased Mr. Disney was to receive my drawing and he said to keep practicing and that to be an artist was a wonderful profession, and that he asked the secretary to send me back my drawing because he knew how important it was for artists to keep their early work. There was enclosed a picture of Mickey Mouse, I guess, with his signature.

"Fourth grade was the first time I entered the sketch book contest which Beulah Bowers had started for the schools. Needless to say, I won a first prize. It did not impress Miss Early.

"Fifth grade was much better. Rose Mulligan was my teacher and if any one teacher in those lower grades stands out in encouraging me in my art, it was Miss Mulligan. She also read aloud to us at the end of every day. I still remember 'The Bird's Christmas Carol.' We dramatized a portion of it for the Christmas assembly. We had lots of assembly programs. Rose Mulligan has no idea how important she would be to solidifying my desire to be an artist—Rose Mulligan and my cousins 'the twins,' Franny and Fuffy McLaughlin. The twins went to Pratt Institute to study art and by the early 1940s had established themselves as top-notch photographers in the magazine world."[1]

The summer between fifth grade and sixth grade brought the end of World War II. "The war being over meant new cars, new bikes, new rollerskates, the 'new look,' sugar and butter, hamburgers, cigarettes, and Wrigley's Spearmint Gum.

"Sixth grade—Miss Viola Burgan. I start writing poetry. I start reading Frank Yerby. Jack Rule and I become *really* good friends. I write a poem about him. He has turtles in pens in his back yard and his grandmother tells me about their ancestors, John Adams and John Quincy Adams. Jeannie Houdlette starts to grow up—faster than me. Carol Morrissey is taller than me too, even though she's younger (it seems as though ALL the girls are taller!).

"Seventh grade—Lincoln Jr. High School. We move from class to class and I have ART for real from Miss Goldman. She's very important to me. Marie Rielly is the music teacher. She also plays the organ at Holy Angels. I get to sing lots of solos! I hate gym. I love shop. I love Miss Hopkins and science. Miss Grace Burke opens up the real world of literature for me. I meet Sheila Rosenthal. We 'go steady' for two years. She's an 'older woman'—one year ahead of me. Her father's a judge and we get free passes to the movies. Every Saturday, we take long walks up Coe Avenue (Sheila lives off the 'Boulevard') and sit under an apple tree. Every Saturday night, we babysit our siblings and talk on the telephone for hours. We pass notes in the hall signed 'Cleo' and 'Marc Antony.' One of our favorite songs is 'Nature Boy.'

"Eighth grade—Sheila and I are still a hot item. My homeroom teacher is Miss Gubala—the 'Bibit' from my childhood and Oak Street days. I still hate gym. Carol and I become even more 'famous.' I'm still the best artist. . . .I make puppets and have a puppet stage in the attic.

De Paola's unpublished drawing "Queen Althea of Pomperania." Submitted to the Illustrators Exhibition at the 1978 Bologna International Children's Book Fair.

"Sheila goes to camp, as she does every summer and I write as I usually do. Her answers are shorter. She comes home from camp and I can tell it's all over. She's met an 'older' man. We break up and I contemplate suicide—but not too seriously. I spend hours in the bathroom just sitting looking at myself in the mirror.

"Ninth grade—I get trench mouth right after school begins and am home for two or three weeks. Mr. Durant who teaches Latin and is my homeroom teacher tells me I'll never catch up. He doesn't like me. I don't like him. I flunk Latin—the first thing I *ever* flunk! Miss Kitty Burke teaches Ancient History. We love each other and she tells me all about Mae West—far more interesting than Caesar. Mr. Dressler teaches algebra and I do catch up (I still hate 'arithmetic'—so algebra is tough)."[1]

A year later the would-be artist wrote to Pratt Institute in New York to tell them that he would be attending their school and "to find out what to take in high school. They answer! That summer I work in the tobacco fields in Portland. It's awful. My dad is now a liquor salesman. We've had a TV for several years—one of the first in Meriden. I send in a poster for Howdy Doody for President—it gets shown on national television. I get over Sheila Rosenthal but have no special girlfriend. We have a Christmas assembly that is very special. Mr. Robert Cyr is teaching music now. Jeannie Houdlette is the Virgin Mary and Edgar Flynn is St. Joseph. Sylvia Petrocelli sings 'O Holy Night' and I sing 'Under the Stars.' We, the ninth graders,

have a St. Patrick's Day Dance after school. My father helps supply some of the decorations—green metallic shamrocks that are part of a promotion for some liquor company. We have lots of parties at our house on Fairmount Avenue—(what else is new?) Tony and Florence Nesci begin a Friday night ritual. They come over to watch the fights on TV. Florence teaches me to pop popcorn. I become hooked for life.

"I loved High School. I was very active. I performed in Props and Paints productions. I sang in special chorus, I made posters, I was decoration chairman for the Junior Prom and the Senior Reception. I was art editor for the 1952 annual. I was in every variety show. I went to almost every basketball game. (I wanted to be the first male cheerleader but the insurance didn't cover me so I wasn't allowed to cheer after weeks of practicing with the cheerleaders.) I still hated gym. I made lots of new friends.

"Graduation night **1952** was awful. I cried and cried and I couldn't stop. I guess somewhere deep deep down I knew that my Meriden years were coming to an end. Something was finished and I was frightened. I didn't want it to end. True, I had won the Maloney Scholarship and was going off to Pratt Institute in the fall to study and become the professional artist I always wanted to be, but things would never be the same. . . . The security of a hometown that knew who I was and where I could go and really feel 'at home' wouldn't be recaptured for many years.

"I was going to have to grow up. And hopefully I did. Pratt was wonderful and trained me well."[1]

"I went off to art school thinking that Norman Rockwell and Jon Whitcomb, famous illustrators at the time, were the zenith. But I learned to keep my mind open and not make any judgments about things until I knew more about them. I was like a vacuum cleaner, devouring everything. It didn't take more than a couple of months before I suddenly discovered Picasso, George Rowe, and Matisse. I said to myself, 'Hey wait a minute, this is something very exciting. I don't know anything about it, but it certainly is appealing to me.'

"Pratt really didn't have dormitories back then, so I lived in a room in the Brooklyn neighborhood. I was a kid from a small town and I loved New York. At that time, the neighborhood was extremely safe. Believe it or not, we used to sit in Fort Green Park at midnight. You can't even do that during the day now. My twin cousins, who had graduated from Pratt in early 1941, advised me to take advantage of New York. So every Saturday morning, I would get on the subway and go into Manhattan. During the fifties, there was so much in New York that was free, and New York was a friendly city. First, I'd go to the Museum of Modern Art, then I'd go to a little French restaurant on 46th St. and have lunch. Then I'd either go window shopping, because I didn't have much money, or I would go see a matinee on Broadway (standing room).

"I started going to art galleries. Because I was very short, and didn't look my age, I began to affect different accents—French or German—just to appear more interesting. Like Sid Caesar. I found that you could have a cocktail at the Rainbow Room, I fancied it was quite the thing to do on a late Saturday afternoon. I'd watch the lights come on and be back in Brooklyn by Saturday night, working away at my drawing board. Or if I was really lucky, I'd stay in Manhattan and do something that night. Then I discovered Greenwich Village. That's where *my* people were.

"For fifty cents, you could have a cappuccino and sit in a coffee house for nine hours. If you sat there long enough, the waitress would fill your cup with regular coffee and sneak a little steamed milk into it. Then she'd ask, 'This piece of baklava is a little old. Do you want it?' Occasionally, a bunch of us would meet and go to an Italian restaurant to have spaghetti. I used to get free glasses of wine a lot. I just loved it."[2]

School was a bit tougher. "Pratt prescribed a very strict course of studies. If you concentrated on illustration, you had to take what they told you to take—drawing, design, and, eventually, painting. I started with figure drawing, clothed and unclothed; I also did animal and perspective drawing. It wasn't four courses a semester; it was nine to five, five days a week."[2]

1955. Earned a scholarship to the Skowhegan School of Painting and Illustration in Maine. "The summer between my Junior and Senior year, I spent ten weeks in Skowhegan, where I was fortunate enough to study with Ben Shahn, who probably had the most impact on me of any of the teachers I had. He told me that being an artist was more than the kind of things you do. 'It's the way you live your life,' he said. I've never forgotten that."[2]

1956. Graduated from Pratt and spent six months in a Benedictine monastery. "Though it was a small monastery, it had a good library. It was like being in a movie—I did a lot of chanting, wore a costume all day long, got a different name and a short haircut. We lived in this little village in Vermont on top of a high hill, complete with snow, cows, and pigs. Actually, I

The person who seemed to be in charge was a handsome, well-dressed, businesslike young woman. (From *Miracle on 34th Street* by Valentine Davies. Illustrated by Tomie de Paola.)

rather liked it. I liked the structure of the day. I don't like to make light of the monastery because I do think that it was a very valid thing for me to do at that age. I think it solidified, not religious, but some deep spiritual values that I have. I have a very strong spiritual life, and meditate very easily. I'm not a fundamentalist, by any means, but I really believe in the strong power of prayer.

"The monastery gave me a way to view life and realize that culture was an important thing as well. If you can add to the culture of the race of man, you're doing a really hot number. It certainly gave me time to delve even more into the study of art; I was sort of the resident artist. The Benedictines are very involved in the arts. I think it also gave me a great deal of respect for work, although I got terrible psychosomatic headaches, so I had to leave."[2]

Returned to secular life, but maintained a connection with the monastery. "I designed fabric for their weaving studio, and started them in a little Christmas card business. Then I began doing all kinds of other art work, and was soon able to make my living as an artist. In the summer I worked in summer theater. Then I got married, for about a year-and-a-half. A friend said it was my brief period. I was briefly in the monastery and briefly married."[2]

1961. Held a one-man art show in Boston. "It was very exciting to have all your things on the wall and all these people coming over, drinking sherry. It went very well. . .I actually sold stuff. I have to admit I made a fairly nice living from my paintings and drawings."[2]

1962. Began teaching college. "I moved from Boston and ended up back in New York. I have the great privilege of saying that I lived down in Soho before it was Soho, in a loft that was only $85 a month. Now if that isn't ancient history, what is?"[2]

In **1964,** de Paola illustrated a picture science book called *Sound* by Lisa Miller, which really was a pen name for Bernice Kohn Hunt, the editor of the series. "I was living in my loft down on Canal Street and had almost given up the idea that I would do books because I had been showing my portfolio around all these years and hadn't got any work. Then someone introduced me to Florence Alexander, the woman who became, and still is, my agent. She took my portfolio and about six weeks later, someone showed interest. Then I got my second book. Before I knew it, I was off and running."[2]

1967. Moved to San Francisco, because "New York wasn't as much fun in the sixties as it had been in the fifties. There was a lot of repression. I tried the monastery again, but stayed an even shorter time than the first. Then I decided to go out to California and get my masters degree. I had been teaching, but with a masters degree, I'd make more money. I also wanted to experience living in a culture totally different than the one I was used to in the northeast. Living in San Francisco at that time was very exciting. It was a terrific, walkable city. In twenty minutes I could be on an isolated beach. It didn't have great museums, but somehow I didn't miss them."[2]

After four years on the west coast, de Paola returned to New Hampshire in **1971.** "There was no edge to my life, which I missed. It was very easy living in California. You had work to do, but then you looked out the window and said, 'Gosh, it's so beautiful I think I'll just go for a walk.'"[2]

In New Hampshire, de Paola settled in a small town. "I like this part of the country. I find it vitalizing. I like the winters, the snow, and the cold weather. And I have very few distractions. There are no movie theaters (though I've discovered the VCR). The other thing is that when you live in the country, you can have space. I have an enormous barn. It's a dream studio. I could never afford it in New York, no matter how successful I was or am. But, I also travel enough so that I don't get cabin fever and I entertain people who visit me for weekends, which is always terrific. I really love having company."[2]

De Paola has illustrated and/or written over one hundred and sixty books. "I started as an illustrator and I still think of myself as an artist first. If I stand in front of the easel or sit at my drawing table and do drawings that aren't book oriented, that's one thing; but in order to do books, I've got to have the words, because I've got to illustrate the words. The story comes first. The hardest part is to try not to see it in pictures until the story is there, especially if I'm writing it myself. That's extremely important because if it doesn't have a good story, no matter how beautiful the pictures are, it's not going to be a good book.

"The idea for *Charlie Needs a Cloak* just appeared one day. I myself learned to spin wool and weave when I lived in Vermont so the story flowed very simply and naturally. I feel that if I don't actually get involved personally with my characters, whether they be human or animal, and find some personal characteristics of either myself or my friends in them, they are

not 'real.' And that is of prime importance to me—that fantasy be 'real,' from the child-in-us-all point of view.

"My Italian grandmother was the model for the heroine [in *Watch Out for the Chicken Feet in Your Soup*]. Like Joey's grandmother in the story she pinched my cheeks, talked 'funny,' and made Easter bread dolls that were a highlight in my young life. . . .

"She always put chicken feet in chicken soup, and I was fascinated. It certainly was something to brag about. I could mow down my opponents with 'My Grandma puts chicken feet in the soup!' Da dah! Stardom. I also remember the wonderful moment when my aunts fought over who was going to get the foot floating in the soup."[3]

De Paola is crazy about colors and style. "My color is quite distinctive. I think my style of illustration has been refined over the years. Style has to do with the kinds of things you are drawn to personally, and I'm drawn to Romanesque and folk art. I think that my style is very close to those—very simple and direct. I simplify.

"I do my books in watercolor-type mediums. I used to love painting in oils, but I'm allergic to the smell of turpentine. So now when I paint, I use acrylic. My favorite medium is that combination of tempera-watercolor-acrylic."

1989. "I have a new book, *The Art Lesson*, which is somewhat autobiographical. It's about not being able to use my Crayola crayons in school. Possibly, the teacher isn't portrayed as one of the great teachers, but when I do a book, I have to be honest about it."[2]

Illustrating and writing has to do with ". . .dreams. A dream that I expressed as a child, that when I grew up I would write and draw pictures for books: a dream that people I've never met would get to know me a little better: a dream that the invisible world could be made visible, and even a dream that I could somehow touch others' lives.

"It's a dream of mine that one of my books, any book, any picture, will touch the heart of some individual child and change that child's life for the better. I don't even have to know about it. I hope it's not a far-fetched dream. Meanwhile, I'll keep working, doing the best I'm capable of."[4]

FOOTNOTE SOURCES

[1]Tomie de Paola, "Autobiography and Friends of Tomie," written for the Tomie de Paola Celebration, September 13-15, 1985, sponsored by the Meriden Public Library, Meriden, Conn.
[2]Based on an interview by Dieter Miller for *Something about the Author*.
[3]*Something about the Author*, Volume 11, Gale, 1977.
[4]Tomie de Paola, "Involved with Dreams," *Books for Your Children*, summer, 1980.

FOR MORE INFORMATION SEE:

Lee Kingman and others, compilers, *Illustrators of Children's Books: 1957-1966*, Horn Book, 1968.
Horn Book, April, 1974, August, 1975, October, 1975.
Dorothy A. Marquardt and Martha E. Ward, *Illustrators of Books for Young People*, Scarecrow, 1975.
Top of the News, April, 1976
Publishers Weekly, July 19, 1976, July 23, 1982.

De Paola's poster for the Children's Theatre Company.

"Children's Book Illustrators Play Favorites," *Wilson Library Bulletin*, October, 1977.

J. Dunning, "Hard Winter's Work," *New York Times Book Review*, November 13, 1977.

L. Kingman and others, compilers, *Illustrators of Children's Books: 1967-1976*, Horn Book, 1978.

S. Hepler, "Profile; Tomie de Paola: A Gift to Children," *Language Arts*, March, 1979.

Richard F. Abrahamson and Marilyn Colvin, "Tomie de Paola: Children's Choice," *Reading Teacher*, December, 1979.

Jacqueline S. Weiss, "Tomie de Paola" (videocassette), Profiles in Literature, Temple University, n.d.

Jim Roginski, compiler, *Newbery and Caldecott Medalists and Honor Book Winners*, Libraries Unlimited, 1982.

Sandra Holmes Holtze, editor, *Fifth Book of Junior Authors and Illustrators*, H. W. Wilson, 1983.

D. L. Kirkpatrick, editor, *Twentieth-Century Children's Writers*, St. Martin's, 1983.

"Illustrious Illustrator," *Hartford Courant* (Conn.), September 13, 1985.

COLLECTIONS

Kerlan Collection at the University of Minnesota.
Osborne Collection, Toronto, Canada.

DINAN, Carolyn

PERSONAL: Born in England. *Education:* Chelsea School of Art, B.A.; graduate study at Royal College of Art. *Home:* Surrey, England. *Office:* Chelsea School of Art, Manresa Rd., London SW3 6LS, England.

CAREER: Free-lance writer and illustrator; Chelsea School of Art, London, England, visiting lecturer in illustration. *Awards, honors:* Other Award from the Childrens' Rights Workshop (Great Britain), 1977, and Carnegie Medal from the British Library Association, 1978, both for *The Turbulent Term of Tyke Tiler; Say Cheese!* was exhibited at the Bologna International Children's Book Fair, 1985.

WRITINGS:

SELF-ILLUSTRATED CHILDREN'S BOOKS

The Lunch Box Monster, Faber, 1983.
Skipper and Sam, Faber, 1984.
Say Cheese!, Faber, 1985, Viking, 1986.
Ada and the Magic Basket, Hamish Hamilton, 1987.
Born Lucky, Hamish Hamilton, 1987.
Ben's Brand New Glasses, Faber, 1987.
A Dog Would Be Better, Hamish Hamilton, 1987.
The Witch's Shopping Spree, Hamish Hamilton, 1988.

ILLUSTRATOR

Charlotte Bronte, *The Search After Hapiness [sic]: A Tale*, Simon & Schuster, 1969.
Catherine Storr, *Puss and Cat*, Faber, 1969.
Janet McNeill, *Umbrella Thursday*, Hamish Hamilton, 1969.
Bianca Bradbury, *Lucinda*, Macdonald, 1969.
Pamela Oldfield, *Melanie Brown Goes to School*, Faber, 1970.
Christobel Mattingley, *The Picnic Dog*, Hamish Hamilton, 1970.
Robert Musman, *Catch a Thief and Other Short Stories*, Longman, 1970.
Cella Turvey, *The Boy and the Donkey*, Longman, 1970.
Helen Cresswell, reteller, *At the Stroke of Midnight, Traditional Fairy Tales*, Collins, 1971.

C. Mattingley, *Worm Weather*, Hamish Hamilton, 1971.
Pamela Rogers, *The Magic Egg*, Lutterworth, 1971.
Gene Kemp, *The Prime of Tamworth Pig*, Faber, 1972.
Pamela Sykes, *The Birthday Glove*, Hamish Hamilton, 1972.
Zinnia Bryan, *Let's Talk to God Again*, Scripture Union, 1972.
P. Oldfield, *Melanie Brown Climbs a Tree*, Faber, 1972.
Ann Staden, *Pepper Face and Other Stories*, Faber, 1972.
G. Kemp, *Tamworth Pig Saves the Trees*, Faber, 1973.
Joan Tate, *Jock and the Rock Cakes*, Brockhampton Press, 1973, Childrens Press, 1976.
Geraldine Kaye, *Tim and the Red Indian Head-Dress*, Brockhampton Press, 1973, Childrens Press, 1976.
P. Oldfield, *The Adventures of Sarah and Theodore Bodgitt*, Brockhampton Press, 1974.
P. Oldfield, *Melanie Brown and the Jar of Sweets*, Faber, 1974.
George P. McCallum, *On Goes the River: An Intermediate Level Reader for Students of English as a Second Language*, Collier, 1974.
C. Mattingley, *The Surprise Mouse*, Hamish Hamilton, 1974.
Ivy Eastwick, *The Toyshop on the Avenue*, Lutterworth, 1974.
Rosemary Weir, *Uncle Barney and the Sleep-Destroyer*, Abelard, 1974.
Joyce Gard, *Handysides Shall Not Fall*, Kaye & Ward, 1975.
The Best Book of Nursery Rhymes, Hodder & Stoughton, 1975.
Boswell Taylor, *Little Donkey*, University of London Press, 1975.
James Thurber, *Many Moons*, Kaye & Ward, 1975.
G. Kemp, *Tamworth Pig and the Litter*, Faber, 1975.
Joy Allen, *Boots for Charlie*, Hamish Hamilton, 1975.
Annie M. G. Schmidt, *Bob and Jilly*, Methuen, 1976.

It seemed as if we glided along in the air for I could hear no sound of our footstep. (From *The Search after Hapiness* by Charlotte Bronte. Illustrated by Carolyn Dinan.)

G. Kemp, *The Turbulent Term of Tyke Tiler*, Faber, 1977.
R. Weir, *Uncle Barny and the Shrink-Drink*, Abelard, 1977.
The Jipijapa Hat, Hodder & Stoughton, 1977.
G. Kemp, *Christmas with Tamworth*, Faber, 1977, published in America as *Christmas with Tamworth Pig*, Merrimack, 1979.
A. M. G. Schmidt, *Bob and Jilly Are Friends*, Methuen, 1978.
The Wardens of the World, Dobson, 1979.
A. M. G. Schmidt, *Bob and Jilly in Trouble*, Methuen, 1980.
G. Kemp, *Dog Days and Cat Naps*, Faber, 1980.
Robin Stemp, *Guy and the Flowering Plum Tree*, Faber, 1980, Atheneum, 1981.
G. Kemp, editor, *Ducks and Dragons: Poems for Children*, Faber, 1980.
G. Kemp, *The Clock Tower Ghost*, Faber, 1981.
Catherine Cookson, *Nancy Nutall and the Mongrel*, Macdonald, 1982.
June Counsel, *But Martin!*, Faber, 1984.
Martin Waddell, *Owl and Billy*, Methuen, 1986.
Dorothy Edwards, *Robert Goes to Fetch a Sister*, Methuen, 1986.
G. Kemp, *Tamworth Pig Stories* (contains *The Prime of Tamworth Pig* and *Tamworth Pig Saves the Trees*), Faber, 1987.

FOR MORE INFORMATION SEE:

Brigid Peppin and Lucy Micklethwait, *Book Illustrators of the Twentieth Century*, Arco, 1984.

DIRKS, Wilhelmina 1916-
(Willy Dirks)

PERSONAL: Born November 6, 1916, in Semarang, Java, Indonesia; daughter of Theodore and Wilhelmina (Legeu) Van Steenbergen; married Adrianus Dirks, December 6, 1939 (died, February 2, 1972); children: Lucy Duke, Anne Bailey, Elizabeth Logan (deceased). *Education:* Attended business college. *Politics:* Liberal. *Religion:* Roman Catholic. *Home:* R.R.1, Thornloe, Ontario, Canada P0T 1S0.

CAREER: Travel agent owner, 1962-75; writer. *Member:* Temiskaming Writers Guild (secretary-treasurer, 1985-89), Women's Institute, Beta Sigma Phi.

WRITINGS:

UNDER NAME WILLY DIRKS

Country Classics Cookbook, Highway Book Shop, 1978.
Suti, a Foster Child, Highway Book Shop, 1980.
Kids in the Kitchen: Recipes from Children for Children, Highway Book Shop, 1981.

Contributor of articles to *Temiskaming Speaker*, *Northern Daily News*, *North Bay Nugget*, and of short stories to *Northern Anthology*.

WORK IN PROGRESS: Research of how Christmas is celebrated in other countries with recipes of Christmas cooking; a book of memories of a travel agent.

SIDELIGHTS: "I have lived in Indonesia for sixteen years, Curacao for six years and in Holland and Canada. I give craft classes including needlework and doll making."

WILHELMINA DIRKS

HOBBIES AND OTHER INTERESTS: Reading, needlework, and other crafts.

DiSALVO-RYAN, DyAnne 1954-

PERSONAL: Born October 3, 1954, in Brooklyn, N.Y.; daughter of Salvatore (a hospital administrator) and Elaine (a para-professional; maiden name, Canonica) DiSalvo; married Edward N. Ryan (an international re-insurance broker), December 26, 1980; children: John Edward, Marja Lewis. *Education:* Attended School of Visual Arts, 1975-77. *Politics:* Democrat. *Religion:* Roman Catholic. *Agent:* Jane L. Feder, 305 East 24th St., New York, N.Y. 10010.

CAREER: Illustrator and author of children's books, 1980—. *Exhibitions:* Master Eagle Gallery, New York, N.Y., 1986, 1987.

WRITINGS:

Uncle Willie and the Soup Kitchen, Morrow, 1990.

ILLUSTRATOR

Patricia Relf, *That New Baby!*, Golden Press, 1980.
Louis Ross, *The Bear under the Bed*, Dutton, 1980.
P. Relf, *The First Day of School*, Golden Press, 1981.
Catherine Kenworthy, *Best Friends*, Golden Press, 1983.
Charlotte Pomerantz, *The Half-Birthday Party* (Junior Literary Guild selection), Clarion Books, 1984.

Marilyn Jeffers Walton, *Those Terrible Terwilliger Twins,* Raintree, 1984.
Mary Pope Osborne, *Mo to the Rescue,* Dial, 1985.
Beatrice Siegel, *Sam Ellis's Island,* Four Winds, 1985.
Richard Wenk, *Adventure at Camp Schoonover,* Scholastic, 1985.
Beverly Cleary, *The Real Hole* (DiSalvo-Ryan was not associated with earlier edition), Morrow, 1986.
B. Cleary, *Two Dog Biscuits* (DiSalvo-Ryan was not associated with earlier edition), Morrow, 1986.
B. Cleary, *The Growing Up Feet,* Morrow, 1987.
B. Cleary, *Janet's Thingamajigs,* Morrow, 1987.
Amy Hest, *The Mommy Exchange,* Macmillan, 1988.
Cathy Warren, *Saturday Belongs to Sara,* Bradbury, 1988.
Abby Levine, *What Did Mommy Do Before You?,* A. Whitman, 1988.
M. P. Osborne, *Mo and His Friends,* Dial, 1989.
A. Hest, *The Best-Ever Good-bye Party,* Morrow, 1989.
Ryerson Johnson, *Why Is Baby Crying?,* A. Whitman, 1989.

SIDELIGHTS: "When I was a little girl growing up in Brooklyn, New York, I never thought that my art work was among the very best. My mother, my father, and my grade school art teacher, Miss Taco, recognized my art ability early on. It was because of their sensitivity—especially my parents—that I eventually began to recognize my talent and enjoy my life as an artist.

"I can remember one day when I was about eight or nine years old looking through a picture book and deciding, 'I can make a better book.' It was from that day on that I knew that I wanted to be a book illustrator.

"In my senior year at Franklin Delano Roosevelt High School, I was awarded the special privilege of taking a six-week etching course on Saturday mornings at John Dewey High School. I liked this very much. My art teacher, Ms. Ann Fleischman, strongly suggested that I look into the School of Visual Arts in Manhattan. Since I was never a very academic student, the thought of four more years of school made my head spin. Luckily, the School of Visual Arts was very appealing to me

DYANNE DiSALVO-RYAN

(From *The Mommy Exchange* by Amy Hest. Illustrated by DyAnne DiSalvo-Ryan.)

and I eventually attended classes on and off for the next two and a half years.

"Through the job opportunity program at the School of Visual Arts I was recruited by Hallmark Cards to work in Kansas City, Missouri. Although the atmosphere and Hallmark art was too restrictive for me, it was at Hallmark Cards, under the supervision of Ms. Linda Smith, that I learned how to set up my palate, remember what colors I mixed so that I could mix them again and to not make my linework so 'organic' when I drew inanimate objects.

"While I was still living in Kansas City, I set up interviews with New York publishers whenever I visited my family back home in Brooklyn. It was during this time that Ms. Bernette Goldsen-Ford, a former editor at Western Publishing, and Ms. Kate Klimo, a former editor at the Gingerbread Division of E. P. Dutton, each gave me my first two manuscripts to illustrate. Both at the same time! I left Hallmark Cards and was teaching grade school math during the day. At night I worked on both books. I can remember feeling quite challenged and satisfied. I had finally achieved my long awaited goal. I was a book illustrator!

"Things haven't changed much since then. I still work on two or three books at one time. Living in New York City brings my art to life. When I ride the subways I sketch the people I see. Friends and family are the inspiration for the world that I create on paper. The house that I grew up in and the block that I played on in Brooklyn as a child are a continuous source of reference for me. My technique of watercolor and pencil is simple. I work quickly and familiarly with my pictures so I never lose the spontaneity that is essential to my characters and color. I hope the pictures I create are timeless. I love my work and feel that it is a great responsibility and honor to be recognized.

"My favorite authors are Mathew, Mark, Luke, and John. The way the narrator speaks often brings my pen to hand. Mavis Jukes, Vera B. Williams, Beverly Cleary, E. E. Cummings, D. H. Lawrence, and Jack Kerouac are inspiring authors to me.

"Music is also an encouraging influence when I am drawing or painting. Sting, the Beatles, Billy Joel, and Bonnie Raitt are good company. My favorite artists are Toulouse-Lautrec, John Sloan, and Maxfield Parish. I admire all performing arts. I especially admire directing, sound, photography, and original screenplays."

HOBBIES AND OTHER INTERESTS: Volunteer in community soup kitchens.

DORIN, Patrick C(arberry)1939-

PERSONAL: Born February 12, 1939, in Chicago, Ill.; son of Aloysius (a production foreman) and Grace (a nurse; maiden name, Maebius) Dorin; married Karen Marie Foley (a preschool teacher), May 13, 1961; children: Thomas, Michael, Susan, Amy, John. *Education:* Northland College, B.S., 1961; Northern Michigan University, M.A., 1966; Michigan State University, Ed.S., 1971; University of Minnesota, Ph.D., 1977, postdoctoral study, 1983-85. *Home:* P.O. Box 667, Superior, Wis. 54880. *Office:* Blaine Elementary School, 823 Belknap St., Superior, Wis. 54880.

CAREER: Elgin, Joliet and Eastern Railway, Joliet, Ill., management trainee and cost analyst, 1961-63; Milwaukee Road, Chicago, Ill., marketing and operations research, 1963-64; U.S. Gypsum Co., Chicago, data processing quality control analyst and freight rate auditor, 1964-65; part-time junior high teacher in Marquette, Mich., 1965-66; elementary teacher in Duluth, Minn., 1966-69; middle school and elementary teacher in East Lansing, Mich., 1969-73; North Branch Public Schools, North Branch, Minn., elementary principal and data processing coordinator, 1973-82; Superior Public Schools, Superior, Wis., elementary principal and community education coordinator, 1982—; University of Minnesota--Duluth, part-time instructor of marketing, transportation, and educational administration, 1983—. Vice-chairman of transportation committee of East Central Minnesota Development Council; vice-president of administration and later president of Lake Superior Transportation Club in Duluth, Minn., 1970s and 1986-88. Consultant for various school districts and industry.

MEMBER: National Association of Elementary School Principals, Wisconsin School Administrators Association, Lake Superior Transportation Club, Railway Locomotive and Historical Society, and various railroad historical and technical societies, including the Soo Line, Chicago and North Western, Milwaukee Road, and Missouri Pacific. *Awards, honors:* Distinguished Service Award from the Minnesota Elementary School Principals' Association, 1982.

WRITINGS:

Lake Superior Iron Ore Railroads, Superior, 1969.
Commuter Railroads, Superior, 1970.
Chicago and North Western Motive Power, Superior, 1971.
The Domeliners, Superior, 1973.
Canadian Pacific Railway, Superior, 1974.
Coach Trains and Travel, Superior, 1975.
The Canadian National Railway's Story, Superior, 1975.
Everywhere West: The Burlington Route, Superior, 1976.
Grand Truck Western, Superior, 1977.
Milwaukee Road East, Superior, 1978.
The Young Railroader's Book of Steam (juvenile), Superior, 1978.
Soo Line Railroad, Superior, 1979.
Amtrak Trains and Travel, Superior, 1979.

Chesapeake and Ohio Railway, Superior, 1981.
Train Watcher's Log, Superior, 1981.
Yesterday's Trains (juvenile), Lerner, 1981.
Yesterday's Trucks (juvenile), Lerner, 1982.
Ontario Northland Railway, Superior, 1987.
Great Northern Railway: Lines East, Superior, 1989.
Everything You Wanted to Know about Elementary Schools, and WERE Not Afraid to Ask, Amidon, 1989.

Contributor of articles to historical, professional and hobby journals and magazines.

WORK IN PROGRESS: A novel; *Louisville and Nashville Railroad;* a series of books about the Norfolk and Western Railway, auto-trains and travel, the Missouri-Kansas-Texas railroad, Missouri Pacific Railroad, and an introduction to railroad, for Superior Publishing.

SIDELIGHTS: "I was born in Chicago and lived there briefly before moving to Ashland, Wisconsin. I spent half of my childhood in that community, with the other half in the steel city of Gary, Indiana. Chicago, Gary, and Ashland played significant roles in my development. I had the best of all worlds; small city and and big city alike.

"One could not live in or visit those three cities and not be exposed to railroads, and as a result of this exposure I developed a deep and lasting interest in them. Because of this interest I decided that it would be best to follow a railroad career. I prepared myself for just such a career by earning a bachelor's

PATRICK C. DORIN

Cover for the 1982 hardcover edition. (From *Yesterday's Trucks* by Patrick. C. Dorin. Photograph courtesy of the American Truck Historical Society.)

degree in business administration with an empahsis on marketing. Upon graduation from Northland College in Ashland, Wisconsin, I went to work for the Elgin, Joliet and Eastern Railway in the Chicago area.

"While working for the E J & E, I was thrust into a role of teaching. I found that I liked it much more than I thought I would. While working in customer relations and marketing research for the Milwaukee Road I made the decision to return to school to become an elementary teacher. It was a decision that I would never regret doing. I earned a degree in elementary education and eventually taught for a total of eight years before deciding to move into the area of school administration.

"Throughout my career in the public school system I retained my interest in railroads. I also felt as though I would like to try

my hand at writing. I decided to combine these two interests and write a book about railroading.

"I began writing my first book shortly after I left the Milwaukee Road in 1964 and completed it in 1968. My intended audience included everyone who might have an interest in railroads from the early ages on up. My purpose was to include not only historical and geographical information about railroads, but also equipment information for model railroaders and a description of railroad operations and services for the shipping and traveling public.

"While teaching I had the desire to return to school. Over the years I earned several more degrees including a doctorate in school administration. Because of my business background, I frequently took additional courses in transportation, marketing, and transportation geography. These courses later influenced my doctoral research, 'A Comparison of Management Activities in Industry and Education,' written in 1977. The business courses that I took, along with my doctoral research ultimately provided me with an opportunity to teach marketing and transportation at the University of Minnesota-Duluth campus. At the same time, I was (and am) working as an elementary principal.

"As part of my duties as a principal I feel as though it is important to get into classrooms and interact with children. Consequently, I never pass up an opportunity to teach, especially reading, but also to go into the classrooms and simply tell stories, either fairy tales or stories of my own experiences on the railroads, or ones that I make up. My experience in the classroom has led me to write some of my books specifically for elementary age children. *Yesterday's Trucks* is one example. I have also attempted some children's fiction, but as of yet I have not published any of this work.

"I feel very strongly about the educational process and believe that it can only be done through a co-operative working relationship between school and home. Toward that end, I wrote a book containing parental questions that have been asked of me again and again over the past twenty plus years.

"I live in Superior, Wisconsin with my wife and family.

"If I were to sum this up, writing is very important to me. It provides me with a bridge for part of my career, in this case railroading. It provides me with an opportunity to teach things that I would not ordinarily be able to do. Writing is also linked with my educational career, not only in terms of books written specifically for elementary age children, but also for my work for parents. It is also an important means of relaxation for me.

"It is my hope that in the future I will continue to write railroad books and at the same time expand into fiction for both the children and the adult markets."

DUNREA, Olivier 1953-

PERSONAL: Surname is pronounced dun-ray; born September 22, 1953, in Virginia Beach, Va.; son of Clarence W. (a baker) and Marian (a homemaker; maiden name, Goodwin) Miller. *Education:* Attended University of Delaware, 1971-73; West Chester State College, B.A., 1975; Washington State University, M.A., 1976. *Home and office:* 214 Wendover St., Philadelphia, Pa. 19128.

CAREER: Washington State University, Pullman, Wash., teaching fellow, 1975-76; Bakerrothschild Horn Blyth, Philadelphia, Pa., administrative assistant and office manager, 1977-78; Friday Architects, Philadelphia, administrative assistant and office manager, 1979-81; Delaware State Arts Council, Wilmington, Del., artist-in-residence, 1981-83; Philadelphia Orchestra Association, Philadelphia, Pa., illustrator, 1981-84; free-lance author and illustrator. *Member:* English-Speaking Union, Philadelphia Children's Reading Round Table. *Awards, honors:* Cooper/Woods Award (travel grant) from the Philadelphia Branch of the English-Speaking Union, 1980; Outstanding Pennsylvania Children's Author, 1985; *Skara Brae* was selected one of Child Study Association of America's Children's Books of the Year, 1987.

OLIVIER DUNREA

WRITINGS:

JUVENILE; ALL SELF-ILLUSTRATED

Eddy B, Pigboy, Atheneum, 1983.
Ravena, Holiday House, 1984.
Fergus and Bridey, Holiday House, 1985.
Mogwogs on the March!, Holiday House, 1985.
Skara Brae: The Story of a Prehistoric Village, Holiday House, 1986.

ILLUSTRATOR

Nathan Zimelman, *The Star of Melvin,* Macmillan, 1987.

Contributor to periodicals, including *Learning,* and *Children's Literature Association Quarterly.*

WORK IN PROGRESS: Series of nonfiction books on prehistoric dwellings, fortifications, burial mounds, huge monuments, etc.

SIDELIGHTS: "I was born in Virginia Beach, Virginia. As a child my major fascination was with farm animals and rocks. Most of my time was spent either taking care of livestock on our homestead or drawing them and making up stories about them. Chickens, geese, and pigs are my favorites. As a child of twelve I had fifteen dogs as companions, in addition to a younger brother, two older sisters, and lots and lots of cousins. However, only my younger brother shared my enthusiasm and love for animals.

They live by the edge of the sea.

(From *Fergus and Bridey* by Olivier Dunrea. Illustrated by the author.)

"I am the only one in my family to have gone to college and then on to graduate school. I majored, not in art or English, but in theatre arts and music. For five years I performed as an actor, singer and dancer, and designed sets and costumes for the professional theatre circuit. In 1972 as an undergraduate at the University of Delaware I won my first travel scholarship to study independently in London and Paris. In 1978 I returned to Britain and spent six weeks in Scotland sketching, painting, and photographing ancient monuments. It was this trip to the British Isles that would most affect my writing and artwork. In 1980 I received the Cooper/Woods Award—a travel grant from the Philadelphia branch of the English-Speaking Union. This grant provided the means for me to return to Scotland, the Orkney Islands, and the Outer Hebrides to further pursue my interest in archaeology and Scottish folklore. I returned to Scotland and the Orkneys in 1981 to do further research.

"I live in Philadelphia and share an old stone house with another writer/illustrator, Edward Boyer, two dogs, one Maine coon cat, and four guinea pigs. When not working on my books or special projects or talking in schools throughout the United States, I spend my time running marathons, camping and canoeing, gardening, reading historical novels and mysteries, and building stone dams on the Wissahickson Creek. Edward and I have constructed over fifty dams!

"I absolutely love children! I think I love them because they (and animals) seem to understand me and my work the best. I don't write books or make pictures for children, I make them for myself. It just so happens that children like what I do as much as I do! Childhood should be a magical time and a special time for children. I remember the books that I most loved as a child. They were either stories about animals (my most favorite is, of course, *Charlotte's Web*) or stories about elves, dragons, ghosts, witches, etc. In the latter part of the twentieth century the world seems so very complicated—to both children and adults alike. My fascination is with the ancient past, when things were more mysterious, more magical, and more permanent. Therefore, my favorite kind of stories to write and illustrate usually center around my own characters that I've created from my imagination. They live in a prehistoric, stony setting. Their dwellings are usually built of stone, quite often

subterranean, and have lots of secret passages and escape tunnels. (I never want to get trapped and neither do any of my characters.)

"The stories I write are fast paced, economically written, and present characters and adventures that I would have liked to have experienced as a child. Each story I write is one that I have dreamed and thought about for a long time before writing it down. I work all the details out in my mind, usually while lying in bed at eleven-thirty in the morning! Then when I know exactly who is going to be in the story, where it takes place, and how it's going to end I sit down and write it. Often, a quick sketch or watercolor study that I do will influence a story idea or a character's name that came to mind.

"While working on a book I tend to live, eat, and breathe the story each and every day. When I'm working at my drawing board I often lose track of time, appointments, forget to eat, but I never forget to walk and play with the dogs because they quite boisterously remind me when it's time to play! I'm a perfectionist to a fault and will often redo an illustration many times before I'm satisfied with it. And even then I often wish I had time to redo it to make it even more perfect with no mistakes in it at all! My writing suffers the same fate. Whenever I reread what I've written I want to rewrite it over and over to absolutely make sure it's right. Writing is easy, it's the rewriting that's always the most difficult. A writer must be careful not to overwrite and lose the spontaneity of what was originally written.

"Whenever I get stuck at the typewriter or blocked at the drawing board I do one of three things (and often all three in rapid succession). I either go for a long ten- to fifteen-mile run to work out the snags in my mind, take the dogs for a long walk in the woods and do some work on my dams, or take out my crazy quilt (king-size) which I've been working on for years and quilt away like mad! Usually after doing all those things I feel ready to tackle the artistic block and get on with the project at hand. However, I'm infamous for missing deadlines because I became too involved in building dams or working on my quilt!

"Finally, I would like to say that perhaps the part I like best about writing and illustrating books is sharing them with children. I enjoy travelling around the country visiting schools, talking about myself and my work, and hearing my readers' responses to my work. I am often impressed with the ideas children tell me and show me that they are working on. I hope to buy a farm near Philadelphia and have classes come out to my studio (barn) for the day and perhaps during the summer months have two or three young writers/artists work in my studio (and on the farm) as apprentices. I feel I have something to offer them and I'm certain they would have something to offer me in terms of creating art and stories."

FOR MORE INFORMATION SEE:

Philadelphia Inquirer, February 26, 1981, February 17, 1982.
"Books Come Alive in Artist's Hands," *Sunday News Journal* (Wilmington, Del.), December 12, 1982.
"Man behind the Mogwog Leaves Bucks Kids Agog," *Bucks County (Pa.) Courier Times,* November 16, 1984.

EDWARDS, Page L., Jr. 1941-

PERSONAL: Born January 15, 1941, in Gooding, Idaho; son of Page Lawrence (a mining engineer) and Mary Elizabeth (a botanist; maiden name, Smith) Edwards; married Diana Elaine Selsor (a writer) August 29, 1987; children: (first marriage) Amy de Forest, Benjamin Carter. *Education:* Stanford University, B.A., 1963; University of Iowa, M.F.A., 1974; Simmons College, M.L.S., 1982. *Home:* P.O. Box 1117, St. Augustine, Fla. 32085. *Agent:* Amanda Urban, International Creative Management, 40 West 57th St., New York, N.Y. 10019. *Office:* St. Augustine Historical Society, 271 Charlotte St., St. Augustine, Fla. 32084.

CAREER: Viking Press, New York, N.Y., editor, 1968; Grossman Publishers, New York, N.Y., editor, 1969-71; University Press of New England, Hanover, N.H., assistant director, 1972-73; David R. Godine, Publishers, Boston, Mass., editor, 1974-75; Haverhill Public Library, Haverhill, Mass., reference librarian, 1975-81; Massachusetts Institute of Technology, Cambridge, archivist, 1981-82; St. Augustine Historical Society, St. Augustine, Fla., director, 1983—. Staff associate, Bread Loaf Writers' Conference, 1982-83. *Military service:* U.S. Navy, 1963-67; became lieutenant junior grade. *Member:* Society of Florida Archivists, Society of American Archivists, Florida Historical Society.

WRITINGS:

The Mules That Angels Ride, J. P. O'Hara, 1972.
Touring, Viking, 1974.
Staking Claims: Stories, Marion Boyars, 1980.
Peggy Salte, Marion Boyars, 1983.
Scarface Joe (young adult), Four Winds, 1984.
The Lake: Father and Son, Marion Boyars, 1985.
American Girl, Marion Boyars, 1990.

Contributor to *Library Journal* and *St. Petersburg Times.*

WORK IN PROGRESS: A novel.

SIDELIGHTS: "I have written one book for young adults, *Scarface Joe,* the story of a young boy who falls in love with a girl a few years older than he at a mining camp in Colorado.

Most of my other novels and stories have been published by Marion Boyars. She is a wonderful editor for my work, and I consider myself very fortunate to have had her support for the past seventeen years. Hers is a small publishing house, but her loyalty to her authors certainly makes up for the size. All of my books are less than 250 pages. I try to distill the story to its bare essentials. However, I write one book on an average of fifteen times from beginning to end to get it right. There are few greater pleasures for me than finishing a new manuscript. My lastest book, *American Girl,* is about a Florida girl who is heiress to the Fountain of Youth."

HOBBIES AND OTHER INTERESTS: Paintings of Edward Hopper, kayaking, sailing, bicycling, trout fishing in Colorado.

ENGELHART, Margaret S(tevens) 1924-

PERSONAL: Born June 19, 1924, in Flint, Mich.; daughter of Henry Hall (in business) and Anita Isabel (a housewife; maiden name, Dever) Stevens; married Carl William Ernst Engelhart (a retired professor), June 11, 1949; children: Anne Engelhart Durant, Steven, Scott, Matthew; (adopted children) Barbara Yokum, Elizabeth Yokum, Daniel Yokum, Geoffrey Yokum, Deborah Yokum. *Education:* University of Michigan, B.A., 1945; Columbia University, M.A., 1947; graduate study at University of Minnesota, 1947- 50. *Politics:* Social Democrat. *Religion:* Unitarian Universalist. *Home:* 72 Brinkerhoff St., Plattsburgh, N.Y. 12901. *Office:* Tundra Books, P.O. Box 1030, Plattsburgh, N.Y. 12901.

CAREER: Henry H. Stevens Moving Co., Flint, Mich., part-time typist, 1940-41; University of Minnesota, Minneapolis, instructor in communications, 1947-49; homemaker, 1950-69; State University of New York College at Plattsburgh, instructor in English, 1969, 1972; Tundra Books of Northern New York, Plattsburgh, editor, 1972—; Nankai University, Tianjin, Peoples Republic of China, teacher of English and American literature, 1985-86. Delegate to National Democratic Convention, 1972. *Member:* National Association for the Advancement of Colored People, Clinton County Historical Association, Society of Genealogists (England), New York Genealogical and Biographical Society, Clinton County Council on the Arts (founding member), Mental Health Association, Plattsburgh (president, 1968-70). *Awards, honors: They Sought a New World* was selected one of New York Public Library's 100 Best Books, and one of Co-op Children's Book Center's (Washington State) Best Books of Year, both 1985.

WRITINGS:

The Mother of Us All (history), Rockland Courier Gazette, 1979.
(With William Kurelek) *They Sought a New World: The Story of European Immigration to North America* (history), Tundra Books, 1985.
(Contributor) *Remove the Blindfold,* Book 1, Oxford University Press (Canada), 1986.
(Contributor) *Doorways,* Macmillan, 1987.

Editor of *Antiquarian,* 1984-86.

WORK IN PROGRESS: A number of articles on children's literature and family history; essays; an Edwardian cookbook.

SIDELIGHTS: "I matured in a household of comfort, the third child of parents, neither of whom graduated from high school.

My father used to say that he went through eighth grade. Later we learned that he had finished only the sixth grade. It was probably at this time that his father left his mother and therefore he needed to go to work. My mother might have finished, but her parents thought she was frail (Grandma's parents had both died of T.B. in Ireland). She always regretted that she had not finished. The strive for education was great in our family. There was never any question whether my older brothers and I would go to university, though my father did warn me that I shouldn't get 'too smart' or no man would marry me.

"We were always read to as children, and we were also encouraged to read by ourselves. Books, dictionaries, and encyclopedias were available at home and we always used the local libraries. My parents were for the most part good role models, patient, helpful to the elderly, aware of others difficulties or problems. They allowed freedom of speech at the dinner table. My brothers were bringing home radical thoughts on politics, religion, and race, and while they didn't perhaps agree, they allowed. I knew all my grandparents, they lived long lives and were all immigrants (Ireland and England), and I remember well sitting with my grandmother, asking questions about her life. Alas, I was not old enough to ask those questions to which I now wish I had the answers. These then are strains of my life, set down early, played out in various ways in the years since then: politics, religion, family and family history, the importance of free speech and individual and minority rights, the importance of the arts.

"There have been (so far!) two profound events in my life: the first was the death of friends after which we adopted their family of five children and tried to create a larger single family. Since family has always been important to both me and my husband, the effort to recreate this larger and infinitely more complex structure was a gigantic effort, for them—all the children—as well as for us. All of these children are now grown and independent, quite splendid in their variety and individuality.

"The second profound experience occurred when my husband and I taught English and American literature to Chinese students at Nankai University, Tianjin, Peoples Republic of China. This opportunity to enter, in a small way, the life and culture of a non-western nation challenged and widened our minds and hearts, even more than our earlier experiences of sabbatic leaves in Germany, Austria and England. China remains very much within me and we hope to return as soon as possible.

"I believe that luck plays a huge role in life. We have little control over many aspects of our lives. It behooves us to catch and use as many as possible of those elements over which we do have control, in order to make intelligent and handsome our personal and community lives.

"*The Mother of Us All* is a history of my husband's family's immigration from Austria to America in 1875. *They Sought a New World,* a book for those ten years old and older, was written because there are few books for children on the subject of immigration. It attempts to give them an idea of the trauma and difficulty of passage from Europe to North America in the nineteenth century, a central experience in the history of both the United States and Canada."

HOBBIES AND OTHER INTERESTS: Gardening, travel, reading.

FOR MORE INFORMATION SEE:

Press Republican (Plattsburgh, N.Y.), March 14, 1987.

ERICKSON, Phoebe

PERSONAL: Born in Baileys Harbor, Wis.; daughter of Axel Eric (a lumberman and farmer) and Emily (a homemaker and farmer; maiden name Anderson) Erickson; married Arthur Blair (an attorney and designer), 1947. *Education:* Attended Chicago Art Institute, 1931-33 and Columbia University. *Politics:* Democrat.

CAREER: Free-lance artist, author, and illustrator of children's books. Archaelogy researcher in Europe, 1960. Instructor at Wesleyan University Writer's Conference, 1980. *Exhibitions—* Group shows: Whitney Museum of American Art, New York, N.Y.; Metropolitan Museum of Art, New York, N.Y.; Chicago Art Institute, Ill.; Davenport Art Museum, Iowa; Institute of Contemporary Art, Boston, Mass.; National Competition of Painters, Alicanti, Spain; Southern Vermont Art Center Galleries, Manchester, Vt.; Region Art Exhibitions, Hopkins Center, Dartmouth College, Hanover, N.H.; One-person shows: Gallery Timmermannen, Uppsala, Sweden; American Swedish Historical Museum, Philadelphia, Pa.; Kansas State Teachers College, Emporia; Historical Galleries, Danbury, Conn.; "Horses in Fantasy, Fact and Fiction," Woodstock Gallery of Art, Vt., 1988. *Member:* American Swedish Historical Foundation, Ridges Wildflower Sanctuary. *Awards, honors:* William Allen White Children's Book Award, 1957, for *Daniel 'Coon: The Story of a Pet Raccoon;* Dorothy Canfield Fisher Children's Book Award, 1960, for *Double or Nothing.*

MARGARET S. ENGELHART

PHOEBE ERICKSON

WRITINGS:

ALL SELF-ILLUSTRATED

Slip, the Story of a Little Fox, Childrens Press, 1945.
Cattail House, Childrens Press, 1949, new editon, 1962.
Black Penny, Knopf, 1951, privately printed, 1982.
The True Book of Animals of Small Pond, Childrens Press, 1953.
Daniel 'Coon: The Story of a Pet Raccoon, Knopf, 1954.
Baby Animal Friends, Wonder Books, 1954.
Double or Nothing, Harper, 1958.
Wildwing, Harper, 1959.
Just Follow Me, Follett, 1961.
Uncle Debunkel: Or, the Barely Believable Bear, Knopf, 1964.
Who's in the Mirror?, Knopf, 1965.

ILLUSTRATOR

Felix Salten, *Bambi's Children,* Random House, 1949.
Thornton Waldo Burgess, *Baby Animal Stories,* Grosset, 1949.
T. H. Burgess, *Nature Almanac,* Grosset, 1949.
Anna Sewell, *Black Beauty,* Random House, 1950.
T. H. Burgess, *Stories around the Year,* Grossett, 1955.
Johanna Dewitt, *Little Reindeer,* Childrens Press, 1957.
Caroline Kramer, *Read-Aloud Nursery Tales,* Random House, 1957.
T. H. Burgess, *Adventures of Peter Cottontail,* Grosset, 1958.

SIDELIGHTS: "Writing evolved in a round-about way for me. When I left New York to live in the country near New Milford, Connecticut, I began keeping a journal which soon became top-heavy with notes and sketches of birds and animals, plants and wild flowers. Childrens Press wanted a story and illustrations about foxes, but since I wasn't a writer and had no time to experiment, I tried to get out of it. But because I had done wildlife illustrations for them, they insisted. So at last I said I'd take a day off and try a story about the red fox family that lived

in a nearby meadow I'd been watching. At dusk the mother fox would bring her kits up to play in the tall grass. With my field glasses I could see them very clearly as they rolled and tumbled in wild happy games. Once I saw the father fox bring them a rabbit, and what furious snarls and yaps were made over that morsel!

"The first necessity was pencil and paper—a lot of paper, I discovered. But eventually I found the technique, to use the term broadly, to be somewhat like that of illustration, where you paint in some scenes carefully and just suggest others. Anyway, the idea became *Slip, the Story of a Little Fox.* It was followed by other books on wildlife. All began with sketches and drawings, so I knew quite a bit about my characters before I began to write. *Black Penny,* the story of a colt I raised and trained, began with hundreds of sketches based on memories of a Wisconsin farm childhood. *Daniel 'Coon* began the same way; in fact, Danny acted out his own story, with a little help from me on the plot.

"Because an artist sees things in pictures, he finds it easy to visualize the scenes he wishes to write about; too easy, sometimes, for there is danger of having the visual image take the place of good, clear writing. His imagination may be used up on the pictures, and leave little of worth in the text. This may not be true for other author-illustrators, so I speak only for myself. But to be able to say what one wants to say, clearly, and with imagination, is the *real* problem, and one that I often struggle with. And by that I do not mean pattern of dialogue, or doubt as to how my characters will react to problems. I have only to 'tune in' on my own self as a child to get that answer. But a book as a whole should have something of worth to say, something that can be felt as a force or aura by the child reading it. And that means the author's whole adult mind must come into play, for no tell-tale sign of a message or object-lesson can show; for that, like the too perfect hero, is dull and unconvincing to the average child.

"The steel trap, one of man's cruelest devices, is used in *Daniel 'Coon* as a symbol; to quote one of the characters in the book: 'Lots of people trap, but I've always thought it was unfair. Killing animals outright is one thing, and torturing them in traps is another.' The callousness it takes to club to death an animal so caught (a common practice) is bound to encourage brutality. Yet sporting magazines make a big thing of youngsters trapping just for the fun of it.

"But gospel such as that is only popped in now and then. My main endeavor was to build up an interesting and exciting story, showing the characteristics of the animals, how lovable they can be, and how close an understanding a child may have with Nature.

"Now I want to say something about a kindred subject, but to say it plainly I must go back a good bit. I was the twelfth child in a family of thirteen. My parents migrated from Sweden in 1880 and settled in what was then wilderness at the tip of the Door County Peninsula in Wisconsin. They built a log cabin, using oxen to clear the land. But money was scarce, so during the long winters my father worked in the lumber camps of upper Wisconsin and Northern Michigan, while mother held the fort at home. And that's what it really amounted to because there were bears and timber wolves in the forest at that time. The roads were mere trails, so it was easier to travel on foot than to push through with wagons and sleighs. So when my father came home to visit his family in their lonely outpost he walked across Green Bay on the ice. Still they were happy in this new land, and did not consider this way of life to be too hard, or even give

Illustration from the fiction-based-on-fact novel showing Erickson and her brother with the colt. (From *Black Penny* by Phoebe Erickson. Illustrated by the author.)

their difficulties much thought. They were doing what they wanted to do, and were young and strong.

"The farm was well developed by the time I came along. My father and brothers worked the land and lumbered. Mother's spinning wheel kept us well supplied with yarn for sweaters, stockings, mittens and caps. Most of our food was raised on the farm. There was a great deal of work, but there was also time for play and reading. We were a family of bookworms though I must say our fare was scant, at least as far as children's books were concerned; except for *Black Beauty, Heidi, Aladdin and His Wonderful Lamp,* we had seen very few. The nearest public library was at that time thirty miles distant, and the tiny bookcase in the one-room school we attended contained slim pickings. We had books at home, but they were for grownups. Still we read some of them, or listened to them being read aloud. Looking back, I don't feel that this was altogether unfortunate, for we attempted books beyond our age level, where both the words and ideas were a challenge. Winter evenings were the best time of all, for then father read aloud to the whirring accompaniment of Mother's spinning wheel. We children half-listened to the accounts of Napoleon's campaigns, Stanley and Livingstone in Africa, the horrors of Andersonville, and the battles of Charles the Twelfth of Sweden. On our own we read the dictionary, the remains of an ancient encyclopedia, and studied the engraving in the huge family Bible, our favorite picture book.

"Once we found a story in a magazine with pictures showing animals wearing clothing. It was a delightful story; we read and reread it, always hoping to find another like it. It took a long time, but for me, that wish was fulfilled the day I walked into the Children's Room at the Evanston Public Library. I had come from my home on the farm to visit an elder sister who lived in Evanston, Illinois. It was my first stay in a real town and I remember walking on people's front lawns because the hard pavement hurt my feet; wearing shoes in the summertime didn't help any either. But all that was forgotten when on the second day of my visit, I discovered the public library. With the help of my sister I soon had a card of my own and promptly lost all interest in sightseeing or even going to the beach. We had miles of beaches at home, but here were miles of books!

"Like Doris Gates, I too have long been on the road to Kansas; for it was at that long ago time, when we children on the farm discovered *The Little Blue Books,* published in Girard, Kansas, and only a nickel a piece. We ordered them by the dozen, with money earned by picking cherries or apples or digging potatoes. They were tiny paperbound books, really meant for adults, but to us, they were not only grist for our reading mill, but were also something we could keep—that really *belonged* to us. There were short stories, plays, poetry, essays and short biographies. In particular I remember Ibsen; *Hedda Gabler* and *The Wild Duck;* plays which seemed tragic, yet wildly exciting—a glimpse into the real grown-up world. We subscribed to the *Haldeman-Julius Weekly,* also published in Kansas. It specialized in literary criticism and book reviews. Magic names like Tolstoi and Dostoyevsky, Joseph Conrad, Matthew Arnold, Jane Austen, and George Eliot, to name but a very few, became important to us, though we seldom laid eyes on the books they had written. Which is probably just as well, because at that age we might have found them dull, and so retained a memory of that dull flavor in after years, and thus have developed a prejudice against them. As it was, we just caught the edge of the aura surrounding them, and felt that they held some secret key to wisdom, which we would someday discover.

"Through reading we became aware of music, other than our own efforts on guitars and accordions, et cetera. In one year of super-colossal effort we saved up enough money to buy a phonograph from Sears & Roebuck, and studied the Victor and Columbia record catalogs. Alas, this behemoth was expensive to feed; the symphonies we wanted were beyond reach—nobody wanted *that* many potatoes dug! So we settled for single records, overtures and arias from operas. I sent for a music correspondence course and pumped through the whole thing on our parlor organ, always having to imagine the sound of the middle B flat, the mice having silenced that key forever. But no matter, I was learning something. I can barely read music now, much less play it; but through reading, the need for music was awakened and developed.

"At thirteen, I finished grammar school, and went to Chicago a year later. After getting a job at a downtown department store, and a card at the public library, my future was settled. Now I could read and study to my heart's content and find out about *everything,* or so I thought. And here again were the librarians to help me. With their training they were able to suggest books and ways of study that I would otherwise have missed. For instance, knowing that I planned to study art, they advised Helen Gardener's great book, *Art through the Ages;* later, at art school, it was the principal text book we used in a course taught by Miss Gardener herself. For years books were almost my only companions; I carried my school under my arm, as a relative quipped. And when at last, in the depths of the Depression, the great day arrived when I could enroll for a year at the Chicago Art Institute, good fortune had placed the building just up the street from the Chicago Public Library.

"In the years following, the Chicago, New York, Connecticut, and now Vermont, public libraries have been, and are, my chief sources for reference and research, as well as for general reading. Many books in my own very modest collection have been purchased after reading a library copy. In fact I never feel at home in a new town until I have visited the library and made the acquaintance of the librarian. Perhaps it is that I feel libraries are doing more 'just plain good' in the world than any other institution, to put it squarely. Another attraction is the sight of books, whole shelves, whole rooms of them; a never-ending supply. For books are a comfort, a stable thing, filled with thoughts and ideas garnered from many minds. An assembly of forces, strong and yet flexible, in that they represent worldwide viewpoints. One may study international politics, or the anatomy of the earthworm.

"How far-reaching was the early guidance of my first librarian! Not because my interests turned toward writing, but because she first opened the way to the wonderful world of words; words to be read, or words to be written.

"As for my book, *Daniel 'Coon,* I hope that children, in reading it, may share with me some of the joys and real responsibilities of owning and caring for, and learning from one of Nature's creatures. I have tried to show compassion and a respect for the dignity of Nature. A reverence for life—all life, not just that of humans. Because I grew up on the land and have always found a deep spiritual comfort in close communion with it, I attempt to bring to the children, both in my writing and in my illustration, a feeling of that companionship. For the earth makes one's joys more joyous and gives depth and meaning to one's sadness. An old Eskimo legend begins with: 'And how did you know what to do, when all this trouble came upon you?' 'The earth told me,' answered the man.

"And so the earth might tell all people if they would only stop to listen.

"I have sometimes been asked how I could write for children since I have none of my own; how could I have any understanding of a child's mind? Well it is a strange thing perhaps, but the ability to write for children seems to devolve on one's ability to recapture one's *own* childhood; to find delight and wonder in things, to come upon them fresh and anew, to be aware of *now,* this moment! Not to have one's reactions always reserved and guarded by one's lifetime experiences, but to be able to look into the mirror, which to some may seem the past, but is in reality the reflection of a certain direct simplicity, a kind of purity of heart. Call it never growing up, if you like. But to me, it seems to be something extra, besides growing up. For that reason I find writing for children something like writing to myself, a feeling that is always with me when I am working on a story, both text and illustrations.

"A point I have noted is that many children do not want the hero, if it be a child, to be a *perfect* little hero, always noble and self-sacrificing. True, that may possibly be their ideal, but such characters seem dull and insincere to them. And children are very quick to detect insincerity. When I was writing *Daniel 'Coon* in New Milford, Connecticut, I read part of an early draft aloud to a sizeable group of children in the library. In one sequence I had Tacks, the boy who owns the coon, act in a submissive way about a fight between the coon and a neighbor's dog. They called me on it at once. Tacks couldn't have acted that way if he really loved his pet. They wanted aggression and controversy, problems to be tackled and solved. As one boy said gloomily, 'It's a good story, but don't make the kids goody-goodies.' Another young philosopher added: 'Make it have a good ending, but have the kids act mean sometimes, like they did in *Black Penny.* That way they seem real.'

"'Horrors!' I can hear some say. With all the trouble in the world, this author wants children shown as disobedient and selfish. In defense, I quote Montaigne, from his essay, *The Art of Conversing:* 'Every day the foolish demeanor of another warns and admonishes me. That which irritates will affect and arouse us more than that which pleases. These times are only good for reforming us backwards. . . .'

"This was written in the sixteenth century, but the group of children in the library had, in effect, said the same thing. Perfection did not impress them because they could not identify themselves with perfection. But they could identify themselves with improvement gained through trial and error. And so *Daniel 'Coon* became somewhat tailored to their ideas of what they would like in a book.

"I don't remember ever having been asked by an artist or a writer how I first began to work in this field, nor have I ever asked the question of them. Maybe we all feel that, like Topsy, we 'just growed.' Well I 'growed' very slowly; my earliest memory of drawing, places me at our kitchen table with a piece of wrapping paper or a bit of white birchbark, struggling to capture the barest semblance of a horse. The number of dicarded attempts proved that my mother was right in not allowing me to use our family writing-paper tablet, or my school tablet, except for a final rendering, which, alas, seldom came. As I look back, this state of affairs seems a virtual paradise, just endless sketches with no deadline, no day of reckoning! Anyway, the weekly output kept growing, and in time even the family accepted the fact that I might someday become an artist. One of my aunts urged me to eat plenty now, because artists always starved. Despite this gloomy warning, the various animals on our farm, as well as members of the family, became models for my ambitious pencil or crayon.

"In particular I remember copying the illustration of the chariot race in *Ben-Hur.* This was a condescension; copying was ordinarily spurned as being less original than my own creations, but since I had never been to Rome, I made an exception in this case. The final drawing, in color, was foisted on my parents as a Christmas present, and was of necessity hung on their bedroom wall. They were proud of it; and so was I—for about a week. Then slowly the awful truth dawned on me: the horses were wooden, the chariots stood still, the drivers were nothing but toys. I tore the picture down from the wall and destroyed it. All was lost—I could never be an artist, because real artists had to be able to put hundreds of things in a picture (or so I thought). That was the test, and I had failed. I could never make a picture like Rosa Bonheur's 'Horse Fair,' a secret ambition, nor like the scenes in our huge illustrated Bible. I was felled by composition, an unknown (at that time) enemy. Still, I must have gone back to drawing of one kind or another, for I recall making many weird sketches of a colt I was training, and of attempting a 'marine' painting with a set of oil colors a well-wisher had given me. In time, art school was possible and after that came the business of making a living in my chosen field. Somehow I did, and finally began to illustrate books for children.

"While doing research for *Animals of Small Pond,* I made weekly trips, over a period of one year, to a pond formed by a beaver dam. Surrounded by great swampy marshes, it had attracted many kinds of wildlife, and as I wanted to do a story covering the cycle of the four seasons, it was a splendid place for observation. But it took patience, and a good deal of time. I used a rowboat, except during the winter when the pond was frozen over, because the muskrat and beaver lodges were some distance from dry land. It is surprising how little attention birds and animals pay to intruders once they become accustomed to them. I had only to remain quiet to see the muskrats and beavers feeding, or working on their lodges, the herons stalking fish, and sometimes the gentle otters at play in the deep water. A pair of Canada geese nested there that summer, parading the pond at sunset with long-drawn plaintive honks. I never went near their nest; the drake can be quite ugly.

"One might fancy this place to be a haven of peace and quiet. Not so at all; except for very early morning, the din was much like a zoo at feeding time; I never did identify all the screeches, whistles, pipings, honkings and groans. Sometimes there were battles, for many of these creatures prey upon one another, which is part of Nature's pattern of checks and balances. One such fight between a mink and a large muskrat ended under the water. But no doubt the mink won, for a mink is a muskrat's most dangerous enemy. The mink, in turn, has enemies, among them the fox, the bobcat, and certain owls. Its speed and ferocity protects it however, and this is an interesting sidelight on the interlocking relationships of wildlife ecology. Much of the mink's diet is made up of rapidly reproducing rodents, amphibians, and animals such as rabbits. This has a tendency to keep these units of the biota from over-production, and is one of the tiny parts of the very complex soil, plant, animal, man, food chain.

"I had first come to the pond to make notes and sketches for my book, but my interests soon widened into a larger field of study. I began to be aware of, and to be curious about, the teeming life the pond supported. I am not a biologist and my studies were not very exacting, or specialized. But a desire to learn can be the beginning of wisdom. I began to see that conservation did not mean just the protection of certain birds, plants, animals and lands because they were *economically useful,* but that all parts of the biota were inter related, and dependent upon one another for healthy functioning, that land is not merely soil, but can be likened to a stream of energy flowing through a circuit of soils, plants, and animals. Natural, or evolutionary changes are slow, the circuits tend to adjust themselves to these changes of give and take. But man's discovery of tools has enabled him to make quick and violent changes over great areas. The bulldozer and the power chain- saw can make short work of removing the land's natural covering.

"I came to writing through illustration. Artists can visualize their material, a great help in writing. A love of poetry is also important. I wrote about animals because I felt I had something to say about them and the children in the stories were a part of that world. Nature plays an important part and that's where my country background as well as my continued country living is a source of inspiration."

HOBBIES AND OTHER INTERESTS: Hiking, gardening, interior design.

FOR MORE INFORMATION SEE:

Bertha M. Miller and others, *Illustrators of Children's Books: 1946-1956*, Horn Book, 1958.
Marjorie S. Grutzmacher, "Phoebe Erickson's *Black Penny* Available Again," *Door County Advocate* (Sturgeon Bay, Wis.), August 10, 1982.

COLLECTIONS

Kerlan Collection at the Univerity of Minnesota.
De Grummond Collection at the University of Southern Mississippi.
Alexis Dupont School, Wilmington, Delaware.

EVANOFF, Vlad 1916-

PERSONAL: Born December 12, 1916, in New York, N.Y.; son of Thomas and Lucy (Zwirka) Evanoff. *Education:* Attended Cooper Union, 1932-35. *Office:* Box 9032, Coral Springs, Fla. 33075.

CAREER: Worked as commercial artist for five years after high school; free-lance writer and illustrator, 1945—. *Military service:* U.S. Army, 1941-45. *Member:* Outdoors Writers Association of America. *Awards, honors: A Complete Guide to Fishing* was named one of New York Public Library's Books for the Teen Age, 1982.

WRITINGS:

Surf Fishing, Ronald, 1948, new edition, Harper, 1974.
How to Make Fishing Lures, Ronald, 1959.
Natural Baits for Fishermen, A. S. Barnes, 1959, published as *Fishing with Natural Baits*, Prentice-Hall, 1975.
A Complete Guide to Fishing, Crowell, 1961, revised edition, 1981.
Modern Fishing Tackle, A. S. Barnes, 1961.
How to Fish in Salt-Water, A. S. Barnes, 1962.
(Editor) *Fishing Secrets of the Experts*, Doubleday, 1962.
Spin Fishing, A. S. Barnes, 1963.
Fresh-Water Fishermen's Bible, Doubleday, 1964, revised edition, 1980.
Hunting Secrets of the Experts, Doubleday, 1964.
1001 Fishing Tips and Tricks, Harper, 1970.
Another 1001 Fishing Tips and Tricks, Harper, 1970.
Best Ways to Catch More Fish in Fresh and Salt Water, Doubleday, 1975.

Make Your Own Fishing Lures, A. S. Barnes, 1975.
(Compiler) *The Fisherman's Catalog*, Dolphin Books, 1977.
Fishing Rigs for Fresh and Salt Water, Harper, 1977.
Five Hundred Fishing Experts and How They Catch Fish, Doubleday, 1978.
Fresh-Water Fishing Rigs, Catchmore, 1984.
Salt-Water Fishing Rigs, Catchmore, 1985.
How to Rig Plastic Worms, Catchmore, 1988.

Contributor to periodicals, including *Salt-Water Sportsman, Motor Boating, True Fishing Yearbook, Sports Afield, Field and Stream,* and *Outdoor Life.*

SIDELIGHTS: "I'm a native New Yorker and started fishing as a boy on nearby farms during summer vacations in New Jersey. This was fresh-water fishing, but when back in the city, I traveled by subway and bus to salt-water fishing spots where I fished from piers, jetties, boats and the beaches in the surf.

"After the War, in 1945, I tried cartooning, free-lance commercial art and some free-lance writing. I decided to write about the subject I knew best—fishing. I wrote and sold some magazine articles on fishing to outdoor and fishing magazines. Then I decided to write and illustrate a book called *Surf Fishing.* The first publisher, A. S. Barnes, accepted it and was published

VLAD EVANOFF

in 1948. It was later revised and published by two other publishers and remained in print for thirty-four years.

"I like all kinds of fresh and salt-water fishing and have traveled to many parts of the country to engage in this and gather material and photos for my magazine articles and books. My favorite method of fishing is surf fishing from the beach, rocky shores, or jetties. I won two striped bass contests in Rhode Island for catching the biggest stripers. One of them weighed forty-nine pounds. A few years later I caught a fifty-two pound channel bass at Cape Hatteras in North Carolina.

"I have been fishing since I was fourteen years old. I have derived so many benefits from it in the study of nature, scenery, making new friends and relaxing, and having a lot of fun that I have felt a constant compulsion to pass these feelings on to others through my writings. If even one or two readers have taken up fishing because of my writings, I feel I have accomplished my mission in this world."

FOR MORE INFORMATION SEE:

Life, April 7, 1961.
Fort Lauderdale News and Sun-Sentinel, December 10, 1978.

COLLECTIONS

De Grummond Collection at the University of Southern Mississippi.

FLEISCHMAN, (Albert) Sid(ney) 1920-

PERSONAL: Born March 16, 1920, in Brooklyn, N.Y.; son of Reuben and Sadie (Solomon) Fleischman; married Betty Taylor, January 25, 1942; children: Jane, Paul, Anne. *Education:* San Diego State College (now University), B.A., 1949. *Home and office:* 305 Tenth St., Santa Monica, Calif. 90402. *Agent:* Bill Berger Associates, Inc., 444 East 58th St., New York, N.Y. 10022.

CAREER: Professional magician; screenwriter; author of books for young people. Magician in vaudeville and night clubs, 1938-41; traveled with a magic show, 1939-40; *Daily Journal,* San Diego, Calif., reporter and rewrite man, 1949-50; *Point* (magazine), San Diego, associate editor, 1950-51; full-time writer, 1951—. Author of scripts for television show "3-2-1 Contact," 1979-82. *Military service:* U.S. Naval Reserve, 1941-45; served as yeoman on destroyer escort in the Philippines, Borneo, and China. *Member:* Authors Guild, Authors League of America, Writers Guild of America West, Society of Children's Book Writers.

AWARDS, HONORS: New York Herald Tribune's Children's Spring Book Festival Award Honor Book, 1962, for *Mr. Mysterious and Company*; Spur Award from the Western Writers of America, Southern California Council on Literature for Children and Young People Award, and Boys' Clubs of America Junior Book Award, all 1964, George C. Stone Center for Children's Books Recognition of Merit Award, 1972, and Friends of Children and Literature (FOCAL) Award from the Los Angeles Public Library, 1983, all for *By the Great Horn Spoon!*; Commonwealth Club of California Juvenile Book Award, 1966, for *Chancy and the Grand Rascal;* Lewis Carroll Award, 1969, for *McBroom Tells the Truth.*

SID FLEISCHMAN

Longbeard the Wizard was selected one of the American Institute of Graphic Arts Children's Books, 1970; *Book World*'s Children's Spring Book Festival Award Honor Book, 1971, for *Jingo Django;* Southern California Council on Literature for Children and Young People Award, 1972, for "Comprehensive Contribution of Lasting Value to the Literature for Children and Young People"; Golden Kite Award Honor Book from the Society of Children's Book Writers, 1974, for *McBroom the Rainmaker;* Mark Twain Award from the Missouri Association of School Libraries, and Charlie May Simon Children's Book Award from the Arkansas Elementary School Council, both 1977, and Young Hoosier Award from the Association for Indiana Media Educators, 1979, all for *The Ghost on Saturday Night*; National Book Award finalist, and *Boston Globe-Horn Book* Award for Fiction, both 1979, both for *Humbug Mountain.*

Newbery Medal from the American Library Association, and selected one of Child Study Association of America Children's Books of the Year, both 1987, both for *The Whipping Boy;* Paul A. Witty Award from the International Reading Association, and Children's Picturebook Award from *Redbook,* both 1988, both for *The Scarebird.*

WRITINGS:

JUVENILE

Mr. Mysterious and Company (*Horn Book* honor list; Junior Literary Guild selection; illustrated by Eric von Schmidt), Atlantic-Little, Brown, 1962.
By the Great Horn Spoon! (Junior Literary Guild selection; illustrated by E. von Schmidt), Atlantic-Little, Brown, 1963, published as *Bullwhip Griffin,* Avon, 1967.
The Ghost in the Noonday Sun (Junior Literary Guild selection; illustrated by Warren Chappell), Atlantic-Little, Brown, 1965, new edition (illustrated by Peter Sis), Greenwillow, 1989.
McBroom Tells the Truth (illustrated by Kurt Werth), Norton, 1966, new edition (illustrated by W. Lorraine), Atlantic-Little, Brown, 1981.

Chancy and the Grand Rascal (*Horn Book* honor list; illustrated by E. von Schmidt), Atlantic-Little, Brown, 1966.

McBroom and the Big Wind (illustrated by K. Werth), Norton, 1967, new edition (illustrated by W. Lorraine), Atlantic-Little, Brown, 1982.

McBroom's Ear (illustrated by K. Werth), Norton, 1969, new edition (illustrated by W. Lorraine), Atlantic-Little, Brown, 1982.

Longbeard the Wizard (Junior Literary Guild selection; illustrated by Charles Bragg), Atlantic-Little, Brown, 1970.

Jingo Django (ALA Notable Book; Junior Literary Guild selection; illustrated by E. von Schmidt), Atlantic-Little, Brown, 1971.

McBroom's Ghost (illustrated by Robert Frankenberg), Grosset, 1971, new edition (illustrated by W. Lorraine), Atlantic-Little, Brown, 1981.

McBroom's Zoo (illustrated by K. Werth), Grosset, 1972, new edition (illustrated by W. Lorraine), Atlantic-Little, Brown, 1982.

The Wooden Cat Man (illustrated by Jay Yang), Atlantic-Little, Brown, 1972.

McBroom's Wonderful One-Acre Farm (includes *McBroom Tells the Truth, McBroom and the Big Wind,* and *McBroom's Ghost;* illustrated by Quentin Blake), Chatto & Windus, 1972.

McBroom the Rainmaker (illustrated by K. Werth), Grosset, 1973, new edition (illustrated by W. Lorraine), Atlantic-Little, Brown, 1982.

The Ghost on Saturday Night (illustrated by E. von Schmidt), Atlantic-Little, Brown, 1974.

Mr. Mysterious's Secrets of Magic (illustrated by E. von Schmidt), Atlantic-Little, Brown, 1975, published as *Secrets of Magic,* Chatto & Windus, 1976.

McBroom Tells a Lie (Junior Literary Guild selection; illustrated by W. Lorraine), Atlantic-Little, Brown, 1976.

Here Comes McBroom (includes *McBroom Tells a Lie, McBroom the Rainmaker,* and *McBroom's Zoo;* illustrated by Q. Blake), Chatto & Windus, 1976.

Kate's Secret Riddle Book, F. Watts, 1977.

Me and the Man on the Moon-Eyed Horse (Junior Literary Guild selection; illustrated by E. von Schmidt), Atlantic-Little, Brown, 1977, published in England as *The Man on the Moon-Eyed Horse,* Gollancz, 1980.

Humbug Mountain (Junior Literary Guild selection; illustrated by E. von Schmidt), Atlantic-Little, Brown, 1978.

Jim Bridger's Alarm Clock and Other Tall Tales (illustrated by E. von Schmidt), Dutton, 1978.

McBroom and the Beanstalk (Junior Literary Guild selection; illustrated by W. Lorraine), Atlantic-Little, Brown, 1978.

The Hey Hey Man (illustrated by Nadine Bernard Westcott), Atlantic-Little, Brown, 1979.

McBroom and the Great Race (Junior Literary Guild selection; illustrated by W. Lorraine), Atlantic-Little, Brown, 1980.

The Bloodhound Gang in the Case of the Flying Clock (illustrated by William Harmuth), Random House/Children's Television Workshop, 1981.

The Case of the Crackling Ghost (illustrated by Anthony Rao), Random House, 1981.

The Case of Princess Tomorrow (illustrated by Bill Morrison), Random House, 1981.

The Case of the Secret Message (illustrated by W. Harmuth), Random House, 1981.

The Case of the 264-Pound Burglar (illustrated by B. Morrison), Random House, 1982.

McBroom's Almanac (illustrated by W. Lorraine), Atlantic-Little, Brown, 1984.

The Whipping Boy (illustrated by P. Sis), Greenwillow, 1986.

The Scarebird (*Horn Book* honor list; illustrated by P. Sis), Greenwillow, 1988.

ADULT NOVELS

The Straw Donkey Case, Phoenix Press, 1948.
Murder's No Accident, Phoenix Press, 1949.
Shanghai Flame, Gold Medal, 1951.
Look Behind You Lady, Gold Medal, 1952, published in England as *Chinese Crimson,* Jenkins, 1962.
Danger in Paradise, Gold Medal, 1953.
Counterspy Express, Ace Books, 1954.
Malay Woman, Gold Medal, 1954, published as *Malaya Manhunt,* Jenkins, 1965.
Blood Alley, Gold Medal, 1955.
Yellowleg, Gold Medal, 1960.
The Venetian Blonde, Gold Medal, 1963.

OTHER

Between Cocktails, Abbott Magic Company, 1939.
(Contributor) Paul Heins, editor, *Crosscurrents of Criticism,* Horn Book, 1977.

SCREENPLAYS

"Goodbye, My Lady" (based on a novel by James Street), 1956.
(With William A. Wellman) "Lafayette Escadrille," 1958.
(With Albert Maltz) "Scalawag," starring Kirk Douglas, Byrna Productions, 1973.

Fleischman's books have been translated into sixteen languages.

ADAPTATIONS:

MOTION PICTURES

(Also author of screenplay) "Blood Alley," starring John Wayne and Lauren Bacall, Batjal Productions, 1955.
(Also author of screenplay) "The Deadly Companions" (based on *Yellowleg*), starring Maureen O'Hara, Carousel Productions, 1961.
"Bullwhip Griffin" (based on *By the Great Horn Spoon!*), Walt Disney, 1967.
"The Ghost in the Noonday Sun," starring Peter Sellers, Cavalcade Films, 1974.

WORK IN PROGRESS: Original screenplay for an animated feature musical, based on characters created by Don Freeman, entitled "Corduroy," for New Visions Pictures.

SIDELIGHTS: Born on **March 16, 1920,** in Brooklyn, New York, Fleischman grew up in San Diego. His father's storytelling influenced his early years.

After graduating from high school, Fleischman travelled with vaudeville and night club acts, perfecting his sleight-of-hand tricks. But shows like these were disappearing rapidly. Fleischman's son, Paul, himself a writer of children's books and a Newbery Award winner, later described this time in his father's life: "I suspect that this stage experience influenced his writing methods as well. He's an improviser and likes to keep himself as interested and in the dark about what's going to happen next as his readers. When he sits down at the typewriter in this silent study, he might as well be a comic stepping on stage in a noisy nightclub, trying to get a read on his audience, always thinking on his feet.

"My father's specialty in magic is sleight of hand. No birthday party was complete without a few tricks; likewise, these days, no school visit, when my father, reenacting his past, takes his act on the road each spring and fall. This style of magic is

"Hey Hey Man," he called softly. "You up there, neighbor?" (From *The Hey Hey Man* by Sid Fleischman. Illustrated by Nadine Bernard Westcott.)

Stored up laughter would pour out his sleeve and keep him awake nights. (From *McBroom Tells the Truth* by Sid Fleischman. Illustrated by Kurt Werth.)

(Fleischman co-wrote the screenplay for the movie "Scalawag." Starring Kirk Douglas, it was released in 1973.)

reflected in his writing. When he gave up being a professional magician, he became instead a prestidigitator of words, palming plot elements, making villains vanish, producing solutions out of thin air. He knows how to keep an audience guessing, how to create suspense, how to keep readers reading. A sleight-of-hand artist must be skilled at misdirection, keeping his audience's eyes away from the real action. My father is a master at doing the same with words, stealthily slipping in a clue, unnoticed by the reader, that will reappear in the book's climax, just as he used to miraculously pull nickels and dimes out of our ears."[1]

1941-1945. During World War II, Fleischman served in the U.S. Naval Reserve on a destroyer escort in the Philippines, Borneo, and China. On January 25, 1942, he married Betty Taylor. They have three children: Jane, Paul, and Anne.

1948. After the war, Fleischman published his first adult book, *The Straw Donkey Case*. "When I knew very little about writing, I wrote very fast. I once did a mystery novel in three weeks. I couldn't do that today. . . .I will rewrite each page until I think it is as good as I can make it before going on to the next. On some days I will get only one page of work finished; on other days, five or six."[2]

1949-1955. Fleischman graduated with a B.A. from San Diego State College and began his writing career as a reporter for the San Diego *Daily Journal* and soon after became associate editor of *Point* magazine in San Diego until 1951 when he

turned to writing full time. His first books were adult mysteries. In 1955 he began a continuing career as a screenwriter when his novel *Blood Alley* was adapted to film.

1962. Fleischman published his first juvenile book, *Mr. Mysterious and Company*, which won *New York Herald Tribune*'s Spring Book Award that year. "I have always wanted to write a book for children, but only after many years of professional writing did I find the courage. It is an axiom among magicians that youngsters are harder to fool than adults. The storyteller and the magician, I have found, have a great deal in common."[3]

1965. An interest in folklore and history prompted the writing of *The Ghost in the Noonday Sun*. For this story, he drew upon the folklore belief that people born at the stroke of midnight were able to see ghosts. "While my books rarely draw upon direct personal experience, I catch ghostly glimpses of my presence on almost every page. The stories inevitably reveal my interests and enthusiasms—my taste for the comic in life, my love of adventure, the seductions (for me) of the nineteenth-century American frontier, and my enchantment with the folk speech of that period. Language is a wondrous toy and I have great literary fun with it.

"Since I don't plot my stories in advance, the experience of writing a book is, for me, very much the same as reading a book. I rarely know what is going to happen next and have to sit at the typewriter to find out. My starting point is almost always a background, such as the California gold rush in *By the Great Horn Spoon!* or the age of piracy in *The Ghost in the Noonday Sun*. On other occasions I begin with an idea for a character: the magician in *Mr. Mysterious and Company,* for example, or a mid-West teller of tall tales as in the McBroom stories."[5]

Most of Fleischman's books are carefully researched and his style is characterized by grandiloquence, hyperbole, exaggeration, and humor. "I am a strong advocate of humor in children's books, which in the past has been regarded as something from the wrong side of the literary tracks. I am delighted to see a growing critical acceptance for this genre. . . .It amazes me that I have written ten McBroom tall tales. . . .It was never my intention to go beyond the first book (*McBroom Tells the Truth*), but a new idea seems to crop up every year or so—an irresistible notion. Sequels can be a treacherous enterprise, for the quality and spontaneity of the first may slip away. I feel that I have been uncommonly fortunate in that McBroom's vitality will not be downed and sees him through from book to book. Nevertheless, I tell myself that each new McBroom tale is *positively* the last—until the next irresistible idea makes a liar of me."[6]

1977. Wrote *Me and the Man on the Moon-Eyed Horse* for the sheer fun of it. "It transforms beyond recognition a frightning experience I had, age sixteen, when a cousin and I were camping on the Arizona desert. A wind sprang up in the night and we were awakened by the sound of man or beast, we didn't know which, crackling through the dry desert growth in our direction. Thump, crackle, thump! Not even the brisk wind could flatten my hair standing on end. And then, as the monster seemed almost upon us in the pale starlight—we saw it. A couple of huge tumbleweeds bouncing along. How powerful imagination can be!

"Later I learned that tumbleweed races were a boyish pastime, which I used in the story, but it was that scary night that really got me thinking about the huge thistles as story material, and gave me the setting. Then, with the comic notion of a character who could clack his teeth in Morse code, I sat down at the typewriter to see what would happen. I never plot a story in advance. A notion or two, a character or two and I'm off. **1979.** Fleischman's *Humbug Mountain* was nominated for the National Book Award and won the *Boston Globe-Horn Book* Award. "*Humbug Mountain* expresses the universal interplay of illusion and reality in our lives— especially in children's lives—though I hadn't the faintest notion that was what I was writing about until the book was finished, and I read it. Don't be too surprised. If novelists really knew what they were doing, they wouldn't be writers. They stumble about in the dark with some sort of internal ouija board sending up messages.

"I was lured into writing *Humbug Mountain* by two words—the title. There stands a real Humbug Mountain in the state of Oregon. I can't explain why the look and sound of those words excited my imagination, but they did. *Humbug* suggested to me a mountain that wasn't really there. And *that* suggested flat scenery—a horizon line that looked drawn with a T square. Oregon simply wouldn't do. With a stroke of the typewriter I moved my mountain to the Great Plains. What majestic powers are available to the novelist!

"Now I had my locale, a sense of place. I had no story, but it would not be fair to say I had no ideas. There were several composting for years in my mind. Perhaps I could adapt a true incident in which a river that defined the borders of two states jumped its banks and gerrymandered a saloon from wet Missouri to bone-dry Kansas. And I had long been interested in the brawling personal journalism of the frontier, with its itinerant printers and raffish newspapermen. My main characters began to emerge. I had enough to begin with, and I typed out page one, chapter one.

"Before long the American myth of the Fool Killer entered the story along with the historic hoax of a petrified man and an enterprising gent selling asbestos-lined coffins to sinners. These were all accidentals during the creative process, and all mysteriously shared the dual themes of illusion—and death. How very clever of me! What economy of symbolism! Except that I was out to lunch at the time, as usual.

"*Humbug Mountain* was a colicky manuscript. Its distresses, its howlings and yowlings, kept me walking the floor. I got my characters into jams and then was unable to find ways to get them out. I took wrong turnings. Story elements wouldn't fit together. Sentences wouldn't write. Paragraphs wouldn't flow. I shelved the mess half-a-dozen times and began to feel a professional rage.

"I had already written a number of novels, and I should have known how it is done. Eudora Welty said in a television interview that a story teaches her how to write that one but not how to write the next one.

"Quite obviously, I did learn how to write *Humbug Mountain*. From the two words that became the title to the last page, I was occupied for three years."[7]

In **1987** Fleischman won the prestigious Newbery Medal for *The Whipping Boy*. "I stumbled across the catapulting idea for *The Whipping Boy* while researching historical materials for another project. I checked the dictionary. 'A boy,' it confirmed, 'educated with a prince and punished in his stead.'

"After about eighteen months, I was still trying to get to the bottom of page five."[4]

He was trying to impose a picture-book length on the story. "Once I took the shackles off, the story erupted. Scenes, incidents, and characters came tumbling out of a liberated imagination. Within a few months I had it all on paper. Susan Hirschman, that gem of an editor, accepted it overnight. Peter Sis delivered his exquisite illustrations. Ava Weiss conceived the beautiful book design."[4]

Then Fleischman was notified that "a book I had struggled with for almost ten years had won the Newbery Medal.

"I don't happen to believe in levitation, unless it's done with mirrors, but for the next few days I had to load my pockets with ballast. The Newbery Medal is an enchantment. It's bliss. It should happen to everyone."[4]

FOOTNOTE SOURCES

[1] Paul Fleischman, "Sid Fleischman," *Horn Book,* July/August, 1987.

[2] "Sid Fleischman," *Something about the Author,* Volume 8, Gale, 1983.

[3] S. Fleischman, from the book jacket of *Mr. Mysterious and Company,* Atlantic-Little, Brown, 1962.

[4] Sid Fleischman, "Newbery Medal Acceptance," *Horn Book,* July/August, 1987.

[5] "Sid Fleischman," *Twentieth-Century Children's Writers,* edited by D. L. Kirkpatrick, St. Martin's 1978.

[6] "Sid Fleischman," *Contemporary Authors New Revision Series,* Volume 5, Gale, 1982. Amended by S. Fleischman.

[7] S. Fleischman, "*Humbug Mountain,*" *Horn Book,* February, 1980.

He sat on the front porch playing his nickle-plated harmonica. (From *The Scarebird* by Sid Fleischman. Illustrated by Peter Sis.)

FOR MORE INFORMATION SEE:

Junior Literary Guild Catalogue, February, 1962, March, 1971.

John Rowe Townsend, *Written for Children: An Outline of English Language Children's Literature,* Horn Book, 1965, revised edition, Lippincott, 1974.

Eleanor Cameron, *The Green and Burning Tree,* Atlantic-Little, Brown, 1969.

Horn Book, April, 1970 (p. 157), August, 1971 (p. 383), December, 1971 (p. 605), February, 1973 (p. 43), August, 1974 (p. 379), October, 1976 (p. 465ff), February, 1980 (p. 94ff), May/June, 1988, September/October, 1988.

Doris de Montreville and Donna Hill, editors, *Third Book of Junior Authors,* H. W. Wilson, 1972.

Cricket, April, 1976 (p. 30).

Publishers Weekly, February 27, 1978 (p. 87ff), January 30, 1987 (p. 292), June 27, 1988.

Language Arts, October, 1982 (p. 754ff).

Jon Tuska and Vicki Pickarski, *Encyclopedia of Frontier and Western Fiction,* McGraw, 1983.

Wilson Library Bulletin, April, 1987 (p. 48).

"Meet the Newbery Author: Sid Fleischman" (videocassette, filmstrip), Pied Piper, 1987.

School Library Journal, May, 1988, August, 1988 (p. 63), September, 1988 (p. 158), November, 1988.

COLLECTIONS

Kerlan Collection at the University of Minnesota.

FORD, Peter 1936-

PERSONAL: Born June 3, 1936, in Harpenden, Hertfordshire, England; son of Fletcher Calvert (an accounts clerk) and Muriel (a housewife; maiden name, Mayo-Smith) Ford; married Laura Geeve (a teacher), August 28, 1960 (divorced); children: Piers, Julian, Isabel. *Education:* Attended school in Harpenden, England. *Politics:* "Green." *Religion:* Buddhist. *Home and office:* 42 Friars St., Sudbury, Suffolk CO10 6AG, England. *Agent:* David Grossman, 110-114 Clerkenwell Rd., London EC1M 5SA, England.

CAREER: Cassell & Co., London, England, assistant editor, 1957-61, Penguin Books, Harmondsworth, and Middlesex, England, senior copy editor, 1961-65; Nelson & Sons, London, senior editor, 1965-71; free-lance writer and editor, 1971—. Consultant to Quartet Books, 1972—, and Plantin Paper Backs, 1987—. *Military service:* British Army, lance bombardier in Royal Artillery, 1955-56; served in Malaya. *Member:* Society of Authors, Royal Commonwealth Society, Folklore Society, Eastern Arts Association.

WRITINGS:

(With Franz Bergel and D. R. A. Davies) *All about Drugs,* T. Nelson, 1970.
(With Max Wall) *The Fool on the Hill,* Quartet Books, 1975.
(With Feliks Topolski) *Topolski's Buckingham Palace Panoramas,* Quartet Books, 1977.
(With Anthony Feldman) *Scientists and Inventors,* Aldus Books, 1979.
(Translator with Kenneth Mitchell) Julius Braunthal, *History of the International: World Socialism, 1943- 1968,* Gollancz, 1980.
(With Michael Howell) *The True History of the Elephant Man,* Penguin, 1980, new edition, Allison & Busby, 1990, another revised edition published as *The Illustrated True History of the Elephant Man,* Penguin, 1983.
The Elephant Man: Retold for Children (illustrated by Robert Geary), Allison & Busby, 1983, Schocken, 1984.
(With M. Howell) *The Beetle of Aphrodite and Other Medical Mysteries,* Random House, 1985, reissued as *The Ghost Disease and Twelve Other Stories of Detective Work in the Medical Field,* Penguin, 1986 (published in England as *Medical Mysteries,* Viking, 1985).
(With John Fisher) *The Picture Buyer's Handbook,* Harrap, 1988.

WORK IN PROGRESS: A book on "future history."

SIDELIGHTS: "Since becoming a full-time freelancer in 1971, I have tended to specialize in co-authorship and to use my editorial skills in assignments on texts that need a degree of special attention or that require a sensitive·application of the invisible editorial hand to make them publishable. Over the years, I have therefore worked on several hundred books, with a

PETER FORD

wide range of London publishers and with authors or would-be authors from a great variety of backgrounds. I have never had a specialist subject *per se.* I have also, through our local regional arts association, Eastern Arts, presented talks and creative writing workshops in schools and other institutions. I am, however, now at the difficult transitional stage where I want to devote more time and energy to my own writing, which means, in turn, some acts of faith and a certain amount of disentangling from the guarantees of fee-paying commissions. We shall see.

"My dog, Max, ensures my life does not become too sedentary. He insists on taking me for at least an hour's walk over our Suffolk meadows in the middle of each day. For leisure, my focus is on theater, cinema, and music, with an interest in amateur drama from time to time."

FORSEY, Chris 1950-

PERSONAL: Born April 5, 1950, in London, England; son of Harold (a factory manager) and Doreen (a homemaker; maiden name, Spillett) Forsey; married Judy Garlick (a book editor), September, 1983; children: Jack, Charlotte. *Education:* Bower Ashton College of Art, diploma in art and education, 1974. *Politics:* "Green." *Religion:* Church of England. *Home and office:* 7 Howard Rd., Dorking, Surrey RH4 3HR, England.

CAREER: NDH Advertising, Bristol, England, advertising trainee, 1968; Health Department Tower Hill Clinic, Bristol, clerk, 1969-71; Mitchell Beazley Publisher, London, England, studio illustrator, 1974-81; free-lance illustrator, 1981—. *Member:* Friends of the Earth.

ILLUSTRATOR

(With others) *Joy of Knowledge,* Mitchell Beazley, 1976.
(Contributor) *International Book of Wood,* Mitchell Beazley, 1977.
Atlas of the Oceans, Mitchell Beazley, 1978.
The Forest, Mitchell Beazley, 1979.
The Great Geographical Atlas, Mitchell Beazley, 1980.
Atlas of the Solar System, Mitchell Beazley, 1981.
(With others) David Lambert, *Dinosaurs,* F. Watts (England), 1982.
(With others) David Jefferis, *Robots,* F. Watts, 1982.
(With Jim Robins) Angela Grunsell, *The Four Seasons,* F. Watts, 1983.
(With others) Martyn Harmer, *Cats,* F. Watts, 1983.
(With others) Dougal Dixon, *Geology,* F. Watts, 1983.
(With J. Robins and others) Gordon Jackson, *Medicine,* F. Watts, 1984.
(With others) D. Dixon, *Geography,* F. Watts, 1984.
(With others) Ifor Evans, *Biology,* F. Watts, 1984.
(With others) Robin McKie, *Technology,* F. Watts, 1984.
(With others) Michael Jay, *Space Shuttle,* F. Watts, 1984.
(With others) Boulton, *Trees,* F. Watts, 1984.
(With others) Pope, *Insects,* F. Watts, 1984.
(With others) Boulton, *Birds,* F. Watts, 1984.
(With others) Leutscher, *Flowering Plants,* F. Watts, 1984.
(With others) Pope, *Seashore,* F. Watts, 1984.
A. Grunsell, *At the Doctor,* F. Watts, 1984.
John Stidworthy, *The Day of the Dinosaurs,* Silver Burdett, 1986.
J. Stidworthy, *The Human Ape,* MacDonald, 1986.
J. Stidworthy, *Mighty Mammals of the Past,* Silver Burdett, 1986.
J. Stidworthy, *Life Begins,* Silver Burdett, 1986.
J. Stidworthy, *When Humans Began,* Silver Burdett, 1986.

D. Savage, *The Adventures of Peregine Piecrust*, Grafton, 1986.

(With Mike Saunders) Kate Petty, *Submarines*, F. Watts, 1986.

K. Petty, *Trucks*, F. Watts, 1987.

J. Stidworthy, Walter Kossman and Joanne Fink, editors, *Creatures from the Past*, Silver Burdett, 1987.

A. J. Wood, *An Elephant Comes to Breakfast*, Macdonald, 1987.

A. J. Wood, *There's a Whale in My Bath*, Macdonald, 1987.

A. J. Wood, *There's a Bear in My Bed*, Macdonald, 1987.

A. J. Wood, *There's a Panda in the Pantry*, Macdonald, 1987.

D. Dixon, *Fossil Detective*, Macmillan, 1988.

The Book of Bears, Crown, 1990.

Contributor of illustrations to *International Book of Wood* published by Mitchell Beazley, 1977.

WORK IN PROGRESS: GAIA Atlas of Planet Management; a children's dinosaur book; a children's history series on architectural reconstructions; an encyclopedia for Guinness Publishing; an atlas of wine; watercolor landscapes for an exhibition.

SIDELIGHTS: "I always loved drawing, but decided to embark on a design career as this seemed the best course to train one for a job. I completed a three-year graphics course and on leaving college was offered a job as a studio illustrator with Mitchell Beazley Publishing. I struggled for the next year learning on the job all the things I should have learned in the illustration course at college.

"Airbrush became a specialty for awhile, even though I didn't really enjoy the process of achieving the result (and still don't in many ways—all that laborious mask cutting!!). But I used to be given the Friday afternoon (deadline day) task of correcting and altering, patching and redoing other people's artwork and this gave me marvellous insights into other people's styles and techniques.

"I still do a lot of airbrush work, mostly for advertising and illustrations for video pack covers, but tend to use it combined with watercolour and gouache as I find pure airbrush tends to make things look too plastic and smooth.

"Working at Mitchell Beazley also gave me the opportunity to 'dabble' in all sorts of subjects and so I was never really pidgeon-holed as an artist. My work, for this reason, has tended to be wide-ranging and various. More and more involvement in children's book work has tended to loosen up my tendency towards the photographic and I now run the two styles of ultra realism with a globby watercolour approach reasonably happily side by side.

"Having a variety of styles up my sleeve and always being ready to experiment has kept me busy most of the time since going free-lance nine years ago. It's the variety that also keeps me interested as, I think, to be continually working in one style would, for me, soon become tedious.

"Delivering work on time, being flexible on price and versatile in style seems to be the way to keep employed.

"I've recently taken up watercolour painting as a hobby and although it is not as lucrative as commercial work at present, it has proved to be quite a successful sideline. The ideal situation would be one where the mix was fifty/fifty between commercial art and painting. I had a painting accepted for the 1989 Royal Institute of Watercolour Annual Exhibition—this giving me confidence to spend more time on the painting side of my work

as it is a bit prestigious to have a painting accepted by this group. I have also produced some work for British Gas—a calendar depicting historic bridges in the southeast of England. These paintings have also been reproduced as greeting cards.

"My interest in 'Green' matters has led to involvement in Friends of the Earth. A recent exhibition of children's paintings, arranged by myself and other Friends of the Earth, proved most interesting. The naivety of their drawing is wonderful, but the message is plain to see as they draw parrots and tigers saying 'Help—the forest is dying.' My involvement in projects for GAIA books, who concentrate mostly on 'Green' publications has also heightened my interest in doing work that could have some influence on the way we live. The thing that worries me is that all these books use paper—and where does the paper come from? Recycling, re-use, and economy of resource must be the answer.

"Photography is an interest that I've kept up, although mostly as a source of reference (along with my sketches) for my paintings, but I still get a thrill from capturing the play of light on a landscape—although it can take nearly as much time and sweat to get a good photo as it does to do a watercolour painting."

HOBBIES AND OTHER INTERESTS: "As an ex-member of a rock band, I still enjoy playing the guitar and harmonica."

FRIEDMAN, Judi 1935-

PERSONAL: Born November 13, 1935, in Milwaukee, Wis.; daughter of Roland Spuhler (a physician) and Florence (a homemaker; maiden name, Schroeder) Cron; married Louis A. Friedman (a former headmaster), December 28, 1957; children: Kimberly, Dana, Seth. *Education:* Vassar College, B.S., 1957; also attended St. Joseph's College, New York University, and Stanford University. *Politics:* Liberal Democrat. *Religion:* "All." *Home and office:* 101 Lawton Rd., Canton, Conn. 06019.

CAREER: Writer. Elementary school teacher in Canton, Conn., 1958-63. President of Canton Educational Research Committee; member of board of directors of Canton Community Kindergarten and Trinity Episcopal Church Nursery School. Vice-president of Canton Land Trust; volunteer worker for Republican Party Minorities Division and Day Care Center for Minority Working Mothers; founder and chairperson of People's Action for Clean Energy. *Awards, honors:* Energy Innovation Award from the State of Connecticut; Award from the American Association of the Advancement of Science and the Children's Book Council, 1974, for *The Eel's Strange Journey;* Award from the American Camping Association magazine, 1988, for an article on peaceful conflict resolution; Governor's Award for Environmental Merit, 1989.

WRITINGS:

The Story of Connecticut, privately printed, 1960.

(Editor with L. K. Porritt) *Tales of Early Life in Connecticut*, privately printed, 1960.

Jelly Jam, the People Preserver (self-illustrated elementary school text; with teacher's guide), Educational Methods, 1972, second edition, 1983.

The ABC of a Summer Pond (juvenile; illustrated with photographs by John Dommers), Johnny Reads, 1975.

The Biting Book (juvenile), Prentice-Hall, 1975.

The Eel's Strange Journey (juvenile; illustrated by Gail Owens), Crowell, 1975.
Noises in the Woods (illustrated by John Hamberger), Dutton, 1979.

Author of environmental television commercials, for Communications Specialists; author of environmental articles.

WORK IN PROGRESS: Siberian Cranes, symbols of peace.

SIDELIGHTS: Friedman writes that her concern for the environment focuses on "alternate energy (sun, wind, wood)" and that she is "violently opposed to nuclear energy." She adds that she believes in "racial equality, children's rights. I want a further understanding of each other, of earth, and of all creatures who inhabit the earth.

"I am especially interested in peace work, having actively participated in six Soviet-American peace missions. My latest book concerns a Soviet-American environmental project about the endangered Siberian crane."

HOBBIES AND OTHER INTERESTS: The outdoors, sports, animals, European and Caribbean travel.

FOR MORE INFORMATION SEE:

Authors in the News, Volume 2, Gale, 1976.

GILMORE, Susan 1954-

PERSONAL: Born September 17, 1954, in Phoenix, Ariz.; daughter of John H. and Marcia (Stransky) Gilmore; married John Paul Lauenstein (a commercial photographer), August 22, 1982. *Education:* University of Nebraska, B.A., 1976; Brooks Institute of Photography, B.A., 1979. *Home:* Minneapolis, Minn. *Office:* 8415 Wesley Dr., Minneapolis, Minn. 55427.

CAREER: Commercial photographer, 1980—. *Member:* American Society of Magazine Photographers.

WRITINGS:

What Goes on at a Radio Station? (self-illustrated with photographs), Carolrhoda, 1984.

Photographs have appeared in many magazines and books.

WORK IN PROGRESS: Commercial photography.

SIDELIGHTS: "I was born in Phoenix, Arizona and raised in Omaha, Nebraska. My interest in radio and in photojournalism made it possible to write and photograph *What Goes on at a Radio Station.* I was able to spend as much time as I needed to follow any one of my choosing at the radio station in order to interview and photograph. I had pages of notes and stacks of proof sheets which I had to edit a great deal in order to tell the story.

"For the past six years I have been doing photography for magazines (local and national), architects, interior designers, advertising agencies, and builders. My photography is mostly architectural but I also photograph people for some publications.

"In doing the radio book, not only did I need to be aware of the photography and good shots, I also had to keep my ears open for comments and quotes for the text. Plus I was in the process of learning about radio stations myself."

HOBBIES AND OTHER INTERESTS: Running, sailing, gardening.

HARRIS, Larry Vincent 1939-

PERSONAL: Born January 20, 1939, in Carnduff, Saskatchewan, Canada; son of Ray Arnold (a farmer) and Blanche (a post mistress; maiden name, Ray) Harris; married Betty Lou Pluim (a homemaker), April 7, 1967; children: Mark Cameron, Kane Bruce, Morgan Gareth. *Education:* University of Alberta, B.Ed., 1965, B.A., 1967; London School of Economics, certificate, 1973. *Politics:* Social Democrat. *Religion:* Christian. *Home and office:* Rivendell Farm, R.R.1, Wetaskiwin, Alberta, Canada T9A 1W8.

CAREER: School administrator and teacher; writer, 1980—. Has held various jobs around the world including weatherman and as an extra in a Japanese movie made in Tokyo. Chairman of Battle Lake Community Church, 1988—. *Member:* Alberta Writers Guild, Alliance of Canadian Cinema, Television and Radio Artists, Alberta Stock Dog Association (director, 1986—.) *Awards, honors:* Honorable Mention from the Alberta Writers Guild, 1985, for *Escape to Honour.*

WRITINGS:

(With Brian Taylor) *Escape to Honour: The Gripping True Story of Hans Nutt, a Young German Who Escaped from the Nazis to Join the French Resistance and Work as a British Spy,* Macmillan of Canada, 1984.
"Etsay Birds" (one-half hour drama), CBC-TV, 1989.

WORK IN PROGRESS: The Southampton Incident, and *The Second Hook,* adult fiction; *Hang in There, Curzon Kids,* junior fiction; "The Daisy Man"; "Unfinished Business," a one-hour screenplay; "Butcher, Baker, Candlestick Maker," and "Night Flight," feature films; *Making the Golden Years Golden,* a nonfiction seniors' survival guide; *An Affair of Honor,* with Brian Taylor; a sequel to *Escape to Honour,* which deals with the post World War II experiences of Hans Nutt as an anti-Soviet agent in East Germany; newspaper and magazine articles.

SIDELIGHTS: "I only wish I'd had the confidence to begin writing sooner, and my advice to any would-be author is to TRY and TRY AGAIN, starting NOW! In my teens and twenties I worked in the Arctic and hitchhiked abroad, visiting a total of sixty countries around the world. Those experiences, coupled with my education and work in various other places have provided me with inspiration and material for a dozen or more writing projects I want to do. The problem is finding the time and energy when I have a family to support. However, I am confident the big break will come now that I've found the courage to try and keep trying.

"My writing is eclectic, which I see as both a strength and a weakness. Probably doing one sort of writing would make me more of an expert in that field, but I see different themes and projects as more suitable to one medium or age group than others, and so far I have just followed my nose about what to write next. A big success in one area would probably focus my attention wonderfully!

"All worthwhile writing carries a message about some aspect of the human condition, which should lead at least a few readers to some greater self understanding, or understanding of others. Obviously it must not be heavily didactic but if it can provoke a sense of curiosity, amusement, or wonder, the reader will be enticed to think about the subject matter and arrive at his or her own conclusions. In an imperfect, pluralistic, and democratic society that is the best we can hope for. It is only by the creation of generations of free thinkers that our liberal societies can stay alive and serve to encourage others to also think for themselves.

"Certainly when I sit down to write I don't consciously think of a message or theme first and write the story after. The process is the opposite. A writer instinctively chooses first what is 'entertaining' in some sense of that word, and out of his or her subconscious builds in a particular vision which carries the message. I call that the writer's 'voice.'

"In the case of *Escape to Honour* I happened, by a wonderful set of chance circumstances, to meet Hans Nutt, the hero. When he told me his story I could hardly believe it. Hans had lived through incredible misadventures but had always stuck to his principles. Doing so almost cost him his life on several occasions. It was a story I just had to tell and I brought in a friend to help me.

"'Etsay Birds' came out of an experience in my Arctic teaching career. In a school I ran were two Inuit children who were being raised by an aged grandfather in difficult circumstances. He was old Josie who carved seagulls for a living. It was known that old Josie was ready to die, but because the children needed him, he was hanging on. This odd little family did succeed because of

LARRY VINCENT HARRIS

their love for one another. Their example was inspiring and the world needed to hear about it.

"'The Daisy Man' is a full-length screenplay of international drama and intrigue. Set in a frightening post-glasnost era, it describes a scenario in which the U.S. is about to elect its first woman president, while a hardline Soviet politburo plans a pre-emptive strike against Washington. To prevent this from happening there is an international plot to assassinate the U.S. president-elect. To save the West, its most important leader must be sacrificed. Only with her out of the way can a strongman vice-president take her place and restrike the balance of terror. 'The Daisy Man' is a provocative film which points out the urgency in meeting glasnost half way.

"From my world travels a multitude of characters and themes are tucked away in my diaries waiting to be set loose in books and stories. It's my hope to live long enough to do justice to them all.

"Other than writing and teaching I spend time in various ways with my family and run a little 125-acre farm. I am a jogger, and a trainer of my first Border Collie stock dog. (There's probably a story there, too.) Story ideas constantly pop into my mind, but that's the easy part. Getting them onto paper is a great deal harder. It is said that blank paper is God's way of telling writers it's not so easy to be God, and you'd better believe it.

"I have many other interests as well, but one life is just too darned short to get involved in them all. As yet, anyway."

HIGHAM, Jonathan Huw 1960-
(Jon Atlas Higham)

PERSONAL: Surname is pronounced *Hie*-am; born November 11, 1960, in Darwen, Lancashire, England; son of Joseph Gowen (a president of an abrasive company) and Joy (a housewife; maiden name, Nobes) Higham. *Education:* Norwich School of Art, B.A. (with honors), 1983. *Religion:* Church of England. *Home:* 28A Redcliffe Sq., London S.W.10, England. *Agent:* Curtis Brown Ltd., 162-168 Regent St., London W1R 5TB, England. *Office:* 2 New Row, London WC2N 4LH, England.

CAREER: Free-lance illustrator, 1983—; author. *Exhibitions:* Brighton Museum, England, 1989.

WRITINGS:

"The Red Desk" (three-act play), first produced in Norwich, England, at Norwich School of Art, February 5, 1981.

UNDER PSEUDONYM JON ATLAS HIGHAM

Aardvark's Picnic (self-illustrated juvenile), Little, Brown, 1986.

ILLUSTRATOR; ALL UNDER PSEUDONYM JON ATLAS HIGHAM

Jeremy Nicholas, *Raspberries and Other Trifles,* Hutchinson, 1984.
Edward Lear, *The Old Man and the Edible Suit,* Macmillan, 1986.
Margaret Ryan, *The Little Cook,* Methuen, 1986.
Ross Francis, *Mick the Dog,* Macdonald, 1988.
Nursery Cats, Gollancz, 1990.

WORK IN PROGRESS: Writing and designing a series of young readers.

SIDELIGHTS: "I was born in 1960, just outside Darwen, in Lancashire, England, the fourth of five children. I come from an artistic family. My parents met at Manchester Art School, my brother is a professional water colorist, and my aunt is a professional writer.

"Due to my father's work in the abrasive industry, our family is now spread over the globe. A posting to France in 1971 and later to America in 1984 has left two sisters in France and one in America. My brother and I remained in England.

"I left Norwich School of Art in 1983 and moved down to London in search of work. Since then I have enjoyed increasing success each year as I have broadened the nature of my work. At present I am completing illustrations for a large series of educational books for Letts, and since being introduced to Gordon Fraser cards early last year, I have produced more than forty greeting cards. I have only written one children's book and instigated another. I have had numerous ideas for other children's books, but find writing a lot harder than drawing! Because of this, I decided to concentrate on illustration alone. I do wish to write again soon, but will not commence until I have a really inspired idea!"

HOBBIES AND OTHER INTERESTS: Computers, cricket, traveling.

HILLER, Ilo (Ann) 1938-

PERSONAL: Given name is pronounced *Eye*-low; born July 28, 1938, in Alexandria, Ind.; daughter of William H. (in sales) and stepdaughter of Dorothy L. (a housewife; maiden name, Baker) Porter; married James E. Hiller (an electrician), February 22, 1957; children: Jay Darrell. *Education:* Attended Durham's Business College, 1986. *Religion:* Protestant. *Home:* 5807 Avenue G, Austin, Tex. 78752. *Office:* Texas Parks and Wildlife Department, 4200 Smith School Rd., Austin, Tex. 78744.

CAREER: University of Texas at Austin, secretary, 1958-62; Texas Parks and Wildlife Department, Austin, magazine office manager, 1964-72, assistant editor of *Texas Parks and Wildlife*, 1972-74, associate editor, 1974-86, statewide coordinator of Project WILD, 1986—. *Member:* Texas Outdoor Writers Association, Texas Outdoor Education Association, Science Teachers Association of Texas. *Awards, honors:* Award of Excellence from the Texas Outdoor Writers Association, National Wildlife Federation's Recommended Nature Book for Young Readers, and Stephen F. Austin School of Forestry Piney Woods Conservation Center's Conservation Award, all 1984, all for *Young Naturalist;* Plaque from the Texas Association of Environmental Education, 1986, for "Recognition of Outstanding Contribution to Environmental Education"; Conservation Educator Award from the Sportsmen Conservationists of Texas, the National Wildlife Federation, and Texas Wildlife Foundation, 1986.

WRITINGS:

Young Naturalist: From Texas Parks and Wildlife Magazine (juvenile), Texas A & M University Press, 1983.
Introducing Birds to Young Naturalists, Texas A & M University Press, 1989.

ILO HILLER

Contributor of more than two hundred articles to magazines. Contributing editor, *Texas Parks and Wildlife*, 1972—; regional field editor, *Hi-Way Herald*, 1984-87.

WORK IN PROGRESS: A book series featuring the natural histories of animals—mammals, insects, reptiles and amphibians, and beach creatures, for young readers and adults.

SIDELIGHTS: "I am employed by the Texas Parks and Wildlife Department as the statewide coordinator of Project WILD, an interdisciplinary, supplementary environmental and conservation education program for educators of young people from kindergarten through high school. It has been my responsibility to establish the guidelines for implementing this educational program in Texas and to coordinate the teaching of Project WILD workshops throughout the state.

"I am also the author of *Young Naturalist*. This book is a collection of nature articles originally published in the *Texas Parks and Wildlife* magazine. The varied subjects were written for young readers who are interested in the outdoors. However, the contents also should appeal to those adults who will admit they still have some of their childhood curiosity. The book is an attempt to answer some of the 'Why, Daddy?' and 'Why, Mommy?' questions most children ask about nature, but for which too few receive answers. Some of these questions may remain unanswered even into adulthood."

HOBBIES AND OTHER INTERESTS: Needlecrafts, camping, reading.

HOFFMAN, Mary (Margaret) 1945-
(Mary Lassiter)

PERSONAL: Born April 20, 1945, in Hampshire, England; daughter of Origen Herman (a railway tele-communications inspector) and Ivegh (a homemaker; maiden name, Lassiter) Hoffman; married Stephen James Barber (a social worker), December 22, 1972; children: Sarah Rhiannon, Rebecca Imogen, Jessica Rowena. *Education:* Newham College, Cambridge, B.A., 1967; University College, London, postgraduate diploma in linguistics, 1970. *Politics:* Greeny. *Religion:* Anglo-Catholic. *Home:* 28 Crouch Hall Rd., London N8 8HJ, England. *Agent:* Pat White, Rogers, Coleridge & White, 20 Powis Mews, London W11, England.

CAREER: Free-lance journalist, 1972—; The Open University, Milton Keynes, England, lecturer in continuing education, 1975-80; reading consultant for British Broadcasting Corp. school television series "Look and Read," 1977—. *Member:* Society of Authors, National Union of Journalists, International Board on Books for Young People (Hans Andersen Medal Panelist, 1981, 1987), London Zoological Society (fellow). *Awards, honors: Nancy No-Size* was shortlisted for the Smarties Prize, 1987.

WRITINGS:

JUVENILE

White Magic, Rex Collings, 1975.
Buttercup Buskers' Rainy Day (illustrated by Margaret Chamberlain), Heinemann, 1982.
The Return of the Antelope (illustrated by Faith Jaques), Heinemann, 1985.
Whales and Sharks, Brimax Books, 1986.
Dangerous Animals, Brimax Books, 1986.
Beware, Princess! (illustrated by Chris Riddell), Heinemann, 1986.
The Second-Hand Ghost (illustrated by Eileen Browne), MMB/Deutsch, 1986.
King of the Castle (illustrated by Alan Marks), Hamish Hamilton, 1986.
A Fine Picnic (illustrated by Leon Baxter), Silver Burdett, 1986.
Animal Hide and Seek (illustrated by L. Baxter), Macdonald, 1986, Silver Burdett, 1987.
The Perfect Pet (illustrated by L. Baxter), Silver Burdett, 1986.
Clothes for Sale (illustrated by L. Baxter), Silver Burdett, 1986.
Nancy No-Size (illustrated by Jennifer Northway), Oxford University Press, 1987.
Specially Sarah (illustrated by Joanna Carey), Methuen, 1987.
My Grandma Has Black Hair (illustrated by Joanna Burroughes), Dial, 1988.
Dracula's Daughter (illustrated by C. Riddell), Heinemann, 1988.
Catwalk (illustrated by J. Burroughes), Methuen, 1989.
All about Lucy (illustrated by J. Carey), Methuen, 1989.
Min's First Jump (illustrated by John Rogan), Hamish Hamilton, 1989.
Mermaid and Chips (illustrated by Bernice McMullen), Heinemann, 1989.
Dog Powder (illustrated by Paul Warren), Heinemann, 1989.

"ANIMALS IN THE WILD" SERIES

Tiger, Belitha/Windward, 1983, Raintree, 1984, revised edition, Belitha/Methuen, 1988.
Monkey, Belitha/Windward, 1983, Raintree, 1985, revised edition, Belitha/Metheun, 1988.
Elephant, Belitha/Windward, 1983, Raintree, 1985, revised edition, Belitha/Methuen, 1988.
Panda, Belitha/Windward, 1983, Raintree, 1985, revised edition, Belitha/Methuen, 1988.
Lion, Raintree, 1985.
Zebra, Raintree, 1985.
Hippopotamus, Raintree, 1985.
Gorilla, Raintree, 1985.
Wild Cat, Raintree, 1986.
Giraffe, Raintree, 1986.
Snake, Raintree, 1986.
Bear, Raintree, 1986.
Wild Dog, Belitha/Methuen, 1987.
Seal, Raintree, 1987.
Antelope, Raintree, 1987.
Bird of Prey, Raintree, 1987.

ADULT

Reading, Writing and Relevance, Hodder & Stoughton, 1976.
(Under name Mary Lassiter) *Our Names, Our Selves,* Heinemann, 1983.
Deadly Letter (anthology), Collins, 1990.

MARY HOFFMAN

"Oh look, there's a zebra!" (From *Animal Hide and Seek* by Mary Hoffman. Illustrated by Leon Baxter.)

Contributor to *Times Educational Supplement*. Reviewer for *School Librarian, British Book News, Guardian,* and other periodicals. Monthly column in *Mother* magazine, 1984-87.

WORK IN PROGRESS: Writing teacher's notes and software user's guides for BBC-TV series "Look and Read"; *Fortune's Favours,* an adult historical romance; *My Grandpa Wears Blue Jeans,* a sequel to *My Grandma Has Black Hair;* picture books; a full-length novel for eight to eleven year olds.

SIDELIGHTS: "On my many visits to schools, children always ask me the same questions and I have been developing a series of stock answers. Why I am a writer is because it's the only thing I am good enough at to do professionally. I am very lucky to do for a job the thing that I enjoy most. I love everything to do with writing—from buying the paper to proof reading. I love reviews (even bad ones); royalty statements (even low ones); phone calls from publishers—everything. You know the way that some people are stage-struck? So much that they'll even make tea or find props? Well, I'm the same about books— page-struck, perhaps? I can never quite believe that this is what I am, this is really what I do and I am not making it up. It still surprises me every time I look at my bookcase that houses my titles.

"You may, by now, have noticed that this is more about *being* a writer than about writing. But fortunately, I do like this bit too. Dr. Johnson, who was prolific, knew himself to be terribly indolent. I am the same. I feel very lazy when I contemplate how much work a new book is going to take and I walk round my study humming or I make a cup of coffee or I decide to ring someone up. (I love ringing people up.)

"But most of my work goes on in my head while I'm on a bus or cooking or having a bath. So if I'm lucky, by the time I can force myself to sit down and start writing, the story comes quite easily.

"Where the ideas come from is very mysterious—when children ask me, I say it is magic. This is the most truthful answer I can manage.

"The only nonfiction I wrote for children is the series of sixteen books in the 'Animals in the Wild' series. These are sharply conservationist, and I do care very much about the way humans treat animals. (This is not the same as *not* caring about the way humans treat humans, by the way.) I am a vegetarian myself and have been for twenty years and I regard fur coats as an ultimate obscenity. The only animals I have are three highly individual Burmese cats. If we lived in the country we would have more.

"Fifteen years ago, I joined an early United Kingdom women's group looking at children's books and discovered them to be sexist, racist, ageist, and classist. In my own books I try for strong and memorable heroines (*Beware, Princess!, Dracula's Daughter*); children of mixed race (*Nancy No-Size*); children whose parents are not well off (*The Second-Hand Ghost*) and I think I may have written the first anti-ageist book (*My Grandma Has Black Hair*). But, I also try to be funny, lively, and linguistically inventive; propaganda is boring.

"When I'm not writing, I like to sing. I sing in a local choir which gives three or four concerts a year. Rehearsing is hard work and requires a lot of concentration. The result is that you can't think about your problems and rehearse properly. So you go home tired, but mentally refreshed.

"I also like cooking, eating, listening to the radio, doing the *Times* crossword, sun-bathing, detective stories, cats, green, buying pictures, and old roses.

"I *don't* like Muzac, blue, transistor radios in public places, crowds, light music, sport and alliterative cliches (strains and stresses, trials and tribulations, kith & kin).

"I do like lots of different kinds of music—Mozart and Messaien, Elvis Presley and Music Hall, Renaissance and Wagner, the Beatles, Benjamin Britten. My favourite writers are Dickens, Joyce, and Proust. I hardly read twentieth-century contemporaries but I love writers who can make me laugh—Malcolm Bradbury, William Cooper, Sue Limb. Can't stand Margaret Drabble or any writer whose purpose is to make the reader miserable (that goes for Flaubert, too)."

HOUSEHOLD, Geoffrey (Edward West) 1900-1988

OBITUARY NOTICE:—See sketch in *SATA* Volume 14. Born November 30, 1900, in Bristol, England; died October 4, 1988, near Banbury, England. Businessman, intelligence officer, and author. Household was an adventure novelist who wrote stories for both young readers and adults. He is best known for his 1939 thriller *Rogue Male,* which was made into a 1941 movie starring Walter Pidgeon and Joan Bennett. Inspired by the author's own wish to eliminate the threat of Nazi leader Adolf Hitler, the book depicts an English big-game hunter who tries to stalk and kill an unnamed European dictator. Household gleaned material for his stories from his own extensive travels. Leaving Oxford in the early 1920s, he worked as a confidential secretary in a bank in Rumania, then moved to Spain and a job with the United Fruit Company marketing bananas in that country as a diet staple for the poor. "I think I can actually say," he once declared, "that I introduced bananas to the masses in Spain." In 1929 he moved to New York City, where he worked briefly as a writer for an encyclopedia and composed children's radio plays for the Columbia Broadcasting System. He also wrote *The Spanish Cave,* an adventure book for children that drew on his experiences in Spain.

Still combining business with writing, Household travelled throughout the Middle East, Europe and South America as a salesman for an English ink manufacturer. During World War II Household had a busy career as a British intelligence officer, serving in Rumania, Greece, Palestine, Syria, and Iraq. Many of his experiences are recounted in his autobiograpy, *Against the Wind,* which was published in 1958. His other books include *The Third Hour, A Rough Shoot, Arrows of Desire,* and *Rogue Justice,* the sequel to *Rogue Male.* For children he wrote *The Exploits of Xenophon, Prisoner of the Indies,* as well as *The Spanish Cave,* and several collections of short stories. The only distinction he made between his adventure writing for youngsters and adults was "to make it faster and simpler for children. I also like to think I'm helping unobtrusively to educate them in the proper use of the English language."

FOR MORE INFORMATION SEE:

Publishers Weekly, April 4, 1977.
Contemporary Authors, Volumes 77-80, Gale, 1979.

OBITUARIES

Times (London), October 6, 1988.
Chicago Tribune, October 7, 1988, October 9, 1988.
Los Angeles Times, October 7, 1988.
New York Times, October 7, 1988.
Washington Post, October 7, 1988.

HUFF, Vivian 1948-

PERSONAL: Born March 5, 1948, in New York, N.Y.; daughter of Hans J. (a scientist) and Ruth (an artist; maiden name, Bronner) Cahnmann; married Travers P. Huff, January 26, 1969 (divorced). *Education:* Attended Hebrew University of Jerusalem, Israel, 1966-67; Philadelphia College of Art, B.F.A., 1971, certificate in art education, 1972, graduate work at University of Pennsylvania, 1972. *Home and office:* 11741 Di Marco Dr., Philadelphia, Pa. 19154.

CAREER: Free-lance photographer and writer, 1968—. Philadelphia Department of Recreation, Pa., arts and crafts teacher, summer, 1968, photographer, summers, 1971, 1972; Williamstown Summer Theatre, Mass., staff photographer, summer, 1970; Jewish Y's and Centres of Greater Philadelphia, Pa., photography teacher, 1972; Philadelphia School District, Pa., elementary and secondary art teacher, 1974—. Photographic work includes greeting cards for Hallmark and Recycled Paper Products, photos for WFIL Radio Station, Eagles football team, and various newspapers, magazines and record companies. Workshop leader. *Exhibitions*—Photographs: Please Touch Museum, Philadelphia, Pa., 1987; Capital Children's Museum, Washington, D.C., 1987. *Member:* Children's Reading Roundtable.

WRITINGS:

SELF-ILLUSTRATED WITH PHOTOS

Let's Make Paper Dolls, Harper, 1978.
(With Jack Dautrich) *Big City Detective,* Lodestar, 1986.

WORK IN PROGRESS: Philadelphia Children at Play or *Street Games* (working titles), a book illustrated with photographs; *Gloria's Day at the Beach,* a photo essay on death for children; *A Building Goes Up,* color photography; *Careers in Federal Law Enforcement,* young adult nonfiction; greeting cards for Hallmark and her own line of photographic greeting cards for Recycled Paper Products; *Mouse Missing a Mate,* a picture book for beginning readers.

SIDELIGHTS: "I was born in New York City and grew up in Bethesda, Maryland. Being raised by a scientist father and an artist mother has provided me with an analytical side and an artistic side. It is this very combination of elements that I strive for in my writing and my photography.

"My parents are European. Consequently, we lived and travelled extensively in Europe and the Middle East. My interest in people and cultures of many lands inspired me to learn to converse in several languages—French, German, Italian and Hebrew. I feel that interaction with people and their different lifestyles sparks creativity on all levels.

"This desire to communicate led me, camera in hand, to all kinds of neighborhoods in Philadelphia to talk with and photograph children playing their favorite street games. (The catalyst for "Philadelphia Children at Play"—a photo exhibit). It also led me to discuss the bewildering subject of death with children of all ages which inspired *Gloria's Day at the Beach,* a children's book about death.

VIVIAN HUFF

"In addition to travel and exploration of people, I have always been interested in children of all ages and their creative activity. Consequently, I teach art in the Philadelphia Public Schools in addition to doing my own work. The electric energy and creativity of children is a constant source of inspiration. My first book *Let's Make Paper Dolls* was a direct result of art classes with young children who expressed a fascination with cut-outs of all kinds. I learned that simplicity is the best learning tool and I followed this pattern with my simple black and white format.

"Recently, I began teaching teenagers and at much the same time, I met Jack Dautrich, a long time detective with the Philadelphia Police Department. Knowing that teenagers are intrigued by detective work and that they are also at an age where future career goals are important, we decided together to attempt a career oriented book explaining all about metropolitan detective work. I felt that lots of 'real' photographs would embellish the text as well as the cover. The resulting book, *Big City Detective* is being enjoyed by teenagers across the country and we are currently working on a similar book about careers in federal law enforcement.

"Throughout the years, while working on a variety of children's photographic picture books, I have dabbled in designing my own greeting cards with accompanying rhymes. This effort came together when Hallmark Cards, Inc. purchased some of my ideas in 1987, and Recycled Paper Products contracted me to do a line of photographic greeting cards in 1989. Now I am thinking that perhaps I will be able to combine some of these designs and rhymes in the creation of a book for young children."

HOBBIES AND OTHER INTERESTS: Travel, photography, aerobic dance.

JEFFERDS, Vincent H(arris) 1916-

PERSONAL: Born August 23, 1916, in Jersey City, N.J.; son of Jerome V. and Jenny Jefferds; married Jean MacBride, December 8, 1946; children: Jean Jefferds Halling, Vincent S., Jenny T. *Education:* Rutgers University, B.A., 1941. *Home:* 182 Tigertail Rd., Los Angeles, Calif. 90049. *Office:* Walt Disney Productions, 500 South Buena Vista St., Burbank, Calif. 91521.

CAREER: Times Square Stores, New York, N.Y., vice-president and director, 1946-51; Walt Disney Productions, Burbank, Calif., beginning 1951, vice-president in sales promotion, 1961-71, vice-president of consumer products division, 1975-79, senior vice-president in marketing, 1980-83, senior marketing consultant, 1983—; free-lance author, 1983—. Artist, with exhibitions in the United States and Europe. *Military service:* U.S. Army, 1942-46; became captain. *Awards, honors:* Named World's Outstanding Licensing Marketer by the Nuremberg Toy Conference, 1968; U.S. Licensing Manufacturers Association Award, 1983, for "Most Creative Merchandiser"; International Award for creative contribution to juvenile publishing, 1983; Award from Procter and Gamble, for most successful marketing program; numerous awards for marketing.

WRITINGS:

Walt Disney's Words That Are Opposites, Danbury Press, 1976.
Disney's Elegant ABC Book, Simon & Schuster, 1983.
Ferdinand and the Robbers (adaption of *The Story of Ferdinand* by Munro Leaf), Random House, 1983.
Winnie-the-Pooh Gets Shipwrecked, Western, 1985.
Peter Pan and the Troll, Western, 1985.
Mickey and Donald in the Tickle Grass, Western, 1985.
The Wooly Bird Meets Winnie-the-Pooh, Western, 1985.
Disney's Elegant Book of Manners, Simon & Schuster, 1985.
A Disney Rhyming Reader (thirty volumes), Grolier, 1988.
Disney's My Very First Dictionary, Abrams, 1989.

SIDELIGHTS: While he was associated with Walt Disney Productions, Jefferds was responsible for initiating such diverse projects as the international Disney book clubs, the international "Disney Ice Show," and the concept of World Showcase at Epcot Center in Florida. He established the Winnie-the-Pooh apparel program at Sears, Roebuck and Company, and created the Orange Bird animated character for the Florida Citrus Commission. Since his retirement, Jefferds has written children's books, which have been published in twelve languages.

JOHN, Joyce

PERSONAL: Born in New York, N.Y.; daughter of Joseph Walter (a manager) and Vera (an artist; maiden name, Penney) Chibatar; married Richard F. John (a data processing manager), June 20, 1964; children: Selina R. *Education:* Attended Philadelphia Museum School of Art. *Home and office:* 2211 Woodlawn Park, McHenry, Ill. 60050.

CAREER: Free-lance illustrator. Falcon Press, Philadelphia, Pa., artist; News Reel Lab, Philadelphia, Pa., animator, designer, 1958-63. Northland Area Art League, Chicago Artists Coalition.

JOYCE JOHN

ILLUSTRATOR

Don Rasmussen and Lynn Goldberg, *A Pig Can Jig,* Science
Research Associates, 1964, new edition, 1970.
Barbara Gregorich, *Sue Likes Blue,* School Zone, 1984.
B. Gregorich, *My Friend Goes Left,* School Zone, 1984.
Thomas Paul Thigpen, *Come Sing God's Song,* David C. Cook,
1987.
Marilyn J. Woody, *High Chair Devotions: God Cares for Me,*
David C. Cook, 1988.
M. J. Woody, *High Chair Devotions: God Made My World,*
David C. Cook, 1988.

WORK IN PROGRESS: Covers, posters, and cards.

SIDELIGHTS: "There was never any doubt in my mind that I
was going to be an artist. While growing up I was always
drawing my sisters and our pets.

"We now live in a home filled with antiques, flowers, assorted
animals, and one daughter, all a constant source of material for
my illustrations, which are mostly collages made with papers I
have textured myself.

"We camp a lot and are fortunate enough to live near
conservation areas and parks in which to walk or bike—I
always take my camera and sketchbook with me.

"My daughter went through phases of liking one particular color
as many children do (and one still hasn't outgrown it). So when I
illustrated *Sue Likes Blue,* I certainly could understand it.

"We live on the river and go boating and canoeing. I especially
like to canoe in the early morning when the mist is coming off
the water. I grow orchids in our little greenhouse and paint them
when I get a chance. When the weather is nice I enjoy sitting
outside and painting the wild life which I use in my illustrations
from time to time."

JOHNSON, Joan J. 1942-

PERSONAL: Born September 8, 1942, in Norwalk, Conn.;
daughter of John L. (a corporation president) and Edith (a
housewife; maiden name, Wood) Irving; divorced; children:
Jedidiah Lincoln David, Nathan Azariah. *Education:* Bethany
College, Bethany, W. Va., B.A., 1964; graduate study at
University of Pennsylvania, 1964-65; Fairfield University,
M.A., 1983. *Politics:* Independent. *Home:* Norwalk, Conn.
Office: Darien High School, School Lane, Darien, Conn.
06820.

CAREER: Ipswich High School, Ipswich, Mass., English
teacher, 1966-70; Goodwin's Carriage House, Auburn, Mass.,
sales representative; Design Trends (interior decorating firm),
Barre, Mass., president, 1970-78; Stauffer Chemical Co.,
Westport, Conn., assistant records administrator, 1978-79;
Darien High School, Darien, Conn., teacher of English and of
talented and gifted program, 1979—; free-lance writer. Speaker. *Awards, honors:* Finalist for the Connecticut Commission
on Arts and *Connecticut Magazine*'s Short Story Contest, 1982,
for "Just Old Junk;" Reiss-Macgregor Scholarship, 1985;
Darien Advocates for Education of the Gifted Grant, 1986, for
"Young Writers Program."

WRITINGS:

The Cult Movement (juvenile), F. Watts, 1984.
Justice (juvenile), F. Watts, 1985.
Combatting Drug Abuse, Silver Burdett, 1989.

WORK IN PROGRESS: Nathan, Buba, and Me, a juvenile
novel about two brothers whose sibling rivalry eventually gets
them in trouble when they cross the path of Buba Jones.

KIMBROUGH, Emily 1899-1989

OBITUARY NOTICE:—See sketch in *SATA* Volume 2: Born
October 23, 1899, in Muncie, Ind.; died of lung cancer,
February 11 (some sources say February 10, or February 12),
1989, in New York, N.Y. Lecturer, editor, radio broadcaster,
and author. Kimbrough was best known for her humorous
lectures and writings. During the 1920s she worked as book
reviewer and editor for *Fashions of the Hour,* a publication of
Marshall Field department stores, and became fashion editor
and managing editor for *Ladies' Home Journal.* Her first book,
Our Hearts Were Young and Gay, recounts her experiences as a
young woman traveling in England and France after leaving
college in 1921. This work, written with actress Cornelia Otis
Skinner, became a motion picture in 1944, whereupon Kimbrough worked in Hollywood as a screenwriter. She later wrote
of her film industry experiences in *We Followed Our Hearts to
Hollywood. It Gives Me Great Pleasure,* describing her
misadventures on the American lecture circuit, formed the basis
for the television series "The Eve Arden Show" on CBS.
Beginning in 1952 she also wrote her own daily radio program
for WCBS-Radio. Among Kimbrough's other writings are
*Through Charley's Door, Forty Plus and Fancy Free, Water,
Water Everywhere,* and *Pleasure by the Busload.* In addition,

she contributed to magazines such as *New Yorker* and *Atlantic Monthly*.

FOR MORE INFORMATION SEE:

Current Biography 1944, H. W. Wilson, 1945.
Who's Who of American Women, 16th edition, Marquis, 1988.

OBITUARIES

New York Times, February 12, 1989.
Chicago Tribune, February, 14, 1989.
Los Angeles Times, February 15, 1989.
Washington Post, February 16, 1989.
Times (London), February 20, 1989.

KLEIN, David 1919-

PERSONAL: Born March 30, 1919, in New York, N.Y.; son of Solomon (a manufacturing jeweler) and Helen (a librarian; maiden name, Schoenberg) Klein; married Marymae Endsley (a textbook editor), December 6, 1942; children: Helen Leslie, Edith Sarah. *Education:* City College of New York (now City College of the City University of New York), B.A., 1940; Columbia University, M.A., 1941; additional graduate study in psychology, New York University, 1962-65. *Politics:* Social Democrat. *Religion:* Humanist. *Home:* 1130 Fifth Ave. S., Edmonds, Wash. 98020. *Agent:* Frances Collin, 110 West 40th St., New York, N.Y. 10018.

CAREER: McGraw-Hill Book Co., New York City, technical editor, 1940-42; Henry Holt & Co., New York City, college textbook editor, 1946-48; Dryden Press, New York City, executive vice-president, 1948-56; Basic Books, Inc., New York City, vice-president, 1956-58; Association for the Aid of Crippled Children, New York City, director of publications, 1958-65; Michigan State University, East Lansing, associate professor, 1965-68, professor of social science, 1968-83, professor of human development, 1970-83, professor emeritus in department of social science, 1983—. Adjunct Professor, School of Public Health, University of North Carolina, 1988—. Instructor and lecturer in English and adult education, City College of New York (now City College of the City University of New York), 1946-56; exchange professor, University of Ryukyus (Okinawa), 1966; visiting professor, Hofstra University, 1970-71; senior lecturer, University of New South Wales, 1972-73; chairman designate at University of Sydney, 1979. *Military service:* U.S. Army, 1942-46; became warrant officer junior grade.

AWARDS, HONORS: Ford Foundation travel grant, 1966; Certificate of Recognition from the National Safety Council, 1966; Fulbright grant from the Australian-American Education Foundation, 1972, 1979.

WRITINGS:

The Army Writer, Military Service Publishing, 1946.
(With Mary Louise Johnson) *They Took to the Sea*, Rutgers University Press, 1948.
Your First Boat, Funk, 1953.
Your Outboard Cruiser, Norton, 1954.
Beginning with Boats, Crowell, 1962.
Helping Your Teenager Choose a College, Child Study Association, 1963.
Great Adventures in Small Boats, Crowell-Collier, 1963.

(With W. Haddon and E. A. Suchman) *Accident Research: Methods and Approaches*, Harper, 1964.
(With S. A. Richardson and B. S. Dohrenwend) *Interviewing: Its Forms and Functions*, Basic Books, 1965.
When Your Teen-ager Starts to Drive, Association for Aid of Crippled Children, 1965.
(With Theodore E. Hughes) *A Family Guide to Estate Planning, Funeral Arrangements, and Settling an Estate after Death*, Scribner, 1983.
(With David Grupper) *The Paper Shtetl: A Complete Model of an Eastern European Jewish Town*, Schocken, 1984.
(With T. E. Hughes) *Ownership*, Scribner, 1984.
(With T. E. Hughes) *The Parents' Financial Survival Guide*, HP Books, 1987.
(With T. E. Hughes) *A Family Guide to Wills, Funerals and Probate: How to Protect Yourself and Your Survivors*, Scribner, 1987.

WITH WIFE, MARYMAE E. KLEIN

Yourself and Others, McDougal, Littell, 1970.
Supershopper, Praeger, 1971.
Yourself Ten Years from Now, Harcourt, 1977.
More for Your Money, Penguin, 1979.
How Do You Know It's True?, Scribner, 1984.
Your Parents and Your Self: Alike/Unlike, Agreeing/Disagreeing, Scribner, 1986.

Contributor of articles on recreation, education, and consumer topics to periodicals, including *Consumer Reports, Ladies' Home Journal, Mademoiselle, New York Times, Fifty Plus*, and *North Carolina Independent*.

WORK IN PROGRESS: More Than Skin Deep: A Guide to Plastic Surgery with Norman Hugo, M.D., for Consumer Reports Books; popular and professional writing on medical issues and consumer affairs.

David Klein with his wife, Marymae.

SIDELIGHTS: "My books for young people, although they differ in subject matter, were all motivated by my desire to teach readers what I think they ought to know. The challenge was to present complicated subjects clearly but without the condescension I find in all too many books addressed to young readers.

"There's nothing dramatic or even interesting about all this, and my wife and I lead rather quiet lives."

HOBBIES AND OTHER INTERESTS: Motorcycling, clock collecting, psychology, sociology, research on risk-taking, and consumer behavior.

KNOX, Mary Eleanor Jessie 1909-
(Mary Shepard)

PERSONAL: Born December 25, 1909, in Surrey, England; daughter of Ernest H. (an illustrator) and Florence Eleanor (an artist; maiden name, Chaplin) Shepard; married Edmund George Valpy Knox (an editor for *Punch;* pseudonym, Evoe), October 2, 1937 (died, January 2, 1971). *Education:* Attended Slade School of Art, London, England. *Politics:* Liberal. *Religion:* Church of England. *Home and office:* 7A Frognal Mansions, 97 Frognal, London NW3 6XT, England. *Agent:* Messrs. N. E. Middleton Ltd., 44 Great Russell St., London WC1B 3PA, England.

CAREER: Illustrator. World Wide Education Service of the Parents' National Education Union, London, England, clerk, 1971-74. *Exhibitions:* Maddox Street Gallery, London, England; Hampstead Library, London.

ILLUSTRATOR

ALL UNDER NAME MARY SHEPARD

Pamela L. Travers, *Mary Poppins,* Reynal & Hitchock, 1934, reissued, Harcourt, 1972, revised edition, 1981.
P. L. Travers, *Mary Poppins Comes Back,* Harcourt, 1935, reissued, 1975.
Arthur Ransome, *Pigeon Post,* Lippincott, 1937.
(With Agnes Sims) P. L. Travers, *Mary Poppins Opens the Door,* Reynal & Hitchcock, 1943, reissued, Harcourt, 1976.
P. L. Travers, *Mary Poppins in the Park,* Harcourt, 1952, new edition, 1980.
P. L. Travers, *Mary Poppins from A to Z,* Harcourt, 1962.
P. L. Travers, *Mary Poppins Story for Coloring,* Harcourt, 1964.
P. L. Travers, *Mary Poppins [and] Mary Poppins Comes Back,* Reynal & Hitchcock, 1937, Harcourt, 1963.
P. L. Travers, *Happy Ever After,* Reynal & Hitchcock, 1940.
Christina Fitzgerald, *Mrs. Killick's Luck,* Methuen, 1960.
A. A. Milne, *Prince Rabbit [and] The Princess Who Could Not Laugh,* Dutton, 1966.
P. L. Travers and Maurice Moore-Betty, *Mary Poppins in the Kitchen: A Cookery Book with a Story,* Harcourt, 1975.
(With A. Sims) P. L. Travers, *The Complete Mary Poppins,* four volumes, Harcourt, 1976.
P. L. Travers, *Mary Poppins in Cherry Tree Lane,* Delacorte, 1982.
P. L. Travers, *Mary Poppins and the House Next Door,* Delacorte, 1989.

SIDELIGHTS: Born on Christmas Day, 1909, "I am the only daughter of illustrator Ernest H. Shepard and artist Florence

Eleanor Jessie Knox with step-granddaughter and husband.

Chaplin Shepard. "My parents met as students at the Royal Academy Schools of Art in Piccadilly, London, and it was not until my mother won a prize for a mural design at Guy's Hospital for the Nurses' Refectory, and my father sold a painting to the Royal Academy, that in 1904 they could afford to marry.

"First, they found a home in Arden Cottage in Shamley Green, a village near Guildford in Surrey, south of London, and began their married life, and in this cottage their only son, Graham Howard Shepard was born in 1907. The family then moved down the road and across the Green to Red Cottage situated in 'Puddleduck Lane,' named for the small stream which ran along an adjacent ditch, and in Red Cottage I was born, I am, told, with a hare-lip. The country general practitioner was skilled at such matters and in a few minutes had me stitched up, protesting no doubt. There were to be no more children.

"A villa, rather than a country cottage, Red Cottage was very ugly (but we liked it), and was built on the site of something more rural, where someone, a long time ago had planted an apple orchard including, by now, a gigantic fruiting white cherry tree. The front porch of Red Cottage was embowered in roses and to the eaves there was a thick growth of ivy which improved its appearance and made it seem less red. The ivy was full of sparrows' nests and our cat, Mumma Diddy, bore her kittens in batches below among the fallen leaves, hoping and getting wind-falls, eggs and chicks. Someone else had planted a hop and a vinegar grape vine at the southeast corner of the house. There was a vinegar factory in the district, and most of the villagers grew a vine to add a little to their very meagre wages.

"Inside our home the rooms were small, where from a dark hallway a short staircase led to four bedrooms, one for our live-in cook-housekeeper from the village, Sara Holden, who had

(From *Prince Rabbit and the Princess Who Could Not Laugh* by A. A. Milne. Illustrated by Mary Shepard.)

won a cookery prize at the new Gas Emporium in Guildford. Sara was with us for over thirty years, a faithful servant, honest and loyal, who I encouraged to spoil me. Once, being thwarted, I pretended to attack her with a knife, growling. Though very small but valiant, she pretended to be afraid, and laughed. The best cure for infantile violence. When she had time, Sara enjoyed a good read, so my mother gave her copies of Jane Austen, which were very much to her taste. To help Sara, girls of tender ages came from the village.

"There was a free-standing studio near what the ancient 'jobbing gardener' called 'the carriage drive,' too narrow for a carriage, with a row of firs and a bed of St. Jonsworth along one side—room for a motor cycle or a Morris Minor. Red Cottage garden was a fair size, with space for vegetables, flowers and chickens which lived in a 'run,' moved every so often for fresh scratching ground, so we had supplies of eggs, meat and fresh vegetables during the first World War. Graham and I were country bred, which toughens the fibres, and could even hear the local Carrier's pigs being killed as we passed without running away. The village pond tadpoles nearby were more interesting.

"The village families were numerous and sometimes without boots or shoes. My mother was very good at visiting—she had a sympathetic nature and an attractive smile, and provided help very tactfully where she could. On the whole the families were healthy, with their own vegetables, a few chickens and perhaps a pig, and rabbits from the neighbouring fields. We turned a

blind eye to poaching, so did the village 'Bobby.' Poachers often had shot-guns and nights were dark."

An admittedly slow learner, Knox was able to absorb and retain in her memory works by Walter de la Mare which she recited, with gestures, when friends came to tea. Taught by her mother, as well as poems, she learnt songs and advanced to 'ellipses'— long shaped ovals—and a teapot in her drawings, and even a few words of French.

"Our parents painted portraits of Graham and me, and we sat for them fairly often, learning to hold poses for quite a long time, with rests. A cat was drawn on the studio wall for me to look at, which gave the sitter rather the appearance of the Infant Samuel. There were studio parties when friends came down for the day from London by train and Bobrick's four wheel cab, horse-drawn, slow but sure, mostly in the summer."

Ernest Shepard was very entertaining as a father when his children were small and before the 1914 War and before the enormous load of work which arrived once his drawings were known and appreciated and commissions poured in, thick and fast. He made a grotto in a wardrobe, after removing the bottom drawer, splendid with imaginary water (glass) and an imaginary mermaid (a cut-out). Both parents encouraged games which were enjoyed by their children and their visiting friends. Plays and charades were organized and an "acting box" was filled with costumes. "*Alice in Wonderland* went down very well.

"The happy childhood was abruptly interrupted by the First World War, when my father went to France, and later to Italy to confront the Italians on the Piave, where he painted mountain scenes with bombardments in watercolour or chalk. Once, for nearly a month, we had no news at all and tried to comfort our mother, but Graham very wisely suggested that daddy was being moved...he was right. For some time being moved always meant tears, as it sometimes does!

"One night, back in Britain, a Zeppelin trundled past Shamley Green, on its way to the target, the Guildford to Kent Railway, which carried munitions for transport to France. My mother woke us and there was the Zeppelin, huge and ponderous in the moonlight. I think it made a humming noise, but can't be sure. It dropped a tiny bomb on Guildford Meadows, scoring a near miss and killing a sheep. Of course the gossips said that a German spy was located in a nearby house, signalling through a roof skylight."

Ernest Shepard was lucky—he returned from the front unwounded, with a Military Cross and a lot of souvenirs. He became an established illustrator for *Punch.*

When Knox was seventeen her mother died suddenly. Her father had already found a site for the building of a house to be called "Long Meadow," nearer to Guildford, thought to be healthier, dry, and on chalk and 500 feet up on a ridge of the North Downs in Surrey. Her mother, however, did not live to see the new house completed. "Sadly, we moved away to what an acquaintance called 'The lamp-post area.' There were four of these necessary objects along the chalky road with its few houses which in those days, ended with Long Meadow."

Holding her hat on with one hand and carrying a bag in the other. (From *Mary Poppins* by P. L. Travers. Illustrated by Mary Shepard.)

Ethel Shepard, a deaconess and her father's only sister, came on furlough from Lahore, India, in 1927, to help the family. "Aunt Ethel took me to my interview with Professor Tonks at the Slade School of Art in Gower Street, London. It was decided that after my disastrous efforts at all the other schools, this might be more in my line. The professor, having been a surgeon chose art and teaching as his career. He joined the Camden Town Group and was a very fine artist with paintings in the Tate Gallery. Some of his braver students would cross the road to University College Hospital to attend dissections for anatomy purposes. Some fainted—I never went."

Knox enjoyed the work at Slade, winning a summer competition prize chosen by Sir George Clausen. "I'm not sure that my father really approved of the Slade School. Aunt Ethel quite evidently hadn't passed on Professor Tonks' unfortunate 'gaffe' (surely not intentionally unkind) when she told him that 'Mary is the daughter of Ernest H. Shepard, the famous artist, you know?' 'Never heard of him,' was the reply. (1) My father was not well known at that time. (2) I do not think that Professor Tonks had ever met a Head Deaconess in full rig before. (3) If he had ever read *Punch,* it would have been in the days of Charles Keene whose work he greatly admired. My admiration for Professor Tonks knew no bounds, he was a splendid teacher and I'm grateful for his help. But my father came to one of the Slade fancy-dress dances as a cricketer with a moustache and a bat, and in the photograph in *The Work of E. H. Shepard,* edited by Rawle Knox, I confront him in Victorian costume and carrying a parasol. I very much doubt that the two artists met. The Slade School was 'avant garde,' not approved of by all! 'Impressionist! Anti-academic!'

"In 1933, Pamela Travers (P. L. Travers) approached my father with her first 'Mary Poppins' book of the series, but he had to turn down the offer because, by this time, he already had too much work in hand, very regretfully."

The assignment was given to Knox. "One of my mother's best friends was also a friend of Pamela's, and I had sent her a Christmas card of a horse bearing a rider with a flag, 'HAPPY CHRISTMAS' (I think), there was snow underfoot and the horse's hoof marks were going the wrong way. This seems to have made no difference, only Pamela's small son spotted the error a good deal later. This was all very exciting, work at last, and great fun. I managed to get a suitable looking Mary Poppins after buying a Dutch-doll and a lot of help and advice from P. L. Travers who then lived in a charming cottage in Mayfield in Sussex (south of London) with her bull dog Cu. Cu and my Albertine, with balloons in their mouths, appear in *Mary Poppins Comes Back.* The stories were really great to illustrate, people did such weird and amazing things, on their heads, up against the ceiling for tea, flying through the air, talking to cats and lions and spinning like tops.

"With the first filming of 'Mary Poppins' by Walt Disney, based on P. L. Travers script, except for Julie Andrews who is a delight to watch and a pleasure to listen to, I think that Pamela was rather upset by the result. Anyway, my drawings were not needed and my agent won me something for compensation. For in the book my idea was to show Mary Poppins' feet in the 'fifth position' as in a ballet, heel to heel and toes facing outwards. Now I have a copyright."

P. L. Travers and Knox have collaborated for more than fifty years, and the 'Mary Poppins' series has been spread out over those years. "It was difficult at times to portray the same characters after a gap in time and keep them looking the same. Pamela always said when the drawing was right, and always praised when praise was due. Very fair.

(The 1964 Walt Disney movie "Mary Poppins," starring Julie Andrews, based its look on Shepard's drawings.)

On sailed the curious figure, its feet neatly clearing the tops of the trees. (From *Mary Poppins Comes Back* by P. L. Travers. Illustrated by Mary Shepard.)

"With the latest book, *Mary Poppins and the House Next Door,* one of my favourites, but which I found the hardest to illustrate, Mary Poppins was to change from flat-as-a-board, angular (but always a comforter in the end) to someone more feminine. So I gave her a frill on her nightdress, and with her sweeping plait of rich black hair (usually in a tight bun on the top of her head), she looked more ladylike. My first instructions had always been 'Mary Poppins must have no figure!' It had been going on for so long, that perhaps she and I must part!"

In 1937, she married Edmund Valpy Knox "Evoe," editor of *Punch* and colleague and friend of her father. To avoid confusion, E. V. Knox had taken the pen name "Evoe," because of the similarity with E. V. Lucas's initials. Edmund Knox was a widower and father of two children. "Evoe's two brilliantly gifted children, a few years younger than myself, Rawle and Penelope received me with great kindness, and always do. At first I was a little afraid of this situation, but I found that fear didn't come into it, only enjoyment. But Rawle and Penelope took it very well, for I was and perhaps still am an inept Surrey bumpkin!

"But happiness was the first thing, and Evoe threw his bowler hat into a garden in St. John's Wood (London), said he wanted a 'Dorah'—cockney for a female companion—and asked me to be his wife. The hat was rescued from the garden and I had to be stopped from laughing before I could answer."

After their honeymoon in Scandinavia where they stayed with a friend's friend, Miss Boeklin, in her glorious farm where each

stair was painted a different colour and where there was a "dig" for a Viking ship in one of the fields, the couple returned to their new flat, quite near to the bowler hat incident, in St. John's Wood. "We had inherited the recent occupant's cook-house-keeper and agreed to have 'brunch' on Sundays so that dear Irish Mary could go to Mass.

"In 1938, war was on the horizon. . . .I was with the ARP (Air Raid Precautions) with a tin hat, called an Air Warden.

"Bad news came for us—it was bad everywhere, but this was worse. Rawle Knox was taken prisoner by the Japanese in Singapore. Would he survive, would Red Cross parcels get through to him? With his exceptional courage and determination, we felt that he had a chance. He has said, modestly, that he survived because he didn't smoke, exchanging cigarettes for food. The news of Graham Shepard's death came in 1942."

In 1945, Knox moved to Hampstead, a North Western suburb of London, with her husband. "After Evoe's retirement, we decided to change our lives, to the extent that Evoe reviewed books for the *Tatler,* temporarily in the place of Elizabeth Bowen and joined every available committee ('they want me on committees because I never say anything') and was co-opted on to the Hampstead Public Libraries, where books were discussed less than drains. Evoe was on the St. John-at-Hampstead Parish Church Council and a Trustee. There was training for the Parish Care Committee which I joined and said even less! There was the children's country Holidays Fund, a favourite charity of the then Vicar, the Rev. Prebendary H. T. Carnegie. At eighty-four, Evoe finished a short book called *The Adventures of a School,* about the Hampstead Parochial School. I got on with some more 'Mary Poppins.'"

After Evoe's death in 1971, Knox took a part-time job and concentrated on editing and publishing a memorial book of Evoe's verse. "When my husband died I joined the Parents' National Education Union (PNEU). I was a part-time clerk and able to pay my rent for three years, at which point I became redundant.

"When I was with the PNEU I would finish at mid-day and come home to work on the memorial book I was doing for Evoe. My step-children and I found a printer, but the whole process took a very long time and the edition didn't appear until 1974. We're just about to publish a paperback edition which the booksellers think will do better."

Knox still does an occasional illustration, but enjoys drawing more for pleasure now. "Years as they pass plunder us of one thing after another."

FOR MORE INFORMATION SEE:

Brian Doyle, editor, *Who's Who of Children's Literature,* Schocken Books, 1968.
Rawle Knox, editor, *The Work of E. H. Shepard,* Schocken Books, 1979.

KUBIE, Nora (Gottheil) Benjamin 1899-1988 (Nora Benjamin)

OBITUARY NOTICE:—See sketch in *SATA* Volume 39: Born January 4, 1899, in New York, N.Y.; died of acute leukemia September 4, 1988, in Westport, Conn. Artist and author. Kubie, who used the pseudonym Nora Benjamin, wrote and illustrated several fiction and nonfiction books for children, including *Roving All Day, The First Book of Israel, The First Book of Archaeology,* and *King Solomon's Navy,* which won the 1955 Isaac Siegel Award for Best Book. Her very first book was a "hand-written 'Stories and Poems' illustrated by the author, at the age of eight or nine." She began her professional career as a free-lance commercial artist until "it occurred to me that I might try to write and illustrate a book of my own." The result was *Hard Alee!,* published in 1939.

Kubie was considered an amateur archaeologist, having participated in ten archaeological digs. "The biggest adventure of my life was the time spent camping in the Dead Sea desert as a member of the volunteer force that excavated the great stronghold of Masada," she once recalled. Her book, *Road to Nineveh* is a biography of archaeologist Austin Henry Layard.

Other books also grew from her interests. She was so fascinated with Israel that she bought a small barn in the Artists' Village of Ein Hod in Israel, had it rebuilt as her studio, and spent several months each year there. "It was a beautiful, crazy, and primitive place. . . .I gardened, swam, made many dear friends, read the Old Testament avidly, wrote *King Solomon's Navy, King Solomon's Horses, The First Book of Israel,* and *The First Book of Archaeology.*"

Kubie was a member of the Author's League of America, Artists Equity, and Artists Village of Ein Hod. Among her other books for children are: *Fathom Five: A Story of Bermuda, Remember the Valley,* and *The Jews of Israel: History and Sources.*

FOR MORE INFORMATION SEE:

Contemporary Authors, Volumes 5-8, Gale, 1969.
Who's Who in World Jewry: A Biographical Dictionary of Outstanding Jews, Olive Books of Israel, 1978.

OBITUARIES

New York Times, September 8, 1988.

LISLE, Janet T(aylor) 1947-

PERSONAL: Born February 13, 1947, in Englewood, N.J.; daughter of Alden M. (an insurance executive) and Janet (an architect; maiden name, MacColl) Taylor; married Richard Lisle (a finance executive), 1976; children: Elizabeth. *Education:* Smith College, B.A., 1969. *Home:* Montclair, N.J.

CAREER: Free-lance writer. Has worked for VISTA, in Atlanta, Ga., and as a reporter. *Awards, honors: Sirens and Spies* was selected one of American Library Association's Best Books for Young Adults, one of *School Library Journal*'s Best Books of the Year, and one of *Booklist*'s Childrens' Editor's Choices, all 1985, and Parents' Choice Award for Children's Literature from the Parents' Choice Foundation, 1986; Golden Kite Honor Book for Fiction from the Society of Children's Book Writers, 1987, and *Booklist* Editor's Choice, 1988, both for *The Great Dimpole Oak.*

WRITINGS:

The Dancing Cats of Applesap (juvenile; illustrated by Joelle Shefts), Bradbury, 1984.

JANET T. LISLE

Sirens and Spies (young adult; ALA Notable Book; Junior Literary Guild selection), Bradbury, 1985.
The Great Dimpole Oak (juvenile; illustrated by Stephen Gammell), Orchard Books, 1987.
Afternoon of the Elves (juvenile), Orchard Books, 1989.

SIDELIGHTS: "Before turning to fiction in the early 1980s, I worked as a newspaper reporter for some ten years. I attended journalism school at Georgia State University, and went on to an internship at the *Atlanta Journal* where I wrote for the 'Women's/Living' section. Later I worked for local newspapers near Atlanta, and after a two-year jaunt to California writing poetry, arrived in Westchester, N.J. and wrote for the *North County News.* Like many writers, I sought free-lance work of all sorts to make ends meet. Over the years I have contributed articles to magazines, directed public relations at an art gallery, and taken on project assignments for high school text books.

"After the birth of my daughter and a move to Montclair, N.J., I began to write fiction for children. At the time, it seemed mostly a good occupation for a house-bound person, but by the end of my second book, *Sirens and Spies,* I realized I'd struck on something I very much liked to do.

"Writing fiction is hard work, harder than writing newspaper stories or public relations releases. To keep my motivation level high, I try to stake out new territory for each book I undertake. Not only must the characters, the plot, and the locales be different, but the sound—or voice—must change with respect to the kind of book being made. Sometimes I'm asked if there will ever be a sequel to one or another of my books. I always reply with great firmness: 'Never.'"

Lisle feels that *The Great Dimpole Oak* "is more aggressive and ambitious than either of the other two [books]. It's really a study of fantasy and of the human mind. . . .Your mind invents certain patterns that place order on the forms; it's a way of making things real and giving them meaning."[1]

FOOTNOTE SOURCES

[1]Ilene Cooper, "New Voices, New Visions: Janet Taylor Lisle," *Horn Book,* November/December, 1988.

LOCKER, Thomas 1937-

PERSONAL: Born June 26, 1937, in New York, N.Y.; son of Bernard (a lobbyist) and Nan (a book dealer; maiden name, Alpern) Locker; married Marea Panares Teske, September, 1964 (divorced, 1971); married Maria Adelman (in dress business); children: (first marriage) Anthony; (second marriage) Aaron, Josh, Jonathan, Gregory. *Education:* University of Chicago, B.A., 1960; American University, Washington, D.C., M.A., 1963. *Politics:* Democrat. *Religion:* Jewish. *Home:* Wykeham Rd., Washington, Conn. 06793. *Office:* 119 Warren St., Hudson, N.Y. 12534.

CAREER: Franklin College, Franklin, Ind., art department chairman, 1963-70; Shimer College, Mt. Carroll, Ill., professor of humanities, 1970-74; free-lance author and illustrator. *Exhibitions:* Rex Evans, Los Angeles, Calif., 1970; Reflections, Atlanta, Ga., 1971; Everett Oschlaeger, Chicago, Ill., 1974, 1976; Merrill Chase, Chicago, 1975, 1976, 1977, 1978; R. S. Johnson, Chicago, 1979, 1980, 1981, 1982; Hammer Gallery, New York, N.Y., 1980, 1982; Alan Jacobs, London, England, 1982. *Military service:* U.S. Army; became private first class. *Member:* Authors League.

AWARDS, HONORS: Where the River Begins was chosen one of *New York Times* Ten Best Illustrated Book of the Year, 1984, received the Parents' Choice Award for Illustration from the Parents' Choice Foundation, selected an Outstanding Science Trade Book for Children by the National Science Teachers Association, *Booklist*'s Children's Reviewer's Choice, American Bookseller Pick of the Lists, and one of Child Study Association of America's Children's Books of the Year, and included in the Biennale of Illustrations, Bratislava, all 1985; *The Mare on the Hill* was exhibited at the Bologna International Children's Book Fair, 1985, was chosen one of Child Study Association of America's Children's Books of the Year, 1986, and Colorado Children's Book Award runner-up from the University of Colorado, and Critici in Erba Honorable Mention from the Bologna Bienale.

WRITINGS:

SELF-ILLUSTRATED

Where the River Begins, Dial, 1984.
The Mare on the Hill, Dial, 1985.
Sailing with the Wind ("Reading Rainbow" selection), Dial, 1986.
Family Farm, Dial, 1988.
(Adapter) Washington Irving, *Rip Van Winkle,* Dial, 1988.
The Young Artist, Dial, 1988.

ILLUSTRATOR

Hans Christian Andersen, *The Ugly Duckling,* retold by Marianna Mayer, Macmillan, 1987.
Lenny Hort, reteller, *The Boy Who Held Back the Sea,* Dial, 1987.

ADAPTATIONS:

"Where the River Begins" (filmstrip with cassette), Random House, 1986.
"The Mare on the Hill" (filmstrip with cassette), Random House, 1986.
"Family Farm" (filmstrip with cassette).

SIDELIGHTS: "After a long career in gallery painting, I discovered the art form of the picture book while reading to my five sons. I gave it a try as a lark and now I devote most of my time to books. I rejoice in the expressive potential of joining words with images and painting in narrative order. I see my books as a kind of bridge between generations and a way to bring fine art to the young mind."

MAESTRO, Betsy C(rippen) 1944-

PERSONAL: Surname is pronounced Ma-*es*-tro; born January 5, 1944, in New York, N.Y.; daughter of Harlan R. (a design consultant) and Norma (in education; maiden name, Sherman) Crippen; married second husband, Giulio Maestro (a free-lance writer and book illustrator), December 16, 1972; children: (second marriage) Daniela Marisa, Marco Claudio. *Education:* Southern Connecticut State College, B.S., 1964, M.S., 1970. *Politics:* Democrat. *Home and office:* 74 Mile Creek Rd., Old Lyme, Conn. 06371.

CAREER: Deer Run School, East Haven, Conn., kindergarten teacher, 1964-75, writer, 1975—. *Member:* National Education Association, Connecticut Education Association. *Awards, honors: Fat Polka-Dot Cat and Other Haiku* was selected one of Child Study Association of America's Children's Books of the Year, 1976, and *The Story of the Statue of Liberty,* 1987; *Lambs for Dinner* was selected a Children's Choice by the International Reading Association and the Children's Book Council, 1979; *Ferryboat* was selected a Notable Children's Trade Book in the Field of Social Studies by the National Council for Social Studies and the Children's Book Council, 1986.

WRITINGS:

JUVENILE PICTURE BOOKS; ALL ILLUSTRATED BY HUSBAND GIULIO MAESTRO

A Wise Monkey Tale (Junior Literary Guild selection), Crown, 1975.
Where Is My Friend? A Word Concept Book (Junior Literary Guild selection), Crown, 1976.
Fat Polka-Dot Cat and Other Haiku, Dutton, 1976.
In My Boat, Crowell, 1976.
Harriet Goes to the Circus: A Number Concept Book, Crown, 1977.
Busy Day: A Book of Action Words (Junior Literary Guild selection), Crown, 1978.
Lambs for Dinner, Crown, 1978.
On the Go: A Book of Adjectives (Junior Literary Guild selection), Crown, 1979.
Harriet Reads Signs and More Signs: A Word Concept Book (Junior Literary Guild selection), Crown, 1981.

(From *On the Town: A Book of Clothing Words* by Betsy Maestro. Illustrated by Giulio Maestro.)

Traffic: A Book of Opposites (ALA Notable Book), Crown, 1981.

The Key to the Kingdom, Harcourt, 1982.

The Guessing Game, Grosset, 1983.

(With G. Maestro) *Just Enough Rosie*, Grosset, 1983.

(With Ellen DelVecchio) *Big City Port*, Four Winds, 1983.

On the Town: A Book of Clothing Words, Crown, 1983.

Around the Clock with Harriet: A Book about Telling Time, Crown, 1984.

Harriet at Play, Crown, 1984.

Harriet at School, Crown, 1984.

Harriet at Home, Crown, 1984.

Harriet at Work, Crown, 1984.

Camping Out: A Book of Action Words, Crown, 1985.

Through the Year with Harriet, Crown, 1985.

Ferryboat (Junior Literary Guild selection), Crowell, 1986.

The Story of the Statue of Liberty, Lothrop, 1986.

The Grab-Bag Party, Golden Press, 1986.

The Pandas Take a Vacation, Golden Press, 1986.

The Perfect Picnic, Golden Press, 1987.

The Travels of Freddie and Frannie Frog, Golden Press, 1987.

A More Perfect Union: The Story of Our Constitution (ALA Notable Book), Lothrop, 1987.

Dollars and Cents for Harriet, Crown, 1988.

Taxi: A Book of City Words, Clarion, 1989.

Temperature and You, Lodestar, 1989.

Snow Day, Scholastic, 1989.

(From *Lambs for Dinner* by Betsy Maestro. Illustrated by Giulio Maestro.)

WORK IN PROGRESS: *Bicycle Trip,* and *Flowers to Fruit,* both for Crowell; *The Discovery of the Americas,* and *The Exploration of the Americas,* both for Lothrop; *Machines and You,* for Lodestar; *Sharks,* for Scholastic; *Delivery Van: Words for Town and Country* and *All Aboard! A Book of Compund Words,* both for Clarion. "The biggest, most complicated book in the works is *The Discovery of the Americas* before the arrival of Christopher Columbus. With the 500th anniversary of his landing coming up in 1992, the subject of Columbus will be very popular. There will, no doubt, be a host of books celebrating him and his achievement. But the discovery of the continent really began in the Ice Age with overland voyages; the Vikings arrived by sea hundreds of years before Columbus; and the continent actually is named for another explorer, Amerigo Vespucci. Perhaps most important, there were major flourishing civilizations in the hemisphere that dramatically pre-dated Columbus. I wanted to include all these things.

"This book will place Columbus in historical context. Too many generations have been educated to believe that 'Columbus discovered America,' as though it all began with him. That simply isn't the case.

"My husband, Giulio, will do the illustrations, as he has for all my books. Visually, it should be very exciting. There will be spreads of stone-age people, the later civilizations, as well as different types of boats and sailing ships at sea.

"We have been doing a series dealing with American history which will continue with this book, and a companion volume will cover later explorers of the continent."

SIDELIGHTS: "My earliest ambition was to be a teacher. My mother was a teacher, later a guidance counselor and school administrator. I didn't have any thoughts of becoming a writer, however.

"My mother was always involved with children and with books. My brother and I had many books, some of which have been passed down to our children, and we spent a lot of time reading. My early favorites were the Margaret Wise Brown books and

the 'Madeline' books. As I got older I turned to Elizabeth Enright, and the 'Nancy Drew' and 'Hardy Boys' series. My nose was always in a book!

"I spent most of my childhood in Brooklyn, New York. We were allowed to go most everywhere by ourselves, not only in Brooklyn, but to Manhattan and other boroughs. There was really nothing to be afraid of then. We rode the subways by ourselves, rode our bikes all the way out on the trails along the Belt Parkway to Coney Island. Saturdays, we would go to the Automat for lunch and then the Young People's Concerts at Carnegie Hall. I had my fair share of lessons, as well: ballet and piano.

"In high school I began working with children during the summers. In fact, all my jobs involved kids: babysitting, tutoring, playground supervisor.

"I majored in early childhood education and for eleven years taught kindergarten and first grade. I was often dismayed by the lack of imaginative nonfiction material available for children. After Giulio, who had been illustrating books for years, and I married, I realized that I had access to a number of editors. So I got up my courage and tried my hand at writing books."[1]

Maestro's first book, *A Wise Monkey Tale*, was illustrated by her husband and based on folk literature. "Since story hour is a part of every day in the kindergarten, I noticed particular favorites with the children, not just individual books, but often types of stories that seem to appeal to them more than others. Certain themes that are recurrent in folk literature, such as the idea of a clever animal outsmarting others, or an animal or person in a serious predicament finding an ingenious solution, always seem to produce fascination and delight in young children."[2]

Maestro collaborated with her husband on her next book as well. She wrote, he illustrated. *Where Is My Friend?* introduced Harriet the elephant, the character for which the Maestros may be most widely known. A spunky, white elephant on roller skates, Harriet navigates through many of the Maestros' concept books, looking for her friend, learning to read signs,

Toot! Toot! Here it comes. (From *Ferryboat* by Betsy Maestro. Illustrated by Giulio Maestro.)

going to the circus. "I don't really remember how we decided to make Harriet an elephant. Giulio loves to do animals and we knew we needed an especially winning character. We also wanted the character to be very graphic. Because Giulio was thinking in terms of bold, bright illustrations. It seemed white would be the best color, so she would really stand out in every spread. Harriet as an elephant rather than a child doesn't pose a problem for kids. They know it's pretend and meant for fun."[1]

The "Harriet" books have won high praise for their clarity, inventiveness and the entertaining way in which they teach basic space, time, and word concepts. "I concentrate on what a given concept means in the life of a young child. For example, I recently did a book on temperature. What are the ways in which a child thinks about temperature? He may consider it in terms of the weather, what garments to wear, whether to go outdoors. The child may associate 'temperature' with fever and being sick. Our concept books are not intended solely to impart information. Of course they accomplish this aim, but always in a way that is closely allied with children's experiences and emotional life.

"In the early days I would come up with an idea, write up the manuscript and immediately send it to my editor in the hope that she would like it. I don't work that way anymore. Now, I am often approached by an editor and asked to do a book on a particular subject. Of course the the idea is always the starting point. At this point, I often confer with Giulio and while he may contribute some suggestions, the emerging project is basically in my hands. Ideas come to me slowly, over time, usually while I'm doing other things. I can't just sit down at my desk and do a draft. A first draft is sometimes done in my head before I even put pencil to paper. For other books, research is the way to begin with lots of note-taking. When finally I am ready to start writing, I do it longhand. The first on-paper draft is usually a mess, with cross-outs and deletions and markings that no one but me would ever understand. Not even Giulio sees this. I revise this initial version by hand several times. Maybe by the third or fourth time around, I'm ready for the typewriter. It is very important for me to read these versions out loud. So many revisions are made on the basis of sound and rhythm.

"As I write, I try to visualize how the text will look on the page, where the page breaks should be and what type of illustrations

The ocean liner has docked. (From *Big City Port* by Betsy Maestro and Ellen DelVecchio. Illustrated by Giulio Maestro.)

we'll want. I divide the text into spreads, and am very conscious of the 'illustratability' of the lines on every page.

"The part of the process I most dislike comes after I've sent the manuscript to my editor. It isn't unusual to wait a number of months for the response. This is why it's important to have many projects going at once; otherwise you could find yourself sitting around with nothing to do.

"Revisions are sometimes a bit like drudgery. My practice is to look quickly at the editor's comments and then put the manuscript away for several days. This gives me time to get perspective on his or her comments. Often a number of people send suggestions: the editor, his or her assistant(s), and for historical books, experts on the particular subject. It can be confusing trying to put all these suggestions together into a coherent whole. Often we end up going back to an earlier version and restoring whole passages that had been changed. I feel frustrated when it seems we're going round and round in circles.

"The process is essentially the same for historical books. The main difference is that the latter require extensive research. For *The Story of the Statue of Liberty* and *The Story of the Constitution*, I spent months in the library reading and filling notebooks. It's almost like taking a course! The primary challenge is to condense vast amounts of information into a lively and simple presentation."[1]

The Story of the Statue of Liberty opens with the inspirational visit of Frederic Bartholdi, the French sculptor who designed and oversaw the erection of the statue to America. It covers not only the exciting and comparatively little-known efforts to raise money to build the statue, but the painstaking labor done by Bartholdi in his Parisian studio. "Children often become frustrated when a project can't be finished instantly. Our book, we hope, will help them appreciate that it took Bartholdi fifteen years to complete the Statue of Liberty. Ambitious projects generally cannot be rushed, but the time taken may be full of drama and excitement. This was certainly true for Bartholdi.

"*The Story of the Constitution* presented different challenges. We didn't have a lot of action to work with. The Constitution was hacked out over many, many meetings. The 'action,' if you will, was mostly intellectual. This was particularly problematic for Giulio. Spreads of men sitting around tables isn't very

As the huge statue grew, all of Paris watched with great fascination. (From *The Story of the Statue of Liberty* by Betsy Maestro. Illustrated by Giulio Maestro.)

exciting visually. So I had to find ways to talk about the making of the Constitution that showed the framers in different settings: their arriving for the Constitutional Convention, for example, gave us the chance to show colonial carriages and views of old Philadelphia."[1]

With the document's bicentennial, the Maestros saw the need "to make the birthday of the Constitution meaningful for the under-ten crowd. . . .As a teacher I learned to distill information and break every concept into smaller ones. Then you can lay down ideas one at a time, like building blocks. That's why just explaining what a compromise is, and showing how the

Constitution was born from compromising, takes so many pages!"[3]

"There seems to be more interest than ever in nonfiction for children. Owing to television, children seem much less sheltered than they once were, and are practically bombarded with information. They're forced to grow up sooner and know about the realities of life, pleasant or not. I don't mean to imply that television is all bad. The high-quality documentaries instill respect for facts and information. Too, school curriculums have changed. Many subjects are approached at lower grade levels than they were before. And events that once were glossed over—particularly in social studies and history—are now treated much more in depth. The quality of textbooks, in my opinion, has risen considerably. There is much more of an attempt to keep up with current research. The publishing industry, responding to changes in the way kids live and are educated, is prioritizing nonfiction.

"Writing for children is much more difficult than most people realize. Picture book authors are often asked, 'Do you plan to write for grown-ups?' as though that would signify 'graduation' for us. In my opinion, most people who ask the question have a low regard for children.

"I have no interest in writing for adults. A good children's book is like poetry: you have comparatively few words to work with, and your text must sing. It must work equally well read silently as read aloud. I love the challenge of taking something complicated and expressing it simply. I hope that my books help give children an early love of reading and learning.

"My number-one leisure activity is still reading. I devour mysteries and historical novels. We like to take trips, usually to cities since we live in the country. We love museums and galleries and ethnic restaurants. For the first time this year we took the children to Europe. Part of the time we spent in Italy, where Giulio has relatives. He and I had both traveled extensively in Europe before marrying and becoming parents, and it was wonderful showing the kids some of our favorite places, as well as discovering new ones with them. We learned so much—maybe there's a book waiting to be written."[1]

FOOTNOTE SOURCES

[1]Based on an interview by Marguerite Feitlowitz for *Something about the Author.*
[2]"A Wise Monkey Tale," *Junior Literary Guild,* September, 1975.
[3]Publicity from Lothrop, Lee & Shepard Books, spring/fall, 1987.

FOR MORE INFORMATION SEE:

Martha E. Ward and Dorothy A. Marquardt, *Authors of Books for Young People,* supplement to the second edition, Scarecrow, 1979.
School Library Journal, November, 1983.
Day (New London, Conn.), November 6, 1986 (p. C1).

MAESTRO, Giulio 1942-

PERSONAL: Given name is pronounced *Jool*-yoh, and surname, Ma-*es*-troh; born May 6, 1942, in New York, N.Y., son of Marcello (a writer) and Edna (Ten Eyck) Maestro; married Betsy Crippen (a kindergarten teacher and writer), December 16, 1972; children: Daniela Marisa, Marco Claudio. *Education:* Cooper Union, B.F.A., 1964; further study in printmaking at Pratt Graphics Center, 1965-68. *Home and office:* 74 Mile Creek Rd., Old Lyme, Conn. 06371.

CAREER: Design Organization, Inc. (advertising design), New York City, assistant to art director, 1965-66; Warren A. Kass Graphics, Inc. (advertising design), New York City, assistant art director, 1966-69; free-lance writer and book illustrator, 1969—. *Exhibitions:* Society of Illustrators Show, New York, N.Y., 1968, 1974; American Institute of Graphic Arts, New York, N.Y., 1974; Art Director's Club, New York, N.Y., 1978, 1982; Fourteenth Exhibition of Original Pictures of International Children's Books, Japan, 1979.

AWARDS, HONORS: From Petals to Pinecones was selected one of Child Study Association of America's Children's Books of the Year, 1969, *Two Good Friends, Number Ideas through Pictures, Gray Duck Catches a Friend,* and *Milk, Butter and Cheese,* all 1974, *Oil, A Pack of Riddles, The Great Ghost Rescue,* and *Who Said Meow?,* all 1975, *Fat Polka-Dot Cat and Other Haiku,* 1976, *Train Whistles, Razzle-Dazzle Riddles, Space Telescope,* and *Hurricane Watch,* all 1986, and *Sunshine Makes the Seasons,* and *The Story of the Statue of Liberty,* both 1987; *The Tortoise's Tug of War* was included in the American Institute of Graphic Arts Children's Book Show, 1971-72, and *Three Kittens,* 1973-74; Merit Award from the Art Directors Club of New York, 1978, for *Harriet Goes to the Circus; Lambs for Dinner* was selected a Children's Choice by the International Reading Association and the Children's Book Council, 1979, *Fiddle with a Riddle,* 1980, *Moonkey,* 1982, and *Halloween Howls,* 1984; *Fish Facts and Bird Brains* was selected an Outstanding Science Trade Book for Children by the National Science Teachers Association, 1985; *Ferryboat* was selected a Notable Children's Trade Book in the Field of Social Studies by the National Council for Social Studies and the Children's Book Council, 1986.

WRITINGS:

JUVENILE; ALL SELF-ILLUSTRATED

(Reteller) *The Tortoise's Tug of War,* Bradbury, 1971.
The Remarkable Plant in Apartment 4, Bradbury, 1973, published in England as *The Remarkable Plant in Flat No. 4,* Macmillan, 1974.
One More and One Less: A Number Concept Book (Junior Literary Guild selection), Crown, 1974.
Leopard Is Sick, Greenwillow, 1978.
Leopard and the Noisy Monkeys, Greenwillow, 1979.
A Raft of Riddles, Dutton, 1982.
Halloween Howls: Riddles That Are a Scream, Dutton, 1983.
(With Betsy Maestro) *Just Enough Rosie,* Grosset, 1983.
Riddle Romp, Clarion, 1983.
What's a Frank Frank? Tasty Homograph Riddles, Clarion, 1984.
Razzle-Dazzle Riddles, Clarion, 1985.
What's Mite Might? Homophone Riddles to Boost Your Word Power, Clarion, 1986.
Riddle Roundup, Clarion, 1989.

ILLUSTRATOR; JUVENILE PICTURE BOOKS BY WIFE, BETSY C. MAESTRO

A Wise Monkey Tale (Junior Literary Guild selection), Crown, 1975.
Where Is My Friend? A Word Concept Book (Junior Literary Guild selection), Crown, 1976.
Fat Polka-Dot Cat and Other Haiku, Dutton, 1976.
In My Boat, Crowell, 1976.
Harriet Goes to the Circus: A Number Concept Book, Crown, 1977.
Busy Day: A Book of Action Words (Junior Literary Guild selection), Crown, 1978.
Lambs for Dinner, Crown, 1978.
On the Go: A Book of Adjectives (Junior Literary Guild selection), Crown, 1979.
Harriet Reads Signs and More Signs: A Word Concept Book (Junior Literary Guild selection), Crown, 1981.
Traffic: A Book of Opposites (ALA Notable Book), Crown, 1981.
The Key to the Kingdom, Harcourt, 1982.
The Guessing Game, Clarion, 1983.
(Ellen DelVecchio, co-author) *Big City Port,* Four Winds, 1983.

Betsy and Giulio Maestro

Ted
fed
Fred
a little **loaf**
of bread.

(From *Your Foot's on My Feet! And Other Tricky Nouns* by Marvin Terban. Illustrated by Giulio Maestro.)

On the Town: A Book of Clothing Words, Crown, 1983.
Harriet at Play, Crown, 1984.
Harriet at School, Crown, 1984.
Harriet at Home, Crown, 1984.
Harriet at Work, Crown, 1984.
Around the Clock with Harriet: A Book about Telling Time, Crown, 1984.
Camping Out: A Book of Action Words, Crown, 1985.
Through the Year with Harriet, Crown, 1985.
Ferryboat (Junior Literary Guild selection), Crowell, 1986.
The Story of the Statue of Liberty, Lothrop, 1986.
The Grab-Bag Party, Golden Press, 1986.
The Pandas Take a Vacation, Golden Press, 1986.
The Perfect Picnic, Golden Press, 1987.
A More Perfect Union: The Story of Our Constitution, Lothrop, 1987.
The Travels of Freddie and Frannie Frog, Golden Press, 1987.
Dollars and Cents for Harriet, Crown, 1988.
Taxi: A Book of City Words, Clarion Books, 1989.
Snow Day, Scholastic, 1989.
Temperature and You, Lodestar, 1989.

ILLUSTRATOR; JUVENILE

Joseph J. McCoy, *Swans*, Lothrop, 1967.
Millie McWhirter, *A Magic Morning with Uncle Al*, Collins & World, 1969.
Katherine Cutler, *From Petals to Pinecones: A Nature Art and Craft Book*, Lothrop, 1969.
Rudyard Kipling, *The Beginning of the Armadillos*, St. Martin's, 1970.
K. Cutler, *Creative Shellcraft*, Lothrop, 1971.
(With others) Richard Shaw, editor, *The Fox Book*, Warner, 1971.
Elyse Sommer, *The Bread Dough Craft Book*, Lothrop, 1972.
Franklyn M. Branley, *The Beginning of the Earth*, Crowell, 1972, revised edition, Crowell, 1987.
Jo Phillips, *Right Angles: Paper-Folding Geometry*, Crowell, 1972.
E. Sommer, *Designing with Cutouts: The Art of Decoupage*, Lothrop, 1973.
E. Sommer, *Make It with Burlap*, Lothrop, 1973.
(With others) R. Shaw, editor, *The Cat Book*, Warner, 1973.
Roma Gans, *Millions and Millions of Crystals*, Crowell, 1973.
Mirra Ginsburg, *What Kind of Bird Is That?*, Crown, 1973.
M. Ginsburg, *Three Kittens* (Junior Literary Guild selection), Crown, 1973.
Vicki Kimmel Artis, *Gray Duck Catches a Friend*, Putnam, 1974.
Tony Johnston, *Fig Tale*, Putnam, 1974.
Judy Delton, *Two Good Friends* (ALA Notable Book; Junior Literary Guild selection), Crown, 1974.
Harry Milgrom, *Egg-Ventures* (Junior Literary Guild selection), Dutton, 1974.
Mannis Charosh, *Number Ideas through Pictures*, Crowell, 1974.
Carolyn Meyer, *Milk, Butter and Cheese: The Story of Dairy Products*, Morrow, 1974.
Sarah Riedman, *Trees Alive*, Lothrop, 1974.
Melvin Berger, *The New Air Book*, Crowell, 1974.
(With others) R. Shaw, editor, *The Bird Book*, Warner, 1974.
Eva Ibbotson, *The Great Ghost Rescue*, Walck, 1975.
Maria Polushkin, *Who Said Meow?* (Junior Literary Guild selection), Crown, 1975.
William R. Gerler, compiler, *A Pack of Riddles*, Dutton, 1975.
R. Gans, *Oil: The Buried Treasure*, Crowell, 1975.
John Trivett, *Building Tables on Tables: A Book about Multiplication*, Crowell, 1975.
E. Sommer and Joellen Sommer, *A Patchwork, Applique, and Quilting Primer*, Lothrop, 1975.

(With others) R. Shaw, editor, *The Mouse Book*, Warne, 1975.
Sigmund Kalina, *How to Make a Dinosaur*, Lothrop, 1976.
R. Gans, *Caves*, Crowell, 1976.
M. Berger, *Energy from the Sun*, Crowell, 1976.
J. Delton, *Two Is Company*, Crown, 1976.
J. Delton, *Three Friends Find Spring* (Junior Literary Guild selection), Crown, 1977.
J. Delton, *Penny-Wise, Fun-Foolish*, Crown, 1977.
Isaac Asimov, *Mars, the Red Planet*, Lothrop, 1977.
Eve Barwell, *Make Your Pet a Present*, Lothrop, 1977.
Caroline Anne Levine, *Knockout Knock Knocks*, Dutton, 1978.
Gail Kay Haines, *Natural and Synthetic Poisons*, Morrow, 1978.
J. Trivett and Daphne Trivett, *Time for Clocks*, Crowell, 1979.
Vicki Cobb, *More Science Experiments You Can Eat*, Lippincott, 1979.
Joanne E. Bernstein, *Fiddle with a Riddle: Write Your Own Riddles* (Junior Literary Guild selection), Dutton, 1979.
I. Asimov, *Saturn and Beyond*, Lothrop, 1979.
Ruth Lerner Perle and Susan Horowitz, adapters, *Little Red Riding Hood with Benjy and Bubbles*, Holt, 1979.
R. L. Perle and S. Horowitz, adapters, *The Fisherman and His Wife with Benjy and Bubbles*, Holt, 1979.
R. L. Perle and S. Horowitz, adapters, *Rumpelstiltskin with Benjy and Bubbles*, Holt, 1979.
R. L. Perle and S. Horowitz, adapters, *Sleeping Beauty with Benjy and Bubbles*, Holt, 1979.
M. Ginsburg, *Kitten from One to Ten*, Crown, 1980.
J. Delton, *Groundhog's Day at the Doctor*, Parents Magazine Press, 1980.
Boris Arnov, *Water: Experiments to Understand It*, Lothrop, 1980.
Andrea G. Zimmerman, *The Riddle Zoo*, Dutton, 1981.
Mike Thaler, *Moonkey*, Harper, 1981.
Marvin Terban, *Eight Ate: A Feast of Homonym Riddles*, Clarion Books, 1982.
M. Terban, *In a Pickle: And Other Funny Idioms*, Clarion, 1983.
C. A. Levine, *The Silly Kid Joke Book*, Dutton, 1983.
Seymour Simon, *Dinosaurs Are the Biggest Animals That Ever Lived: And Other Wrong Ideas You Thought Were True*, Lippincott, 1984.
F. M. Branley, *Comets*, Crowell, 1984.
M. Terban, *I Think I Thought and Other Tricky Verbs*, Clarion, 1984.
Helen Roney Sattler, *Fish Facts and Bird Brains: Animal Intelligence*, Dutton, 1984.
F. M. Branley, *Space Telescope: A Voyage into Space Book*, Crowell, 1985.
F. M. Branley, *Sunshine Makes the Seasons*, revised edition, Crowell, 1985 (Maestro was not associated with the earlier edition).
H. R. Sattler, *Train Whistles: A Language in Code*, revised edition, Lothrop, 1985.
M. Terban, *Too Hot To Hoot: Funny Palindrome Riddles*, Clarion, 1985.
F. M. Branley, *Hurricane Watch*, Crowell, 1986.
M. Terban, *Your Foot's on My Feet! And Other Tricky Nouns*, Clarion, 1986.
M. Terban, *Mad as a Wet Hen and Other Funny Idioms*, Clarion, 1987.
F. M. Branley, *Rockets and Satellites*, revised edition (Maestro was not associated with the earlier edition), Crowell, 1987.
M. Terban, *Guppies in Tuxedos: Funny Eponyms*, Clarion, 1988.
F. M. Branley, *Tornado Alert!*, Crowell, 1988.
M. Terban, *Superdupers*, Clarion, 1989.

(From *Comets* by Franklyn M. Branley. Illustrated by Giulio Maestro.)

Some of Maestro's work has been published in Germany, France, Spain, The Netherlands, England, and Japan.

WORK IN PROGRESS: "My wife, Betsy, and I are collaborating on *Bicycle Trip,* and *Flowers to Fruit,* both for Crowell, *Sharks,* for Scholastic, *Delivery Van: Words for Town and Country,* and *All Aboard! A Book of Compound Words,* both for Clarion, *Machines and You,* for Lodestar, and *The Exploration of the Americas,* and *The Discovery of the Americas,* both for Lothrop. The last deals with America before the arrival of Christopher Columbus. I've always thought it fun to ponder the Native Americans discovering the Europeans. How strange the Europeans must have seemed to them!"

SIDELIGHTS: "From the time I was a child I always held a pencil, crayon or paintbrush in my hand. My boyhood idols were Walt Disney and Walt Kelly, and I even wrote to the Disney studio and to Kelly personally. The Disney studio sent me illustrative material, and Walt Kelly wrote me a letter personally, saying 'If you really want to do this, you have to draw everyday. You really have to keep at it.' Enclosed was an

original drawing as well. A letter from Walt Kelly—it's hard to put into words what a thrill that was for me. It lent weight to all the drawing I was doing. I always assumed that I would grow up to become an artist as well. Thinking back to Kelly's kindness to me, I make it a point to answer every letter I receive from kids, and to enclose a drawing or poster.

"In high school I realized that my talent extended beyond cartooning. I could draw realistically or abstractly in a number of mediums. It felt great, but it certainly didn't help me figure out what I 'would do in life.' If anything it confused the issue somewhat, because my options had increased.

"I majored in art at Cooper Union, renowned for its studio school and faculty members who were all working artists. The one drawback was that the faculty members had narrow viewpoints about art—you did it their way, or they didn't bother with you. When I think back on it, I remember how angry I was. Students would be praised by one teacher and criticized by the next for the same work. It was confusing at the time. Now I realize that all the personal opinions and 'visions' of the various teachers were useful, though at the time it seemed impossible to reconcile them. I can remember endless discussions on the

Fritzi froze her nose. (From *I Think I Thought and Other Tricky Verbs* by Marvin Terban. Illustrated by Giulio Maestro.)

The wind pushes sea water toward the shore. (From *Hurricane Watch* by Franklyn M. Branley. Illustrated by Giulio Maestro.)

subject of 'what is art.' I recall one teacher saying that if you had a drawing board covered with paint splatters and you randomly selected one square inch and put it up on the wall, it would be art. The role of randomness in art was a very big topic in those days. These discussions would have been much more fruitful if one of our teachers had had a sense of humor, and admitted that there were no hard answers.

"During my senior year, there was a commercial art course that some students took. There were the inevitable discussions about fine art verses commercial art. People would sometimes draw a distinction betwen 'fine art' and illustration. The assumption was that so-called fine artists have more talent. I feel that all artists are illustrators. The only really valid distinction has to do with money. Commercial artists get paid for their work, which is not necessarily the case with artists who make art for themselves. The idea that when you are getting paid you are compromising your principles isn't necessarily true. After all Michelangelo was compensated for painting the Sistine Chapel.

"I prepared a portfolio during my senior year at Cooper and landed a job as soon as I graduated. For the next five years I worked in advertising, starting with layout, design, type design, and so on. This was all useful experience but I was doing virtually no drawing on the job, and I was expending an awful lot of energy on projects I didn't care very much about.

"I hoped that the book field would offer me what I most wanted, which was a career as an illustrator. Unfortunately all my samples were from the advertising firm. Gradually I got to know people, started to get book jacket assignments, and then finally in 1970 my first book, *The Beginning of the Armadillos* by Rudyard Kipling. With my first publication, I was able to completely change careers. I was extremely fortunate."[1]

Giulio Maestro is renowned for his extraordinary artistic range and the variety of mediums and techniques in which he works. He has illustrated a number of books by other authors, has illustrated all of Betsy Maestro's works to date, and has illustrated a number of his own books as well. "There are two reasons why I like to work in a variety of styles: It keeps the art interesting and lively for me, and because I spend many hours in the studio every day, working with different materials and techniques helps to keep me fresh. Secondly, it enables me to illustrate books by quite a wide range of writers. It would be boring to do the same kind of project over and over again, and becoming 'typecast' could be a danger in this field. In order to make a nice living with book illustration, you have to be able to hustle, do a number of projects every year for different publishers. However, if all your work looks the same, you can quickly 'saturate' the market. That's why I try to vary my approach to each book, according to whatever the text seems to require. For example, some of my books are illustrated much more realistically than others.

"Over the course of a year I like to mix my projects—a nonfiction book, a picture book, a riddle book, all for different age groups. I usually average five to seven books a year. I always have many projects in different stages. There'll be initial sketches at one publisher while I'm doing the finishes for another and Betsy and I are discussing yet another collaboration.

(From *Through the Year with Harriet* by Betsy Maestro. Illustrated by Giulio Maestro.)

"Betsy and I have evolved a very good way of working together. We talk at the conceptual stage of a book, but I don't interfere with her writing if I can help it. Neither does she interfere with my drawings. But from the outset we agree on an overall visual style for the book. Betsy is very sensitive to the visual requirements of a good children's book—the balance between type and illustrations, how many lines a given page can comfortably accommodate, and rhythm, which is so important for a book intended to be read aloud. She has come to know what kind of language poses problems in terms of illustration (overly descriptive writing, for example) and what kind of writing is especially conducive to being illustrated. She visualizes the whole book as she writes and even includes page breaks.

"My first step on a new project generally is to make a color sketch. This sets a tentative style and palette for the book. Often this first sketch is in watercolor with pen and ink, sometimes in poster paint or in colored pencil. At the same time, I'll do a pencil rough of the whole book showing where the page breaks will be, where the drawings and type will sit. My background in advertising has proved tremendously helpful in terms of selecting and designing lettering. The elements of a book—drawings, typeface, lettering, page size—should be in constant balance for no one element should drown out any other.

"I send the initial color sketch and pencil rough to the publisher and turn to other projects while waiting for a response. Sometimes they love everything and I can go full steam ahead.

Important men began arriving in Philadelphia. (From *A More Perfect Union: The Story of Our Constitution* by Betsy Maestro. Illustrated by Giulio Maestro.)

Sometimes things are 'flagged' for comments or suggested revisions. The next step is to do a full set of careful drawings on tracing paper, or on paper that really pins down the layout of each page. When that is approved, I proceed to the final drawings and all the color work on good drawing paper.

"I like to save color for last. If I used it during the whole series of initial drawings, I'd get 'burned out.' I want the drawings not only to look spontaneous to others, but to feel spontaneous for me. I try not to labor on the drawings, I like lightness and quickness. I've developed a sort of 'mass market' technique of working stage by stage. When the drawings and layouts are completely set I start at the beginning and do the color work straight through page by page. All along I've had a sense of what the palette will be, but here again I like to surprise myself in the execution."[1]

The Maestro team is particularly well-known for their award-winning concept books. "Of course, every book for kids could be called a concept book. When Betsy and I describe one as such, it simply means that we have set out to present a given concept in a coherent and concentrated way. It doesn't mean that the book is preachy or resembles a textbook. These books aim to marry education and entertainment. However, the story line or entertainment aspect never overshadows the concept being presented. For example, in the 'Harriet' books we try to have no distracting visual elements, and a small unexpected surprise at the end of the book.

"I don't remember exactly how we decided to make Harriet an elephant. One consideration was to have a figure that would stand out on the page against simple color backgrounds. When we came up with the idea of a white elephant as the main character for the book, *Where Is My Friend?*, we didn't realize that she would grab the attention of children and become the star of a whole series of books. I liked the fact that Harriet was an off-beat character and could do things like hold her umbrella in her trunk or wear roller skates. Visually the books have a strong abstract quality. The sky is not necessarily blue, for instance; it might be orange or magenta; the sun might be green; the road might be purple. We knew we wanted bold colors and a flat,

two- dimensional perspective. Harriet, we decided, would stand out best if she were pure white, and help keep our color options open. Too, Harriet the elephant has more range flexibility than a human character. The idea has always been that Harriet would be an abstract semi-child figure, not engaged in adult activities. Yet alone in a house she has much more independence than any 'real' child would ever have. Casting Harriet as an animal simply eliminates a lot of off-the-point quibbles having to do with 'reality.' My guiding principle for the "Harriet" illustrations (as well as all our concept books) is: 'Keep it simple.' Don't introduce anything that will confuse, clutter or distract from the text."[1]

"For example, each picture in *Busy Day* was carefully composed to illustrate the particular action described by the word in large type at the bottom of the page. Extraneous details were eliminated, however humorous they might be. Instead, the offbeat team of characters, a clown and an elephant who are good friends, were used to add interest to normal circus activities. Following their progress through the day, we see them **eat** breakfast together, **work** at raising the circus tent, **swing** on trapezes, **jump** on a trampoline, and so on. While some of the activities may be unusual for an elephant, they are performed in a manner clearly identified by the reader. The typeface used in *Busy Day* was chosen for clarity, and the overall format determined in two ways: the fairly small page size allows for a book that is easily managed by small hands; the unobtrusive border on each page confines each word-concept to that page, so that there can be no confusion."[2]

"My latest book written by my wife and frequent collaborator, is about a day in the life of a taxi cab. From one page to another the cab takes us to different parts of a big city. The book is not completely realistic because a cab driver normally makes a hundred or so runs a day. Betsy had to pick and choose a far fewer number of trips. But visually it is quite realistic. It starts early in the morning, gradually gets brighter, then a little darker, then there's a shower, then it clears, then the sun goes down. The interplay of light presented a wonderful challenge. Because the taxi is always on the move, the book has a natural flow.

"First and foremost I'm an illustrator. I don't put myself in the same category with Arnold Lobel whose writing and drawing were equally brilliant. I don't fancy myself a great storyteller, but I love words and word play. My first-reader stories are fine, but haven't been terribly successful in the marketplace. The riddle and word concepts books fare much better. The riddle books are full of homonyms, puns, and plays-on-words, often fairly sophisticated. They're intended not only to be brain-teasers to the reader, but also good ammunition for stumping friends. I'm happy that my publishers didn't attempt to lower the difficulty level of these books. One of my pet peeves is that too often educators and publishers expect too little of kids. The ability to use language effectively has to be nurtured. Young minds should be encouraged to think more complex thoughts and exposed to rich language in reading materials. I hope my word-play books, through humor in text and pictures, help children to take joy in the subtleties of language and word meanings.

"As to hobbies, I do some woodworking—not fine cabinetry however—and I'm the resident fix-it person at home. As a change from working I sometimes make jam. I don't grow the fruit because it's a complicated operation requiring too much time. I just buy fruit from the local farm markets. Making jam is wonderfully therapeutic—I enjoy the colors, textures, fabulous aromas. And of course the compliments on the final product don't exactly hurt! Another hobby is gardening. After hours and hours at the drawing table or writing desk, it's great to go outside and work with a shovel, get my hands in the dirt, or fix a brick walk. It's a good change of pace.

"I think back a lot to the advice Walt Kelly gave me. After decades as an artist, his words ring truer today and bear repeating: 'Draw every day. Draw anything and everything you like. The important thing is to draw every day.' It's the same advice I now give children who ask me how they can learn to draw well. I tell them 'practice, practice, practice!'"[1]

FOOTNOTE SOURCES

[1]Based on an interview by Marguerite Feitlowitz for *Something about the Author*.
[2]*Junior Literary Guild*, March, 1978.

FOR MORE INFORMATION SEE:

Horn Book, April, 1972.
Martha E. Ward and Dorothy A. Marquardt, *Illustrators of Books for Young People,* Scarecrow Press, 1975.
Lee Kingman and others, compilers, *Illustrators of Children's Books: 1967-1976,* Horn Book, 1978.
Day, (New London, Conn.), November 6, 1986 (p. C1).

COLLECTIONS

De Grummond Collection, University of Southern Mississippi.
Kerlan Collection, University of Minnesota.

MALORY, (Sir) Thomas 1410(?)-1471(?)

PERSONAL: Born about 1410, at Newbold Revel, Warwickshire, England; son of Sir John Malory (a sheriff); died about 1471, in Newgate Prison, London, England; married wife, Elizabeth; children: Robert.

CAREER: British knight, known for his rendition of the Arthurian legends based mainly on French romances, completed about 1469 while he was imprisoned. Most scholars attribute him to a knight of Newbold Revel, Warwickshire, England, who succeeded to his father's estates in 1434, became a member of parliament in 1445, turned to outlawry about 1451, and spent most of the last years of his life in and out of prison on charges ranging from assault to extortion.

WRITINGS:

The Book of King Arthur and His Noble Knights of the Round Table, c. 1469, first printed and slightly revised by William Caxton as *Le morte d'Arthur,* [Westminster], 1485, facsimile reprinted as *Le Morte Darthur* (illustrated by Aubrey Beardsley), Dent, 1893, (from the Pierpont Morgan manuscript), introduction by Paul Needham, Scolar Press, 1976 [facsimile reprint from the Winchester manuscript published as *The Winchester Malory: A Facsimile,* introduction by N. R. Ker, Oxford University Press, 1976].

EDITIONS ADAPTED FOR YOUNG READERS

Sidney Lanier, editor, *The Boy's King Arthur* (illustrated by Alfred Kappes), Scribner, 1880 [later editions include those illustrated by N. C. Wyeth, Scribner, 1917, reissued, 197(?); Florian Kraner, Grosset, 1950].
Mary McLeod, editor, *The Book of King Arthur and His Noble Knights* (illustrated by A. G. Walker), E. & J. B. Young, 1900 [later editions include those illustrated by Henry C. Pitz, Lippincott, 1949; Alexander Dobkin, World Publishing, 1950; Herschel Levit, Macmillan, 1963; Howard Pyle, Parents Magazine Cultural Institute, 1964].
Howard Pyle, *The Story of King Arthur and His Knights* (self-illustrated), Scribner, 1903.
Andrew Lang, *The Tales of King Arthur and the Round Table* (illustrated by H. J. Ford), Longmans, Green, 1905.
H. Pyle, *The Story of the Champions of the Round Table* (self-illustrated), Scribner, 1905.
H. Pyle, *The Story of Sir Launcelot and His Companions* (self-illustrated), Scribner, 1907.
A. L. Hayden, *Stories of King Arthur* (illustrated by Arthur Rackham), Cassell, 1910.
H. Pyle, *The Story of the Grail and the Passing of Arthur* (self-illustrated), Scribner, 1910.
Henry Burrowes Lathrop, editor, *Malory's King Arthur and His Knights* (illustrated by Reginald Birch), Baker & Taylor, 1911.
Clifton Johnson, editor, *King Arthur and the Knights of the Round Table* (illustrated by Rodney Thompson), Macmillan, 1916.
Alfred W. Pollard, *The Romance of King Arthur and His Knights of the Round Table* (illustrated by A. Rackham), Macmillan, 1917, published as *Le morte d'Arthur: The Book of King Arthur and His Knights of the Round Table,* University Books, 1961.
Rupert S. Holland, editor, *King Arthur and the Knights of the Round Table* (illustrated by Lancelot Speed), G. W. Jacobs, 1919.
Philip Schuyler Allen, editor, *King Arthur and His Knights: A Noble and Joyous History* (illustrated by Meade Schaeffer and John R. Neill), Rand, McNally, 1924.
Enid Blyton, *The Knights of the Round Table* (illustrated by Kathleen Gell), Latimer House, 1950.
Roger Lancelyn Green, reteller, *King Arthur and His Knights of the Round Table* (illustrated by Lotte Reiniger), Penguin, 1953.
Barbara L. Picard, reteller, *Stories of King Arthur and His Knights* (illustrated by Roy Morgan), Oxford University Press, 1955.

(From the movie "The Sword in the Stone," an animated version of the legend of King Arthur. Copyright 1962 by Walt Disney Productions.)

Keith Baines, *Le morte d'Arthur: King Arthur and the Legends of the Round Table* (illustrated by Enrico Arno), C. N. Potter, 1962.

Barbara Schiller, reteller, *The Kitchen Knight* (illustrated by Nonny Hogrogian), Holt, 1965.

Jay Williams, *The Sword of King Arthur* (illustrated by Louis Glanzman), Crowell, 1968.

B. Schiller, reteller, *The Wandering Knight* (illustrated by H. Levit), Dutton, 1971.

John Steinbeck, *The Acts of King Arthur and His Noble Knights,* Farrar, Straus, 1976.

ADAPTATIONS:

"Knights of the Round Table" (motion picture), starring Robert Taylor and Ava Gardner, Metro-Goldwyn-Mayer, 1953.

RECORDINGS

"Le morte d'Arthur," adapted by John Barton, music by Thurston Dart, dramatized by Harry Andrews, William Squire, Joan Hart, and Tony White, Argo, 1963.

"Le morte d'Arthur: Launcelot and Guenever," edited by Barbara Holdridge, read by Siobhan McKenna, Caedmon, 1972.

SIDELIGHTS: Much speculation surrounds the true identity of the author of the written version of the Arthurian legends. According to most scholars, however, Sir Thomas Malory was

a knight, soldier, and a member of Parliament, who was born in Warwickshire, England about 1410. He was the son of Sir John Malory of Newbold Revel, Warwickshire, the local sheriff and a man of modest means. Malory's boyhood companions probably included the children of servants and landowners who worked at his family's manor and tended its fields.

Sometime in his youth it is thought that he served as a soldier under the banner of King Henry V. Scholars believe that Malory was a member of the great Earl of Warwick, Richard Beauchamp's company and that he was a part of the battle of Agincourt and might have witnessed the burning at the stake of Joan of Arc. Three times in Malory's stories of King Arthur and the Knights of the Round Table women are bound to the stake and condemned to death, but unlike the tragic Joan of Arc, they are always saved at the last minute.

Malory returned to Warwickshire after the end of the fighting in France. When his father died in 1434, he inherited the estates and may also have succeeded to a title of knight. A few years later he married a woman named Elizabeth who bore him a son, Robert, who died before him. In 1445, he became a member of the Parliament at Westminster.

Thereafter, records show that his life took a downward turn. From legal archives of the time, he is cited in lawsuits, charged with rape, robbery, extortion, cattle stealing, and with breaking

Beardsley's double-page illustration for the Arthurian legend. (From *Le Morte Darthur* by Thomas Malory. Illustrated by Aubrey Beardsley.)

into the Abbey of Coombe. For his various crimes, Malory served at least four prison sentences in the last twenty years of his life.

According to a legal document from Northampton, Sir Thomas Malory, along with a companion, was charged with having by force and arms insulted and wounded the plantiff at Sprotton in Northants, and stolen his goods. In 1454 he was released from prison on bail, but proceeded to steal cattle and other personal property. Malory was subsequently imprisoned in Colchester; escaped, but was recaptured and sent to Marshalsea Prison, which housed all types of criminals—debtors, murderers, thieves. It was located in Southwick, just southeast from the inn where Chaucer and his pilgrims were supposed to have met.

In 1456, Malory was released through a royal pardon and sent to Ludgate, a debtor's prison. The following year he was released on bail, but soon returned to prison, again at Marshalsea. The last recorded arrest came in 1460, when he was sent to Newgate Prison, where he translated from the French *Le morte d'Arthur*. In the book, Malory gives the only recorded information about his life. Referring to himself as the "knight prisoner," Malory implores the reader: "I praye you all jentylmen and jentylwymmen that redeth this book of Arthur and his knyghtes from the begynnyng to the endynge, praye for me whyle I am on lyve that God send me good delyveraunce. And whan I am deed, I praye you all praye for my soule. For this book was ended the ninth yere of the reygne of King Edward the Fourth, by Syr Thomas Maleore, knyght, as Jesu helpe hym for His grete myght, as he is the servaunt of Jesu bothe day and nyght."[1]

In 1471, he died at Newgate, probably due to plague. He was buried near the prison at Grey Friars Chapel.

Le Morte d' Arthur was the forerunner for all the Arthurian legends that followed. (From *The Story of the Champions of the Round Table* by Howard Pyle. Illustrated by the author.)

Fourteen years later, in 1485, William Caxton, the first English printer, published *Le morte d'Arthur*. Probably better known than any other English literary work of the Middle Ages except Chaucer's *Canterbury Tales,* it has been continuously in print ever since. Malory's *Le morte d'Arthur* is a compilation of Arthurian material from many sources telling the story of Arthur, the legendary king of Britain and his company of knights. Now approximately 500 years old, the book has been remarkably popular and has exerted a strong influence over many writers, including T. S. Eliot, Mark Twain, and Alfred Lord Tennyson. T. S. Eliot described Malory as one of his favorite authors.

In 1934, it was found that a fourteenth-century manuscript at Winchester College was a much fuller version than Caxton's, and contained sufficient biographical material to establish the author's identity. Although this manuscript is probably still not exactly what Malory originally wrote, it is closer to the original than Caxton's edited version. Eugene Vinaver, dean of Malory scholars and important interpreter of medieval French romances, commented on the longevity of the *Morte d'Arthur:* "Many writers had worked on the French Arthurian prose romances between the thirteenth and the fifteenth centuries; there had been adaptations of it in Spain and in Germany. All this is now dead and buried, and Malory alone stands as a rock defying all changes of taste and style and morals; not as a grand paradox of nature, but as a lasting work of art."[2]

Malory's work is the first English prose epic and the source of English Arthurian legend. Together with Chaucer in the fourteenth century, it laid the basis for modern English narrative.

Although there are very few concrete facts about Thomas Malory, his work has been well documented. Scholars know that *Le morte d'Arthur* was completed in 1469-70, and that its author was a knight prisoner while he wrote some or all of his book. Its principal source was a so-called "French Book," which contained several lengthy prose romances. It also draws heavily on two English poems that were written in Yorkshire and shows that its author had extensive knowledge of other northern English romances. It exemplifies medieval chivalry.

Only two copies are recorded of William Caxton's first edition of *The Noble and Ioyous Book Entytled Le Morte Darthur Notwythstondyng It Treateth of the Byrth Lyf and Actes of the Sayd Kyng Arthur of his Noble Knyghtes of the Rounde Table Theyr Mervayllous Enquestes and Adventures Thachyevyng of the Sankgreal and in Thende the Dolorous Deth and Departyng out of Thys World of Them Al Whiche Book Was Reduced in to Englysshe by Syr Thomas Malory Knight* (Westminster, 1485), and they are housed at John Rylands University Library in Manchester, England and the Pierpont Morgan Library in New York.

FOOTNOTE SOURCES

[1]William Matthews, *The Ill-Framed Knight: A Special Inquiry into the Identity of Sir Thomas Malory,* University of California Press, 1966.
[2]Edmund Reiss, *Sir Thomas Malory,* Twayne, 1966.

FOR MORE INFORMATION SEE:

Vita D. Scudder, *Le Morte d'Arthur of Sir Thomas Malory and Its Sources,* Dutton, 1917.
Edmund K. Chambers, *Sir Thomas Malory,* Oxford University Press, 1922, reissued, Folcroft, 1977.
George L. Kittredge, *Sir Thomas Malory,* privately printed, 1925, reissued, Folcroft, 1974.

(From the John Boorman film "Excalibur," starring Nigel Terry, Nicol Williamson and Nicholas Clay. An Orion/Warner Bros. release, 1981.)

Edward Hicks, *Sir Thomas Malory, His Turbulent Career: A Biography,* Harvard University Press, 1928, reissued, Octagon, 1970.

Eugene Vinaver, *Malory,* Clarendon Press, 1929, reissued, Folcroft, 1977.

Speculum: A Journal of Mediaeval Studies, January, 1933 (p. 3ff).

Robert H. Wilson, *Characterization in Malory,* Folcroft, 1934, reissued, Porter, 1982.

E. Vinaver, editor, *The Works of Sir Thomas Malory,* three volumes, Clarendon Press, 1947, revised edition, Oxford University Press, 1967, reissued, 1977.

"Education," *Time,* December 18, 1950.

Richard D. Altick, *Scholar Adventurers,* Macmillan, 1950.

Stanley J. Kunitz and Howard Haycraft, editors, *British Authors before 1800,* H. W. Wilson, 1952.

Frank N. Magill, editor, *Cyclopedia of World Authors,* Harper, 1958.

R. M. Lumiansky, editor, *Malory's Originality: A Critical Study of "Le morte d'Arthur,"* Johns Hopkins University Press, 1964.

Cornelia Meigs, editor, *A Critical History of Children's Literature,* Macmillan, 1966.

The McGraw-Hill Encyclopedia of World Biography, Volume 7, McGraw-Hill, 1973.

Ian Scott-Kilvert, editor, *British Writers,* Volume 1, Scribner, 1979.

Elva S. Smith, *The History of Children's Literature,* revised by Margaret Hodges and Susan Steinfirst, American Library Association, 1980.

JUVENILE

Margaret Hodges, *Knight Prisoner: The Tale of Sir Thomas Malory and His King Arthur* (illustrated by Don Bolognese and Elaine Raphael), Farrar, Straus, 1976.

MANGIN, Marie France 1940-

PERSONAL: Born June 30, 1940, in Yaounde, France; daughter of Jean (an administrator) and Marguerite (Guenet) Dupertuis; married Claude Mangin (a foreman), February 8, 1964; children: Herve, Muriel, Nicholas. *Home:* 39 rue du Chene Feuillu, Acheres, France 78260. *Agent:* Gautier Languereau, 18 rue Jacob, Paris, France.

CAREER: Free-lance author, 1969—. Has worked as a French teacher in Forbach, France, 1960-64, and as an editor in Paris, France, 1964-66.

WRITINGS:

Plume et pomme (title means "Feather and Apple"), Pomme d'Api, 1969.

Roux Roux Roux (title means "Red, Red, Red"), Pomme d'Api, 1970.

Mirabelle et les bonbons (title means "Mirabelle and the Candies"), Pomme d'Api, 1971.

Baille-Baille Annelyse (title means "Annelyse Is Always Sleeping"), Fleurus, 1972.

Grand mere et les Roses (title means "Grandmother and the Roses"), Fleurus, 1972.

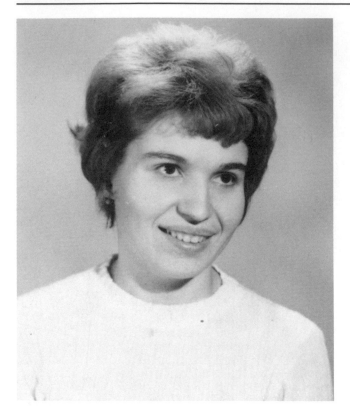

MARIE FRANCE MANGIN

Touroux le lievre (title means "Touroux the Hare"), Fleurus, 1973.

Un petit bout de printemps (title means "Something about Spring"), Fleurus, 1974.

Nono le rhino (title means "Nono, the Rhino"), Editions GP, 1977.

Zip l'hirondelle (title means "Zip, the Swallow") Editions GP, 1978.

Amusons nous (title means "Let's Have Fun"), Gautier-Languereau, 1978.

Crincrin le cactus (title means "Crincrin, the Cactus"), Editions GP, 1979.

Suzette et Nicholas et L'horloge des 4 saisons (illustrated by Satomi Ichikawa), Gautier-Languereau, 1978, translation published as *Suzanne and Nicholas and the Four Seasons*, F. Watts (London), 1978, adaptation by R. B. Wilson published as *Sophie and Nicky and the Four Seasons*, Heinemann, 1981, translation by Joan Chevalier published in America as *Suzette and Nicolas and the Seasons Clock*, Philomel, 1982.

(With Michele Lochak) *Suzette et Nicolas et le Cirque des Enfants*, Gautier-Languereau, 1979, translation by J. Chevalier published as *Suzette and Nicholas and the Sunijudi Circus*, Philomel, 1980.

Suzette et Nicholas au marche (title means "Suzette and Nicolas at the Market"), Gautier-Languereau, 1979.

Sophie bout de chou (title means, "Sophie, Little Darling"; illustrated by S. Ichikawa), Gautier-Languereau, 1987.

Le chamois de Lise (title means, "Lise's Chamois"; illustrated by Gerda Muller), Gautier-Languereau, 1988.

Contributor to anthology *Petite pomme*, 1989.

SIDELIGHTS: "I'm a rather shy, somewhat unsociable person, and I like to write because it's a satisfying way to express myself, and I feel rewarded, especially when my readers enjoy my books. As a child I was always inventing stories. My grandmother, who raised me, was sometimes irritated because she thought I was too much of a dreamer. As soon as I was able to, I read many books aloud from my grandmother's bookshelves. I gained a great deal from this activity.

"I started writing, poetry, then later, children's stories. I sent several of my stories to various publishers selected at random. The newspaper *Pomme d'Api* was the first to take an interest in my work, and the result was the publication of *Plume et pomme*. I was very proud! Then the publisher, GP, contacted me. I wrote four books for them.

"My first story, *Plume et pomme* was published in 1969. It's the story of a friendship between a little boy who was unhappy at being as light as a feather and a little girl who was always being teased because she was as round as an apple. It is my lucky story.

"While watching television one day, I heard Mrs. Gaillard (head of Gautier Languereau Publishing Company) speak on the role of children's books. What she said gave me some hope, and I sent her a series of little poems: 'La ronde des saisons.' They were never published (maybe some day?). But Mrs. Gaillard asked me to write a text for Satomi Ichikawa, an already well-known and very talented children's illustrator. I was very fortunate. My 'lucky-book' is *Suzette and Nicholas and the Seasons Clock*. I presented it to the school of the small town I live in.

"I have a small office in the attic of our house, and it's there that I give life to the characters and the situations I've created. I get so involved and time goes by so quickly that sometimes I've forgotten to prepare lunch for my youngest son when he comes home from school at lunchtime. He says, 'I see, you were writing again.'

"Occasionally I write text to go with illustrators' pictures. I'm very conscientious with that kind of work but always feel a little frustrated when the book comes out without my name on the cover, but am quite happy when that sort of writing job allows us to spend a week at the mountains. However, being a writer is much more rewarding morally than economically. Fortunately my husband is there to support the family with his own career. I only take care of the 'extra.'

"A future project is to write a novel about my childhood, but I don't yet feel quite mature enough to tackle that. . .will I ever be? I regret not being able to draw, but, after all, other people do it very well for me. A goal is to pass on my stories to my grandchildren (I don't have any yet!) and who knows, to my great grandchildren.

"I think that in order to write children's stories, one must remain a little bit of a child. I myself never quite grew up. My wish, of course, is to keep on being inspired to write interesting stories that will interest publishers and illustrators, the latter playing a quite important role in a children's book. My dream is to move or to make smile as many young readers as possible. That would make me quite content!"

McCLOY, James F(loyd) 1941-

PERSONAL: Born February 13, 1941, in Collingswood, N.J.; son of Charles Dunham (a credit manager) and Evelyn (a housewife; maiden name, Floyd) McCloy; married Virginia Stap (an accounting clerk), August 21, 1965; children: Karen, David. *Education:* Glassboro State College, B.A., 1964,

M.A., 1967. *Home:* 402 Rosewood Dr., Pilgrim Gardens, Newark, Del. 19713. *Office:* DDS/VR, Box 8862, Wilmington, Del. 19899.

CAREER: Teacher at public schools in Magnolia, N.J., 1964-65, and Edgewater Park, N.J., 1966-68; Glassboro State College, Glassboro, N.J., graduate assistant, 1965-66; Wilmington College, New Castle, Del., assistant professor of history, 1968-74, adjunct professor, 1976—; Delaware Department of Labor, Newark, Del., interviewer, 1975-83, Wilmington, Del., disability adjudicator, 1983—. Member of New Jersey folklife advisory council of New Jersey Historical Commission. *Member:* New Jersey Folklore Society. *Awards, honors: Dogs at Work* was selected one of Child Study Association of America's Children's Books of the Year, 1979.

WRITINGS:

(With Ray Miller, Jr.) *The Jersey Devil*, Middle Atlantic Press, 1976.

Dogs at Work (juvenile; illustrated by Sheila Beatty), Crown, 1979.

Delaware Periodical Director, Wilmington College Library, 1981.

Contributor of short story "Carranza's Last Flight," in *Focus on Reading*, Level III, edited by Thomas G. Gunning, Merrill Publishing, 1989. Contributor of more than a hundred articles to history and education journals and other periodicals.

WORK IN PROGRESS: A sequel to *The Jersey Devil*.

SIDELIGHTS: "*The Jersey Devil* is about a legendary creature that dates back at least to 1735. The story of the legend, once confined mostly to New Jersey, is now becoming nationally known as interest in monsters and the supernatural is increasing.

"*Dogs at Work* is an illustrated children's book that describes eleven breeds of dogs that have worked for people in the past and that continue to work for people in different but equally important ways today. I find research as challenging and stimulating as writing. I always have to become enthusiastic over a subject before working on it."

McFARLAN, Donald M(aitland) 1915-

PERSONAL: Born October 20, 1915, in Aberdeen, Scotland; son of Donald (a clergyman) and Mary Proudfoot (a housewife; maiden name, Maitland) McFarlan; married Elspeth G. McQueen (a teacher), December 1, 1942; children: Donald R. McQueen. *Education:* University of Glasgow, M.A. (with honors), 1937, diploma in divinity (with distinction), 1940, Ph.D., 1957. *Home:* 94 Southbrae Dr., Glasgow G13 1TZ, Scotland.

CAREER: Ordained Church of Scotland clergyman, 1940; educational missionary in Calabar, Nigeria, 1940-51; Jordanhill College of Education, Glasgow, Scotland, lecturer, 1951-65, senior lecturer, 1965-67, principal lecturer in religious education, 1967-81. External lecturer at University of Ibadan and University of Ife. Convener of business committee of general council of University of Glasgow, 1974-77, Host of "Fireside Sunday School," a children's program on British Broadcasting Corp. (BBC)— Scotland, 1959-70. Member of Court of University of Glasgow, 1984-88. *Member:* Field Society of Nigeria, Royal Scottish Automobile Club, Boys' Brigade (honorary vice-president).

WRITINGS:

JUVENILE

The Greatest Book in the World, Sheldon Press, 1944.
Write Good Engish, Sheldon Press, 1946.
World Travellers, Sheldon Press, 1946.
Calabar: The Church of Scotland Mission, T. Nelson, 1946, 2nd edition, 1957.
The Story of Trade, Sheldon Press, 1947.
Saint Columba, Sheldon Press, 1947.
The Story of Writing, Sheldon Press, 1948.
A Book of Bible Prayers, Sheldon Press, 1948.
Elephant's Birthday Party, T. Nelson, 1948.
Stumpy Sings on Wednesdays, Too, T. Nelson, 1948.
The Secret of the Drum, T. Nelson, 1948.
Timothy Wins a Medal, T. Nelson, 1948.
Pioneers of Health, T. Nelson, 1948.
Trading through the Ages, T. Nelson, 1948.
The Story of Healing, Sheldon Press, 1949.
The Story of Education, Sheldon Press, 1949.
Cross River Tales, two volumes, T. Nelson, 1950.
Jacob and Esau, T. Nelson, 1950.
Moses the Leader, T. Nelson, 1950.
Joseph and His Brothers, T. Nelson, 1950.
The Story of Joshua, T. Nelson, 1950.
David the Shepherd Boy, T. Nelson, 1950.
Elijah the Prophet, T. Nelson, 1950.
Four Great Leaders, T. Nelson, 1950.

DONALD M. MCFARLAN

The Pilgrim's Progress, T. Nelson, 1950.
Countryside Bible Book, Stirling Tract Enterprise, 1954.
Countryside Bible Prayers, Stirling Tract Enterprise, 1957.
White Queen: The Story of Mary Slessor, Lutterworth, 1957.
Mackay of Uganda, Lutterworth, 1958.
The Lively Oracles: The Story of the National Bible Society of Scotland, T. Nelson, 1959.
Highway to the Bible, Books 1-4, Blackie, 1962.
A Bible Reference Book, Blackie, 1973.
Who and What and Where in the Bible, John Knox, 1974, reissued, Blackie, 1982.
The Nazarene File, Blackie, 1978.
Live and Learn, Blackie, 1980.
The Founders' File, Blackie, 1982.
First for Boys: The Story of the Boys' Brigade, Collins, 1982.
Concise Bible Dictionary, Twenty-third Publications, 1986.
Search: The Christian Experience, Blackie, 1983, revised edition, 1989.

MELVILLE, Herman 1819-1891

PERSONAL: Born August 1, 1819, in New York, N.Y.; died September 28, 1891, in New York, N.Y.; son of Allan (an importer) and Maria (Gansevoort) Melville; married Elizabeth Knapp Shaw, August 4, 1847; children: Malcolm, Stanwix, Elizabeth, Frances. *Education:* Attended New York Male High School, and Albany Classical School. *Religion:* Dutch Reformed Church. *Residence:* New York, N.Y.

CAREER: Writer, 1844-91; Customhouse, New York, N.Y., inspector of customs, 1866-85. Worked in various occupations and professions, including bank clerk, assistant clerk in a fur store, farmer, teacher, cabin boy, and seaman. Lecture tour, 1857-60.

WRITINGS:

NOVELS

Typee: A Peep at Polynesian Life, 2 volumes, Wiley & Putnam, 1846, revised edition published as *Typee; or, A Narrative of a Four Months' Residence among the Natives of a Valley of the Marquesas Islands*, 2 volumes, John Murray [London], 1846, published as *Typee: A Romance of the South Seas*, Harcourt, 1920, new edition published as *Typee: Four Months Residence in the Marquesas*, Pacific Basin Books, 1985 (other editions include those illustrated by H. Moore, D. C. Heath & Co., 1902, Mead Shaeffer, Dodd, 1923, Miguel Covarrubias, Limited Editions Club, 1935, and with woodcuts by Elaine Raphael and Don Bolognese, Franklin Library, 1979, published as *Typee*, illustrated by Robert Shore, Bantam, 1958, and Jacques Boullaire, Folio Press, 1974.)
Omoo: A Narrative of Adventure in the South Seas, Harper & Brothers, 1847, Dutton, 1907, new edition, Pacific Basin Books, 1985 (other editions published as *Omoo* illustrated by Mead Schaeffer, Dodd, 1924, and with wood engravings by Reynolds Stone, Limited Editions Club, 1961).
Mardi: And a Voyage Thither, 2 volumes, Harper & Brothers, 1849, St. Boltolph Society, 1923, New American Library, 1964, new edition published as *Mardi*, Hendricks House, 1987.
Redburn: His First Voyage, Harper & Brothers, 1849, Doubleday, 1957, Holt, 1971, (another edition illustrated by Frank T. Merrill, St. Botolph Society, 1924).

White Jacket; or, The World in a Man-of-War, Harper & Brothers, 1850, United States Book Co., 1892, Northwestern University Press, 1970.
Moby-Dick; or, The Whale, Harper & Brothers, 1851, Dutton, 1907, Dodd, 1979, (published in England as *The Whale*, 3 volumes, Richard Bentley, 1851), published as *Moby-Dick*, illustrated by Seymour Fleishman, Scott, Foresman, 1948, adapted for young readers by Felix Sutton (illustrated by H. B. Vestal), Grosset, 1956, adapted by Patricia Daniels, Raintree, 1981, adapted by Joanne Fink (juvenile edition; illustrated by Hieronimus Fromm), Silver, 1984 (other editions include those illustrated by I. W. Taber, Scribners, 1899, Mead Schaeffer, Dodd, 1922, Rowland Hilder, Knopf, 1926, John D. Whiting, J. H. Sears, 1928, Rockwell Kent, Random House, 1930, Alfred Staten Conyers, Saalfield Publishing, 1931, Anton Otto Fischer, Winston, 1931, Raymond Bishop, A. & C. Boni, 1933, Rockwell Kent, Modern Library, 1944, Thomas G. Fraumeni, Globe Book Co., 1950, Boardman Robinson, Heritage Press, 1956, A. S. M. Ronaldson, Longmans, Green, 1959, Robert Shore, Macmillan, 1962, LeRoy Neiman, Artist's Limited Edition, 1975, Warren Chappell, Norton, 1976, Barry Moser, Arion Press, 1979).
Pierre; or, The Ambiguities, Harper & Brothers, 1852, Dutton, 1929, new edition edited by Henry A. Murray, Farrar, Straus, 1949.
Israel Potter: His Fifty Years of Exile, Putnam, 1855, Doubleday, 1965, published as *The Refugee*, T. B. Peterson & Brothers, 1865, published as *His Fifty Years of Exile (Israel Potter)*, Sagamore Press, 1957.
The Piazza Tales (includes "Benito Cereno" and "Bartleby the Scrivener"), Dix & Edwards, 1856, Russell, 1963, (another editon illustrated by Benj Greenstein, Elf Publishers, 1929).
The Confidence Man: His Masquerade, Dix & Edwards, 1857, Holt, 1964, new edition published as *Confidence-Man*, Archon Books, 1987.
Billy Budd and Other Prose Pieces, edited by Raymond W. Weaver, Constable, 1924, published as *Billy Budd and Other Tales*, New American Library, 1961, published as *Billy Budd, Sailor*, edited by Harrison Hayford and Merton M. Sealts, Jr., University of Chicago Press, 1962, also published as *Billy Budd, Foretopman* (illustrated by Robert Quackenbush), F. Watts, 1968, published as *Billy Budd: An Inside Narrative*, Bobbs-Merrill, 1975, text edition with student activity book published as *Billy Budd*, Pendulum Press, 1979.
Benito Cereno (illustrated by E. McKnight Kauffer), Nonesuch Press, 1926, another edition illustrated with wood engravings by Garrick Palmer, Imprint Society, 1972.

POETRY

Battle-Pieces and Aspects of the War, Harper & Brothers, 1866, School Facsimiles, 1979.
Clarel: A Poem and Pilgrimage in the Holy Land, Putnam, 1876, new edition edited by Walter E. Bezanson, Hendricks House, 1973.
John Marr and Other Sailors with Some Sea Pieces, DeVinne Press, 1888, Folcroft, 1975, published as *John Marr and Other Poems*, Princeton University Press, 1922, published as *John Marr*, Menhaden Press, 1980.
Timoleon, Caxton, 1891, published as *Timoleon*, Folcroft, 1976.

OTHER

The Apple-Tree Table and Other Sketches, Princeton University Press, 1922, Greenwood, 1969.

Herman Melville, 1870.

(From the 1930 Warner Bros.' movie "Moby Dick," starring Joan Bennett and John Barrymore.)

Family Correspondence of Herman Melville 1830-1904, edited by Victor H. Paltsits, New York Public Library, 1929, Haskell, 1976.

Journal Up the Straights: October 11, 1856-May 5, 1857, edited by R. Weaver, Cooper Square, 1935.

Journal of a Visit to London and the Continent 1849- 1850, edited by Eleanor Melville Metcalf, Harvard University Press, 1948.

Journal of a Visit to Europe and the Levant, October 11, 1856-May 6, 1857, edited by Howard C. Horsford, Princeton University Press, 1955, Greenwood, 1976.

The Letters of Herman Melville, edited by Merrell R. Davis and William H. Gilman, Yale University Press, 1960.

Herman Melville: Authentic Anecdotes of Old Zack, edited and with an introduction by Kenneth Starosciak, privately printed, 1973.

Stuart M. Frank, *Herman Melville's Picture Gallery: Sources and Types of the "Pictorial" Chapters of Moby-Dick*, E. J. Lefkowicz, 1986.

The Essential Melville, edited by Robert Penn Warren, Ecco Press, 1987.

COLLECTIONS

The Works of Herman Melville, 16 volumes, Constable, 1922-24.

John Marr and Other Poems, introduction by Henry Chapin, Princeton University Press, 1922.

Poems, Containing Battle-Pieces, John Marr and Other Sailors, Timoleon, and Miscellaneous Poems, Constable, 1924, Russell, 1963.

Shorter Novels of Herman Melville, Liveright, 1928, new edition, 1978.

Romances of Herman Melville: Typee, Omoo, Mardi, Moby Dick, White Jacket, Israel Potter, Redburn, Pickwick Publishers, 1928.

Billy Budd, Benito Cereno, [and] The Enchanted Isles, Press of the Readers Club, 1942.

Selected Poems of Herman Melville, edited by William Plomer, Hogarth Press, 1943.

Selected Poems, edited by F. O. Matthiessen, New Directions, 1944.

Collected Poems of Herman Melville, edited by Howard P. Vincent, Packard & Co., 1947.

Complete Works of Herman Melville, 7 volumes, Hendricks House, 1947-69.

The Complete Stories of Herman Melville, edited by Jay Leyda, Random House, 1949.

Billy Budd and Other Stories, Lehmann, 1951.

The Complete Stories, edited by J. Leyda, Eyre and Spottiswoode, 1951.

Selected Writings of Herman Melville: Complete Short Stories, Typee, [and] Billy Budd, Foretopman, Modern Library, 1952.

The Portable Melville, edited by Jay Leyda, Viking, 1952, Penguin, 1978.

Billy Budd [and] The Piazza Tales, Anchor Books, 1956.

Typee [and] Billy Budd, edited by Milton R. Stern, Dutton, 1958.

Four Short Novels, Bantam, 1959.

Selected Tales and Poems, edited by Richard Chase, Rinehart, 1960.

Three Shorter Novels of Herman Melville, Harper, 1962.

Billy Budd [and] Typee, Washington Square Press, 1962.

Herman Melville: Stories, Poems, and Letters, edited by R. W. B. Lewis, Dell, 1962.

Melville: The Best of Moby Dick and Typee; also Billy Budd Complete Plus More, [illegible], 1964.

Selected Poems, edited by Hennig Cohen, Doubleday, 1964.

Cover for the New American Library softcover edition. (From *Billy Budd and Other Tales* by Herman Melville. Illustrated by Fitz Hugh Lave.)

Billy Budd [and] Benito Cereno (illustrated with paintings by Robert Shore), Heritage Press, 1965.

Billy Budd, [and] The Encantadas, Airmont, 1966.

Great Short Works, Harper, 1966.

Three Stories (illustrated with wood engravings by Garrick Palmer), Folio Society, 1967.

Five Tales, Dodd, 1967.

Billy Budd, Sailor and Other Stories, edited by Harold Beaver, Penguin, 1967.

The Writings of Herman Melville, 6 volumes, edited by H. Hayford, Hershel Parker and G. Thomas Tanselle, Northwestern University Press, 1968-71.

Billy Budd and Other Stories, Houghton, 1970.

Great Short Works of Herman Melville, edited by Warner Berthoff, Harper, 1970.

Herman Melville: Voyages, Hallmark Editions, 1970.

Selected Poems of Herman Melville, edited by Robert Penn Warren, Random House, 1970.

On the Slain Collegians, edited and illustrated with woodcuts by Antonio Frasconi, Farrar, Straus, 1971.

Selected Poems, edited by F. O. Matthiessen, Folcroft, 1972.

Poems of Herman Melville, edited by Douglas Robillard, College & University Press, 1976.

Billy Budd, Sailor; The Piazza Tales (illustrated by J. William Myers), Franklin Library, 1978.

Collected Poems, edited by H. P. Vincent, Hendricks House, 1981.

Typee, Omoo, Mardi, edited by G. Thomas Tanselle, Library of America, 1982.

Typee: A Peep at Polynesian Life; Omoo: A Narrative of Adventures in the South Seas: Mardi: And a Voyage Thither, Cambridge Press, 1982.

Redburn, His First Voyage; White Jacket, or, The World in a Man-of-War; Moby-Dick, or, The Whale, Cambridge Press, 1983.

Moby Dick; The Confidence Man; The Piazza Tales; Billy Budd, Octopus, 1984.

Pierre, Israel Potter, The Piazza Tales, The Confidence Man, Billy Budd, Uncollected Tales, edited by H. Hayford, Library of America, 1985.

The Piazza Tales and Other Prose Pieces: 1839-1860, edited by H. Hayford and H. Parker, Northwestern University Press, 1986.

Suddenly sweeping his sickle-shaped lower jaw beneath him, Moby Dick had reaped away Ahab's leg. (From Moby Dick; or, The White Whale by Herman Melville. Illustrated by Ambroise Louis Garneray.)

Contributor to Literary World, Yankee Doodle, Putnam's Monthly, and Harper's Monthly.

ADAPTATIONS

MOTION PICTURES

"The Sea Beast" (based on Moby Dick; silent film), starring John Barrymore, 1926.

"Moby Dick; or, The White Whale," starring John Barrymore and Joan Bennett, Warner Bros., 1930.

"Omoo-Omoo, the Shark God," starring Ron Randell, Devera Burton, and Trevor Bardette, Elsa Pictures, 1949.

"Herman Melville's Moby Dick," Contemporary Films, 1954.

"Moby Dick," starring Gregory Peck and Richard Basehart, Warner Bros., 1956.

"Enchanted Island" (based on Typee), Warner Bros., 1958.

"Bartleby" (based on a tale by Melville), Audio-Visual Services, 1962.

"Billy Budd" (based on the play by Louis O. Coxe and Robert H. Chapman from the novel Billy Budd, Foretopman), starring Robert Ryan, Peter Ustinov, Melvyn Douglas, and Terence Stamp, Allied Artists, 1962.

"The Trial of Billy Budd, Sailor," Teaching Film Custodians, 1965.

"A Discussion of Herman Melville's Bartleby," Encyclopaedia Britannica Educational Corp, 1969.

"Books Alive: Moby Dick," Bailey Films, 1969.

"The Great American Novel: Moby Dick," Bailey Films, 1969, BFA Educational Media, 1971.

"Bartleby by Herman Melville," Encyclopaedia Britannica Educational Corp., 1969.

FILMSTRIPS

"Moby Dick," Fletcher Smith Studios, 1946, Simon & Schuster, 1957, Brunswick Productions, 1967, Educational Dimensions, 1968, Random House, (transparencies), Creative Visuals, 1969, (videocassette; still illustrations with narration), Congress Video Group.

"Billy Budd," Brunswick Productions, 1969.

"Moby Dick, or the Whale: Analysis and Evaluation," Society for Visual Education, 1970.

"Bartleby the Scrivener" (with cassette), Prentice-Hall Media, 1977.

PLAYS

Henry Reed, Moby Dick, a Play for Radio, J. Cape, 1947.

Louis O. Coxe and Robert Chapman, Billy Budd, a Play in Three Acts, Princeton University Press, 1951.

"Moby Dick," adapted by Orson Welles, produced at Duke of York's Theatre, London, June 16, 1955, produced in New York at Ethel Barrymore Theatre, starring Rod Steiger, November 28, 1962.

Moby Dick—Rehearsed: A Drama in Two Acts, Samuel French, 1965.

Robert Lowell, The Old Glory (theater trilogy based on stories by N. Hawthorne and a novella by Melville), Noonday Press, 1966, revised edition, Farrar, Straus, 1968.

James M. Salem, Herman Melville's The Court Martial of Billy Budd: A Play in One Act, Dramatic Publishing, 1969.

"Pequod" (based on Moby Dick; or, The Whale), produced at Mercury Theatre, New York, N.Y., June 29, 1969.

Guy Williams, adaptor, Billy Budd; and, Moby Dick: Adapted for the Stage, Macmillan (London), 1969.

RECORDINGS

"Moby Dick," Decca, 1960, Spoken Arts, 1963, (cassette), Caedmon.

"Billy Budd, Stereo Drama," General Electric, 1963.

"Moby Dick: Selections," Folkways Records, 1965.

The *Essex* stove by a whale. (From *Moby Dick; or, The Whale* by Herman Melville. Illustrated by Barry Moser.)

"Moby Dick by Herman Melville," adapted by Brainerd Duffield, Listening Library, 1971.

"Moby Dick" (excerpts), Caedmon, 1975.

"Billy Budd, Foretopman" (record; cassette), Listening Library, 1977.

"Billy Budd" (record; cassette), Caedmon, (cassette), Listen for Pleasure.

"The Confidence Man: A Comic Fable: Opera in Two Parts," T. Presser Co., 1982.

SIDELIGHTS: **August 1, 1819.** Born on Pearl Street in New York City, Herman Melville was the third child of Allan and Maria Gansevoort Melvill. (The final "e" was added to the family name after 1832.) Both parents came from distinguished and patriotic families, with two claims to historical distinction of which Melville took great pride. His maternal grandfather was a hero of the American Revolution, and his paternal grandfather a participant at the Boston Tea Party. Upon the birth of his son, Allan Melvill wrote to his brother-in-law: "With a grateful heart I hasten to inform you of the birth of another Nephew, which joyous event occurred at 1/2 past 11 last night—our dear Maria displayed her accustomed fortitude in the hour of peril & is as well as circumstances & the intense heat will admit—while the little Stranger has good lungs, sleeps well & feeds kindly, he is in truth a chopping Boy."[1]

Melville's mother, a domineering woman, raised her children in accordance with the strict Calvinist ethics of the Dutch-Reformed church to which she belonged. His father, whom he idolized, began his career as an importer of French millinery items, then as the owner of a dry-goods store in New York City. He was a travelled man of some culture and an engaging story-teller who entertained his children with tales of his sea voyages.

1825. Melville entered New York Male High School. During a summer visit to the Albany side of the family, Allan Melvill sent a letter to his brother-in-law: "I now consign to your especial care & patronage, my beloved Son Herman, an honest hearted double rooted Knickerbocker of the true Albany stamp, who I trust will do equal honour in due time to his ancestry parentage & Kindred—he is very backward in speech &

somewhat slow in comprehension, but you will find him as far as he understands men & thinks both solid & profound, & of a docile & amiable disposition. . . ."[1]

A few years later, he reported: "Herman I think is making more progress than formerly, & without being a bright Scholar, he maintains a respectable standing, & would proceed further, if he could be induced to study more—being a most aimiable & innocent child, I cannot find it in my heart to coerce him, especially as he seems to have chosen Commerce as a favorite pursuit, whose practical activity can well dispense with much book kowledge."[1]

Melville's childhood was secure and comfortable until 1830 when his father suffered severe business losses. Having borrowed considerable amounts of money over the years, Allan Melvill closed his business in New York, and moved to Albany with his family. There, he attempted to recover financially by going into the fur business.

January 28, 1932. Mentally and physically exhausted, Allan Melvill died, deep in debt, leaving behind his widow and eight children. For several years the family lived in financial uncertainty, relying on the help of well-to-do relatives. Melville was forced to leave school and take a job first as a clerk in his Uncle Peter Gansevoort's bank, then on his Uncle Thomas's farm near Pittsfield, Massachusetts.

January, 1835. Entered the Albany Classical School while working part time in the family cap and fur store run by his elder brother, Gansevoort. Two years later, in the face of a deepening national crisis, the family business collapsed. Melville relinquished his formal education and accepted a teaching position at a school near Pittsfield to help support his family. "My school is situated in a remote & secluded part of the town about five miles from the village, and the house at which I am now boarding is a mile and a half from any other tenement whatever—being located on the summit of as savage and lonely a mountain as ever I ascended. The scenery however is most splendid & unusual,—embracing an extent of country in the form of an Amphitheatre sweeping around for many miles.

(From the movie "Billy Budd," starring Terence Stamp and Melvyn Douglas. Released by United Artists, 1962.)

"My scholars are about thirty in number, of all ages, sizes, ranks, charaterrs [sic], & education; some of them who have attained the ages of eighteen can not do a sum in addition, while others have travelled through the Arithmatic: but with so great swiftness that they can not recognize objects in the road on a second journey: & are about as ignorant of them as though they had never passed that way before.

"The man with whom I am now domicilated is a perfect embodiment of the traits of Yankee character,—being shrewd bold & independant, carrying himself with a genuine republican swagger, as hospitable as 'mine host' himself, perfectly free in the expression of his sentiments, and would as soon call you a fool or a scoundrel, if he thought so—as, button up his waistcoat.—He has reared a family of nine boys and three girls, 5 of whom are my pupils—and they all burrow together in the woods—like so many foxes."[2]

1839. "Fragments from a Writing Desk," written under a pseudonym, was published in *Democratic Press and Lansingburgh Advertiser*.

Melville went to New York where, partly from financial necessity, he signed on for his first voyage as a cabin boy on the *St. Lawrence,* sailing for Liverpool. The trip, which instilled in him a love of the sea, was both traumatic and romantic. It later served as a basis for *Redburn*, in which he recreated this experience in detail, through the eyes of a sailor-boy narrator. "Yes! yes! give me this glorious ocean life, this salt-sea life,

this briny, foamy life, when the sea neighs and snorts, and you breathe the very breath that the great whales respire! Let me roll around the globe, let me rock upon the sea; let me race and pant out my life, with an eternal breeze astern, and an endless sea before!

"But how soon these raptures abated, when after a brief idle interval, we were again set to work, and I had a vile commission to clean out the chicken coops, and make up the beds of the-pigs in the long-boat.

"Miserable dog's life is this of the sea! commanded like a slave, and set to work like an ass! vulgar and brutal men lording it over me, as if I were an African in Alabama. Yes, yes, blow on, ye breezes, and make a speedy end to this abominable voyage!"[3]

October 1, 1839. Returning home to find his mother living in extreme poverty, he again taught school. "My son Herman," his mother wrote to her brother, "is now doing well and will be able to allow me from $150. to $200. a year. Allan will soon be able to earn more than he needs for Clothing and will be able to assist me also. In a few years with Gods blessing we will be able to relieve you both entirely from this unpleasant Charity. Herman will need nearly the whole of his first quarters salary after paying his board, to procure necessary clothing &c."[1]

The school closed down before the completion of the term and neglected to pay Melville's salary. Unemployed, he travelled West, and visited his Uncle Thomas now living in Illinois.

(From the 1926 silent film "The Sea Beast," starring John Barrymore in the role of Ahab.)

Finding that his Uncle could not secure his future, he returned to New York in the fall of **1840** where he was unsuccessful in finding work. Once again, Melville turned to the sea and on **January 3, 1841,** he sailed to the South Seas on the whaler, *Acushnet.* New England's whaling fleet was at its peak, and little experience was required to become a crew member. He was gone for nearly four years, travelling through Rio, around Cape Horn, and up the coast of South America to the Galapagos Islands. Several of his novels, including *Moby Dick* and the autobiographical *Typee,* were shaped by this adventure. In *Typee,* Melville described life on board the whaler: "The usage on board of her was tyrannical; the sick had been inhumanly neglected; the provisions had been doled out in scanty allowance; and her cruizes were unreasonably protracted. The captain was the author of these abuses; it was in vain to think that he would either remedy them, or alter his conduct, which was arbitrary and violent in the extreme. His prompt reply to all complaints and remonstrances was—the butt- end of a hand-spike, so convincingly administered as effectually to silence the aggrieved party.

"To whom could we apply for redress? We had left both law and equity on the other side of the Cape; and unfortunately, with a very few exceptions, our crew was composed of a parcel of dastardly and mean-spirited wretches, divided among themselves, and only united in enduring without resistance the unmitigated tyranny of the captain. It would have been mere madness for any two or three of the number, unassisted by the rest, to attempt making a stand against his ill usage. They would

only have called down upon themselves the particular vengeance of this 'Lord of the Plank,' and subjected their shipmates to additional hardships."[4]

July 9, 1842. Jumped ship at Nukahiva, Marquesas Islands, with his friend Richard Tobias Greene, the "Toby" of *Typee.* "Placed in these circumstances then, with no prospect of matters mending if I remained aboard the *Dolly,* I at once made up my mind to leave her: to be sure it was rather an inglorious thing to steal away privately from those at whose hands I had received wrongs and outrages that I could not resent; but how was such a course to be avoided when it was the only alternative left me? Having made up my mind, I proceeded to acquire all the information I could obtain relating to the island and its inhabitants, with a view of shaping my plans of escape accordingly."[4]

Melville and Greene stumbled into the path of the fierce and supposedly cannibalistic, Taipis. Contrary to its reputation, the tribe proved to be extremely friendly but made it quite clear to its guests that they would never be allowed to leave. In *Typee,* Melville described his "attendant": "Kory-Kory, though the most devoted and best natured serving-man in the world, was, alas! a hideous object to look upon. He was some twenty-five years of age, and about six feet in height, robust and well made, and of the most extraordinary aspect. His head was carefully shaven, with the exception of two circular spots, about the size of a dollar, near the top of the cranium, where the hair, permitted to grow of an amazing length, was twisted up in two

A silvery jet was seen far in advance. . . .Lit up by the moon it looked celestial. (From *Moby Dick; or, The Whale* by Herman Melville. Illustrated by Rockwell Kent.)

The whale swam upwards, turning on its back, and. . . .

Look out, captain!

His jaws slowly closed on the boat. . .but one of his teeth caught on an oarlock.

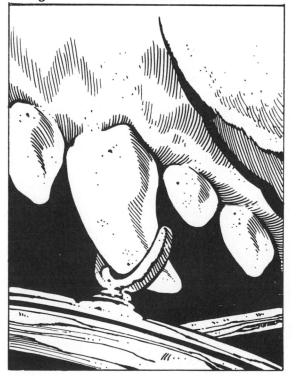

Ahab grabbed the long tooth trying to work it free.

Blast it, to hold me helpless in your very jaws.

(From *Moby Dick* by Herman Melville. Illustrated by Alex Nino.)

prominent knots, that gave him the appearance of being decorated with a pair of horns. His beard, plucked out by the root from every other part of his face, was suffered to droop in hairy pendants, two of which garnished his upper lip, and an equal number hung from the extremity of his chin."[4]

August 9, 1842. Escaped, but had to kill one of the Taipi villagers who had befriended him. He was picked up by an Australian whaler, *Lucy Ann,* on which conditions proved to be intolerable. When the ship arrived at Tahiti, eleven men, including Melville, were put ashore and imprisoned for mutiny. He escaped with a shipmate to the island of Eimo where he worked on a potato farm.

November, 1842. Shipped on a third whaler and travelled through the southern Pacific Ocean.

1843. Visited the Sandwich Islands before enlisting at Honolulu as an ordinary seaman aboard the frigate, *United States.* This voyage, with a different kind of hierarchy at sea, served as inspiration for his novel *White Jacket.*

October 14, 1844. Discharged from the U.S. Navy in Boston. Melville belittled his years at sea, claiming that his real education in life began after his return home. "Until I was twenty-five, I had no development at all. From my twenty-fifth year I date my life. Three weeks have scarcely passed, at any time between then & now, that I have not unfolded within myself."[2]

His family was now prospering, and his brother Gansevoort was a respected and powerful figure in Democratic circles. Encouraged by his family and friends, Melville began working on the narrative to be later titled, *Typee.*

July, 1845. Gansevoort, appointed Secretary of the American Legation to England, took the manuscript of *Typee* to the London publisher, John Murray, who had a reputation of only accepting books relating to personal experiences. Although he published *Typee,* he still requested reassurance of its authenticity. Melville responded: "You ask for 'documentary evidences' of my having been at the Marquesas—in *Typee.*—Dear Sir, how indescribably vexatious, when one really feels in his very bones that he has been there, to have a parcel of blockheads question it!.

"I know not how to set about getting the evidence—How under Heaven am I to subpoena the skipper. . .who by this time is the Lord only knows where, or Kory-Kory who I'll be bound is this blessed day taking his noon nap somewhere in the flowery vale of Typee.

"Typee's honesty must at last be believed on its own account—they believe here now—a little touched up they say but *true.*"[2]

July, 1846. Richard Tobias Greene appeared in Buffalo and verified the authenticity of *Typee.* Melville conveyed this information to his editor of Wiley and Putnam's, Evert A. Duycknck. "What will the politely incredulous Mr Duycknck now say to the true Toby's having turned up in Buffalo. . . .Give ear then, oh ye of little faith—especially thou man of the Evangelist—and hear what Toby has to say for himself."[2]

Toby's reappearance inspired Melville to write a sequel to the revised edition titled, *The Story of Toby.* "I entertain no doubt but that the simple story of Toby will add very much to the interest of the book, especially if the public are informed of the peculiar circumstances connected with it. If you [Duycknck] publish it, you will reap this benefit, whatever it may be in a

The young man's name was Billy Budd. His story is still told on English ships today.

(From *Billy Budd* by Herman Melville. Adapted by Stella Houghton Alico. Illustrated by Vicatan.)

pecuniary way; and altho' you will not be bound to pay me any thing for the Sequel, still, should you make use of it, I rely not a little upon your liberality.

"I have another work now nearly completed which I am anxious to submit to you before presenting it to any other publishing house. It embraces adventures in the South seas (of a totally different character from *Typee*) and includes an eventful cruise in an English Colonial Whaleman (A Sydney Ship) and a comical residence on the island of Tahiti."[2]

December, 1846. Completed *Omoo,* another autobiographical narrative, and offered it to Harpers and Murray who accepted it. "I think you will find it a fitting successor to *Typee;* inasmuch as the latter book delineates Polynisian Life in its primitive state—while the new work, represents it, as affected by intercourse with the whites. It also describes the 'man about town' sort of life, led, at the present day, by roving sailors in the Pacific—a kind of thing, which I have never seen described anywhere."[2]

June 11, 1847. Melville's sister, Helen, reported the success of *Omoo.* "In one week after it was issued the whole edition of 3000; or 3,500 was disposed of and another was put in progress. It has been more highly spoken of on both sides of the Atlantic than its predecessor even, as containing more instructive matter. He bears himself very meekly under his honors however, and to prove it to you, I may mention casually, that he is now at work in the garden, very busy hoeing his favorie tomatoes."[1]

August 4, 1847. Married Elizabeth Shaw in Boston. After a honeymoon in northern New England and Canada, the Melville's set up house in New York.

1848. Discovered Shakespeare's writings, and in doing so, acquired deeper and more rewarding insights into his own craft. "Dolt and ass that I am. I have lived more than twenty-nine years, and until a few days ago, never made close acquaintance with the divine William. Ah, he's full of sermons-on-the-mount, and gentle, ay, almost as Jesus. I take such men to be inspired. I fancy this Mons. Shakespeare in heaven ranks with Gabriel, Raphael, and Michael. And if another Messiah ever comes he will be in Shakespeare's person."[5]

February, 1849. *Mardi,* Melville's first attempt to find his own "voice" as a writer, was published. "The critics. . .seem to have fired quite a broadside into *Mardi;* but it was not altogether unexpected. In fact the book is of a nature to attract compliments of that sort from some quarters; and as you may be aware yourself, it is judged only as a work meant to entertain. And I can not but think that its having been brought out in England in the ordinary novel form must have led to the disappointment of many readers, who would have been better pleased with it, perhaps, had they taken it up in the first place for what it really is.—Besides, the peculiar thoughts & fancies of a Yankee upon politics & other matters could hardly be presumed to delight that class of gentlemen who conduct your leading journals; while the metaphysical ingredients (for want of a better term) of the book, must of course repel some of those who read simply for amusement.—However, it will reach those for whom it is intended; and I have already received assurances that *Mardi,* in its higher purposes, has not been written in vain."[2]

In the same month that *Mardi* was published, a son, Malcolm, was born. Although this was a source of great joy, Melville felt the pressure to command a much larger income.

June, 1849. Published *Redburn,* a return to his autiobiographical narrative form. "For *Redburn* I anticipate no particular reception of any kind. It may be deemed a book of tolerable entertainment;—& may be accounted dull.—As for the other book [*White Jacket*], it will be sure to be attacked in some quarters. But no reputation that is gratifying to me, can possibly be achieved by either of these books. They are two *jobs,* which I have done for money.

"The book *Redburn* to my surprise (somewhat) seems to have been favorably received. I am glad for it—for it puts money into an empty purse. But I hope I shall never write such a book again—tho' when a poor devil writes with duns all round him, & looking over the back of his chair—& perching on his pen & diving in his inkstand—like the devils about St: Anthony— what can you expect of that poor devil?—What but a beggarly *Redburn!*"[2]

August, 1849. Completed *White Jacket,* an indictment of an authoritarian Navy serving democratic society. This book later influenced the abolition of flogging in the American Navy.

October 11, 1849. Sailed to England to arrange publication of *White Jacket.* "At 5 in the morning was wakened by the Captain in person, saying we were off Dover. Dressed in a hurry, ran on deck, & saw the lights ashore. A cutter was alongside, and after some confusion in the dark, we got off in her for the shore. A comical scene ensued. The boatmen saying we could not land at Dover, but only at Deal. So to Deal we went, & were beached there just at break of day. Some centuries ago a person called Julius Caesar jumped ashore about in this place, & took

possession. It was Guy Fawke's Day also. Having left our baggage. . .to go round by ship to London, we were wholly unincumbered; & I proposed walking to Canterbury—distant 18 miles, for an appetite to breakfast."[1]

Visited a prospective London publisher and wrote of the experience to the novelist, Richard Henry Dana: "I was ushered into one of those jealous, guarded sanctums, in which these London publishers retreat from the vulgar gaze. It was a small, dim, religious looking room—a very chapel to enter. Upon the coldest day you would have taken off your hat in that room, tho' there were no fire, no occupant, & you a Quaker.—You have heard, I dare say, of that Greenland whaler discovered near the Pole, adrift & silent in a calm, with the frozen form of a man seated at a desk in the cabin before an ink-stand of icy ink. Just so sat Mr Moxon in that tranced cabin of his. I bowed to the spectre, & received such a galvanic return, that I thought something of hurrying out for some Officer of the Humane Society, & getting a supply of hot water & blankets to resuscitate this melancholy corpse. But knowing the nature of these foggy English, & that they are not altogether impenetrable, I began a sociable talk, and happening to make mention of Charles Lamb, and alluding to the warmth of feeling with which that charming punster is regarded in America, Mr Moxon brightened up—grew cordial— hearty;—& going into the heart of the matter—told me that he (Lamb) was the best fellow in the world to 'get drunk with' (I use his own words) & that he had many a time put him to bed."[1]

Took an excursion to the Continent and came back to London to learn that no satisfactory offer had been made for *White Jacket.* This meant the end of his trip and financial prospect. For most of his life, Melville was haunted by the spectre of never having quite enough money. "I very much doubt whether Gabriel enters the portals of Heaven without a fee to Peter the porter— so impossible is it to travel without money. Some people (999 in 1000) are very unaccountably shy about confessing to a want of money, as the reason why they do not do this or that; but, for my part, I think it such a capital clincher of a reason for not doing a thing, that I out with it, at once."[2]

Bently finally accepted *White Jacket* for publication. "I am in a very painful state of uncertainty. I am all eagerness to get home—I ought to be home—my absence occasions uneasiness in a quarter where I most beseech heaven to grant repose. Yet here I have before me an open prospect to get some curious ideas of a style of life, which in all probability I shall never have again. I should much like to know what the highest English Aristocracy really & practically is. And the Duke of Rutland's cordial invitation to visit him at the Castle furnishes me with just the thing I want. If I do not go, I am confident that hereafter I shall upbraid myself for neglecting such an opportunity of procuring '*material.*' And Allan & others will account me a ninny.—I would not debate the matter a moment, were it not that at least three whole weeks must elapse ere I start for Belvoir Castle—three weeks! If I could but get over *them!* And if the two images [his wife and son] would only *down* for that space of time.—I must light a second cigar & revolve it over again. . . .The Three Weeks are intolerable. Tomorrow I shall go down to London Dock & book myself for a state-room on board the good ship *Independence.*"[1]

February 1, 1850. Arrived back in New York and began work on his sixth book about whaling. In May, he reported on the book's progress: "About the 'whaling voyage'—I am half way in the work. . . .It will be a strange sort of a book, tho', I fear; blubber is blubber you know, tho' you may get oil out of it the poetry runs as hard as sap from a frozen maple tree;—& to cook the thing up, one must needs throw in a little fancy, which from

New York May 1st 1850

My Dear Dana —
About the "whaling voyage" – I am half way in the work, & am very glad that your suggestion so jumps with mine. It will be a strange sort of book, tho'. I fear; blubber is blubber you know; tho' you may get oil out of it, the poetry runs hard as sap from a frozen maple tree; — & to cook the thing up, one must needs throw in a little fancy, which from the nature of the thing, must be ungainly as the gambols of the whales themselves. Yet I mean to give the truth of the thing, spite of this.

Sincerely Yours
H Melville

Melville as a young man alongside a copy of his letter to Richard Henry Dana, author of *Two Years before the Mast.*

the nature of the thing, must be ungainly as the gambols of the whales themselves. Yet I mean to give the truth of the thing, spite of this."[2]

June 27, 1850. Wrote to his London publisher about his forthcoming book: "In the latter part of the coming autumn I shall have ready a new work; and I write you now to propose its publication in England.

"The book is a romance of adventure, founded upon certain wild legends in the Southern Sperm Whale Fisheries, and illustrated by the author's own personal experience, of two years & more, as a harpooneer.

"Should you be inclined to undertake the book, I think it will be worth to you 200 pounds. Could you be positively put in possession of the copyright, it might be worth to you a larger sum—considering its great novelty; for I do not know that the subject treated of has ever been worked up by a romancer; or, indeed, by any writer, in any adequate manner. But as things are, I say 200 pounds, because that sum was given for *White Jacket;* but it does not appear, as yet, that you have been interferred with in your publication of that book; & therefore there seems reason to conclude, that, at 200 pounds, *White Jacket* must have been, in some degree, profitable to you."[2]

Melville, who felt isolated in his quest for honesty and truth, read Nathaniel Hawthorne's now published *The Scarlet Letter,* discovering a kindred spirit in this previously unread author. "A man of deep and noble nature has taken hold of me in this

seclusion, his wild, witch-voice rings through me; or, in softer cadences, I seem to hear it in the songs of the hillside birds that sing in the larch trees at my window."[5]

August, 1850. Pseudonymously reviewed Hawthorne's *Mosses from an Old Manse* for the *Literary World.* The review, a tribute to Hawthorne, also included Melville's hope for a more authentic American literature. "Let America then prize and cherish her writers; yea, let her glorify them. They are not so many in number as to exhaust her good will. And while she has good kitch and kin of her own, to take to her bosom, let her not lavish her embraces upon the household of an alien. For believe it or not, England, after all, is, in many things, an alien to us. China has more bowels of real love for us than she. But even were there no strong literary individualities among us, as there are some dozen at least, nevertheless, let America first praise mediocrity even, in her own children, before she praises (for everywhere, merit demands acknowledgmeent from every one) the best excellence in the children of any other land. Let her own authors, I say, have the priority of appreciation."[6] Melville and Hawthorne became friends.

Purchased a farm, "Arrowhead," near Pittsfield, Massachusetts. "I have a sort of sea-feeling here in the country, now that the ground is all covered with snow. I look out of my window in the morning when I rise as I would out of a port- hole of a ship in the Atlantic. My room seems a ship's cabin; & at nights when I wake up & hear the wind shrieking, I almost fancy there is too much sail on the house, & I had better go on the roof & rig in the chimney.

John Huston and Ray Bradbury co-wrote the screenplay for the 1956 re-make of "Moby Dick," which starred Orson Welles (above)

"I rise at eight—thereabouts—& go to my barn—say good-morning to the horse, & give him his breakfast. (It goes to my heart to give him a cold one, but it can't be helped.) Then, pay a visit to my cow—cut up a pumpkin or two for her, & stand by to see her eat it—for it's a pleasant sight to see a cow move her jaws—she does it so mildly & with such a sanctity.—My own breakfast over, I got to my workroom & light my fire—then spread my M.S.S on the table—take one business squint at it, & fall to with a will. At 2 1/2 P.M. I hear a preconcerted knock at my door, which (by request) continues till I rise & go to the door, which serves to wean me effectively from my writing, however interested I may be. My friends the horse & cow now demand their dinner—& I go & give it them. My own dinner over, I rig my sleigh & with my mother or sisters start off for the village—& if it be a Literary World day, great is the satisfaction thereof.—My evenings I spend in a sort of mesmeric state in my room—not being able to read—only now & then skimming over some large-printed book."[2]

The spring of **1851** was an intense time for Melville, sitting at his desk all day working on *Moby Dick*. He first intended the book to be a whaling document until he altered his design to turn it into a tragic drama of monumental proportion. "How then with me, writing of this Leviathan? Unconsciously, my chirography expands into placard capitals. Give me a condor's quill! Give me Vesuvius' crater for an inkstand. Friends! hold my arms! For in the mere act of penning my thoughts of this Leviathan, they weary me, and make me faint with the outreaching comprehensiveness of sweep, as if to include the whole circle of the sciences, and all the generations of whales, and men, and mastodons, past, present, and to come, with all the revolving panoramas of empire on earth, and throughout the whole universe, not excluding its suburbs."[5]

"In a week or so, I go to New York, to bury myself in a third-story room, and work and slave on my 'Whale' while it is driving through the press. *That* is the only way I can finish it now,—I am so pulled hither and thither by circumstances. The calm, the coolness, the silent grass-growing mood in which a man *ought* always to compose,—that, I fear, can seldom be mine. Dollars damn me; and the malicious Devil is forever grinning in upon me, holding the door ajar. . . .I shall at last be worn out and perish, like an old nutmeg-grater, grated to pieces by the constant attrition of the wood, that is, the nutmeg. What I feel most moved to write, that is banned,—it will not pay. Yet, altogether, write the *other* way I cannot. So the produce is a final hash, and all my books are botches.

"But I was talking about the 'Whale.' As the fishermen say, 'he's in his flurry.' I'm going to take him by his jaw, however, before long, and finish him up in some fashion or other. What's the use of elaborating what, in its very essence, is so short-lived as a modern book? Though I wrote the Gospels in this century, I should die in the gutter."[2]

Moby Dick, originally titled *The Whale,* was published **October, 1851** in London. That November the American edition was published and dedicated to Hawthorne. "It is not a peice [sic] of fine feminine Spitalfields silk— but is of the horrible texture of fabric that should be woven of ships' cables & hawsers. A Polar wind blows through it, & birds of prey hover over it. Warn all gentle fastidious people from so much as peeping into the book—on risk of a lumbago & sciatics."[2]

Although *Moby Dick* brought Melville personal satisfaction, it was not well received by the reviewers. "But I dont know but a book in a man's brain is better off than a book bound in calf—at any rate it is safer from criticism. And taking a book off the brain, is akin to the ticklish & dangerous business of taking an old painting off a panel—you have to scrape off the whole brain in order to get at it with due safety- -& even then, the painting may not be worth the trouble."[7]

Shortly after the completion of *Moby Dick,* the Hawthornes moved. Although Melville had noted Hawthorne's growing remoteness, he sent him a brave farewell. "I dont know when I shall see you. I shall lay eyes on you one of these days however. Keep some Champagne or Gin for me. . . .If you find any *sand* in this letter, regard it as so many sands of my life, which ran out as I was writing it."[7]

December, 1851. Fighting despair and in a state of mental and physical exhaustion, he immediately began work on his next book, based partly on his family. Under the prevailing circumstances, the quality of this new work, to be titled, *Pierre,* suffered. "My development has been all within a few years past, I am like one of those seeds taken out of the Egyptian Pyramids, which, after being three thousand years a seed & nothing but a seed, being planted in English soil, it developed itself, grew to greenness, and then fell to mould."[2]

February 20, 1852. Received a five-hundred-dollar advance on *Pierre* from Harpers, agreeing to have it available for publishing in August. The book was eventually published by the London representatives of Harpers, but by then Melville's nerves were verging on a state of total collapse.

Plagued by sciatica and declining health, he was unable to work his farm. A house full of women and children and his writing often strained him. His father-in-law stepped in and lent him money to finance a trip to Europe and the mid-East.

1857. Published *The Confidence Man,* which explores in an allegorical and satirical manner, the notion of confidence and Melville's outlook on life. The book was badly received, did not earn Melville one penny, and marked the end of his career in fiction. He returned to New York in the fall and accepted an engagement for a series of lectures based on his travels in Europe and the South Seas, enjoying more than moderate success.

1860. Melville, whose interest in poetry had been growing for some time, attempted to publish a volume, but it was rejected. He then embarked on a long voyage aboard *The Meteor,* captained by his brother, Thomas.

April, 1861. At the outbreak of the Civil War, Melville sought a naval appointment but was rejected.

1863. Sold his farmhouse and moved the family to New York.

December 5, 1866. Took an oath of office as Inspector of Customs at the Port of New York.

September 11, 1867. Son Malcolm was found dead of a self-inflicted pistol-wound. "I wish you could have seen him as he lay in his last attitude, the ease of a gentle nature. Mackie never gave me a disrespectful word in his life, nor in any way ever failed in filialness."[1]

1872. Melville's brother, Allan, died in February, and his mother in April. The Great Boston Fire destroyed his wife's Boston properties in the fall, seriously depleting the family income.

February, 1876. The long poem *Clarel* was particularly painful to finish. His wife, who had copied the manuscript for the printer, wrote her sister-in-law: "The fact is, that Herman,

Gregory Peck, as the crazed Ahab, rides the great white whale in the 1956 movie "Moby Dick."

poor fellow, is in such a frightfully nervous state, & particularly now with such an added strain on his mind, that I am actually *afraid* to have any one here for fear that he will be upset entirely, & not be able to go on with the printing. . . . If ever this dreadful *incubus* of a *book* (I call it so because it has undermined all our happiness) gets off Herman's shoulders I do hope he may be in better mental health—but at present I have reason to feel the gravest concern & anxiety about it—to put it in mild phrase."[7] The book was published in June.

The Customhouse, where he spent nineteen years, was notoriously corrupt and Melville was subject to political pressures that occasionally threatened his position. "Whoever is not in the possession of leisure can hardly be said to possess independence. They talk of the *dignity of work*. Bosh. True Work is the *necessity* of poor humanity's earthly condition. The dignity is in leisure. Besides, 99 hundredths of all the *work* done in the world is either foolish and unnecessary, or harmful and wicked."[2]

Summer, 1878. Friend and colleague, Evert Duycknck, died as did Elizabeth Melville's aunt. She left her niece a large amount of money. This financial independence took considerable pressure off Melville and made it possible for him to resign his post as Customs Inspector, which he did, on **December 31, 1885.**

November 16, 1888. Melville began composition of *Billy Budd,* a work containing themes of his earlier books, now reinterpreted and resolved into a powerful work.

April, 1891. *Billy Budd* was completed, and Melville submitted a volume of verse, *Timoleon,* for private printing, dedicated to Elizabeth who so ably managed its production. She reported on Melville's state of health to a relative: "I have been thinking for some days of writing you— because I dont want you to hear in any other or exaggerated way that Herman has been pretty ill for the last week or so—when he had a turn of dizziness or vertigo in the night—which the Dr feared might eventuate in a serious way—but now I am glad to say that his strength which seemed to leave him in one night has gradually returned and he is improving every day—he has not been out yet or even down stairs, but the Dr says there seems to be no reason why he should not entirely recover and be as well as before."[1]

September 28, 1891. Melville died of heart failure in New York City in almost total obscurity. His death brought about a mild interest in his early narrative works, but this was short lived. The deeper aspects of his craft remained generally hidden until about 1919 (the centenary of his birth) before he became the most reknowned and widely-read American author of the nineteenth century. "All Fame is patronage. Let me be infamous; there is no patronage in *that.* What 'reputation' H.M. has is horrible. Think of it! To go down to posterity is bad enough, any way; but to go down as a 'man who lived among the cannibals!'"[2]

FOOTNOTE SOURCES

[1]Jay Leyda, *The Melville Log: A Documentary Life of Herman Melville, 1819-1891,* Harcourt, 1951.

[2]Menrell R. Davis and William H. Gilman, editors, *The Letters of Herman Melville,* Yale University Press, 1960.

[3]Herman Melville, *Redburn: His First Voyage,* Harper & Brothers, 1850.

[4]H. Melville, *Typee: A Peep at Polynesian Life,* Harper & Brothers, 1849.

[5]Lewis Mumford, *Herman Melville,* Harcourt, 1929.

[6]"Hawthorne and His Mosses," *Literary World,* August 17-24, 1850.

[7]Eleanor Melville Metcalf, *Herman Melville: Cycle and Epicycle,* Harvard University Press, 1953.

FOR MORE INFORMATION SEE

BOOKS

R. M. Weaver, *Melville, Mariner and Mystic,* Doran, 1921.

Victor Hugo Paltsits, editor, *Family Correspondence of Herman Melville 1830-1904,* New York Public Library, 1929.

Willard Thorp, *Herman Melville,* American Book, 1938.

C. R. Anderson, *Melville in the South Seas,* Columbia University Press, 1939, Dover, 1966.

W. E. Sedwick, *Herman Melville: The Tragedy of Mind,* Harvard University Press, 1944.

Elizabeth Rider Montgomery, *The Story Behind Great Books* (juvenile), McBride, 1946.

Charles Olson, *Call Me Ishmael,* Reynal & Hitchock, 1947.

George Dixon Snell, *Shapers of American Fiction 1798- 1947,* Dutton, 1947.

Geoffrey Stone, *Melville,* Sheed & Ward, 1949.

Newton Arvin, *Herman Melville,* William Sloan, 1950.

William H. Gilman, *Melville's Early Life and Redburn,* New York University Press, 1951.

M. R. Davis, *Melvilles "Mardi": A Chartless Voyage,* Yale University Press, 1952.

C. L. R. James, *Mariners, Renegades, and Castaways,* James, 1953, 2nd edition, Bewick Editions, 1978.

Robert Cantwell, *Famous American Men of Letters* (juvenile), Dodd, 1956.

Jean Gould, *Young Mariner Melville* (juvenile), Dodd, 1956.

David Edward Scherman and Rosemarie Redlich, *America: The Land and Its Writers* (juvenile), Dodd, 1956.

M. R. Stern, *The Fine Hammered Steel of Herman Melville,* University of Illinois Press, 1957.

Merton M. Sealts, Jr., *Melville as Lecturer,* Harvard University Press, 1957.

Henry Beetle Hough, *Melville in the South Pacific* (juvenile), Houghton, 1960.

Frances Helmstadter, *Picture Book of American Authors* (juvenile), Sterling, 1962.

Tyrus Hillway, *Herman Melville,* Twayne, 1963, revised edition, 1979.

Andrew Curtin, *Gallery of Great Americans* (juvenile), F. Watts, 1965.

Charlotte E. Keyes, *High on the Mainmast: A Biography of Herman Melville,* College & University Press, 1966.

Nora Stirling, *Who Wrote the Classics?,* Volume II (juvenile), Day, 1968.

John T. Winterich, *Writers in America* (juvenile), Davey, 1968.

Meade Minnigerode, *Some Personal Letters of Herman Melville and a Bibliography,* Books for Libraries, 1969.

"Melville" (filmstrip), Thomas S. Klise, 1970.

William Bixby, *Rebel Genius: The Life of Herman Melville,* McKay, 1970.

John Freeman, *Herman Melville,* Folcroft, 1970.

Gay Wilson Allen, *Melville and His World,* Viking, 1971.

M. M. Sealts, Jr. *The Early Lives of Melville: Nineteenth-Century Biographical Sketches and Their Authors,* University of Wisconsin Press, 1974.

Edwin Haviland Miller, *Melville: A Biography,* Braziller, 1975.

Carla Hancock, *Seven Founders of American Literature* (juvenile), Blair, 1976.

Edward H. Rosenberry, *Melville,* Methuen, 1979.

Leon Howard, *Herman Melville: A Biography,* University of California Press, 1981.

"Herman Melville: Damned in Paradise" (videocassette), Pyramid, 1986.

(Program cover for Orson Welles' stage version of "Moby Dick." Starring Rod Steiger [above], as Ahab, it opened November 28, 1962.)

"Herman Melville" (filmstrip, cassette, and guide) Jan Productions, 1987.
Geoffrey Wolff, *Herman Melville: Biography,* Viking, 1987.

PERIODICALS

New England Quarterly, January, 1929 (p. 120ff).
American Literature, May, 1952 (p. 224ff), November, 1953 (p. 307ff), January, 1958 (p. 463ff), November, 1971 (p. 239ff).
American Heritage, December, 1960 (p. 110ff), June-July, 1986.
Reader's Digest, March, 1965 (p. 182ff).
C. S. Cambareri, "The Herman Melville Papers: Literary Treasure in a Barn, *American History Illustrated,* October, 1984.

COLLECTIONS

Houghton Library of Harvard University.
Duyckinck Collection and Berg Collection at New York Public Library.
Newberry Library.

MESSENGER, Charles (Rynd Milles) 1941-

PERSONAL: Born May 11, 1941, in Fulmer, England; son of Toby (an army officer) and Peggy (Rynd) Messenger; married Anne Falconer (a business proprietor), 1968, children: Emma, Rawdon, Harriet. *Education:* Oxford University, B.A. (with honors), 1965, M.A., 1973. *Address:* c/o Royal Bank of Scotland PLC, Holts Farnborough Branch, 31-37 Victoria Rd., Farnborough, Hampshire, England.

CAREER: British Army, Royal Tank Regiment, career officer, 1959-80, retiring as major, served in Near East, Germany, and United States, and held technical and non-technical positions with Ministry of Defence; military historian and defense analyst, 1980—. Historical and defense lecturer and editorial consultant. *Member:* Royal United Services Institute for Defence Studies (research fellow, 1982-83), International Institute for Strategic Studies. *Awards, honors:* Murray Naval History Prize from Exeter College, Oxford, 1964.

WRITINGS:

Trench Fighting, 1914-1918, Ballantine, 1972.
The Art of Blitzkrieg, Scribner, 1976.
The Observer's Book of Tanks, Warne, 1981.
Terriers in the Trenches: The Post Office Rifles at War, 1914-1918, Picton Publishing, 1982.
Cologne: The First 1,000 Bomber Raid, Ian Allan, 1982.
The Unknown Alamein, Ian Allan, 1982.
The Tunisian Campaign, Ian Allan, 1982.
The New Observer's Book of Tanks, Warne, 1984, reissued, 1987.
Bomber Harris and the Strategic Bombing Offensive, 1939-1945, St. Martin's Press, 1984.
Armies of World War 3, Bison/Hamlyn, 1984.

CHARLES MESSENGER

Modern Combat Weapons: Combat Aircraft (illustrated by Nick May and others), F. Watts, 1984.

Tanks, Kola Books, 1984.

Modern Combat Weapons: Helicopters (illustrated by Rob Shone and others), F. Watts, 1985.

The Commandos, 1940-1946, Kimber, 1985.

Modern Combat Roles: Anti-Armour Warfare, Hippocrene, 1985.

Northern Ireland: The Troubles, Bison/Hamlyn, 1985.

The Steadfast Gurkha: Sixth Queen Elizabeth's Own Gurkha Rifles, 1948-1982, Leo Cooper/Secker & Warburg, 1985.

A History of the British Army, Presidio, 1986, new edition, 1988.

The Second World War, F. Watts, 1987.

The Pictorial History of World War II, Gallery Books, 1987.

The Middle East, F. Watts, 1988.

Hitler's Gladiator: The Life and Times of Oberstgruppenfuehrer and Panzergeneraloberst der Waffen SS Sepp Dietrich, Brassey's, 1988.

Middle East Commandos, Kimber, 1988.

World War Two Chronological Atlas, Macmillan, 1989.

Contributor to *Purnell's History of the First World War.* Contributor of articles and book reviews to various historical and military journals. Associate editor, *Current Military Literature;* editorial consultant, *World War Investigator.*

WORK IN PROGRESS: New edition of *The Art of Blitzkrieg; The Iron Division: A History of the 3rd Division, 1809-1987*, for Ian Allan; *The Queen's Men: The History of the Household Division*, for Patrick Stephens; *For Love of Regiment: The History of British Infantry*, for Leo Cooper/Heinemann; *The Last Prussian: The Life of Field Marshal von Rundstedt*, for Brassey's; *War Strategies: Close Air Support; Arms and Armour.*

SIDELIGHTS: "I have been fascinated by war from a very early age and coming from a family with a tradition of service to the Crown, soldiering was in my blood. In recent years what has increasingly interested me most is the fact that combat exerts the most intense stress on the individual. Indeed, it is difficult to think of another human activity which creates so much pressure. By exploring how human beings stand up to this stress we can learn much about ourselves.

"I am also a strong believer in the study of war in order to create peace. Sadly, we have short memories and quickly forget the horrors of war. If we had these more in the forefront of our minds we might pause more before resorting to armed conflict as a way of solving our problems.

"To be a successful writer the first and foremost factor that one must have in one's mind is the reader. It is very easy to write solely to satisfy oneself, but this does not necessarily create a work that will be enjoyed by others. I find myself writing for a variety of audiences, ranging from the expert in the field to the person who knows nothing about the subject in question. Thus my books have ranged from the scholarly to the 'coffee table' pictorial.

"Of all my audiences, however, children are the most demanding and most difficult to write for. On the other hand, they are also the most rewarding. A child will never allow a writer to get away with a loose or sloppy statement, especially when it concerns modern technology or a complex politico-military situation.

"Indeed, the hardest book I have ever had to write was the one on the Middle East. There are few adults who can claim with any confidence to have a firm grasp of the whys and wherefores of the Middle East today. To try and produce a clear and comprehensive account that would totally satisfy today's demanding and sharp teenager stretched my capabilities to the limit—I am still uncertain as to whether I got it right in the end! Luckily, I do have my own sample readership by me—my own children, who are certainly most perceptive critics. Thus, in order to successfully write factual books for children, the writer must have a thorough grasp of the subject and the ability to communicate in simple, easy to understand language."

HOBBIES AND OTHER INTERESTS: My work, convivial company.

MITCHELL, Kathy 1948-

PERSONAL: Born July 27, 1948, in Cincinnati, Ohio; daughter of Gerald Paige (an engineer) and Velma Alice (a hospital administrator; maiden name, Bleier) Clary; married Terence Nigel Mitchell (a graphic designer), February 2, 1978; children: Jessica Rose. *Education:* University of Cincinnati, B.A. (cum laude), 1971. *Politics:* Democrat. *Home:* 828 21st St., 6, Santa Monica, Calif. 90403. *Agent and office:* Michael Brodie, Artists International, 7 Dublin Hill Dr., Greenwich, Conn. 06830.

CAREER: Lippincott and Margulies, New York, N.Y., graphic designer, 1971; Allied International Designers, London, England, graphic designer, 1972; Movea, George, Briggs, London, graphic designer, 1973-75; Leprevost and Leprevost, Beverly Hills, Calif., graphic designer, 1975-76; *Phonograph Record* (magazine), Los Angeles, Calif., art director, 1976; Walter Morgan Associates, Santa Monica, Calif., associate graphic designer, 1977-80; free-lance children's book illustrator and journalistic and advertising illustrator, 1981—.

ILLUSTRATOR

L. Savryn, editor, *Once Upon a Cat*, Platt and Munk, 1983.

Charlotte Bronte, *Jane Eyre*, Grosset, 1983.

Lewis Carroll, *Alice in Wonderland and Through the Looking Glass*, Western, 1986.

L. Frank Baum, *The Wizard of Oz*, Golden Press, 1986.

Frances H. Burnett, *The Secret Garden*, Grosset, 1987.

Edith Kunhardt, *Kittens, Kittens, Kittens*, Golden Books, 1987.

Maida Silverman, *My Bible Alphabet*, Golden Books, 1987.

Isabelle Holland, *The Christmas Cat*, Golden Books, 1987.

The Story of Christmas, Western, 1989.

Contributor of illustrations to *The Illustrated Treasury of Fairy Tales*, edited by T. A. Kennedy.

WORK IN PROGRESS: Silent Night, for Aladdin.

SIDELIGHTS: "I have always been interested in art, and as a child, I remember trying to copy the 'doodles' my mother used to draw when on the phone. By the age of four I was relating stories to my mother, who would write them down—then I would illustrate them.

"My two loves through high school were ancient Egypt and art, so it was no surprise to my parents when I was torn between archaeology and art as a college major. I entered college as a graphic design major on the advice of my high school

KATHY MITCHELL

NAKAE, Noriko 1940-
(Noriko Ueno)

PERSONAL: Born September 29, 1940, in Irima-shi, Saitama-ken, Japan; daughter of Koichi and Kimiko Ueno; married Yoshio Nakae (a graphic designer), December 4, 1966. *Education:* Nihon University, B.A., 1962. *Home and office:* 22-7 Satsukigaoka, Midoriku Yokohama-shi, Kanagawa-ken, Japan.

CAREER: Free-lance artist, 1962—. Exhibitor in Tokyo Biennale, 1974. *Member:* Japanese Water Color Painting League, Japanese Illustrators Council. *Awards, honors:* Japanese Water Color Painting League Award, 1963; Ministry of Foreign Affairs Prize, 1973, for international exhibit; Picture Book of Japan Prize, 1987.

WRITINGS:

UNDER NAME NORIKO UENO

Elephant Buttons (self-illustrated), Harper, 1973.

instructor—a move that kept me away from illustration for a number of years, but proved an invaluable background for illustration.

"After working in New York and London, I moved to Los Angeles, where my husband and I opened our own graphic design firm. As a designer, I commissioned many artists to illustrate album covers, ads, etc. for me, and I all the more admired the creativity and versatility of illustration. One Christmas, I was given a book of illustrations by Brian Froud, and was so enamored by his work that I started to illustrate in my spare time.

"After sending my work to an agent in New York and getting a commission for a children's book, I've never looked back. There is something very rewarding in being able to illustrate for children. Pictures can teach the love of art and creativity and enhance the love of reading.

"Now that I have a young daughter, whom I often use as my model, I feel that I would now like to write as well as illustrate."

HOBBIES AND OTHER INTERESTS: Archaeology, antiques.

(From *Elephant Buttons* by Noriko Ueno. Illustrated by the author.)

ILLUSTRATOR; ALL BY HUSBAND, YOSHIO NAKAE, EXCEPT AS NOTED

Pera Pera no Sekai (title means "The Flimsy World"), Atelier Chemia, 1965.

Mayoi Konda Doubutsutachi (title means "Animals That Visited Chiko"), Atelier Chemia, 1966.

Marutshushi (title means "Magician"), Atelier Chemia, 1967.

Shouchu (title means "Microcosm"), Atelier Chemia, 1971.

Nezumikun no Chokki (title means "The Vest of Mr. Mouse"), Poplar Publishing (Tokyo), 1974.

Kuroboushi-chan (title means "Little Black Hat"), Bunka, 1974.

Yoshitomo Imae, *Soyokaze to Watashi* (title means "A Gentle Breeze and I"), Poplar Publishing, 1974.

Itazura lala-chan (title means "Lala, the Naughty Girl"), Poplar Publishing, 1986.

WORK IN PROGRESS: Designing puppets for a television show; illustrations for television commercials and other advertisements.

NEIER, Aryeh 1937-

PERSONAL: Born April 22, 1937, in Berlin, Germany; son of Wolf (a teacher) and Gitla (a housewife; maiden name, Bendzinska) Neier; married Yvette Celton (a merchandiser), June 22, 1958; children: David. *Education:* Cornell University, B.S., 1958. *Office:* Human Rights Watch, 36 West 44th St., New York, N.Y. 10036.

CAREER: League for Industrial Democracy, New York, N.Y., executive director, 1958-60; *Current* (magazine), associate editor, 1960-63; American Civil Liberties Union, New York, N.Y., field director, 1963-64, executive director, 1965-70, national executive director, 1970-78; New York Institute for the Humanities, New York University, New York, N.Y., director and fellow, 1978-81, professor of law, 1978— ; Human Rights Watch, New York, N.Y., executive director, 1981—. *Member:* Council on Foreign Relations. *Awards, honors:* Gavel Award from the American Bar Association, 1974; honorary L.L.D., Hofstra University, 1975, Hamilton College, 1979, State University of New York, 1988; *Defending My Enemy* was named one of New York Public Library's Books for the Teen Age, 1980, 1981, and 1982.

WRITINGS:

Dossier: The Secret Files They Keep on You, Stein & Day, 1975.

Crime and Punishment: A Radical Solution, Stein & Day, 1976.

Defending My Enemy, Dutton, 1979.

Only Judgment, Wesleyan University Press, 1982.

Contributor to more than twenty books. Contributor of more than 300 articles to magazines, including *Civil Liberties Review, Crime and Delinquency, New York Review of Books, New York Times Magazine* and *Nation,* to newspapers, including *Village Voice, Washington Post, Los Angeles Times* and *New York Times,* and to law reviews including *Michigan Law Review, New York University Law Review* and *Criminal Law Bulletin.*

ROY PAUL NELSON

NELSON, Roy Paul 1923-

PERSONAL: Born June 17, 1923, in Portland, Ore.; son of Roy P. (a crane operator) and Esther F. (a housewife; maiden name, Rood) Nelson; married Marie Helen Frazier (a secretary), February 24, 1951; children: Chris Marie, Robin Rood, Tracy Joan, Bryan James. *Education:* Attended University of Southern California, 1943-44; University of Oregon, B.S., 1947, M.S., 1955; attended Art Center School, Los Angeles, Calif., 1947-48. *Politics:* Republican. *Religion:* Protestant. *Home:* 2175 Onyx St., Eugene, Ore. 97403. *Office:* School of Journalism, University of Oregon, Eugene, Ore. 97403.

CAREER: McCann-Erickson (advertising agency), Portland, Ore., copywriter, 1947; United Press, Salt Lake City, Utah, reporter, 1948-49; American Forest Products Industries, Washington, D.C., assistant editorial director, 1949-53, district manager in San Francisco, Calif., 1954-55; University of Oregon, Eugene, instructor, 1953-57, assistant professor, 1957-63, associate professor, 1963-68, professor of journalism, 1968-87, professor emeritus, 1988—. Free-lance cartoonist, 1940—; graphic design consultant, 1955—. *Military service:* U.S. Naval Reserve, 1944-47; became lieutenant junior grade.

WRITINGS:

Fell's Guide to the Art of Cartooning, Fell, 1962.

(With Byron Ferris) *Fell's Guide to Commercial Art,* Fell, 1966.

The Design of Advertising, W. C. Brown, 1967, 6th edition, 1989.

Visits with Thirty Magazine Art Directors, Magazine Publishers Association, 1968.

(With John L. Hulteng) *The Fourth Estate,* Harper, 1971, 2nd edition, 1983.

Publication Design, W. C. Brown, 1972, 4th edition, 1987.

Cartooning, Regnery, 1975.

(Contributor) Joan Valdes and Jeanne Crow, *The Media Reader,* Pflaum/Standard, 1975.

Articles and Features, Houghton, 1978.

Comic Art and Caricature, Contemporary Books, 1978.

(Contributor) D. Earl Newsom, editor, *The Newspaper,* Prentice-Hall, 1981.

(With Roy H. Copperud) *Editing the News,* W. C. Brown, 1983.

Humorous Illustration and Cartooning, Prentice-Hall, 1984.

(Contributor) Melvin Helitzer, *Comedy Techniques for Writers and Performers,* Lawhead Press, 1984.

Contributor to *World Book Encyclopedia* and *Academic American Encyclopedia.* Author of regular columns for *Communication World* and *Magazine Design and Production.* Contributor of articles and reviews to professional journals, general magazines, and newspapers, including *Step-by-Step Graphics,* and *Publishers Weekly.*

WORK IN PROGRESS: Revision of *Publication Design,* for W. C. Brown.

SIDELIGHTS: "I started drawing before I went to school and in high school began selling gag cartoons to magazines. I also developed an interest in writing, becoming editor of my high school newspaper. As a journalism major in college, I edited the yearbook and wrote and drew for the college daily.

"I knew that I probably wouldn't be able to make a living as a cartoonist, so I wrote advertising copy for McCann-Erickson, became a reporter for United Press, and worked as a public relations man for the lumber paper industry's trade association in Washington, D.C. With my art background, I began designing the magazines and direct-mail pieces this organization published.

"Eventually I became a professor at the University of Oregon's School of Journalism, where I taught both writing and graphic design courses and launched a cartooning course. My first published book in 1962, *Fell's Guide to the Art of Cartooning,* gathered together many of the editorial cartoons I did on a freelance basis for the Eugene *Register-Guard.* Writing that book was largely a matter of arranging the cartoons in a logical order and connecting them with rambling captions. It was a homey book and fun to write because it was largely autobiographical. I was able to work in a lot of anecdotes. I have written three other books on cartooning, but these are less personal and show the work of many other cartoonists.

"The cartooning books have put me in touch with many other cartoonists and brought writing assignments from magazines, news services, encyclopedias, and other publications. The books also involve me in correspondence with readers. One fourteen-year-old boy became a long-term pen pal and a professional cartoonist whose works later appeared in my books. I am one of three judges in the annual Charles M. Schulz Award competition that honors the nation's outstanding young cartoonists.

"I have written a number of college textbooks on writing and graphic design, trying to keep them less stuffy than typical textbooks. They are written with a light touch and are profusely illustrated.

"Having grown up with the books of P. G. Wodehouse, Robert Benchley, James Thurber, Ring Lardner, and later stumbling onto Peter DeVries, I consider humor an important ingredient in all writing, including textbooks. The trick is to keep the humor low key. Understatement is better than exaggeration in a book because it lasts longer.

"A lover of country and western music as well as jazz from the 1930s and 1940s, I am convinced that an appreciation of music is also important to a writer. The rhythm of the sentence is important. A good sentence ought to make you want to tap your foot as you read it.

"There is a connection between writing and drawing. You should create pictures with your words, pictures in the reader's mind. And if you want to become a cartoonist, you had better have something to say. There isn't much room in the business for people who merely draw well."

HOBBIES AND OTHER INTERESTS: Singing; playing a Martin guitar; penmanship and fountain pen collecting; automobile design; print media art, design, and humor; painting; museums and art galleries; baseball; evangelical Christianity.

FOR MORE INFORMATION SEE:

Ken Muse, *The Secrets of Professional Cartooning,* Prentice-Hall, 1981.

K. Muse, *The Total Cartoonist,* Prentice-Hall, 1984.

NIXON, Kathleen Irene (Blundell) 1894-1988(?)
(K. Nixon)

OBITUARY NOTICE:—See sketch in *SATA* Volume 14: Born in 1894 in London, England; died about 1988. Illustrator and author. Nixon lived in India for twenty-five years during which time she worked for *Times of India Press* and designed color posters of animals and birds for the Indian State Railways. She is best known for the numerous children's books that she wrote and illustrated under the name K. Nixon beginning in the 1950s after her return to England. These titles include: *Pushti* and *Pindi Poo,* inspired by her pets, *The Bushy Tail Family, Animal Legends,* and *Strange Animal Friendships.* Her animal pictures were also exhibited in several cities, including Melbourne, London, and Paris.

FOR MORE INFORMATION SEE:

Contemporary Authors, Volumes 73-76, Gale, 1978.

OBITUARIES

Times (London), October 6, 1988.

OATES, Stephen B. 1936-

PERSONAL: Born January 5, 1936, in Pampa, Tex.; son of Steve Theodore and Florence (Baer) Oates; married Marie

Phillips (a personnel administrator), May 16, 1987; children: (previous marriage) Gregory, Allen, Stephanie. *Education:* University of Texas at Austin, B.A. (magna cum laude), 1958, M.A., 1960, Ph.D., 1969. *Home:* 10 Bridle Path, Amherst, Mass. 01003. *Office:* Department of History, University of Massachusetts, Amherst, Mass. 01003.

CAREER: Arlington State College (now University of Texas at Arlington), Arlington, instructor, 1964-67, assistant professor of history, 1967-68; University of Massachusetts, Amherst, assistant professor, 1968-70, associate professor, 1970-71, professor of history, 1971—, adjunct professor of English, 1980—, Paul Murray Kendall Professor of Biography, 1985—. Guest lecturer at numerous colleges, universities, societies and associations throughout the United States; has made numerous guest appearances on radio and television programs. Honorary member of board of directors, Abraham Lincoln Association. American history and biography consultant to various commercial and university presses, and consultant to National Endowment for the Humanities for various book, museum, television, and motion-picture projects. *Member:* Society of American Historians, American Antiquarian Society, Texas Institute of Letters, Phi Beta Kappa.

AWARDS, HONORS: Texas State Historical Association Fellow, 1968; Texas Institute of Letters Fellow, 1969; Guggenheim Fellow, 1972; Chancellor's Medal for Outstanding Scholarship from the University of Massachusetts, 1976; Christopher Award, 1977, and Barondess/Lincoln Award from the New York Civil War Round Table, 1978, both for *With*

STEPHEN B. OATES

Malice toward None; National Endowment for the Humanities Senior Summer Fellow, 1978.

The Fires of Jubilee was named one of New York Public Library's Books for the Teen Age, 1980, 1981, and 1982; Distinguished Teaching Award from the University of Massachusetts, 1981; Litt.D., Lincoln College, 1981; Graduate Faculty Fellowship from the University of Massachusetts, 1981-82; Christopher Award, and *New York Times Book Review* Notable Book, both 1982, Robert F. Kennedy Memorial Book Award, and Chancellor's Certificate of Recognition from the University of Massachusetts, both 1983, all for *Let the Trumpet Sound;* Institute for Advanced Studies in the Humanities Fellow, 1984; Author's Award for the Best Article of the Year from *Civil War Times Illustrated*, 1984, for "Abraham Lincoln: Man and Myth"; University of Massachusetts Presidential Writers Award, 1985; Master Teacher Award from the University of Hartford, 1985; Silver Medal from the Council for Advancement and Support of Education, 1986, for Professor of the Year, and semi-finalist, 1987.

WRITINGS:

Confederate Cavalry West of the River, University of Texas Press, 1961.
(Editor and author of introduction and commentary) John Salmon Ford, *Rip Ford's Texas*, University of Texas Press, 1963, reissued, 1987.
(Editor and contributor) *The Republic of Texas*, American West, 1968.
Visions of Glory: Texans on the Southwestern Frontier, University of Oklahoma Press, 1970.
To Purge This Land with Blood: A Biography of John Brown, Harper, 1970, 2nd edition, University of Massachusetts Press, 1984.
(Editor) *Portrait of America*, Volume 1: *From the European Discovery to the End of Reconstruction*, Volume 2: *From Reconstruction to the Present*, Houghton, 1973, 4th revised edition, 1987.
The Fires of Jubilee: Nat Turner's Fierce Rebellion, Harper, 1975.
With Malice toward None: The Life of Abraham Lincoln, Harper, 1977.
Our Fiery Trial: Abraham Lincoln, John Brown, and the Civil War Era, University of Massachusetts Press, 1979.
Let the Trumpet Sound: The Life of Martin Luther King, Jr., Harper, 1982.
Abraham Lincoln: The Man behind the Myths, Harper, 1984.
(Editor, author of prologue, and contributor) *Biography as High Adventure: Life-Writers Speak on Their Art*, University of Massachusetts Press, 1986.
William Faulkner: The Man and the Artist, Harper, 1987.

Editor with Paul Mariani of the "Commonwealth Classics in Biography" series for University of Massachusetts Press, 1986—. *With Malice toward None* has been published in French, Spanish, and Polish; *Let the Trumpet Sound* has been published in French, German, and Arabic; *William Faulkner* has been translated into French, German, Portuguese, and Spanish. Contributor to *Dictionary of American Biography, Supplement Eight*, edited by John A. Garraty and Mark C. Carnes, Scribner, 1988, to many anthologies, and to numerous periodicals, including *American Heritage, American History Illustrated, American West, Civil War History, Timeline*, and *Nation*.

WORK IN PROGRESS: Voices of the Storm: A Biographical History of the Civil War Era, for Harper.

SIDELIGHTS: "I've loved storytelling ever since I was a child, both hearing stories and telling them myself. I recall spending a good bit of my time in the early part of junior high school in the library reading biographies and novels, and, later on, narrative histories. I had a fantastic English teacher my senior year who is still living in my hometown of Pampa, Texas. We are still in touch with one another. He gave me a sense of language and a sense of the importance of literature. That same year I had a history teacher who turned me on to something I had loved for years, history itself. History and literature have been my twin loves since I've been old enough to remember."[1]

Today Oates is a distinguished educator and biographer whose books include: *To Purge This Land with Blood: A Biography of John Brown, The Fires of Jubilee: Nat Turner's Fierce Rebellion, With Malice toward None: The Life of Abraham Lincoln,* and *Let the Trumpet Sound: The Life of Martin Luther King, Jr.* "All four of those men were deeply spiritual. Two of them were ministers: Nat Turner was a slave preacher. While Lincoln did not belong to any official church, he was deeply religious and deeply spiritual. John Brown, a Congregationalist Calvinist of the old style, truly believed himself an instrument of God called to Harpers Ferry to help put an end to slavery. There's that common theme with all of them. Too, they were brooding men who were deeply worried about the injustice of slavery and racial discrimination in this country, about the country's failure to live up to the promise of the Declaration of Independence.

"Certainly Nat Turner, King, and Lincoln were extraordinary human beings with a deep sense of history and a deep insight into what their lives might amount to. And I guess I would include old John Brown in that. Though he failed in most business enterprises he tried, he was spectacularly successful in igniting humanitarian and liberal communities and abolitionists in the North to contribute money and weapons to his cause, and he was able to attract a number of idealistic young men to follow him to Harpers Ferry—several of them young blacks."[1]

An educator as well as a biographer, Oates has been the Paul Murray Kendall Professor of Biography at the University of Massachusetts since 1985. He finds teaching and writing mutually enriching activities. "I try to take the same approach in both. I've gone out to talk with students and teach them, and they've raised questions which I've then gone back to try to answer in writing my biographies. When I get them answered, I can take the books back to the students and see what they think. For me, teaching and writing are symbiotic—mutually beneficial and reinforcing. I might add that I teach a year-long graduate seminar in the art and technique of biography, the only course in the country, we think, which not only probes the extant literature, but tries to teach the principles of biographical research and narrative biographical writing. Many of my students have published books and articles that originated in the seminar. Several of us (myself and seminar graduates actively writing biography) also belong to the New England Creative Biography Group, whose monthly meetings are devoted to readings and constructive criticism by the members."[1]

The experiences of writing biographies has "reenforced my life-long conviction that the people of the past have never really died. For they enjoy a special immortality in biography, in our efforts to touch and understand them and so to help preserve the [illegible] said the 'nothing exists but a stream of souls, that all knowledge is biography.'"[1]

Cover for the 1982 paperback. (From *Let the Trumpet Sound: The Life of Martin Luther King, Jr.* by Stephen B. Oates.)

FOOTNOTE SOURCES

[1]"Stephen B. Oates," *Contemporary Authors, New Revision Series,* Volume 26, Gale, 1989.

FOR MORE INFORMATION SEE:

Antioch Review, summer, 1970, fall, 1984.
Newsweek, July 6, 1970.
Best Sellers, August 15, 1970.
Nation, March 29, 1971.
New York Times Book Review, October 5, 1975, March 13, 1977, September 12, 1982, October 28, 1984, September 20, 1987.
Saturday Review, February 5, 1977.
Christian Science Monitor, February 28, 1977.
Book World, March 6, 1977.
New York Times, March 12, 1977, August 25, 1982, August 3, 1987.
American Historical Review, October, 1977.
Chicago Tribune Book World, August 8, 1982, September 18, 1983, April 22, 1984.
Publishers Weekly, August 27, 1982, June 28, 1985.
Los Angeles Times Book Review, August 29, 1982.
New Republic, September 13, 1982.
Chronicle of Higher Education, November 3, 1982.
American History Illustrated, January, 1986.
Book Forum, Volume VII, number 4, 1986.
Globe & Mail (Toronto), August 23, 1986.

Atlantic, July, 1987.
Chicago Tribune, July 26, 1987.

O'CONNOR, Jane 1947-

PERSONAL: Born December 30, 1947, in New York, N.Y.; daughter of Norman and Dovie (Brandt) Abramson; married Jim O'Connor, December 9, 1973; children: Robert, Teddy. *Education:* Smith College, B.A., 1969. *Home:* New York, N.Y. *Office:* Random House, 201 East 50th St., New York, N.Y. 10022.

CAREER: Books for Young Readers, Random House, New York, N.Y., executive editor, 1968-88, editor-in-chief, 1988—. *Awards, honors:* New York Academy of Sciences Honor Book, 1981, for *Magic in the Movies;* Golden Sower Award from the Nebraska Library Association, 1982, for *Yours Till Niagara Falls, Abby;* Children's Choice from the International Reading Association, 1989, for *The Ghost in Tent Nineteen.*

WRITINGS:

JUVENILE

Yours Till Niagara Falls, Abby (illustrated by Margot Apple), Hastings House, 1979.
(With Katy Hall) *Magic in the Movies: The Story of Special Effects,* Doubleday, 1980.
Just Good Friends, Harper, 1983.
(With Joyce Milton) *The Dandee Diamond Mystery,* Scholastic, 1983.
(With J. Milton) *The Amazing Bubble Gum Caper,* Scholastic, 1984.
(With husband, Jim O'Connor) *The Magic Top Mystery,* Scholastic, 1984.
Lulu and the Witch Baby (illustrated by Emily A. McCully), Harper, 1986.
(Reteller) *The Teeny Tiny Woman* (illustrated by R. W. Alley), Random House, 1987.
Lulu Goes to Witch School (illustrated by E. A. McCully), Harper, 1987.
Sir Small and the Dragonfly (illustrated by John O'Brien), Random House, 1988.
(With J. O'Connor) *The Ghost in Tent Nineteen* (illustrated by Richard Williams), Random House, 1988.

WORK IN PROGRESS: The Amazing Adventures of Super Cluck, with son Robert O'Connor, for Harper; a sequel to *The Ghost in Tent Nineteen,* with husband, Jim O'Connor.

OGLE, Lucille Edith 1904-1988

OBITUARY NOTICE: Born September 20, 1904, in Cleveland, Ohio; died December 17, 1988, in Pontiac, Michigan at the age of eighty-four. Publisher. Ogle was the co-creator of the "Golden Books" series with George Duplaix. She began her publishing career in the late 1920s as editor-in-chief of Harter Publishing Company in Cleveland. By 1936 she had moved to New York City and Western Publishing Company, where as vice-president, she oversaw the development of Golden Books. First published in 1942, the popular series of children's books was among the first juveniles with full-color illustrations. Ogle was also a member of the board of directors of Artists and Writers Press from 1948 to 1968, and Odyssey Press from 1959 to 1968, as well as the vice-president of Golden Press from 1957 to 1968.

FOR MORE INFORMATION SEE:

OBITUARIES

School Library Journal, February, 1989.

OSBORNE, Charles 1927-

PERSONAL: Born November 24, 1927, in Brisbane, Australia; son of Vincent Lloyd (a barrister) and Elsa (a musician; maiden name, Raumer) Osborne. *Education:* Attended University of Queensland, 1944-45. *Politics:* Undoctrinaire liberal. *Home:* 125 St. George's Rd., London SE1 6HY, England. *Agent:* Aitken and Stone Ltd., 29 Fernshaw Rd., London S.W.10, England.

CAREER: Began career as writer and actor in Australia; Ballad Bookshop, Brisbane, Australia, co-owner, 1947-51; writer and editor in London, England, 1953—; assistant editor, *London Magazine,* 1957-66; chief editor for Alan Ross Ltd. (publishers), 1965—; writer on European musical events for *New York Times,* 1986—; chief drama critic, *London Daily Telegraph.* Broadcaster of musical and literary programs, British Broadcasting Corp., 1957—. Arts Council of Great Britain, assistant literature director, 1966-71, literature director, 1971-86; director, Poetry International, 1967-70. *Member:* P.E.N., Poetry Book Society (secretary, 1971- 86). *Awards, honors:* Yorkshire Post Music Award, 1981, for *The Complete Operas of Puccini.*

WRITINGS:

(With Brigid Brophy and Michael Levey) *Fifty Works of English and American Literature We Could Do Without,* Rapp & Carroll, 1967, Stein & Day, 1968.
Kafka, Oliver & Boyd, 1967, Barnes & Noble, 1968.
Swansong: Poems, Shenval, 1968.
The Complete Operas of Verdi, Gollancz, 1969, Knopf, 1970.
Ned Kelly, Anthony Blond, 1970.
(Reviser) Dyneley Hussey, *Verdi,* 5th Edition, Dent, 1973.
The Concert Song Companion: A Guide to the Classical Repertoire, Gollancz, 1974, Da Capo, 1985.
Richard Wagner and His World, Scribner, 1977 (published in England as *Wagner and His World,* Thames & Hudson, 1977).
Verdi, Macmillan (London), 1978.
The Complete Operas of Mozart: A Critical Guide, Atheneum, 1978.
Rigoletto: A Guide to the Opera, Barrie & Jenkins, 1979, Silver Burdett, 1980.
W. H. Auden: The Life of a Poet, Harcourt, 1979.
The Opera House Album: A Collection of Turn-of-the- Century Postcards, Taplinger, 1979.
The Complete Operas of Puccini: A Critical Guide, Gollancz, 1981, Atheneum, 1982.
The Life and Crimes of Agatha Christie, Collins (London), 1982, Holt, 1983.
The World Theatre of Wagner: A Celebration of One Hundred Fifty Years of Wagner Productions, Macmillan, 1982.
The Dictionary of the Opera, Simon & Schuster, 1983.
Collected Poems, 1941-1981, Riverrun Press (New York), 1984.
How to Enjoy Opera, Salem House, 1984.
Schubert and His Vienna, Knopf, 1985.
Giving It Away (memoirs), Secker & Warburg, 1986.
Verdi: A Life in the Theatre, Knopf, 1987.

(From *Rigoletto: A Guide to the Opera* by Charles Osborne. Photograph by Rudolf Betz.)

The Complete Operas of Richard Strauss, Trafalgar Square, 1988.

EDITOR

Australian Stories of Today, Faber, 1962.
Twelve Poets, Poetry Book Society (London), 1967.
Australia, New Zealand and the South Pacific: A Handbook, Praeger, 1970.
Letters of Giuseppe Verdi, Gollancz, 1971, Holt, 1972.
(And author of introduction) *Richard Wagner—Stories and Essays*, Library Press, 1973.
The Bram Stoker Bedside Companion: Ten Stories by the Author of Dracula, Taplinger, 1973.
New Poems, 1973, Poetry Book Society, 1973.
(With Peter Porter) *New Poetry: An Anthology*, Arts Council of Great Britain, 1975.
The Dictionary of Composers, Bodley Head, 1977, Taplinger, 1978.
(And compiler with Kenneth Thomson) *Klemperer Stories. Anecdotes, Sayings, and Impressions of Otto Klemperer*, Robson Books (London), 1980.

TRANSLATOR FROM THE GERMAN

Frida Leider, *Playing My Part*, Da Capo, 1978.
Arthur Schnitzler, *The Round Dance*, Riverrun Press, 1982.

Also author of *Masterpieces of Nolan, Masterpieces of Drysdale*, and *Masterpieces of Dobell*, all 1976. Plays include "Actor by Moonlight," and "Platonov." Contributor to numerous anthologies, including *Australian Poetry, 1951-52, Oxford Book of Australian Verse*, 1956, *The Queensland Centenary Anthology*, 1959, and *Australian Writing Today*, 1968. Also contributor to *Chambers Encyclopedia Yearbook* and to *Enciclopedia dello spettacolo;* and to numerous newspapers and periodicals, including *Times Literary Supplement, Observer, Guardian, Spectator, London Magazine, Encounter*, and *New Statesman*. Editor of *Opera*, 1966.

WORK IN PROGRESS: A book on composer Wagner.

HOBBIES AND OTHER INTERESTS: Travel—especially to and through the United States, reading, theatre and opera-going, watching old movies on television, visiting Austrian baroque churches, writing.

FOR MORE INFORMATION SEE:

New York Times Book Review, January 18, 1970, November 11, 1979.
Times Literary Supplement, January 22, 1970, January 8, 1971, March 7, 1980, September 24, 1982.
Time, November 19, 1979.
Nation, November 24, 1979.
New York Times, November 30, 1979, December 11, 1979.
New Republic, December 1, 1979.
Chicago Tribune Book World, December 9, 1979.
Washington Post Book World, December 23, 1979.
Saturday Review, January 5, 1980.
Times (London), March 6, 1980, September 9, 1982.
New York Review of Books, October 23, 1980.
Charles Osborne, *Giving It Away,* Secker & Warburg, 1986.

OZER, Jerome S. 1927-

PERSONAL: Born July 18, 1927, in New York, N.Y.; son of Isidore Meyer (a tailor) and Lena (a social worker; maiden name, Brusensky) Ozer; married Harriet Leibow (a nurse), October 31, 1953; children: Joseph, Ira. *Education:* City College (now of the City University of New York), B.S.S., 1948; Cornell University, M.A., 1949, Ph.D., 1952. *Politics:* Democrat. *Religion:* Jewish. *Home and office:* Jerome S. Ozer Publishers, Inc., 340 Tenafly Rd., Englewood, N.J. 07631.

CAREER: Arno Press, New York, N.Y., executive vice-president, 1968-70; Jerome S. Ozer Publishers, Inc., Englewood, N.J., president, 1970—; John Harms Center for the Arts, Englewood, N.J., house manager, 1987—; Bergen Community College, N.J., adjunct instructor, 1988—. Publishing director of Boardroom Books, 1980-81. Member of board of trustees of Englewood Public Library, 1977—. *Military service:* U.S. Army, 1945-46. *Member:* American Historical Association, Organization of American Historians, Immigration History Society, American Film Institute.

WRITINGS:

American Mosaic: Immigrants in American History, Macmillan, 1975.
(With Shirley Blumenthal) *Coming to America: Immigrants from the British Isles,* Dial, 1980.

Editor of *Film Review Annual,* 1981—. Editor of *Opera Annual,* 1984—.

PARISH, Peggy 1927-1988

OBITUARY NOTICE:—See sketch in *SATA* Volume 17: Born July 14, 1927, in Manning S.C.; died of a ruptured abdominal aneurysm on November 19, 1988, in Manning, S.C. Author and teacher. Parish was the author of more than thirty children's books and the creator of the popular "Amelia Bedelia" series. After graduating from the University of South Carolina in 1948, Parish taught English and creative dancing in the Oklahoma panhandle country and third grade in Kentucky before moving to New York City where she taught third grade at the Dalton School. It was while teaching at the Dalton School that she had her first book published in 1962, *My Golden Book of Manners,* illustrated by Richard Scarry. "Children have always been my life," said Parish, "so writing stories for children came

naturally. I do have special feelings about writing for children. I don't try to teach anything in my stories—I write for fun."

Her first "Amelia Bedelia" book was published in 1963. Since then, books about the daffy maid who causes havoc by taking all instructions literally (when asked to 'dust the furniture,' she throws dust on it) have sold over seven million copies. The most recent "Amelia Bedelia" book was *Amelia Bedelia's Family Album,* which was published in August, 1988.

Besides her series about the literal-minded maid, Parish wrote a "Granny" series about Granny Guntry, a tough old lady who finds herself in hair-raising situations. She also wrote stories for children such as: *The Cats' Burglar, Mr. Adams's Mistake, No More Monsters for Me,* and *Zed and the Monsters,* and *I Can—Can You* (four baby books). Her nonfiction books include such titles as: *Let's Celebrate: Holiday Decorations You Can Make, December Decorations: A Holiday How-to-Book,* and *The Story of Grains: Wheat, Corn, and Rice.* In 1984 Parish received the Milner Award, and in 1988 a nationwide celebration of Amelia Bedelia's twenty-fifth birthday was sponsored by her principal publishers.

FOR MORE INFORMATION SEE:

Contemporary Authors, Volumes 73-76, Gale, 1978.
Shirley Norby and Gregory Ryan, *Famous Children's Authors,* Dennison, 1988.

OBITUARIES

New York Times, November 22, 1988.
Newsweek, December 5, 1988.
School Library Journal, January, 1989.
Horn Book, March/April, 1989.

PARKER, Kristy (Kettelkamp) 1957-

PERSONAL: Born May 3, 1957, in Decatur, Ill.; daughter of James F. (a university dean of admissions) and Emily (a teacher; maiden name, Siegrist) Kettelkamp; married Thomas E. Parker (an engineer), August 19, 1978; children: Erin, Andy, Sara. *Education:* Attended Millikin University, 1975-77; University of Illinois at Urbana-Champaign, B.S., 1979. *Religion:* Presbyterian. *Home:* 4897 Chimney Springs Dr., Greensboro, N.C. 27407.

CAREER: Writer, 1979—; Dubuque Community School System, Dubuque, Iowa, teacher's aide, 1979-80; North Scott Community School System, Scott County, Iowa, substitute teacher, 1980-81. *Member:* Juvenile Forum Writers Group, National League of American Penwomen. *Awards, honors:* First prize in beginner's category from Mississippi Valley Writer's Conference, 1985, for essay "Lookout Superman"; Honorable Mention in Religious Category for essay "The One Who Suffered First," 1985, and Honorable Mention for essay, "Tender Moments," 1986, both from the National League of American Penwomen.

WRITINGS:

I Talked with God (choral arrangement), Alfred Publishing, 1979.
My Dad the Magnificent (juvenile; illustrated by Lillian Hoban), Dutton, 1987.

Also author in collaboration with singer/song-writer Mary Larson of folk songs "Gramma's Quilt" and "Brothers," 1987.

WORK IN PROGRESS: Picture books for children.

SIDELIGHTS: "My childhood was that of an every day, average, American kid, growing up in a close-knit family in the Midwest. As unremarkable as that sounds, it has probably contributed greatly to the kinds of stories that I write.

"I think I have always been a writer. My first publication, 'I Like to Ride on the Bus,' appeared in the PTA newsletter when I was in the third grade! From that time on, I have always been compelled to express myself through writing.

"During my teenage years, my interests turned toward song-writing. I purchased a guitar for forty dollars with money earned from detasseling corn. I then started writing songs that my two sisters and I sang for church services. 'I Talked with God,' a four-part song that I wrote for my high school choir was eventually published by Alfred Publishing in 1979.

"An interest in children and helping others through education led me to earn a degree in elementary education with a concentration in language arts. I think my exposure to both children and the books they read inspired me to try writing my own books.

KRISTY PARKER

"I began writing for children in 1982 when my oldest daughter was a year old. I took a course through Scott Community College in Davenport, Iowa. *My Dad the Magnificient* was written as an assignment for that class. My teacher encouraged me to submit it, and in 1987 it became a book!

"I feel that my personal involvement with children is the main thing that inspires me to write. Many of my ideas for stories come from moments spent with my own children. When I write about these moments, it is a way for me to preserve them and keep them alive, and for my thoughts and feelings about these times to be shared with others.

"I feel that my stories are reflections of the everyday experiences that many children have. I recently wrote a story about our move from Iowa to North Carolina which I feel addresses the many concerns that a small child has about moving. It is my hope that the words I write will touch the people that read them in some good and positive way. It is rewarding to me to think that somewhere a parent and child might be sharing my book, and talking about how it makes them feel, and enjoying their time together."

HOBBIES AND OTHER INTERESTS: Camping with my family, swimming, singing in the church choir, movies, cross-stitch.

FOR MORE INFORMATION SEE:

Milliken Quarterly, summer, 1987.

PATERSON, Diane (R. Cole) 1946-

PERSONAL: Born July 23, 1946, in Brooklyn, N. Y.; daughter of A. R. and T. E. (Isaacs) Cole; divorced, 1978; married John Mannion, 1982; children: (first marriage) Elizabeth, Jana. *Education:* Attended Pratt Institute, 1966-68; State University of New York—New Paltz, B.A., 1985. *Home:* Gardiner, N.Y. *Agent:* Libby Ford, Kirchoff/Wohlberg, Inc., 866 United Nations Plaza, New York, N.Y. 10017.

CAREER: Author and illustrator of children's books. *Awards, honors: Fiona's Bee* was selected one of Child Study Association of America's Children's Books of the Year, 1975, and *Skunk for a Day,* 1976; *Smile for Auntie* was included in the Children's Book Showcase of the Children's Book Council, 1977; *I Hate Kisses* was selected a Children's Choice by the International Reading Association, 1982.

WRITINGS:

SELF-ILLUSTRATED CHILDREN'S BOOKS

The Biggest Snowstorm Ever, Dial, 1974.
Eat!, Dial, 1975.
Smile for Auntie (Junior Literary Guild selection), Dial, 1976.
If I Were a Toad (Junior Literary Guild selection), Dial, 1977.
Wretched Rachel, Dial, 1978.
The Bathtub Ocean, Dial, 1979.
Hey, Cowboy!, Knopf, 1983.
Soap and Suds, Knopf, 1984.

ILLUSTRATOR

Susan Pearson, *Monnie Hates Lydia,* Dial, 1975.
Beverly Keller, *Fiona's Bee* (Junior Literary Guild selection), Coward, 1975.

DIANE PATERSON

Roger Caras, *Skunk for a Day*, Dutton, 1976.

Robert Kraus, *Kittens for Nothing*, Windmill Books, 1976.

R. Caras, *Coyote for a Day*, Dutton, 1977.

Barbara Greenberg, *The Bravest Babysitter* (Junior Literary Guild selection), Dial, 1977.

S. Pearson, *Everybody Knows That!*, Dial, 1978.

Brothers Grimm, *The Golden Goose*, Troll Associates, 1981.

Robie H. Harris, *I Hate Kisses*, Knopf, 1981.

B. Keller, *Fiona's Flea* (Junior Literary Guild selection), Coward, 1981.

B. Keller, *The Bee Sneeze*, Coward, 1982.

Nathan Zimelman, *If I Were Strong Enough*, Abingdon, 1982.

Carlo Collodi, *Pinocchio and the Puppet Show*, adapted by David E. Cuts, Troll Associates, 1982.

C. Collodi, *Pinocchio and the Great Whale*, adapted by D. E. Cutts, Troll Associates, 1982.

C. Collodi, *Pinocchio Goes to School*, adapted by D. E. Cutts, Troll Associates, 1982.

C. Collodi, *Pinocchio Meets the Cat and Fox*, adapted by D. E. Cutts, Troll Associates, 1982.

Janet Lorimer, *The Biggest Bubble in the World*, F. Watts, 1982.

Judith G. Collins, *Josh's Scary Dad*, Abingdon, 1983.

Caroline Bauer, *Too Many Books!*, Warne, 1984.

Ski Michaels, *The Big Surprise*, Troll Associates, 1986.

Michael J. Pellowski, *The Duck Who Loved Puddles*, Troll Associates, 1986.

S. Michaels, *Fun in the Sun*, Troll Associates, 1986.

Robyn Supraner, *Kitty: A Cat's Diary*, Troll Associates, 1986.

Erica Frost, *The Littlest Pig*, Troll Associates, 1986.

M. J. Pellowski, *The Messy Monster*, Troll Associates, 1986.

ADAPTATIONS:

"A Smile for Auntie," Weston Woods.

WORK IN PROGRESS: The Diane Paterson Storybook; Sylvia's Sunday.

SIDELIGHTS: "My own childhood floods my mind when I'm working on picture books. Seen through the distance of time and experience, my childhood seems to have been magical. I vividly recall the way things looked to me when I was small: the trees were gigantic, and ceilings were very high, faces came looming down out of the sky to say 'Hello'—fish-eye-lense-scale. I remember the sound of the snow shovel scraping the sidewalks early in the morning. Snow! Now that's a magical event to a child. It's satisfying to me to share this vision with my own children, and with others."[1]

"Until I was six my parents and I lived with my paternal grandparents, aunts, uncles, and cousins in a marvellous Brooklyn brownstone with skylights, an Oriental carpet runner in the hall, books, and plants. I was the youngest child and terribly spoiled. My grandfather was involved with importing bulbs from Holland. We had a backyard full of tulips and daffodils. My grandmother, a very creative, artistic lady, was

"I'd rather wait for someone to drop by," Fiona thought. (From *Fiona's Bee* by Beverly Keller. Illustrated by Diane Paterson.)

"We're going to the country—to Uncle Jack's lake!" (From *Monnie Hates Lydia* by Susan Pearson. Illustrated by Diane Paterson.)

very traditional serving a proper Victorian high tea at four every afternoon. She sewed beautifully and made patchwork quilts. At Christmas our decorations were lavish; I remember helping make the table napkins.

"I was the resident artist of the family and took myself seriously in that position. I can't recall a time when I didn't draw or paint and make things. My mother always had me make cards for birthdays and other holidays. Encouragement came early on from my teachers and peers. As a girl I was aware that the great painters we studied were all men. On some level, I must have been wondering where the women artists were. There was a general assumption that in order to be great you had to be male. Even so, I was determined to become the finest artist I could.

"When I was in high school I won a summer scholarship to the New York Phoenix School of Design. About halfway through the term, all the other students had dropped out. So for all intents and purposes I had private instruction. I spent the mornings drawing from a model and then from a plaster bust; the afternoons at the Metropolitan Museum of Art. I'd sit for

hours in a little seat reserved for art students, copying Degas sculptures or Greek statuary.

"I was accepted to Pratt ·after graduation. Their graphics department deservedly has always been renowned and was very receptive to women. We had a more difficult time of it in the fine arts department, however. The first year was especially intense. We stayed up all night as a regular way of life. They wanted us to know our maximum work capacity and to work continually at that intense level.

"One of my most important teachers was Martha Earlbacher. For one of the first assignments we had to draw a plot of grass of the same dimensions. I remember drawing every blade meticulously—Earlbacher brought that quality out in us. She made us see. We would do self-portraits, and in fact, she kept one I did of myself in hair curlers.

"To this at Pratt that I took my first course in typography, learned how to bind books, and went to the Museum of Modern Art to study and touch the books by Matisse.

Smile for Auntie.

(From *Smile for Auntie* by Diane Paterson. Illustrated by the author.)

"I married after graduation and with my new husband moved to Canada. We lived in a tent on a Nova Scotia beach that first summer. It was a simple life and I was constantly doing illustrations. I started my own business doing illustrations, posters, and public relations for the Blue Nose Sailboat in Halifax Harbor. I even got to steer the boat into its berth.

"My next artistic phase consisted of large-scale dot paintings. Each dot was carefully placed according to a system of color vibrations. The technique began to drive me crazy, so I stopped. I mean, I put hundreds of jillions of millions of dots on those canvases. Enough was enough! Beautiful as these paintings were, they weren't likely to earn a living for me. They took too long to execute and catered to a very specialized taste. I also did pen-and-ink dot drawings. My agent took one look, and said, 'Draw characters. Draw the same character in a number of different positions.' Well, I was highly insulted. Then, he opened a textbook, pointed to a line drawing, and said, 'Can you do this?' Of course I could. So I figured as long as I was drawing one character in different positions, I might as well throw in some words. I made several books out of my agent's assignment—did the calligraphy, the illustrations, cloth-bound them, made dust covers and then made boxes with slip cases for them. Then my agent took them to Phyllis Fogelman who bought all of them on the spot. *The Biggest Snowstorm Ever*, my first published book, was in that original batch.

"Phyllis became my editor. She and the other staff members at Dial were fabulous. The art director took me over every little line and detail. They taught me the whole process from mechanics to overlays."[2]

With *Smile for Auntie*, the writing and drawing "happily happened quite simultaneously. First I drew a fat woman with a polka-dotted babushka and galoshes, and then I drew a very sad-looking baby sitting next to her. I named the woman Auntie and proceeded to have her torment the poor baby into smiling. Of course the baby was too young to talk, so it was a monologue with Auntie talking and the baby only able to answer with grimaces and other facial contortions."

"The book was animated for Weston Woods by a Czechoslovakian who drew exactly as I did. They also hired a famous Czech actress to model Auntie for the animations. The movie looks very much like my book, and if that weren't so wonderful, it would almost be eerie."[2]

"When my daughters were preschool age,. . .we spent many hours playing a favorite game together. They would think of an animal or an object and try to make me guess what it was by acting it out. They went through fantastic contortions trying to be spiders, frogs, chickens, and even coat hangers and books.

"I did find it difficult to guess when they were being telephone poles. They fooled me many times. *If I Were a Toad* was written directly from these very happy memories. . . .Maybe someday I'll write a book about coat hangers and telephone poles."

"After these many years of drawing, I think I have a pretty good sense of what I can do. For a long time I drew from models or pictures. I still do that, but feel increasingly confident of my ability to make a realistic drawing directly from my imagination. It's very liberating.

"Watercolors have become a very important passion, and recently I joined a watercolor club. I always keep my paints and a pad in my car. I do a lot of small paintings from nature that way, or else I'll go hiking through Hudson Valley with my

Lisa and Heather snuggled together in the soft armchair. (From *The Bravest Babysitter* by Barbara Greenberg. Illustrated by Diane Paterson.)

paints in my backpack. In the winter I paint the most incredible blossoms in the local greenhouse. I love the shape of boats and their reflections on water. I am trying to train myself to make one watercolor a day as a sort of journal for myself. Martha Earlbacher is still an important inspiration for me. In fact, it was seeing her work in a book of watercolors that compelled me to get started in this medium."[2]

Paterson divides her professional time between picture books, fine art, and textbook illustrations. "I've got two daughters in college, so for the next few years I'll continue with textbooks. Basically textbooks are bread and butter, but they don't offer much in the way of artistic satisfaction. The publishers are so worried about offending racial, sexual, and ethnic groups that they bend over backwards to satisfy everyone. They have rigid quotas for the black, white, Oriental, Indian, as well as old, young, and handicapped characters. For an assignment that consisted of drawing rabbits I was told a certain number had to be brown and a certain number white. It is so inhibiting. Math textbooks are generally the worst because you end up doing scores of flutes or ducks or ladybugs, or whatever. They do not encourage fanciful pictures.

"I decided at one point to go back to school for a degree in English. It exposed me to writers and ideas I would otherwise not be exposed to. I have also wanted to write adult books, an illustrated adult novel, in fact. I find it a good deal harder to write for adults, because my imagination is largely pictorial, I tend to use too many adjectives. I admire the apparent simplicity of William Carlos Williams and Marianne Moore's language. I particularly love Moore's poems about animals.

"One of the most fulfilling projects I have done for my college courses involved a history assignment calling for research of our own families. At thirty-six, the age at which my maternal grandmother died, I began a project on her life. Rose Burton Isaacs was married to a coal miner who eventually died of black lung disease. They lived in Kentucky in considerable poverty. They had six children, the last of whom was a breach birth; she hemorrhaged and died not long after. For the time (1900-1936) and place, this would not have been an extraordinary story. But Rose Burton Isaacs was a poet and a schoolteacher in a one-room schoolhouse. As family history has it, the family was so poor she couldn't afford paper on which to write her poetry and used an enamel table top, instead. Later she'd copy her poems on the meat wrapping from the butcher. We still have those poems, written in brown ink. I went to Kentucky and spoke with as many relatives and descendants as I could. This is the legacy I grew up with. The events were painful for my mother, since she was called upon to care for her siblings after her mother's death. My daughters, too, have grown up with Rose's story. One of them has also written about her, approaching her life and work in the context of the American Dream.

"I feel privileged to have had such a grandmother. Her example is a sobering inspiration binding generations of women in my family. Thinking of Rose Burton Isaacs makes me thankful for the times in which I live, and determined to work very, very hard."[2]

Paterson's recent project, *Sylvia's Sunday*, inspired by Gabriel Garcia Marquez's *One Hundred Years of Solitude* where he concluded that every day is the same day, started out as six double-spaced typewritten pages. "I sent it to my editor who liked the idea but said it was too long. I've now got it down to two or three pages. It's interesting to see my art work affecting the way I edit. I took out a lot of descriptive language, the content of which would only be repeated in the illustrations. Now I am finding that the illustrations inspire language. It's an interesting interaction that I want to explore further. For me, I think it's probably best to work on text and pictures simultaneously. The work becomes seamless and progresses more easily. I would like to do the illustrations in full watercolor, with some black line work. Increasingly, however, I find I'm working without the black line, using just watercolor. In terms of words and pictures, it's an exciting time. I feel poised on the brink of change."[2]

"The first solo exhibition of my watercolors at the Mark Gruber Gallery in New Paltz, N.Y. (1989) has been a major cause of change in my work. My illustrations are crossing over into the boundaries of fine art. I am thrilled with the positive reaction to these works. My next goal is to use this highly developed style in my picture books. Great things are in the works."

FOOTNOTE SOURCES

[1]Lee Kingman and others, compilers, *Illustrators of Children's Books: 1967-1976*, Horn Book, 1978.
[2]Based on an interview by Marguerite Feitlowitz for *Something about the Author*.

PATTERSON, Charles 1935-

PERSONAL: Born August 5, 1935, in New Britain, Conn.; son of Robert F. (a lawyer and businessman) and Ann Janet (a housewife; maiden name, Wilson) Patterson. *Education:* Amherst College, B.A., 1958; Columbia University, M.A., 1960, Ph.D., 1970; Episcopal Theological School, Cambridge, Mass., B.D., 1963. *Home:* 545 West End Ave., New York, N.Y. 10024.

CAREER: St. Stephen's School, Rome, Italy, teacher of ancient and biblical history, 1964-65; American Universities Field Staff, New York City, editor and assistant director, 1967-69; New School for Social Research, New York City, part-time teacher of history, religion, and literature, 1971-82; Trinity School, New York City, part-time English and comparative religions teacher, 1972-74; Hunter College of the City University of New York, New York City, adjunct assistant professor of literature of the Bible, 1974-75; New Lincoln School, New York City, teacher of history and English, 1976-78; Birch Wathen School, New York City, teacher of history and writing, 1978-80; free-lance editor and writer, 1980-81, 1984—; Calhoun School, New York City, teacher of history and English, 1981-84; Charles Scribners & Sons (publishers), New York City, assistant editor, 1985-86; Adelphi University, Long Island, New York, adjunct faculty member, 1985-86. *Member:* PEN, Authors Guild, National Writers Union, Forum of Writers for Young People.

WRITINGS:

Anti-Semitism: The Road to the Holocaust and Beyond, Walker, 1982.
(Contributor) *World History: Patterns of Civilization* (textbook), Prentice-Hall, 1983.
Thomas Jefferson, F. Watts, 1987.
Marian Anderson, F. Watts, 1988.
Asad of Syria, Simon & Schuster, 1990.

Contributor of articles and reviews to newspapers and journals, including *Jewish World, Judaica Book News, West Side Spirit*, and *Martyrdom and Resistance*. Assistant editor, *Dictionary of the Middle Ages*, twelve volumes, Scribner, 1985-86.

CHARLES PATTERSON

WORK IN PROGRESS: A historical novel about King Herod and his family "caught between the pressures of Roman rule and the Jewish aspirations of Jesus, John the Baptist, and the Essenes."

SIDELIGHTS: "The idea for my book on anti-Semitism came to me when I was teaching history to high school students. I looked for, but could not find, a good readable history of the Holocaust and what led up to it for my classes. I am not Jewish, but I had done a great deal of reading on the subject. Also, meeting Holocaust survivors—one of whom became a very good friend—made the story of that great tragedy even more real. At the theological seminary I attended some years earlier, I had become fascinated by Judaism and by the Old Testament and the way they contributed so much to Christianity, but I also came to see the role that certain church teachings played in portraying Jews in such a negative way and in creating anti-Semitic attitudes in Europe. Recently I have come to realize more and more that the seeds of my interest in the Holocaust go back to my childhood. My father, who was a major in the U.S. Army in Europe, never returned from World War II. I'm sure my own sense of loss has made me feel a special bond to all the victims of that time.

"Anyway, convinced there was a need for such a book, I sent a book proposal around to various publishers. Walker & Company liked the idea and helped convince me to make it a book on the long history of anti-Semitism that began in ancient times and that unfortunately continues to this day. The research was a lot

of work, but I have no regrets. The book has been recommended by the Anti-Defamation League of B'nai B'rith. At a time when young people need to understand how such a thing could have happened and to be the ones who will make sure that it will never happen again, I am proud that I have been able to make my own small contribution."

FOR MORE INFORMATION SEE:

Social Education, May, 1983.
History Teacher, November, 1983.
Judaica Book News, fall/winter, 1983-84.
Booklist, May 15, 1987.
School Library Journal, June-July, 1987.

REESE, (John) Terence 1913-

PERSONAL: Born August 28, 1913, in Epsom, England; son of John (a confectioner and hotelier) and Anne (a hotelier; maiden name, Hutchings) Reese; married Alwyn Sherrington, 1970. *Education:* Attended Bradfield College and New College, Oxford. *Politics:* Conservative. *Religion:* Agnostic. *Home:* 23 Adelaide Crescent, Flat 5, Hove BN3 2JG, Sussex, England.

CAREER: Writer and bridge expert. Bridge correspondent for *Evening News,* London, 1948-80, *Observer,* London, 1950—, *Lady,* 1954—, *Standard,* 1980—, and *Sunday Mirror,* 1989—. *Awards, honors:* Winner of numerous British, European, and world bridge championships.

WRITINGS:

(With Hubert Phillips) *The Elements of Contract,* British Bridge World, 1937, revised edition, Eyre & Spottiswoode, 1948.
(With H. Phillips) *How to Play Bridge,* Penguin Books, 1945, revised edition, Parrish, 1958.
Reese on Play: An Introduction to Good Bridge, Edward Arnold, 1947, 2nd edition, R. Hale, 1975.
(With H. Phillips) *Bridge with Mr. Playbetter,* Batchworth Press, 1952.
The Expert Game, Edward Arnold, 1958, new edition, R. Hale, 1973.
Master Play, the Expert Game: Contract Bridge, Coffin, 1960, reissued as *Master Play in Contract Bridge,* Dover, 1974.
Play Bridge with Reese, Sterling, 1960.
Modern Bidding and the Acol System, Nicholson & Watson, 1960.
Bridge, Penguin Books, 1961, new edition, Hodder & Stoughton, 1980.
Develop Your Bidding Judgment, Sterling, 1962, reissued as *Bidding a Bridge Hand,* Dover, 1972.
The Game of Bridge, Constable, 1962.
(With Anthony Watkins) *Poker, Game of Skill,* Faber, 1962, Merrimack Book Service, 1964.
Learn Bridge with Reese, Faber, 1962, revised edition, Hamlyn/American, 1978.
(With A. Watkins) *Secrets of Modern Poker,* Sterling, 1964.
Bridge for Bright Beginners, Sterling, 1964.
Your Book of Contract Bridge, Faber, 1965, Transatlantic, 1971.
Story of an Accusation, Heinemann, 1966, Simon & Schuster, 1967.
(With Boris Schapiro) *Bridge Card by Card,* Hamlyn/American, 1969.
(Adapter from the French) Benito Garozzo and Leon Yallouze,

The Blue Club (with foreword by Omar Sharif), Faber, 1969.

C. C. Wei's Precision System, M. Lisa Precisions, 1970.

Precision Bidding and Precision Play, W. H. Allen, 1972, Sterling, 1973, 2nd edition, R. Hale, 1980.

Advanced Bridge (adapted from *Play Bridge with Reese* and *Develop Your Bidding Judgment*), Sterling, 1973.

(With Robert Brinig) *Backgammon: The Modern Game*, W. H. Allen, 1975, Sterling, 1976.

Play These Hands with Me, W. H. Allen, 1976.

Bridge by Question and Answer, Arthur Barker, 1976.

Bridge at the Top (autobiography), Merrimack Book Service, 1977.

Begin Bridge with Reese, Sterling, 1977.

Winning at Casino Gambling: An International Guide, Sterling, 1978.

The Most Puzzling Situations in Bridge Play, Sterling, 1978.

(With Jeremy Flint) *Trick Thirteen* (novel), Weidenfeld & Nicolson, 1979.

(With Patrick Jourdain) *Squeeze Play Made Easy: Techniques for Advanced Bridge Players*, Sterling, 1980 (published in England as *Squeeze Play Is Easy*, Allen & Unwin, 1980).

Bridge Tips by World Masters, R. Hale, 1980, Crown, 1981.

(With Eddie Kantar) *Defend with Your Life*, Merrimack Book Service, 1981.

(With David Bird) *Miracles of Card Play*, David & Charles, 1982.

(With D. Bird) *Bridge: The Modern Game*, Faber, 1983.

Unholy Tricks, Gollancz, 1984, revised edition, 1988.

(With D. Bird) *How the Experts Do It*, Faber, 1985.

Omar Sharif's Life in Bridge, Faber, 1985.

TERENCE REESE

(With Julian Pottage) *Positive Defence*, Gollancz, 1985.

(With J. Pottage) *Positive Declarer's Play*, Gollancz, 1986.

What Would You Bid?, Faber, 1986.

Master Plays in a Single Suit, Gollancz, 1987.

(With D. Bird) *The Hidden Side of Bridge*, Faber, 1988.

Master Deceptive Plays, Gollancz, 1988.

Bridge for Ambitious Players, Gollancz, 1988.

(With D. Bird) *Doubled and Venerable: Further Miracles of Card Play*, Gollancz, 1988.

Bridge: Tricks of the Trade, Gollancz, 1989.

Do You Really Want to Win at Bridge?, Gollancz, 1989.

ALL WITH ALBERT DORMER

Bridge Player's Dictionary, Sterling, 1959, revised and enlarged edtion, 1963, adaptation published as *Bridge Conventions, Finesses, and Coups*, Sterling, 1965.

Blueprint for Bidding: The Acol System Applied to American Bridge, Sterling, 1961.

The Acol System Today, Edward Arnold, 1961, revised edition published as *Bridge, the Acol System of Bidding: A Modern Version of the Acol System Today*, Pan Books, 1978.

The Play of the Cards, Penguin Books, 1967, new edition, R. Hale, 1977.

Bridge for Tournament Players, R. Hale, 1968.

How to Play a Good Game of Bridge, Heinemann, 1969.

How to Play a Better Game of Bridge, Stein & Day, 1969.

Practical Bidding and Practical Play, Sterling, 1973.

The Complete Book of Bridge, Faber, 1973, Saturday Review Press, 1974.

The Bridge Player's Alphabetical Handbook, Merrimack Book Service, 1981.

ALL WITH ROGER TREZEL

Safety Plays in Bridge, Fell, 1976.

Elimination Play in Bridge, Fell, 1976.

Blocking and Unblocking Plays in Bridge, Fell, 1976.

Snares and Swindles in Bridge, Fell, 1976.

When to Duck, When to Win in Bridge, Fell, 1978.

Those Extra Chances in Bridge, Fell, 1978.

The Art of Defence in Bridge, Gollancz, 1979.

Master the Odds in Bridge, Gollancz, 1979.

The Mistakes You Make in Bridge, Gollancz, 1984.

EDITOR

Ely Culbertson, *Contract Bridge Self-Teacher*, revised edition, Faber, 1965.

E. Culbertson, *Contract Bridge Complete*, 7th edition, Faber, 1965.

Alfred Sheinwold, *Improve Your Bridge*, Jenkins, 1965.

Josephine Murphy Culbertson, *Contract Bridge Made Easy, the New Point Count Way*, Faber, 1966.

Former editor of *British Bridge World*.

WORK IN PROGRESS: Bridge in Thirty Days with David Bird, for Faber; *Acol in the Nineties* with D. Bird, for Hale.

SIDELIGHTS: "My mother was keen on bridge and I started young, at the age of seven, when I jealously sorted my cards behind a cushion. I played (successfully) for Oxford University in the first university match with Cambridge, 1935. After a year at Harrods I became a professional bridge player and writer. 'Waste of a good brain,' my father always said.

"Since 1976 I have played very little bridge and prefer to lose my money at backgammon. Tournament bridge is being ruined by the World Bridge Federation with its ghastly regulations, screens, and so forth."

RICHARDSON, Jean (Mary)

PERSONAL: Born in London, England; daughter of Frederick Haig (a master silversmith) and Lena Jessie (a civil servant; maiden name, McClellan) Richardson. *Education:* University of Birmingham, B.A. (with honors); graduate study at St. Hilda's College, Oxford. *Religion:* Church of England. *Home:* 6 Culford Grove, London N1 4HR, England.

CAREER: Free-lance editor and writer. Has worked as a book reviewer for *Birmingham Post*, and *BBC World Service*.

WRITINGS:

JUVENILE

Enjoying Ballet, Beaver Books, 1977.
Beaver Book of the Seaside, Beaver Books, 1978.
Enjoying Music (illustrated by Clive Spong), Beaver Books, 1979.
The First Step (illustrated by Priscilla Lamont), Hodder & Stoughton, 1979.
Dancer in the Wings (illustrated by Jane Bottomley), Hodder & Stoughton, 1981.
One Foot on the Ground (illustrated by J. Bottomley), Hodder & Stoughton, 1982.
Careers in the Theatre, Kogan Page, 1983.
Careers in Dance, Kogan Page, 1984.
(Editor and contributor) *Cold Feet* (anthology), Hodder & Stoughton, 1985.
Clara's Dancing Feet (illustrated by Joanna Carey), Putnam, 1986.
(Editor and contributor) *Beware! Beware!* (anthology), Hamish Hamilton, 1987, Viking, 1989.
Tall Inside (illustrated by Alice Englander), Putnam, 1988.
Musical Chairs, Methuen, 1988.
Jenny and the Tooth Fairy (illustrated by Mike Dodd), Oxford University Press (New York), 1988.
A Dog for Ben (illustrated by J. Carey), Methuen, 1988.
Playing a Part, Hodder & Stoughton, 1989.

Contributor to periodicals, including *Egon Ronay Guides* and *British Book News*.

WORK IN PROGRESS: Nicholas and the Amazing Rocking Horse, A Day for the Lighthouse, and *Thomas's Minder,* picture books for Dent; an anthology of ballet stories, for Kingfisher; an anthology of theatre and dance stories, for Hamish Hamilton; other picture books; an adult novel.

SIDELIGHTS: "So far, my fiction has been for children and reflects three areas of special interest: the performing arts, which I find fascinating both as a spectator and because they demand the same kind of total dedication as writing (*The First Step, Dancer in the Wings,* and *One Foot on the Ground* are a trilogy about a young girl's struggle to become a dancer, *Musical Chairs* is about a competition for young musicians, and *Playing a Part* is a love story with a theatrical background); the supernatural, which has provided the theme for two anthologies and is an interest that developed from my friendship with the writer Robert Aickman; and animals, which provided the idea for *A Dog for Ben,* and which I hope to write more about. I was an only child, and for as long as I can remember, books have brought me more pleasure than anything else in life. Writing is perhaps a way of trying to repay this debt.

JEAN RICHARDSON

"I am a home-based person. I have a large flat on several floors in a Victorian house, and enjoy beautifying it and looking after the garden. It's full of books, and I spend a lot of time reading and listening to music. I go to the theatre, opera, and ballet as much as possible, and also like to draw and paint and look at pictures."

FOR MORE INFORMATION SEE:

Times Literary Supplement, November 20, 1987.
British Book News, March, 1988.
Junior Bookshelf, April, 1988.
Books for Your Children, autumn, 1988.
Books for Keeps, January, 1989.

RICHARDS, R(onald) C(harles) W(illiam) 1923-
(Allen Saddler, K. Allen Saddler)

PERSONAL: Born April 15, 1923, in England; son of Charles James (a shopkeeper) and Alice (Bloomfield) Richards; married Doris Edmondson (a registered nurse), August 18, 1945; children: Richard Samuel. *Education:* Attended elementary schools in South London, England. *Politics:* Labour. *Religion:* Agnostic. *Home:* 5 St. John's Hall, Station Rd., Totnes, Devon

TQ9 5HW, England. *Agent:* Serafina Clarke, 98 Tunis Rd., London W12 7EY, England.

CAREER: Writer and theatre critic. Critic for *Guardian, Stage, Plays & Players,* and *Plays International,* 1972—. Former printer in London, England. *Member:* National Union of Journalists, Writers' Guild.

WRITINGS:

JUVENILE; ALL UNDER PSEUDONYM ALLEN SADDLER

Mr. Whizz (illustrated by Doreen Caldwell), Blackie & Son, 1982.
Jerry and the Monsters (illustrated by Terry MacKenna), Methuen, 1986.
Smudger's Seaside Spectacular (illustrated by Ian Newsham), Blackie & Son, 1986.
The Relay Race (illustrated by Gareth Floyd), Methuen, 1986.
Jerry and the Inventions (illustrated by T. MacKenna), Methuen, 1988.
Smudger's Saturday Special (illustrated by I. Newsham), Blackie & Son, 1988.

"THE KING AND QUEEN" SERIES; ALL UNDER PSEUDONYM ALLEN SADDLER; ALL ILLUSTRATED BY JOE WRIGHT

The Archery Contest, Oxford University Press, 1982.
The King Gets Fit, Oxford University Press, 1982.
The Fishing Competition, Oxford University Press, 1983.
The King and the Invisible Dwarf, Oxford University Press, 1983.
The King at Christmas, Oxford University Press, 1984.
The Queen's Painting, Oxford University Press, 1984.

NOVELS; ALL UNDER PSEUDONYM K. ALLEN SADDLER

The Great Brain Robbery, Elek, 1965.
Gilt Edge, Elek, 1966.
Talking Turkey, M. Joseph, 1968.
Betty, Sphere Books, 1974.

RADIO PLAYS; ALL UNDER PSEUDONYM ALLEN SADDLER

"The Penstone Commune," British Broadcasting Corp., 1973.
"Willie Banks and the Technological Revolution," British Broadcasting Corp., 1973.
"Who Needs Money?," British Broadcasting Corp., 1974.
"The Road," British Broadcasting Corp., 1974.
"Willie Banks and the Administrative Machine," British Broadcasting Corp., 1977.
"Penstone Revisited," British Broadcasting Corp., 1977.
"Ahead of the Game," British Broadcasting Corp., 1978.
"Archie's Watergate," British Broadcasting Corp., 1979.
"Revolution at the Palace," British Broadcasting Corp., 1979.
"The Giveaway," British Broadcasting Corp., 1979.
"The Price Strike," British Broadcasting Corp., 1981.
"Daddy Good," British Broadcasting Corp., 1982.
"Old and Blue," British Broadcasting Corp., 1982.
"Undesirable Alien," British Broadcasting Corp., 1982.
"Arson in Berlin," British Broadcasting Corp., 1983.
"The Day War Breaks Out," British Broadcasting Corp., 1983.
"Working the System," British Broadcasting Corp., 1984.
"Up against the Wall," British Broadcasting Corp., 1985.
"Man of the People," British Broadcasting Corp., 1986.
"I Should Say So" (comedy monologues; two series), British Broadcasting Corp., 1986-88.
"Spring," British Broadcasting Corp., 1987.
"Second Chance," British Broadcasting Corp., 1988.

PLAYS; ALL UNDER PSEUDONYM ALLEN SADDLER

"Them," first produced at Plymouth Art Centre, England, 1976.
"All Basic Comforts," first produced in North Devonshire, England at the Lobster Pot, 1977.
"Naf," first produced in Plymouth, England, 1979.
"The Puppet Man," first produced in 1981.
"Kindly Leave the Stage," first produced in Paignton, Devonshire, England at Palace Avenue Theatre, 1986.
"The King and Queen Show" (juvenile), first produced in Bridgwater, Somerset, England at Art Centre, 1987.

Author of television documentary script "The Concert Party," 1980, and with Doris Richards, television comedy show "Barnet," 1985. Contributor of reviews and features to periodicals, including *Guardian, Plays & Players, Stage, Sunday Times, Observer,* and *Radio Times.*

WORK IN PROGRESS: "Captain Cockle," children's book series; *Gloria,* a novel; "The Sponsor," a radio comedy; *Writing for a Living,* a textbook.

SIDELIGHTS: "I am a working writer, willing to tackle anything between masterpieces and matchbox labels."

ROSENTHAL, M(acha) L(ouis) 1917-

PERSONAL: Born March 14, 1917, in Washington, D.C.; son of Jacob (a salesman) and Ethel (Brown) Rosenthal; married Victoria Himmelstein (a senior psychiatric social worker), January 7, 1939; children: David, Alan, Laura. *Education:* University of Chicago, B.A., 1937, M.A., 1938; New York University, Ph.D., 1949; additional study at University of Michigan and Johns Hopkins University. *Home:* 17 Bayard Lane, Suffern, N.Y. 10901. *Agent:* A. L. Hart, Fox Chase Agency, Public Ledger Bldg., Independence Square, Philadelphia, Pa. 19106. *Office:* Department of English, New York University, 19 University Place, New York, N.Y. 10003.

CAREER: Poet, critic, editor, and teacher. Michigan State University, East Lansing, instructor in English, 1939-45; New York University, New York City, 1946—, began as instructor, professor of English, 1961—, Poetics Institute, founder, 1977, director, 1977-79. Visiting specialist, U.S. Cultural Exchange programs, Germany, 1961, Pakistan, 1965, Poland, Rumania, Bulgaria, 1966, Italy, France, 1980, 1988; visiting professor, University of Pennsylvania, 1974, University of Zurich, 1984; visiting poet, Israel, 1974, Yugoslavia, 1980; Moss Chair of Excellence in English, Memphis State University, 1989. Director, National Endowment for the Humanities Seminars, 1981, 1983; Distinguished Scholar Exchange Program, China, 1982; director, National Endowment for the Humanities Institute, 1985. *Member:* Modern Language Association of America, P.E.N., American Association of University Professors, Poetry Society of America (board of governors and vice-president, 1989—), Phi Beta Kappa. *Awards, honors:* American Council of Learned Societies Fellow, 1941-42, 1951-52; Guggenheim fellowship, 1960-61, 1964-65; Explicator Foundation Award, 1984; Rockefeller Foundation residency, Bellagio, Italy, 1988.

WRITINGS:

(With W. C. Hummel and V. E. Leichty) *Effective Reading: Methods and Models,* Houghton, 1944.

(With A. J. M. Smith) *Exploring Poetry*, Macmillan, 1955, 2nd edition, 1973.

The Modern Poets: A Critical Introduction, Oxford University Press, 1960.

A Primer of Ezra Pound, Macmillan, 1960.

Blue Boy on Skates: Poems, Oxford University Press, 1964.

The New Poets: American and British Poetry since World War II, Oxford University Press, 1967.

Beyond Power: New Poems, Oxford University Press, 1969.

The View from the Peacock's Tail: Poems, Oxford University Press, 1972.

Randall Jarrell, University of Minnesota Press, 1972.

Poetry and the Common Life, Oxford University Press, 1974, revised edition, Schocken, 1983.

She: A Sequence of Poems, BOA Editions, 1977.

Sailing into the Unknown: Yeats, Pound, and Eliot, Oxford University Press, 1978.

Poems 1964-1980, Oxford University Press, 1981.

(Translator) Carlo Collodi, *The Adventures of Pinocchio: Tale of a Puppet* (illustrated by Troy Howell), Lothrop, 1983.

(With Sally M. Gall) *The Modern Poetic Sequence: The Genius of Modern Poetry*, Oxford University Press, 1983, new edition, Galaxy Books, 1986.

The Poet's Art, Norton, 1987.

As for Love: Poems and Translations, Oxford University Press, 1987.

EDITOR

(With T. Jameson) *A Selection of Verse*, Littlefield, 1952. (And author of introduction) William Butler Yeats, *Selected Poems and Two Plays*, Macmillan, 1962, published without plays as *Selected Poems*, Franklin Library, 1979, latest revised edition published as *Selected Poems and Three Plays of William Butler Yeats*, Macmillan, 1986.

(With Gerald De Witt Sanders and John Herbert Nelson) *Chief Modern Poets of England and America*, Macmillan, 1962,

revised edition published as *Chief Modern Poets of Britain and America*, 1973.

The William Carlos Williams Reader, New Directions, 1966.

The New Modern Poetry: British and American Poetry since World War II, Macmillan, 1967, new edition published as *The New Modern Poetry: An Anthology of American and British Poetry since World War II*, Oxford University Press, 1969.

100 Postwar Poems: British and American, Macmillan, 1968.

Poetry in English: An Anthology, Oxford University Press, 1987.

Contributor of poems, articles, and reviews to journals and magazines, including *New Yorker*, *New Statesman*, *Poetry*, *Spectator*, and *Quarterly Review of Literature*. Poetry editor, *Nation*, 1956- 61, *Humanist*, 1970-78, and *Present Tense*, 1973— .

ADAPTATIONS:

"Pound and Eliot" (recording), Gould Media.

WORK IN PROGRESS: The Present State of Criticism, The Contemporary Poets, The Poetry and Poetic Drama of W. B. Yeats, and *At the Last: New Poems*, all for Oxford University Press.

SIDELIGHTS: Rosenthal, a critic, editor, teacher, and poet, was born in "Washington, D. C. and taken fairly quickly to nearby Mount Rainier and Brentwood, Maryland. In Brentwood I entered kindergarten and—to quote Hart Crane. . .—I 'quickly fled.' That is, I walked home at recess-time the same morning, satisfied I had experienced 'school' for what it was worth and that was that.

"And then—the tranquility of Woodbridge [Connecticut]: a pet turtle; fishing with a bent pin from a small 'wood bridge'; the dirt road rising into the hillside; West Rock, where 'Judges Cave' (hiding place of regicide judges protected and fed by local farmers) is still, I should hope, commemorated; the marsh at the foot of the hill where I first found water lilies; the small, hospitable, tomato-fragrant farms all along the road; the Italian farmers scattered here and there with their scrappy little sons who taught me that 'Jew' was an insult and that the price of friendship was an obligatory fight. Thither we were brought. . .by my stepfather.

"I could return in memory to Woodbridge and live there forever. It seems to me the matrix both of my dream-life and my education in the world's larger realities.

"Jobs became scarce in the New Haven area, and so we moved on after the fourth grade to Passaic [N.J.], and thence to Newark, and thence to Boston, and thence to Cleveland, and thence to Chicago. We were extremely poor. My mother occasionally took menial jobs; and I earned some money as a newsboy, and by hauling blocks of ice in my small wagon for the neighbors and delivering suits and dresses that had been cleaned and pressed or repaired by a tailor, or tutoring other children. Yet we never considered ourselves *needy*, or even insecure, but rather as persons of privilege in transit.

"Summers and at Christmas break I would be put on a train to visit my father in Washington. *He* was hardly wealthy either, but he was neither bohemian nor proletarian. . . .[He was] a talented salesman with undeveloped musical gifts. He dreamed of setting up his own business and occasionally, in a small way, did so. He was made for high talk and good song, not the

M. L. ROSENTHAL

"But—where's the Field of Miracles?" he asked. (From *The Adventures of Pinocchio: Tale of a Puppet* by C. Collodi. Translated from the Italian by M. L. Rosenthal. Illustrated by Troy Howell.)

loneliness and hard, unrewarding work in which he was trapped.

"I had felt the vocation of a writer—and a poet especially— since childhood. The vocation itself was my special secret privilege, for it made me sure of myself in some strange way, persisting independently of whatever circumstances I found myself in. . . .I was always absorbed in literature, and scholarships and fellowships came my way, and so I became a graduate student while writing my poetry.

"Self-education has always been my instinctive critical purpose. It is inseparable from an almost helpless participation in any poem I read, as though I had merged with its author and were in some sense thinking my way into it once more. From one perspective, every poem is a draft that might have gone beyond its present point and might have been altered in some

interesting way or other; and so we cannot respond fully to its quality, or respect its elastic integrity, without understanding the tentative nature of even the most accomplished writing. It's for this reason, I think, that I've never felt a conflict, except of time, between my vocations as poet and critic or teacher: that is, between writing poems and thinking or talking about them.

"Everything flows together, no matter how disparate one's experiences and activities. . . .All the experiences. . .have in one way or another entered my poems or shaped (or distorted, or eroded, or reoriented) my thinking."[1]

FOOTNOTE SOURCES

[1]*Contemporary Authors Autobiography Series*, Volume 6, Gale, 1987.

ROSTKOWSKI, Margaret I. 1945-

PERSONAL: Surname is pronounced Ros-*kow*-ski; born January 12, 1945, in Little Rock, Ark.; daughter of Ralph Carlisle (a pathologist) and Charlotte (a registered nurse; maiden name, Leuenberger) Ellis; married Charles Anthony Rostkowski (a director of a shelter for the homeless), September 12, 1970; children: David Lee. *Education:* Middlebury College, B.A., 1967; University of Kansas, M.A.T., 1971. *Politics:* Democrat. *Religion:* Society of Friends (Quakers). *Home:* 2830 Marilyn Dr., Ogden, Utah 84403. *Agent:* Ruth Cohen, P.O. Box 7626, Menlo Park, Calif. 94025. *Office:* Ogden High School, 2828 Harrison Blvd., Ogden, Utah 84403.

CAREER: Washington Junior High School, Ogden, Utah, reading teacher, 1974-84; Mount Ogden Middle School, Ogden, teacher of English and French, 1979-84; Ogden High School, Ogden, teacher of English and writing, 1984—. Member of Ogden City Board of Adjustments, and Friends of Weber County Library. *Member:* National Education Association, Society of Children's Book Writers, National Council of Teachers of English, League of Women Voters, Utah Education Association, Ogden Education Association, Delta Kappa Gamma, Phi Delta Kappa. *Awards, honors:* Golden Kite Award (fiction category) from the Society of Children's Book Writers, one of American Library Association's Best Books for Young Adults, and one of *Booklist*'s Children's Editor's Choices, all 1986, and Children's Book Award from the International Reading Association, and Jefferson Cup Award from the Virginia Library Association, both 1987, all for *After the Dancing Days*.

WRITINGS:

After the Dancing Days (young adult novel; ALA Notable Book; Junior Literary Guild selection), Harper, 1986.
The Best of Friends (young adult novel), Harper, 1989.

WORK IN PROGRESS: A young adult novel.

SIDELIGHTS: "I came to writing relatively late in life, beginning *After the Dancing Days* at age thirty-seven. Yet, I am not sorry that I put off writing so long, for I believe that everything in my life up to now has been a preparation for writing, an accumulation of moments worth reconstructing on paper.

"As a child I was a reader, *Little Women* when I was ten, *War and Peace* when I was sixteen, volumes of historical fiction I checked out from the Carnegie Free Library. We lived in the foothills of the Wasatch Mountains and our backyard was literally sagebrush, rock and rattlesnake. My mother's constant refrain was 'put down your book and go outside and play, you'll ruin your eyes.' She was right about the eyes, and maybe I should have spent more time in the woods, as they are now the setting for much of my writing.

"I use family stories in my books. My mother and father's family have lived in the Kansas City area since before the Civil War. My mother had young uncles who fought in World War I, who were gassed, who caught measles, and my father's father rode a motorcycle to his teaching job. All these were woven into *After the Dancing Days.* The facts were important, but more vital for the writing were the feelings that moved these family stories: the fear I see in the face of a great-aunt standing between her two brothers who were about to go to France, the joy in the faces of my mother and her sister, little girls of seven and nine,

sitting on the grass on either side of their uncle, back safe from France.

"I find families fascinating to write about, living as I do in a family that is so close we often grate on each other. I do not write *about* my family, but again, I use the emotions that operate in any family, to bring my characters to life. Now, as mother and aunt of teenagers, I see family life from many perspectives: child, parent, sister, aunt, wife, daughter. I have never liked books for young people that portray adults as ineffectual or evil, instead of people still struggling to learn the best way to lead their lives. We all struggle, every day, and if we are lucky, we all learn, every day.

"My formal writing education began in high school, when a wonderful man, George Taylor, taught me all the important things I needed to know about writing and teaching writing. In the years between high school and that January day that I began *After the Dancing Days,* I attended Middlebury College in Vermont and the University of Kansas, married, taught school, traveled, loved all the animals and friends that entered my life. In short, I prepared to write.

"And now I write—at cost to a lot of other things. My son, David, and husband, Chuck, keep the house going so I can stare at my computer screen or take long walks through the foothills (to which I have returned, never feeling at home anywhere else) trying to work out just why the characters are acting that way. I have much less time for things I used to enjoy, some community work, more time with friends. I am constantly trying to find a balance in my life.

"Teaching also enriches my life and my writing. I have the best teaching assignment possible: working both with ninth graders who are still excited and alive to learning and with older students who want to write. So I get to spend my teaching days with my first loves: books and writing. My students give me ideas and models and language for my books. They also help me know which questions and issues are important to people of their age.

"My books begin with questions, with things I want to explore and learn more about. *After the Dancing Days* began when I wondered what life would be like for a young soldier who had to return from a war so badly wounded that people turned away from him in horror. And *The Best of Friends* began for me when my students asked me to write about the period of the Vietnam War, a time they are very curious about but find few adults willing to discuss. My next novel, one I am not quite ready to discuss, will again revolve around the workings of a family, specifically two sisters.

"I enjoy all parts of the writing process, from the first excitement of meeting and falling in love with characters, to the thrashing out of the plot, to the search for the right expression. I even enjoy revision for it is then when I do the hard work, when I find the feeling that is buried beneath the surface of the moment.

"My hobbies reflect my passion for writing: I have always read and loved young adult books; currently I am broadening my acquaintance with the work of the outstanding authors who live here in Utah. I also love nothing better than a long conversation with another writer about the work that we both do."

FOR MORE INFORMATION SEE:

Claudia Lepman-Logan, "Books in the Classroom: Moral Choices in Literature," *Horn Book,* January-February, 1989.

ROTHBERG, Abraham 1922-

PERSONAL: Born January 14, 1922, in New York, N.Y.; son of Louis (a garment worker) and Lottie (a housewife; maiden name, Drimmer) Rothberg; married Esther Conwell (a physicist), September 30, 1945; children: Lewis. *Education:* Brooklyn College (now Brooklyn College of the City University of New York), B.A., 1942; University of Iowa, M.A., 1947; Columbia University, Ph.D., 1952. *Politics:* Independent. *Religion:* Jewish. *Home and office:* 340 Pelham Rd., Rochester, N.Y. 14610. *Agent:* Joan Raines, Raines & Raines, 71 Park Ave. S., New York, N.Y. 10016.

CAREER: Hofstra College (now University), Hempstead, N.Y., instructor in English and humanities, 1947-51; Columbia University, New York City, instructor in creative writing, 1948; Free Europe Press (publications division of Radio Free Europe), New York City, editor-in-chief of press and of *East Europe* (magazine), and senior political counselor to Free Europe Committee, 1952-59; George Braziller, Inc. (publishers), New York City, managing editor, 1959; *New Leader,* New York City, managing editor, 1960-61; roving correspondent in Europe for *National Observer* and *Manchester Guardian,* 1962-63; writer and editorial consultant, 1964-65; Bantam Books, Inc., New York City, senior editor, 1966-67; full-time writer, editor, and editorial consultant, 1968-72; St. John Fisher College, Rochester, N.Y., professor of English, 1973-83, chairman, English department, 1981-82. Visiting professor and distinguished writer-in-residence, Wichita State University, Kan., 1985. Chairman, editorial board, *Stateside* magazine, 1947-49. *Military service:* U.S. Army, 1943-45; became sergeant.

MEMBER: Authors League, P.E.N. *Awards, honors:* Ford Foundation Fellow, 1951-52; John H. McGinnis Award for short story, 1969, for essay, 1974; Annual Literary Award of the Friends of the Rochester Library for a body of work, 1980.

WRITINGS:

Abraham (juvenile), Behrman, 1952.
An Eyewitness History of World War II, four volumes, Bantam, 1962.
The Thousand Doors (novel), Holt, 1965.
The Heirs of Cain (novel), Putnam, 1966.
The Song of David Freed (novel), Putnam, 1968.
The Boy and the Dolphin (juvenile), Norton, 1969.
The Other Man's Shoes (novel), Simon & Schuster, 1969.
The Sword of the Golem (novel), McCall, 1971.
Aleksandr Solzhenitsyn: The Major Novels (literary criticism), Cornell University Press, 1971.
Heirs of Stalin: Dissidence and the Soviet Regime, 1953-1970 (history), Cornell University Press, 1972.
The Stalking Horse (novel), Saturday Review Press, 1972.
The Great Waltz (novel), Putnam, 1978.
The Four Corners of the House (short story collection), University of Illinois Press, 1981.

ABRAHAM ROTHBERG

EDITOR

(With Martha Foley) *U.S. Stories: Stories of the 48 States,* Farrar, Straus, 1949.
Flashes in the Night: Contemporary Hungarian Short Stories, Random House, 1958.
A Bar-Mitzvah Companion, Behrman, 1959.
Anatomy of a Moral: The Political Essays of Milovan Djilas, Praeger, 1959.
Call of the Wild, Bantam, 1963.
White Fang, Bantam, 1963.
Dr. Jekyll and Mr. Hyde, Bantam, 1967.
Great Adventure Stories of Jack London, Bantam, 1967.
(With Solomon Simon and Morrison Bial) *The Rabbis' Bible:* Volume II, *The Early Prophets,* Behrman, 1969, (with S. Simon) Volume III, *The Later Prophets,* 1974.

Contributor of short stories, essays, poems, articles and reviews to magazines, including: *Yale Review, Stateside, American Hebrew, Menorah Journal, Opinion, Hairenik Weekly, Congress Weekly, Antioch Review, University of Kansas City Review, New Mexico Quarterly, New Leader, National Observer, Christian Century, Commonweal, Interplay, Sunday Times Book Review, Southwest Review* and *Saturday Evening Post;* his magazine writing has been included in a number of anthologies. Consultant, *The New Union Prayer Book,* Central Conference of American Rabbis, 1975. Chairman of editorial board, *Stateside,* 1947-49.

WORK IN PROGRESS: The Inland Sea, a novel set in Japan which explores differences between Americans and Japanese; *Coming to Terms,* a novel of the conflict between the World War II generation and the Vietnam generation in the way they see the world and their personal relations; a novel set in the late 1940s and early 1950s about a group of World War II veterans who return to an America they never made and who go about trying to remake it and/or themselves.

SIDELIGHTS: "When I was a child, my father and my uncle and my early Hebrew school teachers taught me the legends of the Prague Golem. In 1963, as a reporter, I was in Prague and went to visit the Jewish Museum there, the old cemetery, the grave of Rabbi Low, and the entire area of the old ghetto. Slowly, a book began to jostle me in the corners of my mind until I had to open the doors and windows in me, as much as I was able, to let the daylight in and the story out. No small part of that jostling was seeing the names, dates of birth and death of thousands and thousands of Jews killed by the Nazis which were inscribed on the 'Wall of Mourning' in that Prague ghetto. It was not a recollection easily put aside.

"Some years later, after much wrestling with the Golem, the novel emerged, a book about peace and violence, about when the sword is to be used, if ever, and when it is to be sheathed, if ever. *The Sword of the Golem* is a modern novel in a medieval

setting, for we live in an extension of the Middle Ages, or perhaps a new Middle Ages. The book concerns itself with the nature of belief—in God, in man, in the state, and in the church, in love—and attempts to explore their ambiguities and complexities, their sustaining qualities and their shortfalls.

"The book is also about love—the love of God, the love of men and women, the love of parents and children, the love of human beings for their own kind and their communities. And because it is about love, it is also about love's obverse, hatred. In exploring the head-on confrontation—to use a modern term—between traditional Judaism and traditional Christianity, between the privileges and obligations of 'creation,' of 'machines' that work for you but can work against you, the novel attempts to see if there is common ground on which can be built what has often been talked about but rarely acted upon, a genuine peace between communities, a genuine Judeo-Christian tradition, a genuine putting aside of violence as an instrument of solving differences of interest and opinion."

HOBBIES AND OTHER INTERESTS: Music, travel, gardening, reading.

FOR MORE INFORMATION SEE:

Harper's, May, 1965.
Best Sellers, December 1, 1966, January 15, 1968, February 15, 1969, February 1, 1971.
Nation, December 5, 1966.
New York Times Book Review, January 14, 1968, February 9, 1969, February 14, 1971.
Newsweek, February 12, 1968.
Hudson Review, autumn, 1968.
Saturday Review, March 8, 1961, January 31, 1971.
Arnold L. Goldsmith, "Abraham Rothberg's *The Sword of the Golem*," in *The Golem Remembered, 1909-1980*, Wayne State University Press, 1981.
Ralph Cohen, "Abraham Rothberg's Moral Vision," *Virginia Quarterly Review*, summer, 1982.

SASEEN, Sharon (Dillon) 1949-
(Sharon Saseen Dillon)

PERSONAL: Born January 23, 1949, in Savannah, Ga.; daughter of Edward James (a businessman) and Lois (a homemaker; maiden name, Howard) Saseen; married Joseph Anthony Dillon, 1972 (divorced, 1978); children: Edward. *Education:* Attended St. Mary's Dominican College, 1966-68; University of Georgia, B.F.A., 1970, regents study abroad program, Cortona, Italy, 1970, M.A.E., 1972; attended Parsons School of Design, 1984; Syracuse University, M.F.A., 1988. *Politics:* Non-partisan. *Religion:* Catholic. *Home and studio:* 242 Habersham St., Savannah, Ga. 31401. *Agent:* Bruce Carter, Fredrich-Carter & Associates, 6815 Forest Park Dr., Savannah, Ga. 31406.

CAREER: James Island Middle School, Charleston, S.C., art teacher, 1973; Chatham County Board of Education, Savannah, Ga., art teacher, 1973-79; Savannah Country Day School, Savannah, art teacher, 1979-84; free-lance artist, 1983—. Artist-in-residence, Savannah Art Association, 1976-79; guest painting instructor and instructor of adult art classes, Armstrong State College, 1978-81. *Exhibitions:* Group shows: "Savannah Artists Show," Savannah College of Art and Design, Ga., 1984; "An Exhibition of Daufuskie Impressions,"

If the music and playing the musical instrument came easily to Basil, the language of the dolphins did not. (From *The Boy and the Dolphin* by Abraham Rothberg. Illustrated by Imero Gobbato.)

SHARON SASEEN

Melrose Company and Pink House Gallery, Hilton Head Island, S.C., 1986. One-person shows: Gallery 209, Savannah, 1979; Savannah College of Art and Design, 1983; Historic Savannah Foundation, 1986.

MEMBER: Gallery 209 (co-operative art gallery, president, 1985), Symphony Women's Guild, Telfair Academy of Arts and Sciences, Junior League of Savannah, National League of American Pen Women, Historic Savannah Foundation, Delta Kappa Gamma. *Awards, honors:* Barney Mindoff Paderewski Memorial Purchase Award from the Savannah Art Association Member's Show, 1976, for painting "Gaston Street East"; Second Prize, Johnny Mercer theme division from the Savannah Arts Festival, 1977, for painting "Moods and Images of Johnny Mercer"; First Prize in the Show Award from the Savannah Arts Festival, 1978, for painting "Victorian Wonderland"; Friedman's Award from the Savannah Arts Festival, 1979, for painting "Cathedral Steeples."

ILLUSTRATOR

(Under name Sharon Saseen Dillon) Audilee Boyd Taylor, *Where Did My Feather Pillow Come From?*, Castlemarsh, 1982.

Designer of posters and prints.

SIDELIGHTS: "My interest in art began at the very sensitive age of twelve. Awkward looking, non-athletic, academically an underachiever, I would entertain myself by drawing pictures of my favorite celebrity, Jackie Kennedy. *Life* magazine was full of stories about the Kennedys. I would study these and then sketch. A supportive aunt, Barbara Saseen White, noticed my newly awakened talent and suggested private art lessons to my father. Sidney Bumann kindled the fire and set me on an artistic path. From her I learned how to use oils, compose pictures, and understand her love of Cezanne. I loved everything she painted—floral, landscapes, and seascapes—and in emulating her work became a little Sidney Bumann. Though Sidney is gone today, my mother recalls her commenting that I wasn't afraid to try anything and was very bold in my art. During my early adolescent years I dreamed of becoming an artist. Adults were very supportive, but my peers found me an oddball.

"Although my high school teachers at St. Vincent's Academy, in Savannah, Georgia were very supportive, we did not have an in-house art teacher. Lessons continued on and off with Sidney as the demands of school and extra-curricular activities took their toll. I continued to draw and paint, working from life. Occasionally I would copy because I had not learned how to use reference material. Accolades continued as I illustrated homework assignments, drew posters for school functions and entered art shows. In my sophomore year I took an art appreciation course with Joan Hardy. I was enthralled by the impressionists and post-impressionists, especially Monet, Renoir, Van Gogh, and Gauguin. Their colors were so inspiring! My senior year culminated with a trip to the National Gallery of Art in Washington, D.C. There I finally got to see firsthand the work of my mentors.

"At the University of Georgia I majored in art education as it seemed the most practical route for me. At that time few artists in the South were self-supportive. However, teaching jobs were plentiful. Enjoying young children as well as the many aspects of creative art—clay, painting, drawing, photography, weaving—I found teaching the perfect role for me at this time. Lamar Dodd, head of the visual arts department and my drawing teacher, greatly influenced my work and philosophy of education. Being a product of the fifties, he was an abstract expressionist. I picked up on his quick gesture lines and gained strength in my ability to see. Another major thrust in my formal education was Frank Wachowiak, author and instructor of art education. He opened up for me the possibilities of children in their art.

"After eight years of teaching in both the public and private schools, I became greatly influenced by the art for and by children. During this time I was also painting and exhibiting my work in local shows and galleries. Sharing my work with my students was a special impetus in this vocation. During this time I was attracted to Peter Spier's whimsical style in illustrating children's books. I also found the oriental prints of Utamaro and Hokusai very appealing. I received commissions to paint the historical houses in Savannah and oriental screens. The fluid line effects of Spier, Utamaro and Hokusai are shown in these works. Egyptian jewelry was another major force in my career. The vibrant colors in their artifacts helped me to awaken my paintings.

"In 1983 I resigned my position as an elementary art teacher to become a full-time artist. The pressures of two careers were cancelling each other out. I feel very fortunate that there is a demand for my original oils and watercolors as well as for my limited edition prints which have enabled me to support myself and my son. There is a continuous need to grow and expand, and the Independent Study Program at Syracuse University provided this. Currently I have twelve prints, two posters, one

The gander protected her and the nest as she sat on the eggs. (From *Where Did My Feather Pillow Come From?* by Audilee Boyd Taylor. Illustrated by Sharon Saseen Dillon.)

children's book which I illustrated, and commissions which are keeping me fluid. In the spring of 1986 my prints were featured in Lord & Taylor's 'Focus America: Savannah' promotion in their Fifth Avenue store."

HOBBIES AND OTHER INTERESTS: Reading, nature, window box gardening.

FOR MORE INFORMATION SEE:

Savannah Morning News, October 19, 1979 (p. A-8), March 14, 1985 (sec. 15C, p. 42).
Savannah News-Press, March 21, 1985 (p. 1ff), February 15, 1987 (sec. G., p. 1).
Opus 91, April, 1985 (p. 7).
Gazette, July 9, 1987 (p. 5ff).
"Savannah's Saseen Captures Feel of Coastal City," *Atlanta Northstar,* September, 1987.
Seabreeze, The Guide to Coastal Living, March- April, 1989 (p. 30).

SCANNELL, Vernon 1922-

PERSONAL: Born January 23, 1922, in Lincolnshire, England; son of James (a photographer) and Elsie Mabel (Wrate) Scannell; married Josephine Higson (a painter), October 1, 1954; children: Jacob, John, Tobias, Nancy, Jane. *Education:* Attended University of Leeds, 1946-47. *Politics:* "Romantic Radical." *Home:* 51 North St., Otley, West Yorkshire LS21 1AH, England.

CAREER: Author. Professional boxer for brief period; Hazelwood School, Limpsfield, Surrey, England, teacher of English, 1955-62. Broadcaster of talks and poetry. *Military service:* British Army, 1941-46. *Member:* Royal Society of Literature (fellow). *Awards, honors:* Heinemann Award for Literature from the Royal Society of Literature, 1960, for *The Masks of Love;* Cholmondoley Poetry Prize, 1974; Society of Authors Travelling Scholarship, 1987.

WRITINGS:

YOUNG ADULT NOVELS

The Dangerous Ones, Wheaton, 1971.
A Lonely Game, Wheaton, 1979.

JUVENILE POETRY

The Apple Raid and Other Poems, Chatto & Windus, 1974.
(With Gregory Harrison and Laurence Smith) *Catch the Light,* Oxford University Press, 1982, Merrimack, 1983.
The Clever Potato (illustrated by Tony Ross), Century Hutchinson, 1988.

ADULT NOVELS

The Fight, Nevill, 1953.
The Wound and the Scar, Nevill, 1954.
The Big Chance, John Long, 1960.
The Shadowed Place, John Long, 1961.
The Face of the Enemy, Putnam, 1961.
The Dividing Night, Putnam, 1962.
The Big Time, Longmans, Green, 1965.
Ring of Truth, Robson, 1983.

ADULT POETRY

Graves and Resurrections, Fortune Press, 1948.

(Contributor) Howard Sergeant and Dannie Abse, editors, *Mavericks: An Anthology,* Editions Poetry and Poverty, 1957.
A Mortal Pitch, Villiers, 1957.
The Masks of Love, Putnam, 1960.
A Sense of Danger, Putnam, 1962.
(Editor with Patricia Beer and Ted Hughes) *New Poems 1962: A P.E.N. Anthology of Contemporary Poetry,* Hutchinson, 1962.
Walking Wounded: Poems 1962-1965, Eyre & Spottiswoode, 1965.
Epithets of War: Poems 1965-1969, Eyre & Spottiswoode, 1969.
Selected Poems, Allison, 1971.
The Winter Man, Allison, 1973.
The Loving Game, Robson, 1975.
New and Collected Poems: 1950-1980, Robson, 1980.
Winterlude, Robson, 1982.
Funeral Games, Robson, 1987.
Soldiering On, Robson, 1989.

OTHER

Edward Thomas (criticism), Longmans, Green, 1963.
(Compiler with Jon Silkin) *Pergamon Poets 8,* Pergamon, 1970.
The Dangerous Ones, Pergamon, 1970.
Mastering the Craft, Pergamon, 1970.
The Tiger and the Rose (autobiography), Hamish Hamilton, 1971.
Not without Glory: Poets of the Second World War (criticism), Woburn, 1976.
A Proper Gentleman (autobiography), Robson, 1977.
(Editor) *Sporting Literature,* Oxford University Press, 1987.
Argument of Kings (autobiography), Robson, 1987.

VERNON SCANNELL

Also author of radio scripts, "A Man's Game," and "A Door with One Eye," and of radio opera, "The Cancelling Dark," with music by Christopher Whelan, performed December 5, 1965. Contributor to *Listener, Encounter, London Magazine, Spectator,* and *Times Literary Supplement.*

WORK IN PROGRESS: Love Shouts and Whispers, poems for children, for Century Hutchinson.

SIDELIGHTS: "My most recent book for young readers, a collection of poems called *The Clever Potato,* was commissioned by an editor at Century Hutchinson. She had seen a children's poem I had written for Anne Thwaite's Annual, *Allsorts,* and thought I might like to use this poem as the center piece for a collection on the prospects of the same theme— food. At first I thought the idea impractical, but after a few days I found myself besieged by ideas and images for 'food poems,' some comic, almost surrealistic, others more serious, dealing with such topics as third world starvation and poverty. I began to write and it seemed that the creative process generated further ideas for poems, and I wrote the whole collection at what was, for me, an extraordinary speed. All of the poems are written in some prescribed form, including sonnets, a villanelle, rhymed couplets, etc. Almost all of them use rhyme. I hope that they will appeal to readers of all ages for I believe, with W. H. Auden, that it is impossible to write a good poem for children that is not also a good poem to an adult."

HOBBIES AND OTHER INTERESTS: Listening to music, watching boxing.

FOR MORE INFORMATION SEE:

Hilary Morrish, "Vernon Scannell," *The Poet Speaks: Interviews with Contemporary Poets,* edited by Peter Orr, Routledge, 1966.
Jeremy Robson, editor, "Vernon Scannell," *Corgi Modern Poets in Focus: 4,* Corgi, 1971.
Phillip Hay and Angharad Wynn-Jones, *Three Poets, Two Children: Leonard Clark, Vernon Scannell, Dannie Abse Answer Questions by Two Children,* edited by Desmond Badham- Thornhill, Thornhill Press, 1975.
New Statesman, October 21, 1977.
Times Literary Supplement, August 1, 1980.

SCHWARTZ, David M(artin) 1951-

PERSONAL: Born November 29, 1951, in New York, N.Y.; son of Morris J. (a furrier and salesman) and Diane (an English teacher; maiden name, Narroff) Schwartz; married Mary Lou Brozena, April 1, 1984 (divorced, 1988). *Education:* Cornell University, B.S., 1973, teacher certification, 1974. *Home and office:* 999 Hartford Turnpike, North Haven, Conn. 06473. *Agent:* Charlotte Sheedy, Charlotte Sheedy Literary Agency, Inc., 145 West 86th St., New York, N.Y. 10024.

CAREER: Elementary schoolteacher in Putney, Vt., 1974-76; worked variously as carpenter, lumberjack, veterinary assistant, environmental educator, and free-lance writer, 1976-78; Marlboro College, Marlboro, Vt., assistant dean and career counselor, 1978-80; Time-Life Books, Alexandria, Va., staff writer, 1900, free-lance writer, 1900—. Yale University, New Haven, Conn., writing tutor, 1986—. *Member:* Authors Guild. *Awards, honors: Booklist* Editors' Choice, 1985, one of Child

Study Association of America's Children's Books of the Year, 1986, and Utah Informational Children's Book Award, 1988, all for *How Much Is a Million?*

WRITINGS:

JUVENILE NONFICTION

How Much Is a Million? (ALA Notable Book; *Horn Book* honor book; illustrated by Steven Kellogg), Lothrop, 1985, large print edition, Scholastic, 1987.
The Hidden Life of the Pond (illustrated with photographs by Dwight Kuhn), Crown, 1988.
The Hidden Life of the Forest (illustrated with photographs by D. Kuhn), Crown, 1988.
The Hidden Life of the Meadow (illustrated with photographs by D. Kuhn), Crown, 1988.
If You Made a Million (illustrated by S. Kellogg), Lothrop, 1989.

OTHER; ALL WITH NEAL WEINER

The Interstate Gourmet: New England, Summit Books, 1983.
The Interstate Gourmet: Mid-Atlantic States, Summit Books, 1983.
The Interstate Gourmet: California and the Pacific Northwest, Summit Books, 1983.
The Interstate Gourmet: Southeast, Summit Books, 1985.
The Interstate Gourmet: Midwest, Summit Books, 1985.

Contributor to magazines, including *Smithsonian, National Wildlife, International Wildlife, Audubon, Travel and Leisure,* and *Country Journal.* Contributing editor of *New England Monthly.*

ADAPTATIONS:

"How Much Is a Million" (cassette), Lothrop, 1987.

WORK IN PROGRESS: Adult books.

SIDELIGHTS: "A biology major in college, I never took a non-required English course, and during those years writing was about as far from my mind as the sky full of stars that inspired *How Much Is a Million?* one beautiful spring evening a few years after I graduated. Seeing it in its crystalline splendor and musing over its enormity brought back my childhood sense of wonder at the magnitude of large numbers. *How Much Is a Million?* resulted when—after years of thinking about it—I finally sat down to write something that might help kids share the awe and comprehend the numbers involved.

"The 'Hidden Life' series sprang from my awe for the opposite end of the quantitative spectrum—small things that, despite their minuteness, hold a world of beauty and detail. Photographer Dwight Kuhn and I had worked together on magazine articles for *Smithsonian* and *Audubon* featuring his masterful close-up photography. We had the idea that we should do nature books focusing on the diminutive animals and plants that many kids (and most adults) overlook in their macro-existence.

"I intend to write more children's concept books, and I also want to tell some surprising but true stories of ordinary people who defied powerful social conventions to achieve remarkable goals. I am working, for example, on a book about Gustaf Hakansson, Sweden's 'Supergrandpa,' who became a national hero in 1951 when he entered a 1,000-mile bicycle race at age sixty-six.

How Big Is a Billion? (From *How Much Is a Million?* by David M. Schwartz. Illustrated by Steven Kellogg.)

"In my writing for adults, I am concentrating on trade in wildlife, both the illegal-but-commonplace and the legal- but-disturbing."

HOBBIES AND OTHER INTERESTS: Morris dancing and other forms of folk dancing, bicycling, hiking, camping, birdwatching and nature observation, "anything else that adds new dimensions to travel."

FOR MORE INFORMATION SEE:

Sally Holmes Holtze, editor, *Sixth Book of Junior Authors and Illustrators,* H. W. Wilson, 1989.

SCHWEITZER, Iris

PERSONAL: Born in Israel; immigrated to the United States.

CAREER: Author and illustrator of children's books. *Awards, honors:* International Board on Books for Young People Honor List, 1968, for *Louie's Lot; Louie's Snowstorm* was chosen one of Child Study Association of America's Children's Books of the Year, 1974.

WRITINGS:

ALL SELF-ILLUSTRATED

In a Forest of Flowers, Putnam, 1974.
Tiglis and the Bird-Machine, Doubleday, 1980.
Hilda's Restful Chair, Collins, 1981, Atheneum, 1982.
Twice beneath the Ornok Tree, Collins, 1984.
Playground Rhymes, Collins, 1987.

ILLUSTRATOR

E. W. Hildick, *Louie's Lot,* Faber, 1965.
E. W. Hildick, *Louie's SOS,* Doubleday, 1968.
E. W. Hildick, *My Kid Sister,* World, 1971.
Molly Cone, *About Learning,* Union of American Hebrew Congregations, 1971.
Martha Bennett Stiles, *Dougal Looks for Birds,* Four Winds, 1972.
E. W. Hildick, *The Active-Enzyme, Lemon-Freshened Junior High School Witch,* Doubleday, 1973.
E. W. Hildick, *Louie's Snowstorm,* Doubleday, 1974.
Eric Lambert, *Eric Lambert's 'The Tender Conspiracy,'* Heinemann Educational, 1975.
E. W. Hildick, *The Top-Flight Fully-Automated Junior High School Girl Detective,* Doubleday, 1977.
Diane Wilmer, *Up Along, Down Along, Under and Over,* Collins, 1985.

Contributor of illustrations to *Book of Nursery Rhymes,* Collins.

SHULMAN, Max 1919-1988

OBITUARY NOTICE: Born March 14, 1919, in St. Paul, Minn.; died of bone cancer, August 28, 1988, in Hollywood (one source says Los Angeles), Calif. Humorist and author. Shulman will be best remembered as the creator of the television and film character Dobie Gillis, a girl-crazy adolescent. A Doubleday book editor who had read Shulman's humor columns in the University of Minnesota student paper urged him to write his first novel, *Barefoot Boy with Cheek,* a best-seller when it was issued in 1943. While in the Army Air Corps during World War II, Shulman wrote two more novels, *The Feather Merchants* and *The Zebra Derby,* both published after the war. In 1951 his next novel, *The Many Loves of Dobie Gillis,* received rave reviews. It spawned a prime-time television series of the same name and a motion picture titled "The Affairs of Dobie Gillis," both of which Shulman scripted. He next won acclaim with the Broadway play "The Tender Trap" written with Robert Paul Smith and later made into the film starring Frank Sinatra and Debbie Reynolds. In the late 1970s he collaborated with Julius Epstein on the screenplay for "House Calls," the comedy featuring Walter Matthau and Glenda Jackson.

Shulman's other writings include the novels *Rally Round the Flag, Boys, Sleep Till Noon,* and *I Was a Teenage Dwarf.* About writing comedy, he once remarked: "I don't think there's any kind of writing more serious than funny writing—nor more difficult or demanding of more dedication and work hours. It's tough to do. . . . You've got all the rules of fiction to follow in humor writing—plus you've got to make somebody laugh, too."

FOR MORE INFORMATION SEE:

Dictionary of Literary Biography, Volume 11: *American Humorists, 1800-1950,* Gale, 1982.
International Motion Picture Almanac, Quigley, 1986.

OBITUARIES

Chicago Tribune, August 29, 1988.
Los Angeles Times, August 29, 1988.
New York Times, August 29, 1988.
Washington Post, August 31, 1988.

STEVENS, Lucile V(ernon) 1899-

PERSONAL: Born March 7, 1899, in St. Paul, Minn.; daughter of J. L. (a salesman) and Mattie (a housewife; maiden name Carter) Vernon; married Harry L. Stevens (a school administrator; deceased). *Education:* Wichita State University, A.B., 1919; University of Arkansas, graduate study, 1954. *Politics:* Democrat. *Religion:* Protestant. *Home:* 550 First Ave. So., Apt. 304, St. Petersburg, Fla. 33701.

CAREER: High school teacher of English and social studies in Kansas, 1919, and 1922-27, Oklahoma, 1921, and Arkansas, 1943-59. *Member:* Pensters (Mobile, Ala.; vice-president, 1970).

WRITINGS:

Death Wore Gold Shoes, Bouregy, 1966.
Love-in-a-Mist, Bouregy, 1967.
Dowry of Diamonds, Bouregy, 1968.
Threads of Gold, Bouregy, 1968.
The Red Tower, Bouregy, 1968.
Crape Myrtle Tree, Bouregy, 1970.
Search through the Mist, Bouregy, 1971.
Home to Cypresswood, Bouregy, 1972.
Green Shadows, Bouregy, 1973.
The Redbird Affair, Bouregy, 1974.
Joni of Storm Hill, Bouregy, 1976.
Phantom Rubies, Bouregy, 1979.
Of Dreams and Danger, Bouregy, 1981.

SIDELIGHTS: "I always wanted to be a writer but life interfered until after I was alone and without obligations. I have been writing steadily since and expect to continue as long as I live, because I like to write. I do not undertake profound work, but I do try to go deeply into human motivation and to have some conflict of spirit, also to bring descriptions of Nature into our cement-and-brick world. I like today's young people—the decent majority. They are strong and wonderful, better than we were.

"My hobbies are many as I am interested in practically everything on earth. I do all my own sewing, do needlepoint and knitting, have polished gems and worked silver to make jewelry, have done ceramics from the clay up, and do beadwork, the French type of bead flowers from tiny beads on fine wire. I enjoy politics, watch television, read mysteries and nonfiction. I am interested in the American West. I have traveled over this country except for the far West."

SUSSMAN, Cornelia (Silver) 1914-
(Cornelia Jessey)

PERSONAL: Born February 9, 1914, in Jeanette, Pa.; daughter of Jesse Charles and Lottie (Rivkind) Silver; married Irving Sussman (a teacher and writer), May 6, 1932. *Education:* University of California, Berkeley, M.A. (cum laude), 1934, general secondary teaching credentials, 1934. *Politics:* Democrat. *Religion:* Roman Catholic. *Home and office:* 259 San Dimas Ave., Oceanside, Calif. 92056.

CAREER: Writer. Former teacher of English to non-English speaking students and of creative writing. *Awards, honors:* Catholic Press Association Award for Best Piece of Artistic Criticism, 1970, for an essay; *Thomas Merton* was chosen one of Child Study Association of America's Children's Books of the Year, 1976, and selected one of New York Public Library's Books for the Teen Age, 1980, 1981, and 1982.

WRITINGS:

FOR YOUNG PEOPLE; WITH HUSBAND, IRVING SUSSMAN

Thomas Merton: Young Man on the Flying Belltower, Macmillan, 1976, revised edition published as *Thomas Merton,* Doubleday, 1980.

OTHER; WITH I. SUSSMAN

(Member of editorial board and contributor) John M. Oesterreicher, editor, *The Bridge: A Yearbook of Judaeo-Christian Studies,* Pantheon, Volume I, 1955, Volume II, 1956, Volume IV, 1962. *How to Read a Dirty Book; or, The Way of the Pilgrim Reader,* Franciscan Herald, 1966.
This Train Is Bound for Glory, Franciscan Herald, 1969.
As Others See Us, Sheed & Ward, 1971.
Spiritual Partners: Profiles in Creative Marriage, Crossroad, 1982.

UNDER PSEUDONYM CORNELIA JESSEY

The Growing Roots, Crown, 1947.
Teach the Angry Spirit, Crown, 1949.
The Treasures of Darkness, Noonday Press, 1953.
The Plough and the Harrow, Harvill Press, 1961, published in America as *Consuela Bright,* Sheed & Ward, 1961.
Profiles in Hope, Veritas, 1978.
The Prayer of Cosa, Harper, 1985.

Cornelia Sussman with husband, Irving.

Contributor to *New Catholic Encyclopedia,* McGraw's *Catholic Youth Encyclopedia,* and to periodicals, including *Saturday Review, Christian Century, Way, Cistercian Studies, Commonweal, Contemplative Review, Spiritual Life,* and *America.* Author of monthly book column in *Franciscan Herald.* Contributor to *Way.*

WORK IN PROGRESS: A novel, entitled *Among the Little Sparrows;* a fiction book for school children tentatively entitled *Two Little Women: Their Tea Party on Planet Earth.*

SIDELIGHTS: "How I came to write my books or anything: I add the words 'or anything' because I write anything. Writing is how I breathe, what I am, as the spider always having to spin. I came to write as part of reading. From age two I started reading, beginning with my sister's blocks. Everybody assumed I was too young to start reading but I seized her blocks and she had a hard time getting them back.

"The alphabet was beautiful just to look at, and putting the letters together made words. They were like an electric charge, or an electric beam. A door opened and I walked out. It was difficult for my mother to tear me away from a book or anything I was reading.

"Stories are fascinating to me, because the place where I am—planet earth—fascinates me, and everything on this earth and in the sea and in the air, the dark spaces beyond, stars, planets, Saturn's rings. Yet, most of all, *people* fascinate me. I see houses and streets, places, and people working as stories.

"So I came to writing from reading. The next question: FOR WHOM I INTEND WHATEVER I WRITE? For anyone who will read whatever I write. As a reader from infancy it was my pleasure to read books that were for children, and books that were for grown-ups, and books that were for teenagers at any age. I write that way: any one interested, at any age, is my reader.

"FROM WHAT EXPERIENCES DO I DERIVE MY MATERIALS? The experiences of all that is on planet earth—people, towns, cities, streets, songs, movies, conversations. I love to walk neighborhood streets in the evening, to see as lights go on in rooms, people, mysterious and strange to me, what kind of life are they living? Or to walk along a small boat marina and see a light on a table inside a little boat, a boy reading, makes me spin a story—is he studying for an exam, or working out the map of a sea voyage, or just dreaming over a book? Once I wrote a book because I saw a bare electric light swinging on a long cord in a dark hall in a small Mexican town, and heard a girl singing.

"Two books I am now writing were triggered by a scene. The first, a novel still in progress, *Among the Little Sparrows,* was seeded by the sight of an old lady waiting patiently to be admitted to a hospice for her last days on planet earth. The second is a children's book seeded by a news item about two girls who survived a small plane crash in the wilderness. The working title: *Two Little Women: Their Tea Party on Planet Earth.* They have to fend for themselves and in the process find a strange house, seemingly a desert ruin, a house without a roof—and they rescue a trapped person."

HOBBIES AND OTHER INTERESTS: Nature; "the Old West from the point of view of the dispossessed, for example, the American Indians. I collect their stories, poems, works of art, and visit their communities."

SUSSMAN, Irving 1908-

PERSONAL: Born December 25, 1908, in New York, N.Y.; son of Samuel A. (a diamond merchant) and Elka (Shurack) Sussman; married Cornelia Silver (a writer), May 6, 1932. *Education:* University of California, Los Angeles, B.A., 1929, M.A., 1932, Ph.D., 1936; also attended University of California, Berkeley, 1930-36, and Boalt School of Law, 1930-35. *Politics:* Democrat. *Religion:* Roman Catholic. *Home:* 259 San Dimas Ave., Oceanside, Calif. 92056. *Office:* Way, 109 Golden Gate Ave., San Francisco, Calif. 94109.

CAREER: MacLoon Productions, Los Angeles, Calif., actor, 1929-32; toured with Stratford-on-Avon Shakespearean Co., 1931, plays included "Outward Bound," "The Star Wagon," "The Copperhead," "The House of Women," "Thought," "The New Moon" (musical), "The Desert Song" (musical), "Arsenic and Old Lace," "The Man Who Came to Dinner," "Blythe Spirit," "Loyalties," "Our Town," and Claudel's "Christopher Columbus" (with the San Francisco Symphony Orchestra); Castlemont High School and Technical High School, Oakland, Calif., English teacher, beginning 1934; Dominican College, San Rafael, Calif., professor of English, 1936-39; Palm Springs High School, Riverside, Calif., English teacher, until 1970, chairman of department, 1950-70. Guest lecturer at colleges and universities in California, Arizona, and Colorado. Producer at Don Quixote Marionette Theatre; director for Oakland Children's Theatre; has appeared in feature films.

MEMBER: International P.E.N., Authors Guild, Authors League of America, Third Order of St. Francis. *Awards, honors: Thomas Merton* was chosen one of Child Study Association of America's Children's Books of the Year, 1976, and selected one of New York Public Library's Books for the Teen Age, 1980, 1981, and 1982.

WRITINGS:

FOR YOUNG PEOPLE; WITH WIFE, CORNELIA SUSSMAN

Thomas Merton: The Daring Young Man on the Flying Belltower, Macmillan, 1976, revised edition published as *Thomas Merton,* Doubleday, 1980.

OTHER; WITH C. SUSSMAN

(Contributor) John M. Oesterreicher, editor, *The Bridge: A Yearbook of Judaeo-Christian Studies,* Pantheon, Volume I, 1955, Volume II, 1956, Volume IV, 1962.
How to Read a Dirty Book; or, The Way of the Pilgrim Reader, Franciscan Herald, 1966.
This Train Is Bound for Glory, Fransiscan Herald, 1969.
As Others See Us, Sheed & Ward, 1971.
Spiritual Partners: Profiles in Creative Marriage, Crossroad, 1982.

PLAYS

"Lot's Wife" (two-act), first produced in Berkeley, Calif., at Little Theatre, 1935.
"Francis and Lady Poverty," first produced in California at San Juan Bautista Mission Auditorium, 1976.

Contributor of several hundred articles, poems, and reviews to magazines, including *Saturday Review, America, Catholic Digest, Commonweal,* and *Desert Call,* and of articles with

IRVING SUSSMAN

Jacket from the 1976 hardcover edition. (From *Thomas Merton: The Daring Young Man on the Flying Belltower* by Cornelia and Irving Sussman. Jacket photograph by John Howard Griffin.)

wife, C. Sussman, to *Catholic Youth Encyclopedia.* Contributing editor of *Way,* and *Living Prayer.*

WORK IN PROGRESS: Two novels, *A Marvelous Piece of Luck,* and *Encounter at the Cornice Hotel;* a book on creative interpretations of literature and Scripture, titled *The Eve Helix and the Damascus Connection.*

SIDELIGHTS: "I have been a 'writer' as far back as my memory goes, and I have been an avid 'reader' long before I so much as understood the meaning of a single word I read. Whether it was my love of reading that made me want to write, or my writing things on a sheet of paper that made me love reading, is pretty much a moot question by now. It is obvious to me that I would not have become a writer if I had not been a reader, and (the other side of the argument) I would never have been a reader were it not that I wanted to read for myself, even though at the age of six I could hardly pronounce, let alone, understand printed words, newspapers my father read, laughing aloud, or swearing under his breath and having to be begged to tell me what made him glad or mad or sad. I wanted to read for myself the exciting books my brother (who was nine or ten) was reading with such pleasure—and not too overjoyed about his trying to tell me what happened to the Count of Monte Cristo, or how did Huck get out of the cave, or what kind of funeral was a Viking Funeral.

"But it takes a catalyst, for better or for worse, to turn a kind of vague wish to be a writer into an obsession. As is probably true with all writers ('successful' or not) the catalyst is generally a teacher, rather than a parent, or a friend, or even a writer—especially a 'successful' one. So it was in my life. As a class essay assignment I wrote in about one hundred words of a dangerous experience my family had gone through in a rowboat on the St. Lawrence River in Canada during a summer vacation. We barely escaped alive. The last sentence of the essay states: 'I saw my father's hair turn grey before my very eyes.' I was in the sixth grade when I wrote that 'masterpiece,' so allowances should be made for a writer's imagination or the desire to add verisimilitude to some bald and unconvincing facts; however, this teacher of blessed memory not only gave the essay a top grade ('excellent plus!') but read the thing to the whole class much to my embarrassment and a few nasty looks from my peers. It inspired the teacher to ask the class what each of us wanted to be when we grew up. To help us make a decision she listed various choices: fireman, policeman, nurse, doctor, businessman, salesman, newspaper reporter, writer, actor, singer, and something we'd never heard of (until five wars later), a military career.

"I had no choice (what with an 'excellent plus!' grade) except to put down writer. What kind of writer? I had no idea. She suggested that perhaps I'd become an essay writer. It's really what I became. I did not, and do not, write for children, nor for young adults, nor for adults, nor for scholars. I write for those who read me, ages eight to eighty. In the book *Spiritual Partners,* the section on Mark Twain and the one on William Blake 'sold' extremely well with readers from ages thirteen to twenty-five; the sections on Nora and James Joyce, Maisie Ward and Frank Sheed was of great interest to writers of all ages; the section of Nadezhda and Osip Mandelstam interested poets, intellectuals, and believers in human rights."

HOBBIES AND OTHER INTERESTS: Painting, wood carving, English Renaissance studies.

TAYLOR, Audilee Boyd 1931-

PERSONAL: Born December 2, 1931, in Sylvania, Ga.; daughter of Crawford Lee (a farmer) and Julia Lucinda (Hickox) Boyd; married Herbert Lee Taylor (president, Nu-South Rentals, Inc.), June 25, 1950; children: Julia Yvonne, Jed Lee, Jon Herbert, Jessica Audilee. *Education:* Attended Draughons Business College, 1948-49; attended writers' workshops and seminars at Oxford College of Emory University, and Armstrong State College. *Politics:* Republican. *Religion:* Southern Baptist. *Address:* c/o Castlemarsh Publications, P.O. Box 60728, Savannah, Ga. 31420.

CAREER: H. L. Taylor Construction Co., Inc., Savannah, Ga, executive assistant, 1963-84; writer, 1977—; Wilmington Island Baptist Church, Ga., children's director, 1980-84; Castlemarsh Publications, Savannah, editor/publisher, 1981—; Citicorp Diners Club, research of rare and unusual titles and book jobber, 1985-87; Nu-South Rentals, Inc., Savannah, vice-president, 1988—. Guest lecturer, Savannah College of Art and Design, schools, libraries, and bookshops. *Member:* Georgia Publishers Association (charter member), Publishers Association of the South (charter member), Southeastern Writers Association, Council of Authors and Journalists, Society of Children's Book Writers, Georgia Historical Society, Historic Savannah Foundation.

WRITINGS:

Where Did My Feather Pillow Come From? (illustrated by Sharon Saseen Dillon), Castlemarsh, 1982.
(Editor) James M. Thomas, *Individual Integrity* (nonfiction), Castlemarsh, 1984.

Contributor of poems and inspirational articles to *Georgia's Coastal Illustrated,* and *Gazette* (Savannah, Ga.). Contributor of poems and sports articles to *Savannah Morning News and Evening Press.* Editorial board, *Spring Tides* (children's literary magazine), 1988—.

WORK IN PROGRESS: The Other Sheep, a picture storybook to be published by Castlemarsh; *The Mulberry Connection,* a junior historical/mystery novel.

SIDELIGHTS: "I was born at home on our farm in Screven County, near Sylvania, Georgia, the only girl with four brothers. I have fond memories of those days. Life was different then, it was a quieter time for growing up. My memories are not so much of things, as seasonal: fall and the smell of burning leaves in the lane; winter and naked trees against a stark sky, the one big snow when I was a girl; spring and flowers in the garden; summertime and revival meeting, visiting friends, swimming, reading, and playing outside in the late afternoon as dusk fell.

AUDILEE BOYD TAYLOR

"Reading was always a favorite pastime. It never occurred to me that someday I would be a writer, nor do I recall it ever being suggested to me as a student. After completion of my schooling in Sylvania, I attended Draughons Business College in Savannah.

"Following several incidental jobs, I settled into working in our family business, which I view as being the best of all worlds. I was able to work, attend to home and family, do volunteer work, and still have time for other interests.

"My husband and I built our home on Wilmington Island near Savannah, on five acres on the marsh, close enough to smell the sea occasionally. We lived there for twenty-one years.

"At forty I had my fourth child. It was in looking for books to read to her that I first thought of wanting to write. In pursuing that goal, I have had my greatest sense of personal achievement and satisfaction.

"I began by attending writers' workshops and seminars, many of which were held at St. Simons Island, Georgia. There was a great sense of community in coming together in a large group with a common interest in writing. Every return to St. Simons prompts a renewal of my creative spirit.

"As a beginning, inexperienced writer, one of the best ways to become published is to contribute articles, especially to small weekly newspapers. I wrote 'A Psalm of Praise' for my Sunday School class, an article on a sports event for my brother, an inspirational article, 'It's Never Too Late,' for myself, and a poem, 'Returning,' for my husband. All of these were published in Savannah and St. Simons Island newspapers as contributions.

"One day when I was playing tennis, I remembered an incident several years earlier when my daughter, Jessica, had asked me at bedtime, 'Mother, where did my feather pillow come from?' It occurred to me this would make a wonderful children's book, thus prompting my first book for children. This book is dedicated to my mother, Julia Lucinda. It is really her story—how she helped care for the geese, and the making of the feather pillows.

"I wanted this book to be dual in its purpose, entertaining and educational. I soon learned my information on geese, their habits and care, was sketchy. As this was a dominant factor in the story, it was necessary to do quite a bit of research.

"Upon completion of the story, I submitted it to a major publishing house. It was exciting to receive my first rejection slip, and my second. I wrote a letter of inquiry to another major publishing house, receiving a letter from the children's editor stating they would be delighted to read my story. At that point, however, I had decided to start my own publishing company, and publish my children's books myself, as well as books by other authors.

"Sharon Saseen Dillon illustrated the book. The grammarian was Janice G. Talley and Deborah Ansel was the graphic artist. Kingsport Press in Tennessee did the color separations, printing and binding. Castlemarsh does not have staff, but uses freelance and professional services. It is important to surround yourself with professionals when publishing your own works, especially because your objectivity needs to be tested.

"Seeing my book in print for the first time was an unforgettable experience. It is hard to explain except to say I felt stunned,

"Take this umbrella with you. Hurry!" (From *Where Did My Feather Pillow Come From?* by Audilee Boyd Taylor. Illustrated by Sharon Saseen Dillon.)

thrilled but stunned. It was really exciting to go to the library and see my book on the COMCAT.

"When I get an idea for a book I make a file and begin to compile information and research on any subject related to that work. Over a period of time, as I live with the subject matter, I begin to write the story in my mind. Then I make an outline, putting down the major headings, or times, and begin to fill in the order of circumstances under these headings. This organization helps me to stay on target with my story, and leaves me free to think.

"I have heard many formulas for being a successful writer. I have been told you will never succeed unless you write every morning from eight until twelve. Some even say 'and from one to whatever.' Not all lives can be so regulated; there are other considerations. Rather than formulas, I find that principles applied are better. There is a need to be consistent, to be a disciplined writer; not to just write when you feel like it, but to keep at it. And finally, to just do it.

"Writing is, in my view, a form of art. An artist paints a picture with brush and canvas; an author paints a picture with words in the imagination. An author has the ability to create, to inspire, to build up or to tear down, to effect other lives with the stroke of a pen. There is great power in the written word. Just as the individual is responsible for what they say, an author is responsible for what he or she writes. It is important to speak with clarity, with clear distinct words that cannot be misinterpreted to mean something different from what was intended.

"I have shared with children and youth of all ages about writing and publishing, exhibiting and explaining what is involved in the making of a book, to whatever degree is appropriate for their age. I have shared this information with school and library groups, college classes, and women's clubs. 1989 is the Year of the Young Reader, and much emphasis is being put on literacy. I am grateful to have the opportunity to influence and encourage young writers."

HOBBIES AND OTHER INTERESTS: Reading, collecting books and shells, gardening, arranging flowers, tennis, swimming.

FOR MORE INFORMATION SEE:

Savannah Morning News and Evening Press, May 30, 1982, November 28, 1982 (section G, p. 6), October 7, 1984 (section G, p. 7).
"Firm Publishes Its First Book," *Hilton Head News,* July 22, 1982.
Atlanta Journal and Constitution, July 24, 1988 (section L, p. 4).

TEITELBAUM, Michael 1953-
(Joanne Louise Michaels, Neal Michaels, Michael Neal, B.S. Watson)

PERSONAL: Born April 23, 1953, in Brooklyn, N.Y.; son of Milton (a teacher) and Lillian (a teacher; maiden name, Klafter) Teitelbaum; married Sheleigh Grube (a vocalist), September 8, 1984. *Education;* Adelphi University, B.A. (magna cum laude), 1975. *Home* 125 East 14th St., 1F, New York, N.Y. 10009.

MICHAEL TEITELBAUM

CAREER: Western Publishing Co., Inc., New York City, editor of periodicals and Golden Books, 1978-84; Putnam Publishing Group, New York City, editor of Grosset & Dunlap, 1984-85, creative director of PlayValue Books, 1985-87; Macmillan Publishing Co., New York City, editor-in-chief of Checkerboard Press, 1987; free-lance writer and editor of juvenile books and magazines, 1987—. Writer and performer for "Family Electric Theatre," a comedy program on WBAI-FM Radio; writer and puppeteer for Bond Street Theatre Coalition. *Member:* Society of Children's Book Writers, Editorial Freelancers Association.

WRITINGS:

JUVENILE

The Neverending Story Picture Album, Golden Press, 1984.
To Catch a Gremlin, Golden Press, 1984.
(Under pseudonym Michael Neal) *A New Friend,* Golden Press, 1984.
Santa Claus the Movie: The Boy Who Didn't Believe in Christmas (illustrated by Barbara Stedman), Grosset, 1985.
The Cave of the Lost Fraggle (illustrated by Peter Elwell), Holt, 1985.
(With Louise Gikow and Joanne Barkan, under joint pseudonym Joanne Louise Michaels) *Baby Gonzo's Treasure Hunt,* Muppet Press, 1986.
An American Tail: Little Lost Fievel (includes cassette), Putnam, 1986.
(Adapter) *An American Tail: Escape from the Catsacks* (includes cassette), Putnam, 1986.
An American Tail: Fievel's New York Adventure, Putnam, 1986.
An American Tail: The Mott Street Maulers, Putnam, 1986.
Tony and Fievel, Putnam, 1986.
Fievel's Boat Trip, Putnam, 1986.
Fievel and Tiger, Putnam, 1986.
Fievel's Friends, Putnam, 1986.
Howard the Duck Read Aloud Storybook, Putnam, 1986.
Meet the Blinkins, Putnam, 1986.
The Magic Light, Putnam, 1986.

The Big Show (includes cassette; illustrated by Carol Bouman and Dick Codor), Putnam, 1986.
Where Is Baby Twinkle? (includes cassette; illustrated by C. Bouman and D. Codor), Putnam, 1986.
Here Come the Blinkins (coloring book), Putnam, 1986.
Holiday Fun All through the Year (coloring book), Marvel Books, 1987.
A Clean Sweep, Marvel Books, 1987.
The Haunted House, Marvel Books, 1987.
Ghostbusters Jokes and Riddles Coloring Book, Simon & Schuster, 1987.
Photon: The Darkness Missiles (illustrated by David Rosler), Putnam, 1987.
Photon: Prisoners of Evil (illustrated by D. Rosler), Putnam, 1987.
The Camel's Birthday: A Raggedy Ann Storybook, Macmillan, 1988.
Little Mouse in the Rocket Ship, Marvel Books, 1988.
Mrs. Goose and the Rock and Roll Band, Marvel Books, 1988.
Junior Karate (nonfiction), KidsBooks, 1988.
The Mystery of Magic Island, Golden Books, 1988.
The Tawny Scrawny Lion Saves the Day, Golden Books, 1989.

Also author of *Danger in the Sky* and, under pseudonym Neal Michaels, *The Duke of Lorin.* Creator of comic strips "Computer Capers," "The Adventures of the MicroKids," and "The Glitch Family," under pseudonym B. S. Watson, for *MicroKids* magazine. Also author of script for a talking plush doll, based on the Steven Spielberg/Don Bluth animated film "An American Tail." Contributor to magazines, including *He-Man, Kirk Cameron Poster* and *Snoopy.* Author of "Willow" coloring books, Random House, 1988, "Mighty Mouse" coloring books, Marvel Books, 1988, "Jetsons" coloring books, Marvel Books, 1988, and "Fraggle Rock" counting and activity books, Henson Associates, 1988. Editor, *Ducktales,* 1988—, and *Ghostbuster,* 1989—.

WORK IN PROGRESS: Four non-fiction books for the Smithsonian Institution about space, wild animals, undersea world, and dinosaurs, for Putnam; *Big Bird's Beep Book of Pets and Farm Animals,* for Western Publishing.

SIDELIGHTS: "I grew up in Brooklyn (who didn't), more a product of radio and television, than of the printed word. In college I studied radio, television, and film. My entry into the publishing world was more coincidental than planned. I started my career editing comic books featuring the great Disney and Warner Bros. cartoon characters. Cartoons remain a passion (animation of all type actually, from experimental stop-motion, computer generated to a 1940s Bugs Bunny cartoon) of mine. My book work has dealt mostly with other people's characters. When I recently became editor of *Ducktales* magazine, it was a nice return to the great characters that I started with. After ten years of writing about other people's characters I have recently begun to write original stories, based on characters of my own creation.

"I love movies (animated and otherwise), playing in the ocean, and baseball. My immediate goals are to get an original story published and to see the Mets in the World Series."

TERKEL, Susan N(eiburg) 1948-

PERSONAL: Born April 7, 1948, in Philadelphia, Pa.; daughter of Sidney A. (in life insurance) and Deborah (a homemaker; maiden name, Burstein) Neiburg; married Lawrence Arthur

Terkel (a business executive); children: Ari, Marni, David. *Education:* Cornell University, B.S., 1970. *Religion:* Jewish. *Home:* 44 West Case Dr., Hudson, Ohio 44236. *Agent:* Andrea Brown, 301 West 53rd St., Suite 13B, New York, N.Y. 10019.

CAREER: Teacher, 1971-72; writer. Coordinator of Northeast Ohio chapter of Gillain Barre Syndrome Support Group; co-director of Spiritual Life Society and Hudson Yoga Center. *Member:* Authors Guild, Society of Children's Book Writers, National Writer's Union.

WRITINGS:

FOR YOUNG PEOPLE

Yoga Is for Me (illustrated by Arthur Klein), Lerner, 1982.
(With Janice E. Rench) *Feeling Safe, Feeling Strong: How to Avoid Sexual Abuse and What to Do If It Happens to You,* Lerner, 1984.
Abortion: Facing the Issues, F. Watts, 1988.
Legalizing Drugs, F. Watts, 1990.

WORK IN PROGRESS: Alexander Johnson, a juvenile novel; *Understanding Custody.*

SIDELIGHTS: "I can still recall the thrill I got when, at the age of six, I completed the last line of my first story. I told myself, 'Susan, you're a writer now.' That conviction has never wavered.

SUSAN N. TERKEL

"I love writing because of the chance I get to create my own world, to rewrite my own past, or to share my views about the real world with others, especially with children. Moreover, I like the work conditions that go along with being a writer—working at home, on my own schedule, never having to face retirement.

"There is a great responsibility, particularly when one is writing for our young people today. While I discovered the truth in writing, especially in fiction, that you cannot manipulate your characters into doing things that they wouldn't do if they were real, I also discovered that it is quite possible to infuse in your characters a sense of hope or sense of despair. I hope my work is evidence that I chose to infuse a sense of hope about the world, whether my book is about sexual abuse survivors or about fantasy. I write to tell each child, each reader, that he or she *can* make a difference in the world."

THORN, John 1947-
(Sanford W. Jones)

PERSONAL: Born April 17, 1947, in Stuttgart, Germany (now West Germany); came to the United States in 1949, naturalized, 1963; son of Richard Berthold (a merchant) and Victoria (a merchant; maiden name, Gruber) Thorn; married Sharon McFarland, September 7, 1968 (divorced, April 30, 1984); married Susan Osenni (a teacher), May 11, 1986; children: (first marriage) Jedediah McFarland, Isaac Turner; (second marriage) Mark David. *Education:* Beloit College, B.A., 1968; graduate study at Washington University, St. Louis, Mo., 1969. *Politics:* Liberal. *Religion:* Jewish. *Home and office:* 18 Virginia Ave., Saugerties, N.Y. 12477. *Agent:* David Reuther, 271 Central Park W., New York, N.Y. 10024.

CAREER: New Leader, New York City, editor, 1969-72; Hart Publishing Co., New York City, editor, 1972-76; writer, 1976—; Professional Ink (book production company), Saugerties, N.Y., president, 1986—. Publications director, Society for American Baseball Research, 1985-87; historical consultant to Major League Baseball, National Baseball Hall of Fame Library, National Baseball Hall of Fame Committee on Baseball Veterans, Canadian Baseball Hall of Fame, *American Heritage, Sports Illustrated* and *National Geographic. Member:* Authors Guild, Society for American Baseball Research, Professional Football Researchers' Association (president, 1987-89), New York Historical Society, New York State Historical Association. *Awards, honors: The Relief Pitcher* was selected one of New York Public Library's Books for the Teen Age, 1980, and *Baseball's Ten Greatest Games* and *Pro Football's Ten Greatest Games,* both 1982; *The Game for All America* was named one of the Fifty Best Books for Adults and Young Adults by the American Library Association, 1988.

WRITINGS:

A Century of Baseball Lore, Hart, 1974, revised edition, Galahad, 1980.
The Relief Pitcher, Dutton, 1979.
Baseball's Ten Greatest Games, Four Winds, 1981.
Pro Football's Ten Greatest Games, Four Winds, 1981.
The Armchair Quarterback, Scribner, 1982.
The Armchair Aviator, Scribner, 1983.
The National Pastime: The Nineteenth Century, Society for American Baseball Research, 1984.

(With David Reuther) *The Armchair Mountaineer,* Scribner, 1984.
(Editor) Jacob Morse, *Sphere and Ash* new edition, Camden House, 1984.
(With Pete Palmer), *The Hidden Game of Baseball,* Doubleday, 1984.
The Armchair Book of Baseball, Scribner, 1985.
The National Pastime: The Dead Ball Era, Society for American Baseball Research, 1986.
(With Terry Brykczynski and D. Reuther) *The Armchair Angler,* Scribner, 1986.
The National Pastime, Warner, 1987.
The Armchair Book of Baseball II, Scribner, 1987.
(With John Holway), *The Pitcher,* Prentice-Hall, 1987.
The National Pastime: The Gotham Game, Society for American Baseball Research, 1988.
(With D. Reuther) *The Armchair Traveler,* Prentice-Hall, 1988.
(With Bob Carroll and P. Palmer) *The Hidden Game of Football,* Warner, 1988.
The Game for All America, Sporting News, 1988.
(With P. Palmer) *Total Baseball,* Warner, 1989.

Contributor to periodicals, including *Sporting News, Sport, American Heritage,* and *New York Times.* Editor, *The National Pastime: A Review of Baseball History,* 1982—.

WORK IN PROGRESS: The Football Abstract, with P. Palmer and B. Carroll.

FOR MORE INFORMATION SEE:

New York Times Book Review, May 6, 1979.
Los Angeles Times Book Review, January 15, 1984.
Washington Post Book World, January 28, 1985.

TOWNSEND, Thomas L. 1944-
(Tammie Lee, Tom Townsend)

PERSONAL: Born January 6, 1944, in Waukegan, Ill.; son of Thomas H. (an army officer) and Edna (Carter) Townsend; married Janet L. Simpson (a chemical operator), April 17, 1964; children: Samantha L. *Education:* Attended military academy in Arkansas. *Home and office:* P.O. Box 905, Kemah, Tex. 77565. *Agent:* Esther Perkins, P.O. Box 48, Childs, Md. 21916.

CAREER: Free-lance military adviser and instructor in Central America, 1975-76; Alden Sailing School, Houston, Tex., sailing and navigation instructor, 1977-79; IDACON Oil Co., Houston, captain of yachts, 1979-81; writer, 1981—; Annapolis Sailing School, Houston, sailing instructor, 1983-84. Consultant on maritime terrorism. *Military service:* U.S. Army, Armor Division, 1962-68; became first lieutenant. *Member:* Romance Writers of America, C.O.M. Writers Group, Golden Triangle Writers Guild, Galveston Novel Writers, Bay Area Writers League. *Awards, honors:* Silver Award for Children's Films from the Houston International Film Festival, 1986, for "Jean Lafitte, Texas Hero"; Juvenile Book Award from the Friends of American Writers, and Texas Bluebonnet Award Nomination, both 1986, both for *Where the Pirates Are;* Texas Institute of Letters Award.

Townsend as he appears in school programs in his role as pirate, Jean Lafitte.

WRITINGS:

JUVENILE NOVELS, EXCEPT AS INDICATED; UNDER NAME TOM TOWNSEND

Where the Pirates Are, Eakin Press, 1985.

(Also producer and actor) "Conversations with Jean Lafitte" (one-man play), on tour of Texas school system, 1986—.

The Dark Ships (illustrated by Mark Mitchell), Eakin Press, 1986.

Trader Wooly and the Secret of the Lost Nazi Treasure, Eakin Press, 1987.

Davy Crockett, an American Hero (juvenile biography), Eakin Press, 1987.

Powderhorn Passage: Sequel to Where the Pirates Are, Eakin Press, 1988.

Trader Wooly and the Terrorists, Eakin Press, 1988.

The Battle of Galveston, (illustrated by Debbie Little), Eakin Press, 1989.

Queen of the Wind (young adult novel), Eakin Press, 1989.

OTHER; UNDER NAME TOM TOWNSEND, EXCEPT AS INDICATED

The Last Grey Wolf (adult novel), Ideas Associates, 1977, revised edition, Larksdale Press, 1982.

Texas Treasure Coast (young adult nonfiction), Eakin Press, 1979.

(Under pseudonym Tammie Lee) *Texas Wild Flower* (historical romance novel), Zebra Books, 1983.

Panzer Spirit (adult novel), Pageant Books, 1988.

Contributor of more than three hundred articles to periodicals.

ADAPTATIONS:

"Jean Lafitte, Texas Hero" (children's documentary film; based on his live performances as Jean Lafitte), RBG Media, 1986.

WORK IN PROGRESS: Episodes for a young adult adventure series entitled "Cadets," for Butterfield Press; *Ghost Flyers* (tentative title), an occult novel; a children's picture book; a documentary video production on the life of Davy Crockett.

SIDELIGHTS: "Hopefully, I write books which leave my readers feeling good. There are plenty of other writers who are more capable than myself of depressing their readers by dealing with all of the real and imagined problems of modern life.

"I believe that the novel is the most complete, as well as the most complex, literary art form known to man. I also believe that it is an art form which has been greatly improved by modern writers, especially in the areas of readability and structure.

"Writing is an obsession with me. I have always been a writer and always will be. Perhaps the most satisfying aspect of writing is being able to do it well enough to make a living at it."

Locally, Townsend is known for his articles on sailing and Texas history, as well as for *Texas Treasure Coast*, which deals with shipwrecks, sunken treasure, and the nautical history of the Texas coast. Townsend lived aboard a forty-eight-foot wooden yawl at Seabrook shipyard for several years. He is a veteran of more than a dozen ocean passages in boats ranging from twenty-three feet up to the one-hundred-fifty-six-foot, three-masted schooner *Artemis*. He has worked as a salvage diver, delivery captain, corporation yacht captain, sailing and navigation instructor, and consultant on maritime security. Townsend is also the author of a college-accredited course in anti-terrorism tactics.

HOBBIES AND OTHER INTERESTS: Musical composition.

FOR MORE INFORMATION SEE:

"Meet the Author" (videocassette), RBG Media, 1987.

TREAT, Lawrence 1903-

PERSONAL: Born December 21, 1903, in New York, N.Y.; son of Henry (a jeweler) and Daisy (a teacher; maiden name, Stein) Goldstone; married Margery Dallet, June, 1930 (divorced, 1939); married Rose Ehrenfreund (an artist), May 7, 1943. *Education:* Dartmouth College, B.A., 1924; Columbia University, L.L.B., 1927. *Politics:* Independent. *Home and office:* RFD Box 475A, Edgartown, Mass. 02539. *Agent:* Don Congdon, 156 Fifth Ave., New York, N.Y. 10010.

CAREER: Author of short stories and mystery novels. Member of Gay Head (Mass.) Zoning Board of Appeals, 1972-74, and Gay Head Finance Committee, 1975-77. *Member:* Mystery Writers of America (founder and past president, director, 1946-84), Boston Authors Club, Martha's Vineyard Charade Club. *Awards, honors:* Edgar Allan Poe Award for Best Mystery Story from the Mystery Writers of America, 1965, for "H as in Homicide," and 1976, for editing the *Mystery Writer's Handbook;* Crime Writers International Conference Short Story Prize, Stockholm, 1981, for "All in Good Taste"; Special Edgar

Allan Poe Award, 1987, for television story "Wake Me When I'm Dead."

WRITINGS:

PUZZLE BOOKS

Bringing Sherlock Home, Doubleday, 1932.
You're the Detective! Twenty-Four Solve-Them-Yourself Picture Mysteries (illustrated by Kathleen Borowik), Godine, 1983.
Armchair Detective, Dorling Kindersley, 1983.
Crime and Puzzlement 1, Godine, 1986.
Crime and Puzzlement 2, Godine, 1986.
Crime and Puzzlement 3, Godine, 1988.

MYSTERY NOVELS

B as in Banshee, Duell, Sloan & Pearce, 1940.
D as in Dead, Duell, Sloan & Pearce, 1941.
H as in Hangman, Duell, Sloan & Pearce, 1942.
O as in Omen, Duell, Sloan & Pearce, 1943.
The Leather Man, Duell, Sloan & Pearce, 1944.
V as in Victim, Duell, Sloan & Pearce, 1945.
H as in Hunted, Duell, Sloan & Pearce, 1946.
Q as in Quicksand, Duell, Sloan & Pearce, 1947.
T as in Trapped, Morrow, 1947.
F as in Flight, Morrow, 1948.
Over the Edge, Morrow, 1948.
Trial and Terror, Morrow, 1949.
Big Shot, Harper, 1951.
Weep for a Wanton, Ace Books, 1956.
Lady, Drop Dead, Abelard, 1960.
Venus Unarmed, Doubleday, 1961.
(Editor) *Murder in Mind: An Anthology of Mystery Stories by the Mystery Writers of America*, Dutton, 1967.
P as in Police, Davis Publications, 1970.
A Special Kind of Crime (anthology), Doubleday, 1982.

Also editor of *Mystery Writer's Handbook*. Many ot Treat's stories have been published in large print editions and Braille. Contributor of several hundred short stories to numerous magazines, including *Woman's Home Companion*, *Redbook*, *Woman's Day*, *Ellery Queen's Mystery Magazine*, *Saint*, and *Alfred Hitchcock's Mystery Magazine*.

SIDELIGHTS: "Like probably half the world, I always wanted to write, although I may have been a little more intense and a little less confident about it than most people. Still, I always loved words, their sound, their meanings, their uses. As a child, I made up stories and bothered people with puns, but who was I, to actually aspire to being an AUTHOR!

"All in good time, I graduated from college with a Phi Beta Kappa key and a fifty-dollar literary prize, but where do you go after that? I chose law, not because I was enamoured of it, but my parents wanted it, so why not?

"I'd practiced law for something less than a year when the firm I was working for split up and the two partners went their separate ways, said they were sorry they'd wasted my time, and handed me a generous check. To me, that was fate. I cashed the check and went to Paris to write.

"Coming from a well-to-do background, I always carried that dream of being a writer. But what to write, with my limited experience in life? I tried to get a broader background. During vacations I shipped out as an ordinary seaman on a freighter, I bummed out west (as far as Denver), I worked as a salesman in a clothing store, and here I was in Paris, still groping. My next

crisis came when my money ran out and I realized that if I was to write, I'd better write something that would sell. A mystery story seemed to be the answer. A plentiful market, and my legal background— perfect! So I wrote a detective story, came back to the United States and sold it. Naturally, I thought I was on my way, and maybe I would have been, but the Depression happened, magazines folded, and there was no story market.

"What to do about it? Try everything you can think of, keep going, and come up with something different—like a pictorial mystery puzzle.

"To sum up the next fifty years, I worked hard and I was lucky, and basically that's my story. I still write and I always will, whether or not I sell. As a friend of mine once put it, if you don't write, you die, and I have too much to live for. I often envy myself for the kind of life I live, here on Martha's Vineyard, with my wife who is an artist, and an interesting one.

"What more could I want?"

Treat is the originator of the police procedural genre with his book *V as in Victim*, and the originator of pictorial mysteries with *Crime and Puzzlement*.

HOBBIES AND OTHER INTERESTS: Mycology, shell fishing, bread baking, travel.

FOR MORE INFORMATION SEE:

Dartmouth Alumni, March, 1975.
Vineyard Gazette, July 24, 1979, November 23, 1984.
Martha's Vineyard Times, December 19, 1985.

TURNER, Gwenda 1947-

PERSONAL: Born May 11, 1947, in Kyogle, New South Wales, Australia; daughter of Walter David (a fisherman) and Mary (a housewife; maiden name, Bugden) Williams; married John Turner (an advertising executive), July 31, 1974. *Education:* Wellington Polytechnic School of Design, Diploma in Graphic Design, 1970. *Home and office:* 18 Greenwood St., Christchurch, Canterbury 1, New Zealand. *Agent:* Anne Bower Ingram, 4/6 Boronia St., Wollstonecraft, Sydney, New South Wales 2065, Australia.

CAREER: Secretary in Brisbane, Australia, 1964-66; graphic design consultant, 1970-74; full-time artist, 1974- 76; full-time writer and illustrator, 1976—. *Member:* Australian Society of Authors, Canterbury Society of Arts. *Awards, honors:* Russell Clark Award for Illustration from the New Zealand Library Association, 1984, and shortlisted for the Australian Children's Book of the Year Award for Best Picture Book, 1985, both for *The Tree Witches*.

WRITINGS:

JUVENILE; ALL SELF-ILLUSTRATED

Daydream Journey, Collins, 1982.
The Tree Witches, Kestrel, 1983.
Creepy Cottage, Omnibus Books, 1983.
Catnip Mice and Tussie Mussies, Omnibus Books, 1983.
New Zealand ABC, Whitcoulls, 1983.
Gwenda Turner's Playbook, Viking/Kestrel, 1983.
Snow Play, Collins, 1986.

GWENDA TURNER

New Zealand 123, Whitcoulls, 1986.
New Zealand ABC Frieze, Pacific, 1986.
New Zealand 123 Frieze, Pacific, 1987.
New Zealand Colours, Penguin, 1989.
Colors, Viking/Kestrel, 1989.
Once Upon a Time, Penguin, 1990.

OTHER; SELF-ILLUSTRATED
Akaroa: Banks Peninsula, New Zealand, John McIndoe, 1977.
Buildings and Bridges of Christchurch, John McIndoe, 1981.

SIDELIGHTS: "Until I was seven our family lived in Byron Bay (New South Wales, Australia). My grandmother lived about six doors down the road and I have very happy memories of those years. Because of my father's ill health, we moved to Brisbane, but spent many holidays at Byron Bay where other aunts, uncles, and cousins usually gathered.

"I have two sisters, one older and the other younger. I played mostly with the three boys who lived over the back fence. They had all the things I didn't have—a bicycle, a sand pit, a mulberry tree, *several* packs of cards including 'Old Maid' and 'Happy Families,' and a mango tree that hung over their fence.

"I had a friend Elaine who introduced me to the series of Enid Blyton books—*The Mystery of. . . .*, *The Famous Five,* and *The Secret Seven*. We were sure that one day, on our way home from school, an adventure was lurking in someone's garden!

"We had no formal art classes at school. I loved drawing maps and doing decorative lettering in my exercise books. At secondary school, typing, shorthand, and bookkeeping were the only subjects. When I left school at the age of sixteen, I worked for three years as a secretary. During that time I drew and painted only as a hobby. I wanted to travel, but I also knew that I wanted to be an artist. Fate led me to New Zealand, where I began a three-year, full-time course at the Wellington Polytechnic School of Design. Included in the seven subjects was photography. I learned a great deal. It was wonderful and I loved it. I feel that it was an advantage having been out in the work force for three years before I took up tertiary education. I knew what I wanted and was prepared to go through the financial difficulties to see myself through the course. I graduated in 1970 with a diploma in graphic design.

"After working at magazine art and advertising art and design for several years, I began drawing old houses and buildings. Many of these buildings had a story behind them, and this led me to write and illustrate my first book. One of the appealing aspects of children's books is that one can work in full colour. In the case of the children's picture book, there are very few restrictions. Design, layout, shape of book, and choice of typeface are just as important to me as the storyline and illustrations. I enjoy producing books because I can bring together all aspects of my creativity and express them in the form of a book.

"My training in graphic design has enabled me to plan and visualize the finished book. Writing, designing, illustrating, and doing the finished art work for my books provides an ever

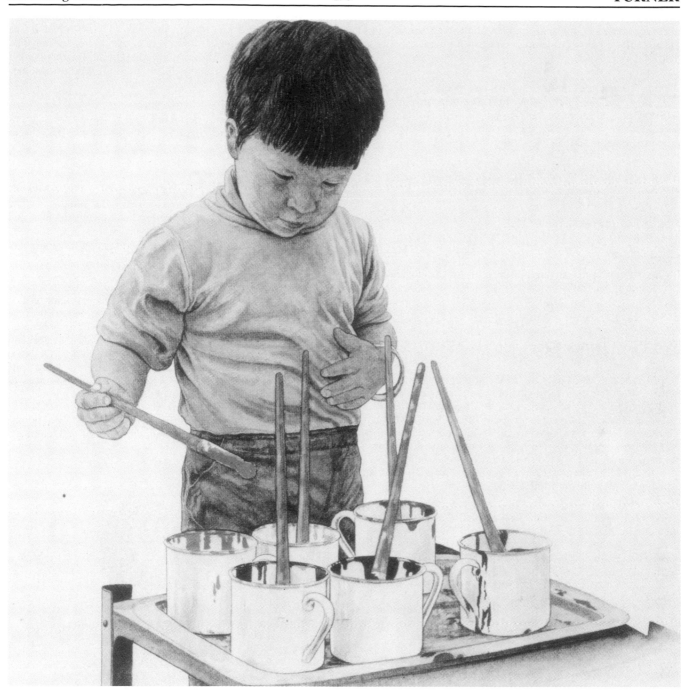

(From *Gwenda Turner's Playbook* by Gwenda Turner. Illustrated by the author.)

increasing challenge to, hopefully, produce new and innovative books, whether they are for adults or children.

"I have been influenced by author/illustrators such as Beatrix Potter, N. C. Wyeth, Howard Pyle, Andrew Wyeth, Carl Larson, Arthur Rackham, Maurice Sendak, John Burningham, Kenneth Grahame, and Norman Lindsay. Potter's work appeals because one feels that she sincerely loved what she wrote and painted. Somehow this comes across in an intangible way. I admire Sendak's work because with each book he has developed and improved his craft.

"I had a very happy and secure childhood. My ideas for stories come from my childhood experiences. I think what is exciting is what sparks off a particular idea for a story. I remember when I

heard the words 'partners in foolishness' in a play on television. I wrote down those words and within a week had written the first draft of *The Tree Witches*.

"After writing my story and planning the illustrations, I then go looking for animals, people, and so forth, because my style of illustrating is true-to-life and I research everything I draw. I enjoy starting work at eight a.m. each day. Very few days pass by when I haven't nibbled away with a pen or brush. I like working to deadlines. Being an author/illustrator is a way of life. There are not enough hours in a day!

"Emerson was correct when he wrote. 'Success is constitutional; depends on a PLUS condition of mind and body, on power of work, on courage.'

"I enjoy working in my studio and looking out into the garden at the bird life. I enjoy gardening—my two burmese cats like to help.

"Things I don't like could perhaps be summed up by saying—I wish more people would grow up liking themselves, having self-esteem, realizing that they are unique. Perhaps then, more people in the world would respect other human beings, their property, animals and all living things."

HOBBIES AND OTHER INTERESTS: Gardening, woodworking, travel, photography.

FOR MORE INFORMATION SEE:

COLLECTIONS

Lu Rees Archives, Canberra College of Advanced Education Library, Australia.

WATTS, James K(ennedy) M(offitt) 1955-

PERSONAL: Born March 20, 1955, in San Francisco, Calif.; son of Malcolm S. M. (a doctor) and Genevieve (Moffitt) Watts; married Aldona J. Koudelka (a homemaker), May 5, 1984; children: Aldona Genevieve, Julian James Gintaras. *Education:* Attended University of Michigan-Sarah Lawrence, summer residency in Florence, 1974; University of California, Berkeley, B.A., 1977; California College of Arts and Crafts, B.F.A., 1979; attended San Francisco Academy of Art, summer scholarship program, 1978.

CAREER: Graphic Traffic, Emeryville, Calif., production manager, 1980-83; free-lance illustrator, 1984—. *Exhibitions:* East Bay Watercolor Society Annual, San Francisco, Calif., 1980; The Art Gallery, San Rafael, Calif., 1980, 1981; "21st Annual Hayward Area Forum for the Arts," 1982; "Bay Arts '82," San Mateo, Calif., 1982; "Northern California Arts 22nd Annual," 1982; "22nd Annual Hayward Area Forum of the Arts," 1983; California State Fair, 1988; "27th Annual Hayward Area Forum of the Arts," 1988. One-man shows: University of California, San Franciso, 1979; San Francisco Preservation Hall, 1980; San Francisco State University, 1984. *Member:* Society of Children's Book Writers. *Awards, honors:* Don Freeman Memorial Grant-in-Aid from the Society of Children's Book Writers, 1983; *Best Friends* was named one of International Reading Association's Children's Choices, 1987.

ILLUSTRATOR

Celeste Stewart, *The Blue Dragon,* Windswept House, 1985.
Alfred Slote, *The Trouble on Janus,* Lippincott, 1985.
Lee Bennett Hopkins, compiler, *Best Friends,* Harper, 1986.
    X. J. Kennedy, *Brats,* Macmillan, 1986.
Jane Louise Curry, reteller, *Back in the Beforetime: Tales of the California Indians,* Macmillan, 1987.
Peggy Parish, *Good Hunting, Blue Sky,* Harper, 1988.
Carol Kendall, *The Wedding of the Rat Family,* Macmillan, 1988.
Shirley Mozelle, *Uncle Jim's Gift,* Harper, 1989.
Victoria Sherrow, *Wilbur Waits,* Harper, 1990.

WORK IN PROGRESS: A picture book, *Charlie Anderson,* for McElderry Books.

SIDELIGHTS: "I was always drawing pictures when I was young. I loved to look at all kinds of books, as long as they had pictures. I would spend hours wandering through history books, art books, and science books, losing myself in the worlds their pictures conjured up.

"When I was ten or so, I began drawing stories on the pages of pads of paper, making them up as I went along. They were usually spy adventures, tales of ancient Greece, or science fiction.

"I didn't draw very much in high school or college. It wasn't encouraged and I became interested in other things. But the margins of my binder paper were covered with doodles and portraits of whoever was being lectured about, and occasionally my reports or papers had glorious illustrations on their title pages.

"In the summer of 1974, after my freshman year of college, I studied for two months in Florence, Italy. I spent a lot of time looking at the frescoes and paintings created by the artists of the Renaissance. I will never forget sitting by myself in the Duomo Cathedral in Florence, looking at a statue carved by Michaelangelo when he was very old, and thinking it was the most beautiful thing I had ever seen. Although I had three more years in college (I majored in history), I think that trip to Florence was a big reason why I went to art school after college.

"At art school I studied drawing and painting and a lot of human anatomy, so that I could draw a human figure without looking at

JAMES K. M. WATTS

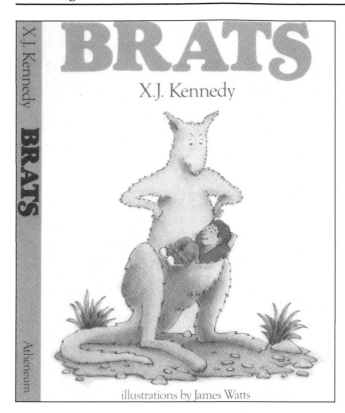

In a kangaroo one day Awful Abner stowed away.... (Jacket illustration by James Watts from *Brats* by X. J. Kennedy.)

one. I discovered how much I missed drawing and painting and I decided to become an artist.

"I enjoy the challenge of bringing a story to life in pictures. When an editor at a publishing company sends me a manuscript to illustrate, the first thing I do is read it over twenty or thirty times. What do the characters look like? What do they wear? Where do they live? I spend a lot of time in the library researching costumes, designs, and anything else I might need or want to know about for my illustrations. Sometimes I go to the zoo to look at an animal that might be in a story. Sometimes I get ideas by looking at the people walking down the street.

"After all my research for a story is done, I sit down and close my eyes and try to imagine the pictures. Then I pick up my pencil and start drawing pictures. It takes a lot of drawings to find the right one.

"When I am happy with the drawings for all the illustrations, I am ready to start the final illustrations. I like to use pencils, watercolors, colored pencils, pastels, and acrylic paints, sometimes all of them at once! It all depends on the effect I'm trying to achieve in the picture.

"The most important parts of the illustrations are the words to the story. The illustrations and the words should fit together perfectly, so that you couldn't imagine the pictures without the story, or the story without the pictures. This is the most difficult part about illustrating a book.

"What's the most exciting part? That happens after I finish all the illustrations. I pack them up carefully and mail them to the editor. The book is designed, printed, and bound. Many months later I receive a box from the publisher with ten or twenty copies of the book. The last time I saw the illustrations they were

paintings on illustration board. Now they are printed on pages with words next to them. It's exciting to open a brand new book that has never been opened before, and see the story and the illustrations together at last!"

WEEVERS, Peter 1944-

PERSONAL: Born April 15, 1944, in Romford, Essex, England. *Education:* Studied graphics and illustration at South East Essex School of Art for five years. *Home:* Entrevaux, France.

CAREER: Illustrator, 1966—. *Awards, honors: The Hare and the Tortoise* was chosen one of Child Study Association of America's Children's Books of the Year, 1986.

WRITINGS:

(With John Bush) *The Christmas Fox*, Hutchinson, 1988.
(With J. Bush) *The March Hare*, Hutchinson, 1989.

ILLUSTRATOR

Anthony Roberts, *Alphonso's Dream*, privately printed, 1974.
Caroline Castle, reteller, *The Hare and the Tortoise*, Hutchinson, 1984, Dial, 1985.
C. Castle, *Herbert Binns and the Flying Tricycle*, Hutchinson, 1986, Dial, 1987.
Lewis Carroll, *Alice's Adventures in Wonderland*, Hutchinson, 1989.

SIDELIGHTS: "I suppose I take my work very seriously, but am seldom entirely satisfied. In my view sensitivity is the main criteria for the appreciation of all art forms, not age or education particularly. Basically there is no difference between adults and children in this regard.

"I began working as an illustrator in London. Approximately a year later, in 1967, I left England to work in Amsterdam, Holland. In 1970 I went to Paris where I freelanced doing book covers and film posters. I went to Monaco, in 1971, where I met my wife, Sylvie. After a few months we went to Amsterdam to work together doing magazine illustration and promotional illustration. In 1974 we 'commuted' between England and France producing, publishing, and even marketing our own work in limited editions. Finally we settled in France where our daughter Tilia was born. We are educating Tilia ourselves for various reasons, including bilingual maintenance.

"*Alice's Adventures in Wonderland* is such a well-known but often glossed over chef-d'oeuvre, written by a brilliant mathematician who was also an extremely imaginative, witty and incorrigible romantic. This is also why Lewis Carroll's most famous and most inspired work is so demanding, challenging, and exciting to illustrate. His imagery is superb and timeless. It is all the more credible because of his often intricate and precise (mathematical) descriptions. One cannot say one is limited by this because such well described, 'logical nonsense' as, for example—a blue caterpillar, three inches long, smoking a hookah on a mushroom is, in a way, fundamental and so evocative that the illustrative possibilities are enormous.

"Naturally every illustrator interprets his or her own way and new publications of *Alice* are nearly always justified because the story is so rich, evocative and timeless. I have tried to illustrate it as completely as possible going as far as I think I can

PETER WEEVERS

without overly distracting from Carroll's text, and naturally without any disrespect for the original Carroll/Tenniel visualization.

"Interests include sculpture, writing, photography—when time permits, gardening, (Bonsai cultivation), cooking."

WIBBELSMAN, Charles J(oseph) 1945-

PERSONAL: Born February 5, 1945, in Cincinnati, Ohio; son of Frederick C. (a postal service employee) and Eve K. (Ries) Wibbelsman. *Education:* Xavier University, A.B. (magna cum laude), 1966; University of Cincinnati College of Medicine, M.D., 1970. *Home:* 2033 Baker St., San Francisco, Calif. 94115. *Agent:* Alice Freid Martell, 555 Fifth Ave., Suite 1900, New York, N.Y. 10017. *Office:* Permanente Medical Group, Inc., 2200 O'Farrell St., San Francisco, Calif. 94115.

CAREER: Massachusetts General Hospital, Boston, pediatric intern, 1970-71; Children's Hospital of Cincinnati, Ohio, resident in pediatrics, 1971- 72; Children's Hospital of Los Angeles, Calif., fellow in adolescent medicine, 1972-74; San Francisco Clinic, Calif., chief of Division of Venereal Diseases Control, 1976-79; Permanente Medical Group, Inc., San Francisco, physician, 1979—. Diplomat of American Board of Pediatrics; chief of Teenage Clinic at Kaiser Permanente Medical Center, 1983—; member of Kaiser Permanente Inter-Regional AIDS Task Force, 1987—. Guest on television programs, including "The Oprah Winfrey Show." *Military*

service: U.S. Navy, pediatrician at U.S. Naval Hospital, Naval Regional Medical Center, Long Beach, Calif., 1974-76; became lieutenant commander. *Member:* American Academy of Pediatrics (fellow), Society for Adolescent Medicine, California Medical Association, San Francisco Medical Association. *Awards, honors: The Teenage Body Book* was selected one of American Library Association's Best Books for Young Adults, 1979, and one of New York Public Library's Books for the Teen Age, 1980, 1981, and 1982.

WRITINGS:

(With Kathy McCoy) *The Teenage Body Book*, Simon & Schuster, 1979, 3rd edition published as *The New Teenage Body Book*, Price, Stern, 1987.
(With K. McCoy) *Growing and Changing: A Handbook for Pre-Teens* (illustrated by Bob Stover), Putnam, 1987.

Author of "Dear Doctor," a column in *Teen*, 1974-76. Contributor to periodicals and medical journals, including *Teen, Journal of the American Medical Association, American Journal of Public Health, Journal of Chemical Endocrinology, Journal of Pediatrics*, and *Journal of Infectious Diseases*.

WORK IN PROGRESS: With Kathy McCoy, *Crisis-Proof Your Teenager: How to Prevent a Parent's Worst Fears*, written specifically for parents of adolescents to alert them of the red flags of teen risk behavior, for Bantam.

SIDELIGHTS: "As a physician specializing in adolescent medicine, I have learned that there is much education that teenagers and their parents need during these turbulent years of rapid physical and emotional changes. Many times the crises of these years can be life-threatening. It is so very important to reach out to these teens and their families beyond what physicians and health care providers can do within the framework of established medical boundaries. Writing to, for, and in answer to young adults is vital and rewarding!"

HOBBIES AND OTHER INTERESTS: Swimming, sailing, downhill skiing, travelling in France.

WILLIAMS, Linda 1948-

PERSONAL: Born January 6, 1948, in Honolulu, Hawaii; daughter of Walter (an attorney) and Ella (a registered nurse; maiden name, Fraser) Ackerman; married Charles Williams (a financial division manager), December 28, 1968; children: Patrick, Nicklaus, Samantha. *Education:* Oregon State University, B.S., 1969. *Home:* 37964 River Dr., Lebanon, Ore. 97355.

CAREER: Writer. Has worked as a preschool teacher and director for twenty years. *Member:* International Reading Association, Oregon Reading Association. *Awards, honors: The Little Old Lady Who Was Not Afraid of Anything* was selected one of Child Study Association of America's Children's Books of the Year, 1987, and received the Keystone to Reading Book Award from the Keystone State Reading Association (Pennsylvania), and runner-up for the Colorado Children's Book Award from the Colorado Council of the International Reading Associaton, both 1988.

WRITINGS:

The Little Old Lady Who Was Not Afraid of Anything (Junior Literary Guild selection; illustrated by Megan Lloyd), Crowell, 1986.

SIDELIGHTS: Williams was born in Hawaii. "It was a wonderful place to grow up. There was space. We hiked mountains and swam under waterfalls that are now state parks charging admission. We skinny-dipped at beaches that now have hundreds of tourists a year.

"I had four older sisters and two younger brothers. My position in the family had lots of advantages. I was able to talk my mother out of the dance lessons and charm classes my four older sisters attended. And I was able to talk my father into hunting and fishing trips with my younger brothers.

"Thus, it didn't seem strange when I attended and graduated from Hawaii Preparatory Academy, a boys boarding school. I loved it! But poetic justice would have its way. With dozens of boys to choose from, I fell in love with one from a different school on a different island!

"College was a happy accident. I went to Oregon State University simply to be with my high school sweetheart. I do not know why I entered the School of Home Economics or why I stayed with it. I simply do not like to cook or sew! Then one day the head of the preschool lab said, 'You are a natural at understanding children.' A compliment! I changed my major and graduated two terms later in nursery school teaching. I also learned the power of an honest compliment. I knew I was where I belonged. Observing and understanding children has caused me to continually think and grow. I learn by teaching and so I teach parents as I learn from their children.

"I married my high school sweetheart just before graduation. We have three children—Patrick, Nicklaus, and Samantha. We have settled in Oregon, a place with space.

"*The Little Old Lady Who Was Not Afraid of Anything* is the first story I sent to a publisher. I have always been fond of stories that children can help me tell. After telling the story to my classes for five years, I typed it up, gave it a good luck kiss, and mailed it to Harper & Row. I will be forever grateful to senior editor Barbara Fenton for choosing Megan Lloyd to illustrate the story. Her illustrations were better than my imagination."

WISMER, Donald (Richard) 1946-

PERSONAL: Surname is pronounced *Whiz*-mer; born December 27, 1946, in Chicago, Ill.; son of Donald Minor and Katherine (Brandstrader) Wismer; married Leah Rubel, December 17, 1976; children: Sarah Miriam, Asher Zvi, Akiva Meir, Aryeh Moshe. *Education:* Indiana University, B.A., 1968, M.A., 1973; Southern Connecticut State College, M.S., 1977. *Home address:* P.O. Box 402, Fallsburg, N.Y. 12733. *Agent:* James Allen, Virginia Kidd Literary Agency, Box 278, 538 East Harford St., Milford, Pa. 18337.

CAREER: Indiana University, Bloomington, library assistant, 1967-73; Harvard University, Cambridge, Mass., stack supervisor at Widener Library, 1974-76; Bigelow Laboratory for Ocean Sciences, West Boothbay Harbor, Maine, librarian, 1977, Maine State Library, Augusta, coordinator for Automated Data Services, 1977-84, division director, Reference and

DONALD WISMER

Information Services, 1984-89. *Member:* Science Fiction Writers of America, Maine Library Association (president of Special Library Group, 1979-80; member of executive board, 1979-83). *Awards, honors:* "Wave's Refuge" was on the preliminary ballot for the Nebula Award, 1986, and *Planet of the Dead*, 1988.

WRITINGS:

The Islamic Jesus: An Annotated Bibliography of Sources in English and French, Garland Publishing, 1977.
Starluck (science-fiction novel), Doubleday, 1982.
Warrior Planet (science-fiction novel), Baen, 1986.
Planet of the Dead (science-fiction novel), Baen, 1987.

Contributor to library science journals. Editor of *Downeast Libraries*, 1981-83. "Wave's Refuge" was included in the anthologies, *Tin Stars*, edited by Isaac Asimov and others, New American Library, 1986 and *Strange Maine* edited by Charles Waugh and others, Lance Tapley, 1986.

WORK IN PROGRESS: A Roil of Stars, a science-fiction novel.

SIDELIGHTS: "I write what I write because I enjoy science fiction and because I think it is good for people. It is the most underrated genre among literary critics, but that's o.k. because they are disregarded by the vast bulk of the reading public anyway. When I speak before school groups, I tell the kids to consider this question: who has a greater impact on society, the author who sells 100,000 copies of his genre novel, or the highly regarded poet who reaches 1500 people? It's not as simple a question as it sounds, but the numbers *are* indicative.

"What is the point of writing in the first place? Many would-be authors would say, 'to get published,' but that's not enough. The motivation has to be to reach people, to stir their minds, to make them think. Of all the arguments I have ever heard on literary merit, the kernel comes to that four word phrase: to make them think.

"The science-fiction genre generally (but not totally) falls into the action/adventure category of fiction, but it is perceptibly a genre of ideas. The excitement of vision permeates all good science fiction, and the reader will find therein anything he or she wants, from deep psychological study to theories of world government and religious truth. Science fiction that lacks such ideological excitement never lasts long, if it gets published in the first place.

"But the ideas don't survive the marketplace unless they are cloaked in a driving plotline; that's why H. G. Wells' fiction reads so poorly today, and Jules Verne's so well. They wrote in the same era, but Verne's attention was on the story, and Wells' on the message. If you want to get a message out, don't worry much about it; write a good story, and the message will come through. The message, however, has to be there, or your story will be a sterile thing.

"I write so-called 'hard' science fiction, space opera, 'Star Warsy' stuff—spaceships and conflict and planets and aliens. If you ask which writers have influenced me the most, I would say: Clifford D. Simak, first and foremost, for his humanity; A. E. Van Vogt, for his lucidity; and perhaps Raphael Sabatini (who did not write science fiction) for his elegance. Lately among science-fiction writers, Alfred Bester and Barrington J. Bayley. As a young adult, the star of the show was Edgar Rice Burroughs—almost any science-fiction writer today would say that.

"My major problem as a writer is time: a forty-hour/week job, four children so far. I squeeze writing into two evenings a week, and that cannot continue indefinitely. Soon I'll have to break out into full-time writing, and then my output will sharply rise.

"My major advice to a fledgling writer: sit down and do it. Begin it, continue it, finish it. Make yourself an expert at goal-setting; there are plenty of books to show you how. And learn to type on a keyboard with all ten fingers; it is a skill that will make you a living regardless of whether you ever get published. Don't let anyone read it until you've finished it. And take all criticism with a shovel of salt; English teachers can't agree on anything."

WOOD, Linda C(arol) 1945-

PERSONAL: Born September 4, 1945, in Smyrna, Tenn.; daughter of Randolph C. (a record and motion picture executive) and Lois H. (Henry) Wood. *Education:* Attended University of California, Los Angeles, 1965-66; University of California, Berkeley, B.A., 1967, M.A., 1969; Sorbonne, University of Paris, Certificat de la Civilisation Francaise, 1967. *Home and office:* 815 1/2 Coast Blvd. S., La Jolla, Calif. 92037. *Agent:* Jane Jordan Browne, Multimedia Product Development, Inc., 410 South Michigan Ave., Room 828, Chicago, Ill. 60605.

CAREER: Free-lance writer; CRM Books, Del Mar, Calif., editor, 1970-73; University of California, San Diego, and La Jolla, editorial consultant for University Extension, 1980-83. *Awards, honors:* Outstanding Science Book for Children from the National Science Teachers' Association and the Children's Book Council 1982, and Distinguished Work of Nonfiction

from the Southern California Council on Literature for Children and Young People, 1983, both for *Windows in Space*.

WRITINGS:

JUVENILE

(With Ann Elwood) *Windows in Space*, Walker, 1982.

OTHER

(Editor) *The Psychology Primer*, Dell, 1975.
(Editor) *A Land Called California*, Pacific Sun Press, 1979.
A Viewer's Guide to Cosmos Carl Sagan, Random House, 1980.
(With A. Elwood) *A Reader/Study Guide for Cosmos Carl Sagan*, Random House, 1980.
(Editor with James O'Toole and Jane L. Scheiber) *Working: Changes and Choices*, Human Sciences Press, 1980.
(With Harding E. Smith) *Understanding Space and Time*, Kendall/Hunt, 1981.
Study Guide for Contemporary Western Europe, Praeger, 1984.
Study Guide for Contemporary China/Japan, Praeger, 1984.

WORTH, Richard 1945-

PERSONAL: Born November 13, 1945, in Hartford, Conn. *Education:* Trinity College, B.A., 1967, M.A., 1968. *Home:* 171 Sycamore La., Fairfield, Conn. 06430.

CAREER: Author, producer of audiovisual programs.

WRITINGS:

YOUNG ADULT

Poland: The Threat to National Renewal, F. Watts, 1982.
Israel and the Arab States, F. Watts, 1983.
The Third World Today, F. Watts, 1983.
The American Family (illustrated with photographs by Robert Sefcik), F. Watts, 1984.
You'll Be Old Someday, Too, F. Watts, 1986.

FOR MORE INFORMATION SEE:

Booklist, July, 1982, June 15, 1983, November 15, 1983, December 1, 1984, May 1, 1986.
Voice of Youth Advocates, February, 1983, February, 1984, April, 1985, December, 1986.
School Library Journal, September, 1983, January, 1984, April, 1984, April, 1985, September, 1986.
Bulletin of the Center for Children's Books, October, 1983.

YAKOVETIC (Joseph Sandy) 1952-
(Joe Yakovetic)

PERSONAL: Accent is on "vet"; born December 12, 1952, in Bridgeport, Conn.; son of John D. (an insurance adjuster) and Madeline (an executive secretary; maiden name, Genito) Yakovetic; married Samii (Sheilah L.) Taylor (a record producer and writer), September 27, 1987. *Education:* California State—Fullerton, B.A., 1976. *Politics:* Republican. *Religion:* "Born Again" Christian. *Office:* c/o Harcourt, Brace, Jovanovich, Inc., 1250 Sixth Ave., San Diego, Calif. 92101.

CAREER: Movieland Wax Museum, Buena Park, Calif., caricature/portrait artist, 1969-70; Movieland Cars of Stars, Planes of Fame, Buena Park, Calif., caricature/portrait artist and manager, 1970-72; Disneyland Hotel, Anaheim, Calif., caricature/portrait artist and manager, 1973-75; NBC-TV, Burbank, Calif., graphic artist, journeyman, courtroom artist, 1976-77; free-lance artist and illustrator, 1977—; Maranatha Music Record Co., Costa Mesa, Calif., product developer, artist, 1986—. Member: American Film Institute. Awards, honors: American Legion School Award, 1968; Outstanding Achievement in Design Award from California State University, 1976.

ILLUSTRATOR

Elspeth C. Murphy, *Barney Wigglesworth and the Birthday Surprise,* Cook, 1988.

E. C. Murphy, *Barney Wigglesworth and the Church Flood,* Cook, 1988.

E. C. Murphy, *Barney Wigglesworth and the Party That Almost Wasn't,* Cook, 1988.

E. C. Murphy, *Barney Wigglesworth and the Smallest Christmas Pageant,* Cook, 1988.

Marian F. Bray, *Springtime of Khan,* Cook, 1988.

M. F. Bray, *Summer by the Sea,* Cook, 1988.

Paula Boussard, *The Great Balloon Adventure,* Cook, 1989.

Also illustrator of book covers for Carolyn Haywood books—four books in the "Betsy" series, two in the "Penny" series, *Two and Two Are Four,* and *Primrose Day;* covers for "Zelda Hammersmith" series.

WORK IN PROGRESS: Promotional art for Disney.

SIDELIGHTS: "I have been 'illustrating' since age two when I drew an entire story on little pieces of paper, stapled them together and then dictated the dialogue for my mother to write down. I was always playing with clay or drawing my toys and television cartoon characters. I was quick to copy Jon Gnagy's 'How to Draw' sessions on television and Walter Lantz's 'Woody Woodpecker' was used as a model for some of my early creations. In grade school, I quickly won popularity with my sophisticated drawings of the Jetsons and the Flintstones.

"Growing up in Buena Park, California I began wearing glasses in third grade and consequently wasn't very athletic. I didn't have a lot of friends, so I was always making up stories and dialogues with my toy figures and building forts and towns for them.

"Since the Book Mobile stopped in front of my house, I read a lot of biographies, fiction and mysteries. I also watched old movies and variety shows on television. I spent a great deal of time day dreaming that I was Gene Kelly, Fred Astaire or Bing Crosby. On Saturday evenings, I used to 'direct' my sister and cousins so we could perform skits or pantomime records to entertain our parents.

"Throughout grade school, I was always an average student. In junior high, with a little 'pressure' from my parents, I buckled down and took school more seriously. No matter how hard I worked, I never managed to get better than a B+ grade. Finally, out of desperation, I began to embellish every paper or project with appropriate artwork. It worked! I got past the B+ mark. Soon I was illustrating reports for history, Spanish and health. By ninth grade (my last year in junior high), I had a 3.5 average and was an Honor Society student. During these years, I had also learned to put on an air of confidence and to boldly step ahead. I also realized I could never be fully accepted by my peers, so I groomed myself to be accepted by those in authority. I began taking risks, too. Not with drugs or alcohol, but by getting in front of people and taking a stand on what I believed, and expressing myself. The result—I became student body president, year book editor, and wrote the school talent show. At graduation, I was awarded the American Legion School Award for honor, courage, patriotism, scholarship and service.

"Entering high school meant that I REALLY had to get serious. College was only three years away and art was not the career I was told to pursue. It was important to have a 'real job.' Excelling in science, I aspired to be a great plastic surgeon. Ironically, I received a scholarship for medical illustrating.

"By my senior year at Western High in Anaheim, California, I had started my first job doing caricatures and portraits at the Movieland Wax Museum. The money was great, so I did caricatures on through college.

"In my second year of college, I decided to change my major to art. My parents were very concerned about our lack of contacts to further a career in art. However, once I was in art, my life changed—I was in my element. I found that grades came easy and I had a knack for illustrating—especially in the children's market.

"During college, I was approached by SHARE, a Beverly Hills charity group who raises money for the Exceptional Children's

YAKOVETIC

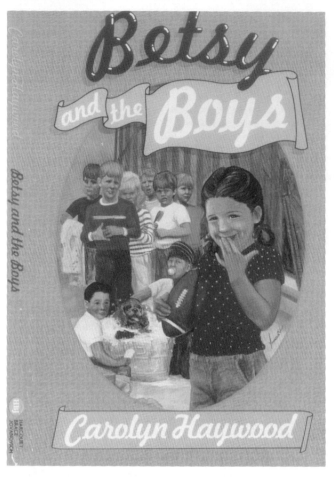

Won't Billy be surprised when he finds out that I have a football. (Cover illustration by Joe Yakovetic from *Betsy and the Boys* by Carolyn Haywood.)

Foundation. I was hired by them to do caricatures and help decorate their annual 'Boomtown Party.' I've been working for them since 1974. This work taught me to be humble and encourage others. These women, many of whom are Hollywood celebrities, would be on their hands and knees working on the show. The ladies of SHARE were and still are very gracious, and have been very supportive to my career.

"I graduated from California State—Fullerton in 1976 with a B.A. in illustration. Minoring in costuming, I spent most of my last two years in the theatre department crewing and assisting, and finally designing costumes for several major stage productions. Upon graduation, I was quite surprised to be awarded the Outstanding Achievement Award in Design from the theatre department.

"My biggest problem in college had been that I lacked an artistic style of my own. I would develop the style for the particular subject I worked on. While this was a constant irritation for my instructors, it helped me to land my job in the graphics department of NBC where one had to accurately copy styles.

"It was through one of the caring ladies of SHARE that I was granted an interview at NBC. Although I was hired to do caricatures for a particular program, I was quickly put to work on many other programs: 'The Dick Van Dyke Comedy Show,' 'The Midnight Special,' 'Sanford and Son,' 'The Rock Music Awards,' 'The 1920s Dean Martin Special,' and numerous other specials.

"One of my favorite NBC jobs was courtroom illustrating for the news. It was a real challenge in the courtroom. I had to draw quickly and accurately everything the newscaster needed to convey his story. My years of caricatures and quick portraits truly came in handy. On one occasion, I was flown to Salt Lake City to draw a judge who had not been photographed in years and refused to allow any artists or photographers in his courtroom. I would sit and observe him, then go out into the hallway to sketch. I ended up going to the library and finding an old photo of him which I was able to copy and age. I then added the sketch to my composites.

"Eventually my free-lance work prompted my leaving NBC. During the next few years, I leaned heavily on caricatures as a source of income. I was even contracted to do caricatures for a television movie—'The Legend of the Golden Gun' (Columbia Pictures).

"In 1980, I accepted Jesus Christ as my Lord and Savior, after many years of spiritual searching. At that time, I knew I couldn't be satisified with the work I was doing. After much prayer and fasting, I laid my talents before the Lord and asked that He either use them or take them away. Within the week, I was hired to do children's album covers and a storybook record for Maranatha Music, a Christian company. I worked almost exclusively for them, designing and illustrating most of their children's products.

"In 1987, I was approached by David C. Cook Publishing (also a result of the Maranatha work). They asked me to design and illustrate the four book 'Barney Wigglesworth' series.

"Two years before, I had met Samii Taylor, a recording engineer who hired me to do artwork for a television pilot she produced. We became best friends and decided to combine our talents to form Yakovetic Productions. We were married in September of 1987. Samii is also a gifted writer with many talents.

"Aside from our business, geared mainly toward youth, we are both actively involved with several charity organizations: SHARE, the Young Musicians Foundation, and United Friends of the Children. Our goal is to serve God and to do the best work in all situations. We hope that His love and truth can reach those with whom we come into contact."

HOBBIES AND OTHER INTERESTS: Water sports, performing, singing, dancing, writing, camping, cooking and entertaining, church music, drama, and socials.

YEPSEN, Roger B(ennet), Jr. 1947-

PERSONAL: Born November 5, 1947, in Schenectady, N.Y.; son of Roger Bennet (a retired business executive) and Natalie (a homemaker; maiden name, Mosher) Yepsen; married Alice Nass (a school counselor), December 6, 1979; children: Metthea, Rhodes. *Education:* Bucknell University, B.A., 1970; additional study, Pennsylvania Academy of Fine Art, 1987—. *Home and office:* R.D. 1, Box 623, Barto, Pa. 19504. *Agent:* McIntosh and Otis, Inc., 310 Madison Ave., New York, N.Y. 10017.

CAREER: Art teacher at elementary and secondary level in Edmeston, N.Y., 1970-71; U.S. Department of Housing and Urban Development, Lewisburg, Pa., housing adviser, 1972-73; Rodale Press, Emmaus, Pa., editor, 1974-86; free-lance writer and editor, 1986—. Professional bass guitar player,

1971-73. *Awards, honors:* Bronze Award from the University of Kansas White Awards, 1988, for an article.

WRITINGS:

JUVENILE; SELF-ILLUSTRATED

Train Talk: An Illustrated Guide to Lights, Hand Signals, Whistles, and Other Languages of Railroading (Junior Literary Guild selection), Pantheon, 1983.
Smarten Up!, Little, Brown, 1989.

OTHER

(Editor) *Home Food Systems: Rodale's Catalog of Methods and Tools for Producing, Processing, and Preserving Naturally Good Foods*, Rodale Press, 1981.
(Editor) *The Durability Factor*, Rodale Press, 1982.
(Editor) *Encyclopedia of Natural Insect and Disease Control*, Rodale Press, 1984.
Boost Your Brain Power, Rodale Press, 1986.

Contributing editor, *Men's Health*, 1987—.

WORK IN PROGRESS: A children's atlas of story settings around the world.

SIDELIGHTS: "I'm working on illustrated books that open up obscure or technical subjects to young readers, as *Train Talk* attempts to do with railroad communications.

"My summer office is the second floor of a pig barn. I can walk there from my house in bare feet—a nice way to commute. In the colder months I work in a loft above the living room, so that I can keep warm and keep an eye on my kids. Both offices are small and cozy and have long views; they remind me of the bedroom I had as a boy."

ZEMACH, Margot 1931-1989

OBITUARY NOTICE:—See sketch in *SATA* Volume 21: Born November 30, 1931, in Los Angeles, Calif.; died of Lou Gehrig's disease, May 21, 1989, in Berkeley, Calif. Illustrator and author. Zemach illustrated and wrote more than forty children's books, including *Duffy and the Devil: A Cornish Tale*, retold by her husband, Harve Zemach, which won the 1974 Caldecott Medal. *The Judge: An Untrue Tale* and *It Could Always Be Worse* were both Caldecott Honor Books.

In 1955 Zemach was awarded a Fulbright Scholarship to the Vienna Academy of Fine Arts. There she met another Fulbright scholar, Harve Fischtrom, whom she married two years later and with whom she collaborated on her first book, *A Small Boy Is Listening* in 1958. That was the beginning of a seventeen-year collaboration. Writing under the name Harve Zemach, her husband retold numerous folktales, which she illustrated, including *Mommy, Buy Me a China Doll* and *The Princess and Froggie*. After his death in 1974, Zemach settled in Berkeley, California with their four daughters. There she continued to illustrate award-winning children's books, often with her own texts or from folktales which she adapted, such as *Hush, Little Baby*, which was chosen to represent the United States on the International Board of Books for Young People in 1978.

Zemach had definite opinions about good illustrations for children, believing that "children are fascinated by detail. . . .In the most elaborate picture, the chances are that what gives special delight is a little fly or a dropped glove. Children need detail, color, excellence—the best a person can do." In recent years she produced *The Little Red Hen: An Old Story* and *The Three Wishes: An Old Story*. At the time of her death she was working on a picture book of Mother Goose rhymes. Her work is included in the Kerlan Collection at the University of Minnesota.

FOR MORE INFORMATION SEE:

Martha E. Ward and Dorothy A. Marquardt, *Illustrators of Children's Books*, Scarecrow, 1975.
Self Portrait: Margot Zemach, Addison-Wesley, 1978.
School Library Journal, February, 1978, February, 1979.
Christian Science Monitor, October 23, 1978.

OBITUARIES

Detroit Free Press, May 24, 1989.
The Times (London), May 25, 1989.
Los Angeles Times, May 27, 1989.
School Library Journal, July, 1989.
Horn Book, September/October, 1989.

Cumulative Indexes

Illustrations Index

(In the following index, the number of the volume in which an illustrator's work appears is given *before* the colon, and the page number on which it appears is given *after* the colon. For example, a drawing by Adams, Adrienne appears in Volume 2 on page 6, another drawing by her appears in Volume 3 on page 80, another drawing in Volume 8 on page 1, and another drawing in Volume 15 on page 107.)

YABC

Index citations including this abbreviation refer to listings appearing in *Yesterday's Authors of Books for Children*, also published by Gale Research Inc., which covers authors who died prior to 1960.

S

Van Sciver, Ruth *37:*162
Van Stockum, Hilda *5:*193
Van Wely, Babs *16:*50
Varga, Judy *29:*196
Vasiliu, Mircea *2:*166, 253; *9:*166; *13:*58
Vaughn, Frank *34:*157
Vavra, Robert *8:*206
Vawter, Will *17:*163
Veeder, Larry *18:*4
Velasquez, Eric *45:*217
Vendrell, Carme Solé *42:*205
Venezia, Mike *54:*17
Ver Beck, Frank *18:*16-17
Verney, John *14:*225
Verrier, Suzanne *5:*20; *23:*212
Versace, Marie *2:*255
Vestal, H. B. *9:*134; *11:*101; *27:*25; *34:*158
Vicatan *59:*146
Vickrey, Robert *45:*59, 64
Victor, Joan Berg *30:*193
Viereck, Ellen *3:*242; *14:*229
Vigna, Judith *15:*293
Vilato, Gaspar E. *5:*41
Villiard, Paul *51:*178
Vimnèra, A. *23:*154
Vincent, Eric *34:*98
Vincent, Félix *41:*237
Vip *45:*164
Vivas, Julie *51:*67, 69
Vo-Dinh, Mai *16:*272
Vogel, Ilse-Margret *14:*230
Voigt, Erna *35:*228
Vojtech, Anna *42:*190
von Schmidt, Eric *8:*62; *50:*209, 210
von Schmidt, Harold *30:*80
Vosburgh, Leonard *1:*161; *7:*32; *15:*295-296; *23:*110; *30:*214; *43:*181
Voter, Thomas W. *19:*3, 9
Vroman, Tom *10:*29

W

Waber, Bernard *47:*209, 210, 211, 212, 213, 214
Wagner, John *8:*200; *52:*104
Wagner, Ken *2:*59
Waide, Jan *29:*225; *36:*139
Wainwright, Jerry *14:*85
Wakeen, Sandra *47:*97
Waldman, Bruce *15:*297; *43:*178
Waldman, Neil *35:*141; *50:*163; *51:*180; *54:*78
Walker, Charles *1:*46; *4:*59; *5:*177; *11:*115; *19:*45; *34:*74
Walker, Dugald Stewart *15:*47; *32:*202; *33:*112
Walker, Gil *8:*49; *23:*132; *34:*42
Walker, Jeff *55:*154
Walker, Jim *10:*94
Walker, Mort *8:*213
Walker, Norman *41:*37; *45:*58
Walker, Stephen *12:*229; *21:*174
Wallace, Ian *53:*176, 177
Wallace, Beverly Dobrin *19:*259
Wallace, Ian *56:*165, 166; *58:*4
Waller, S. E. *24:*36
Wallner, Alexandra *15:*120
Wallner, John C. *9:*77; *10:*188; *11:*28; *14:*209; *31:*56, 118; *37:*64; *51:*186, 187, 188-189, 190-191, 192-193, 194, 195; *52:*96; *53:*23, 26
Wallower, Lucille *11:*226
Walters, Audrey *18:*294
Walther, Tom *31:*179
Walton, Tony *11:*164; *24:*209
Waltrip, Lela *9:*195
Waltrip, Mildred *3:*209; *37:*211
Waltrip, Rufus *9:*195
Wan *12:*76
Ward, Fred *52:*19
Ward, John *42:*191
Ward, Keith *2:*107
Ward, Leslie *34:*126; *36:*87
Ward, Lynd *1:*99, 132, 133, 150; *2:*108, 158, 196, 259; *18:*86; *27:*56; *29:*79, 187, 253, 255; *36:*199, 200, 201, 202, 203, 204, 205, 206, 207, 209; *43:*34; *56:*28
Ward, Peter *37:*116
Warner, Peter *14:*87

Warren, Betsy *2:*101
Warren, Marion Cray *14:*215
Warshaw, Jerry *30:*197, 198; *42:*165
Washington, Nevin *20:*123
Washington, Phyllis *20:*123
Waterman, Stan *11:*76
Watkins-Pitchford, D. J. *6:*215, 217
Watson, Aldren A. *2:*267; *5:*94; *13:*71; *19:*253; *32:*220; *42:*193, 194, 195, 196, 197, 198, 199, 200, 201; *YABC* *2:*202
Watson, Gary *19:*147; *36:*68; *41:*122; *47:*139
Watson, J. D. *22:*86
Watson, Karen *11:*26
Watson, Wendy *5:*197; *13:*101; *33:*116; *46:*163
Watts, Bernadette *4:*227
Watts, James *59:*197
Watts, John *37:*149
Webber, Helen *3:*141
Webber, Irma E. *14:*238
Weber, Erik *56:*19, 20
Weber, Florence *40:*153
Weber, William J. *14:*239
Webster, Jean *17:*241
Wegner, Fritz *14:*250; *20:*189; *44:*165
Weidenear, Reynold H. *21:*122
Weihs, Erika *4:*21; *15:*299
Weil, Lisl *7:*203; *10:*58; *21:*95; *22:*188, 217; *33:*193
Weiman, Jon *50:*162, 165; *52:*103; *54:*78, 79, 81
Weiner, Sandra *14:*240
Weiner, Scott *55:*27
Weinhaus, Karen Ann *53:*90
Weisgard, Leonard *1:*65; *2:*191, 197, 204, 264-265; *5:*108; *21:*42; *30:*200, 201, 203, 204; *41:*47; *44:*125; *53:*25; *YABC* *2:*13
Weiss, Ellen *44:*202
Weiss, Emil *1:*168; *7:*60
Weiss, Harvey *1:*145, 223; *27:*224, 227
Weiss, Nicki *33:*229
Weissman, Bari *49:*72
Wells, Haru *53:*120, 121
Wells, Frances *1:*183
Wells, H. G. *20:*194, 200
Wells, Rosemary *6:*49; *18:*297
Wells, Rufus III *56:*111, 113
Wells, Susan *22:*43
Wendelin, Rudolph *23:*234
Wengenroth, Stow *37:*47
Werenskiold, Erik *15:*6
Werner, Honi *24:*110; *33:*41
Werth, Kurt *7:*122; *14:*157; *20:*214; *39:*128
Westerberg, Christine *29:*226
Weston, Martha *29:*116; *30:*213; *33:*85, 100; *53:*181, 182, 183, 184
Wetherbee, Margaret *5:*3
Wexler, Jerome *49:*73
Whalley, Peter *50:*49
Wheatley, Arabelle *11:*231 *16:*276
Wheeler, Cindy *49:*205
Wheeler, Dora *44:*179
Wheelright, Rowland *15:*81; *YABC* *2:*286
Whelan, Michael *56:*108
Whistler, Rex *16:*75; *30:*207, 208
White, David Omar *5:*56; *18:*6
White, Martin *51:*197
Whitear *32:*26
Whithorne, H. S. *7:*49
Whitney, George Gillett *3:*24
Whittam, Geoffrey *30:*191
Wiberg, Harald *38:*127
Wiese, Kurt *3:*255; *4:*206; *14:*17; *17:*18-19; *19:*47; *24:*152; *25:*212; *32:*184; *36:*211, 213, 214, 215, 216, 217, 218; *45:*161
Wiesner, David *33:*47; *51:*106; *57:*67; *58:*55
Wiesner, William *4:*100; *5:*200, 201; *14:*262
Wiggins, George *6:*133
Wikkelsoe, Otto *45:*25, 26
Wikland, Ilon *5:*113; *8:*150; *38:*124, 125, 130
Wilbur, C. Keith, M.D. *27:*228
Wilburn, Kathy *53:*102
Wilcox, J.A.J. *34:*122
Wilcox, R. Turner *36:*219
Wild, Jocelyn *46:*220-221, 222
Wilde, George *7:*139
Wildsmith, Brian *16:*281-282; *18:*170-171
Wilhelm, Hans *58:*189, 191

Wilkin, Eloise *36:*173; *49:*208, 209, 210
Wilkinson, Barry *50:*213
Wilkinson, Gerald *3:*40
Wilkoń, Józef *31:*183, 184
Wilks, Mike *34:*24; *44:*203
Williams, Ferelith Eccles *22:*238
Williams, Garth *1:*197; *2:*49, 270; *4:*205; *15:*198, 302-304, 307 *16:*34; *18:*283, 298-301; *29:*177, 178, 179, 232-233, 241-245, 248; *40:*106; *YABC* *2:*15-16, 19
Williams, J. Scott *48:*28
Williams, Kit *44:*206-207, 208, 209, 211, 212
Williams, Maureen *12:*238
Williams, Patrick *14:*218
Williams, Richard *44:*93
Williams, Vera B. *53:*186, 187, 188, 189
Willmore, J. T. *54:*113, 114
Wilson, Charles Banks *17:*92; *43:*73
Wilson, Dagmar *10:*47
Wilson, Edward A. *6:*24 *16:*149; *20:*220-221; *22:*87; *26:*67; *38:*212, 214, 215, 216, 217
Wilson, Forrest *27:*231
Wilson, Gahan *35:*234; *41:*136
Wilson, Jack *17:*139
Wilson, John *22:*240
Wilson, Maurice *46:*224
Wilson, Patten *35:*61
Wilson, Peggy *15:*4
Wilson, Rowland B. *30:*170
Wilson, Sarah *50:*215
Wilson, Tom *33:*232
Wilson, W. N. *22:*26
Wilwerding, Walter J. *9:*202
Winchester, Linda *13:*231
Wind, Betty *28:*158
Windham, Kathryn Tucker *14:*260
Wing, Ron *50:*85
Winslow, Will *21:*124
Winsten, Melanie Willa *41:*41
Winter, Milo *15:*97; *19:*221; *21:*181, 203, 204, 205; *YABC* *2:*144
Winter, Paula *48:*227
Wise, Louis *13:*68
Wiseman, Ann *31:*187
Wiseman, B. *4:*233
Wishnefsky, Phillip *3:*14
Wiskur, Darrell *5:*72; *10:*50; *18:*246
Wittman, Sally *30:*219
Woehr, Lois *12:*5
Wohlberg, Meg *12:*100; *14:*197; *41:*255
Woldin, Beth Weiner *34:*211
Wolf, J. *16:*91
Wolf, Linda *33:*163
Wolff, Ashley *50:*217
Wondriska, William *6:*220
Wonsetler, John C. *5:*168
Wood, Audrey *50:*221, 222, 223
Wood, Don *50:*220, 225, 226, 228-229
Wood, Grant *19:*198
Wood, Ivor *58:*17
Wood, Muriel *36:*119
Wood, Myron *6:*220
Wood, Owen *18:*187
Wood, Ruth *8:*11
Woodson, Jack *10:*201
Woodward, Alice *26:*89; *36:*81
Wool, David *26:*27
Wooten, Vernon *23:*70; *51:*170
Worboys, Evelyn *1:*166-167
Worth, Jo *34:*143
Worth, Wendy *4:*133
Wosmek, Frances *29:*251
Wrenn, Charles L. *38:*96; *YABC* *1:*20, 21
Wright, Dare *21:*206
Wright, George *YABC* *1:*268
Wright, Joseph *30:*160
Wright-Frierson, Virginia *58:*194
Wronker, Lili Cassel *3:*247; *10:*204; *21:*10
Wyatt, Stanley *46:*210
Wyeth, Andrew *13:*40; *YABC* *1:*133-134
Wyeth, Jamie *41:*257
Wyeth, N. C. *13:*41; *17:*252-259, 264-268; *18:*181; *19:*80, 191, 200; *21:*57, 183; *22:*91; *23:*152; *24:*28, 99; *35:*61; *41:*65; *YABC* *1:*133, 223; *2:*53, 75, 171, 187, 317

Author Index

The following index gives the number of the volume in which an author's biographical sketch, Brief Entry, or Obituary appears.

This index includes references to all entries in the following series, which are also published by Gale Research Inc.

YABC—*Yesterday's Authors of Books for Children: Facts and Pictures about Authors and Illustrators of Books for Young People from Early Times to 1960,* Volumes 1-2

CLR—*Children's Literature Review: Excerpts from Reviews, Criticism, and Commentary on Books for Children,* Volumes 1-19

SAAS—*Something about the Author Autobiography Series,* Volumes 1-9

Author Index

H

Hall, Marjory
    See Yeakley, Marjory Hall
Hall, Rosalys Haskell 1914- 7
Hallard, Peter
    See Catherall, Arthur
Hallas, Richard
    See Knight, Eric (Mowbray)
Hall-Clarke, James
    See Rowland-Entwistle, (Arthur) Theodore
    (Henry)
Haller, Dorcas Woodbury 1946- 46
Halliburton, Warren J. 1924- 19
Halliday, William R(oss) 1926- 52
Hallin, Emily Watson 1919- 6
Hallinan, P(atrick) K(enneth) 1944- 39
    Brief Entry 37
Hallman, Ruth 1929- 43
    Brief Entry 28
Hall-Quest, (Edna) Olga W(ilbourne)
    1899-1986 11
    Obituary 47
Hallstead, William F(inn) III 1924- 11
Hallward, Michael 1889- 12
Halsell, Grace 1923- 13
Halsted, Anna Roosevelt 1906-1975
    Obituary 30
Halter, Jon C(harles) 1941- 22
Hamalian, Leo 1920- 41
Hamberger, John 1934- 14
Hamblin, Dora Jane 1920- 36
Hamerstrom, Frances 1907- 24
Hamil, Thomas Arthur 1928- 14
Hamil, Tom
    See Hamil, Thomas Arthur
Hamill, Ethel
    See Webb, Jean Francis (III)
Hamilton, Alice
    See Cromie, Alice Hamilton
Hamilton, Charles Harold St. John
    1875-1961 13
Hamilton, Clive
    See Lewis, C. S.
Hamilton, Dorothy 1906-1983 12
    Obituary 35
Hamilton, Edith 1867-1963 20
Hamilton, Elizabeth 1906- 23
Hamilton, Mary (E.) 1927- 55
Hamilton, Morse 1943- 35
Hamilton, Robert W.
    See Stratemeyer, Edward L.
Hamilton, Virginia (Esther) 1936- 56
    Earlier sketch in SATA _4_
    See also CLR _1, 11_
Hamley, Dennis 1935- 39
Hammer, Charles 1934- 58
Hammer, Richard 1928- 6
Hammerman, Gay M(orenus) 1926- 9
Hammond, Winifred G(raham) 1899- 29
Hammontree, Marie (Gertrude) 1913- ...13
Hampson, (Richard) Denman 1929- 15
Hampson, Frank 1918(?)-1985
    Obituary 46
Hamre, Leif 1914- 5
Hamsa, Bobbie 1944- 52
    Brief Entry 38
Hancock, Mary A. 1923- 31
Hancock, Sibyl 1940- 9
Handforth, Thomas (Schofield) 1897-1948 42
Handville, Robert (Tompkins) 1924- 45
Hane, Roger 1940-1974
    Obituary 20
Haney, Lynn 1941- 23
Hanff, Helene 11
Hanlon, Emily 1945- 15
Hann, Jacquie 1951- 19
Hanna, Bill
    See Hanna, William
Hanna, Nell(ie L.) 1908- 55
Hanna, Paul R(obert) 1902- 9
Hanna, William 1910- 51
Hannam, Charles 1925- 50
Hano, Arnold 1922- 12
Hansen, Caryl (Hall) 1929- 39
Hansen, Joyce 1942- 46
    Brief Entry 39
Hansen, Ron 1947- 56
Hanser, Richard (Frederick) 1909- 13

Hanson, Joan 1938- 8
Hanson, Joseph E. 1894(?)-1971
    Obituary 27
Harald, Eric
    See Boesen, Victor
Harcourt, Ellen Knowles 1890(?)-1984
    Obituary 36
Hardcastle, Michael 1933- 47
    Brief Entry 38
Harding, Lee 1937- 32
    Brief Entry 31
Hardwick, Richard Holmes, Jr. 1923- ...12
Hardy, Alice Dale [Collective pseudonym] 1
Hardy, David A(ndrews) 1936- 9
Hardy, Jon 1958- 53
Hardy, Stuart
    See Schisgall, Oscar
Hardy, Thomas 1840-1928 25
Hare, Norma Q(uarles) 1924- 46
    Brief Entry 41
Harford, Henry
    See Hudson, W(illiam) H(enry)
Hargrave, Leonie
    See Disch, Thomas M(ichael)
Hargreaves, Roger 1935(?)-1988
    Obituary 56
Hargrove, James 1947- 57
    Brief Entry 50
Hargrove, Jim
    See Hargrove, James
Hark, Mildred
    See McQueen, Mildred Hark
Harkaway, Hal
    See Stratemeyer, Edward L.
Harkins, Philip 1912- 6
Harlan, Elizabeth 1945- 41
    Brief Entry 35
Harlan, Glen
    See Cebulash, Mel
Harman, Fred 1902(?)-1982
    Obituary 30
Harman, Hugh 1903-1982
    Obituary 33
Harmelink, Barbara (Mary) 9
Harmer, Mabel 1894- 45
Harmon, Margaret 1906- 20
Harnan, Terry 1920- 12
Harnett, Cynthia (Mary) 1893-1981 5
    Obituary 32
Harper, Anita 1943- 41
Harper, Mary Wood
    See Dixon, Jeanne
Harper, Wilhelmina 1884-1973 4
    Obituary 26
Harrah, Michael 1940- 41
Harrell, Sara Gordon
    See Banks, Sara (Jeanne Gordon Harrell)
Harries, Joan 1922- 39
Harrington, Lyn 1911- 5
Harris, Aurand 1915- 37
Harris, Catherine
    See Ainsworth, Catherine Harris
Harris, Christie 1907- 6
Harris, Colver
    See Colver, Anne
Harris, Dorothy Joan 1931- 13
Harris, Geraldine (Rachel) 1951- 54
Harris, Janet 1932-1979 4
    Obituary 23
Harris, Joel Chandler 1848-1908
    See ....YABC _1_
Harris, Jonathan 1921- 52
Harris, Larry Vincent 1939- 59
Harris, Lavinia
    See Johnston, Norma
Harris, Leon A., Jr. 1926- 4
Harris, Lorle K(empe) 1912- 22
Harris, Marilyn
    See Springer, Marilyn Harris
Harris, Mark Jonathan 1941- 32
Harris, Robie H.
    Brief Entry 53
Harris, Rosemary (Jeanne) 4
    See also SAAS _7_
Harris, Sherwood 1932- 25
Harris, Steven Michael 1957- 55
Harrison, C. William 1913- 35

Harrison, David Lee 1937- 26
Harrison, Deloris 1938- 9
Harrison, Edward Hardy 1926- 56
Harrison, Harry 1925- 4
Harrison, Molly 1909- 41
Harrison, Ted
    See Harrison, Edward Hardy
Harshaw, Ruth H(etzel) 1890-1968 27
Hart, Bruce 1938- 57
    Brief Entry 39
Hart, Carole 1943- 57
    Brief Entry 39
Harte, (Francis) Bret(t) 1836-1902 26
Hartley, Ellen (Raphael) 1915- 23
Hartley, Fred Allan III 1953- 41
Hartley, William B(rown) 1913- 23
Hartman, Evert 1937- 38
    Brief Entry 35
Hartman, Jane E(vangeline) 1928- 47
Hartman, Louis F(rancis) 1901-1970 22
Hartshorn, Ruth M. 1928- 11
Harvey, Edith 1908(?)-1972
    Obituary 27
Harwin, Brian
    See Henderson, LeGrand
Harwood, Pearl Augusta (Bragdon) 1903- ...9
Haseley, Dennis 1950- 57
    Brief Entry 44
Haskell, Arnold 1903- 6
Haskins, James 1941- 9
    See also CLR _3_
Haskins, Jim
    See Haskins, James
    See also SAAS _4_
Hasler, Joan 1931- 28
Hassall, Joan 1906-1988 43
    Obituary 56
Hassler, Jon (Francis) 1933- 19
Hastings, Beverly
    See James, Elizabeth
Hatch, Mary Cottam 1912-1970
    Brief Entry 28
Hatlo, Jimmy 1898-1963
    Obituary 23
Haugaard, Erik Christian 1923- 4
    See also CLR _11_
Hauman, Doris 1898- 32
Hauman, George 1890-1961 32
Hauptly, Denis J(ames) 1945- 57
Hauser, Margaret L(ouise) 1909- 10
Hausman, Gerald 1945- 13
Hausman, Gerry
    See Hausman, Gerald
Hautzig, Deborah 1956- 31
Hautzig, Esther 1930- 4
Havenhand, John
    See Cox, John Roberts
Havighurst, Walter (Edwin) 1901- 1
Haviland, Virginia 1911-1988 6
    Obituary 54
Hawes, Judy 1913- 4
Hawk, Virginia Driving
    See Sneve, Virginia Driving Hawk
Hawkesworth, Eric 1921- 13
Hawkins, Arthur 1903- 19
Hawkins, Quail 1905- 6
Hawkinson, John 1912- 4
Hawkinson, Lucy (Ozone) 1924-1971 21
Hawley, Mable C. [Collective pseudonym] 1
Hawthorne, Captain R. M.
    See Ellis, Edward S(ylvester)
Hawthorne, Nathaniel 1804-1864
    See ....YABC _2_
Hay, John 1915- 13
Hay, Timothy
    See Brown, Margaret Wise
Haycraft, Howard 1905- 6
Haycraft, Molly Costain 1911- 6
Hayden, Gwendolen Lampshire 1904- ...35
Hayden, Robert C(arter), Jr. 1937- 47
    Brief Entry 28
Hayden, Robert E(arl) 1913-1980 19
    Obituary 26
Hayes, Carlton J. H. 1882-1964 11
Hayes, Geoffrey 1947- 26
Hayes, John F. 1904- 11

Author Index